Entrepren

This book addresses the burgeoning interest in organizational learning and entrepreneurship, bringing together for the first time a collection of new papers dealing explicitly with entrepreneurial learning. Where past books have examined learning in a corporate context, Harrison and Leitch instead focus on the learning process within entrepreneurship and the small business. Areas covered include:

- A review of the concept of entrepreneurial learning and the relationship between entrepreneurial learning and the wider literatures on management and organizational learning,
- A review and development of a number of conceptual models of the process of learning in entrepreneurial contexts,
- An illustration of the applications of the concept of the entrepreneurial learning in a range of contexts,
- An international perspective on entrepreneurial learning.

This book will be of great interest to students and researchers engaged with entrepreneurship, management learning, organizational learning and adult education.

Richard T. Harrison is Professor of Management and Head of Queen's University Management School, Belfast, and is Visiting Professor in Entrepreneurship and Innovation at Edinburgh University Management School.

Claire M. Leitch is Senior Lecturer and Director of Education (Postgraduate Studies and Executive Education) at Queen's University Management School, Belfast, and is Visiting Professor at the Centre for Organizational Renewal and Evolution, University of Aarhus.

Routledge Studies in Entrepreneurship

Edited by Jay Mitra (Essex University, UK) & Zoltan Acs (George Mason University, USA)

Entrepreneurial Learning

Conceptual frameworks
and applications

Edited by Richard T. Harrison
and Claire M. Leitch

Routledge
Taylor & Francis Group

LONDON AND NEW YORK

First issued in paperback 2011

First published 2008
by Routledge
2 Park Square, Milton Park,
Abingdon, Oxon, OX14 4RN

Simultaneously published in the USA and Canada
by Routledge
270 Madison Avenue, New York, NY 10016

Routledge is an imprint of the Taylor & Francis Group

© 2008 selection and editorial matter, Richard T. Harrison and
Claire M. Leitch; selection and editorial matter; individual chapters, the contributors.

Typeset in Times New Roman by Keyword Group Ltd.,

British Library Cataloguing in Publication Data
A catalogue record for this book is available from the British Library

Library of Congress Cataloging-in-Publication Data
Entrepreneurial learning: conceptual frameworks and applications/edited by Richard T. Harrison and
Claire M. Leitch.
p. cm. -- (Routledge advances in management and business studies)
Includes bibliographical references and index.
ISBN 978-0-415-39416-1 (hbk.) -- ISBN 978-0-203-93192-9 (ebk) 1. Entrepreneurship.
2. Organizational learning. I. Harrison, Richard T., 1955- II. Leitch, Claire M.
HB615.E59745 2008
658.3'124--dc22   2007032091

ISBN 10: 0-415-39416-3 (hbk)
ISBN 10: 0-415-61931-9 (pbk)
ISBN 10: 0-203-93192-0 (ebk)

ISBN 13: 978-0-415-39416-1 (hbk)
ISBN 13: 978-0-415-61931-8 (pbk)
ISBN 13: 978-0-203-93192-9 (ebk)

Contents

Figures

Tables

Contributors

Robert Chia is Professor of Management at the University of Aberdeen Business School, Scotland. He holds a PhD in Organization Studies and is a Fellow of the Royal Society of Arts. His research interests include the study of peripheral vision and strategic foresight, entrepreneurial learning, East–West mentalities and business practices, and the role of management education. He is the author/editor of three books and numerous international journal articles as well as book chapters in a variety of management sub-fields.

E-mail: r.chia@abdn.ac.uk

Michael J. Christie is City of Mandurah Chair in Entrepreneurship and Business Innovation at Murdoch University, Australia. He focuses his research on entrepreneurship and economic development. Originally a practitioner in these areas, he has taught entrepreneurship at Murdoch University, Australia, and at Queensland University of Technology, Newcastle University and the University of New England. He completed his PhD on the strategic management processes of boards of regional development agencies. His research interests are economic development, entrepreneurship and commercialization.

E-mail: m.christie@murdoch.edu.au

Marc Compeau is an Instructor and Director of Entrepreneurship Programs in the School of Business at Clarkson University, Potsdam, New York. His research interests include micro-business, particularly in rural settings; entrepreneurial education and development at the undergraduate level; and the study of management competencies.

E-mail: compeaum@clarkson.edu

Andrew C. Corbett is an Assistant Professor of Entrepreneurship and Strategic Management at Rensselaer Polytechnic Institute's Lally School of Management and Technology. His research centres on learning and knowledge-based inputs to the process of entrepreneurship and strategic renewal. His work has appeared in *Entrepreneurship: Theory and Practice, Management Communication Quarterly, Journal of Small Business Management* and others.

E-mail: corbea@rpi.edu

Mark Easterby-Smith is Past-President of the British Academy of Management, and Professor of Management Learning at Lancaster University. His main research interests are in management research methods and organizational learning. He has published many papers and several books, including *Management Research: An Introduction* (Sage, 2002), and the *Handbook of Organizational Learning and Knowledge Management* (Blackwell, 2003). In 2003 he was appointed a Senior Fellow of the UK's Advanced Institute of Management (AIM) research initiative, and is currently leading a research team that is using case studies and thematic analysis to investigate the principles and practice of 'dynamic capability' across a range of large and small organizations.

E-mail: m.easterby-smith@lancaster.ac.uk

Ignatius Ekanem is a Senior Researcher at the Centre for Enterprise and Economic Development Research (CEEDR), Middlesex University Business School, London. He specializes in economic regeneration and small business research, with a particular focus on the financial management practices of small businesses. His research interests also include business support needs of minority business groups such as women and second-generation ethnic minorities.

E-mail: i.ekanem@mdx.ac.uk

Sandra L. Fisher is an Assistant Professor of Organizational Studies in the School of Business at Clarkson University. She earned her PhD in Industrial/Organizational Psychology from Michigan State University. Her research interests include examining the effects of technology on people in organizations, the impact of business outsourcing on employment relationships, and the development of entrepreneurs. Her papers have appeared in journals such as *Personnel Psychology* and *Human Resource Management*. She has over five years experience consulting with government and private-sector organizations in performance management, training and technology implementation.

E-mail: sfisher@clarkson.edu

Paul N. Friga is a Clinical Associate Professor at the Kelley School of Business at Indiana University in Bloomington, Indiana, where he teaches courses in strategy and management consulting. He researches strategic decision-making, knowledge transfer, intuition and entrepreneurship. He completed his PhD and MBA at the University of North Carolina at Chapel Hill and previously worked as a management consultant for PricewaterhouseCoopers and McKinsey & Company. His undergraduate degree (Honors Program) is from Saint Francis University, where he graduated magna cum laude with a double degree in Management and Accounting.

E-mail: pfriga@indiana.edu.

Jeanette W. Gilsdorf is Professor in the Department of Information Systems at California State University–Long Beach. With research interests in persuasion, business lexicon and usage, communication aspects of knowledge management, corporate policy on communicating and intercultural communication she has published articles in *Management Communication Quarterly, Journal of Business Communication, Business Communication Quarterly, IEEE Transactions on Professional Communication, Business Horizons* and others. She is a past president of the Association for Business Communication.

E-mail: gilsdorf@earthlink.net

Edward Gonsalves is Board Trustee and Director at Yaa Asantewaa Arts, London, and Founding Director of Vinbra UK Ltd. He is a visiting lecturer on the European Business School's MA in Entrepreneurial Management programme. His research interests include strategic management of SMEs, organizational learning, inter-corporate mentoring and the growth of ethnic minority enterprise clusters in the UK.

E-mail: gonsalve@regents.ac.uk

Mary E. Graham is Newell Associate Professor in the School of Business at Clarkson University. She earned her PhD from the School of Industrial and Labor Relations at Cornell University, with concentrations in human resource studies and organizational behavior. She teaches courses at the undergraduate and graduate levels in human resource management, rewards management and organizational behavior. She has publications on incentive pay programs, gender-related pay disparities and perceptions of corporate reputation, including papers in the *Journal of Organizational Behavior, Organizational Research Methods, Organization Science* and *Eastern Economic Journal*. She is an associate editor of *Human Resource Management* journal and on the editorial board of *Human Resource Management Review*. She is a member of the Academy of Management and the Society for Human Resource Management (SHRM).

E-mail: graham@clarkson.edu

Colin Gray is a Professor of Enterprise Development in the Innovation, Knowledge and Enterprise academic centre of the Open University Business School. His research interests include the determinants of small business growth and entrepreneurship; the effects of the adoption of information and communication technologies (ICT) on small firm performance, networking and strategy; and the development and effects of organizational learning and absorptive capacity in small firms. He is also the President of the Institute for Small Business and Entreprneurship (ISBE) and a Trustee of the Small Enterprise Research Team (SERTeam).

E-mail: c.w.j.a.gray@open.ac.uk

Richard T. Harrison is Professor of Management and Director of the Management School at Queen's University Belfast, Northern Ireland. His current research interests fall into a number of broad themes that can be linked by a unifying interest in the nature of the entrepreneurial process as it is reflected in business development, and in the implications of research and theorizing for practice and public policy. Much of his research interests in learning in entrepreneurial contexts are a development of his extensive involvement in executive education and development. In addition, he is a leading authority on business angel and early-stage venture finance and has advised governments, development agencies and business groups internationally on risk capital and venture finance issues. He is founding co-editor of the research journal *Venture Capital: An International Journal of Entrepreneurial Finance*, the leading publisher of academic research on risk capital.

E-mail: r.harrison@qub.ac.uk

René J. Jorna is full Professor in Knowledge Management and Cognition at the Faculty of Management & Organization of the University of Groningen. He studied Analytic Philosophy and Logic (Master in 1981) and Experimental Psychology (Master in 1982) and had his PhD in 1989 in Cognitive Science on knowledge representation. His research and publications refer to cognition, semiotics, knowledge management, sustainable innovation, knowledge technology and decision support systems, especially related to planning and scheduling. In 1990 he published *Knowledge Representation and Symbols in the Mind* (Stauffenburg) and in 1994 *Semiotic Aspects of Artificial Intelligence* (Walter de Gruyter). From 1990 until 1995 he was manager of a large research project on planning and scheduling (DISKUS), which resulted in commercial software and five dissertations. From 2001 until 2004 he was programme manager of the NIDO project on Sustainable Innovation. In 2006 the book *Planning in Intelligent Systems* (Wiley) appeared (together with van Wezel and Meystel; Wiley, New York) and in 2006 also *Sustainable Innovation: The human, organizational and knowledge dimension* (Greenleaf Publishing Cie). He has also published more than 100 scientific articles and book chapters. He supervises 9 PhD projects on sustainable innovation, planning, scheduling and cognition and social simulation.

E-mail: r.j.j.m.jorna@rug.nl

Claire M. Leitch is a Senior Lecturer in Management at Queen's University Belfast, Northern Ireland. Her research interests include developing an understanding of the learning company and applying it as a company development process; the application of action learning and other client-centred learning approaches, within entrepreneurial and executive education and development; gaining a deeper knowledge of the dynamics of leadership in the process of organizational transformation; entrepreneurial learning and business development; and developing a fuller understanding of the academic technology transfer process.

E-mail: c.leitch@qub.ac.uk

Benyamin B. Lichtenstein is an Assistant Professor of Management and Entrepreneurship at the University of Massachusetts in Boston. His research utilizes insights from complexity science to explore the dynamics of new venture creation, and the processes that support learning, change and development in entrepreneurial ventures. He has published over 30 refereed journals articles, conference proceedings and book chapters, including articles in *Organization Science, Journal of Business Venturing, Entrepreneurship Theory and Practice, Human Relations* and *Academy of Management Executive*, where he received the 'Article of the Year' award in 2000.

E-mail: Benyamin.bar1@gmail.com

G. T. Lumpkin is an Associate Professor of Management and Entrepreneurship at the University of Illinois at Chicago. His primary research interests include entrepreneurial orientation, opportunity recognition, entrepreneurial learning, new venture strategies and strategy-making processes. He received his PhD in Business Administration from the University of Texas at Arlington and his MBA from the University of Southern California. His research has been published in the *Academy of Management Review, Academy of Management Journal, Entrepreneurship Theory and Practice, Journal of Business Venturing, Journal of Management,* and *Strategic Management Journal.* Recently, he has co-authored a textbook entitled *Strategic Management: Creating Competitive Advantages.*

E-mail: tlumpkin@uic.edu

Joyce McHenry is an Associate Professor at the Oslo School of Management (Oslo Markedshøyskole), Oslo, Norway. Her research interests include gaining a deeper knowledge of the dynamics of managing knowledge and learning; the design and application of competence models; managing change as a social learning activity; contributing to a wider discussion on formal and informal learning in a European context; and developing a fuller understanding of practice-based theorizing on learning and knowledge.

E-mail: joyce.mchenry@omh.no

Diamanto Politis is a Research Fellow at the Scandinavian Institute for Research in Entrepreneurship (SIRE) at Halmstad University, Sweden. She received her PhD in Business Administration from Lund University, Sweden. Her dissertation topic focused on the process of entrepreneurial learning. Other fields of interests are venture capital, entrepreneurial career development, and issues of resource acquisition and competence development in new ventures. Her research has been published in *Entrepreneurship Theory and Practice, Venture Capital* and *Frontiers of Entrepreneurship Research.*

E-mail: diamanto.politis@fek.lu.se

Theo Postma is Associate Professor of Strategic Management at the Faculty of Management and Organization, University of Groningen. He received his PhD in business economics from the University of Groningen in 1989. His research interests involve strategy (i.e. absorptive capacity as a dynamic capability), technology assessment, scenario development, strategic learning in and between organizations. His current research interests also focuses on corporate governance, innovation and strategic management in SMEs. His work appeared in journals such as *European Management Journal, Eastern Economic Journal, International Studies of Management and Organization, European Journal of Health Economics, Technological Forecasting and Social Change, Organization Studies, Venture Capital, Entrepreneurship Theory and Practice, and Journal of Small Business Strategy.*

E-mail: t.j.b.m.postma@rug.nl

Patricia A. Rowe is a Lecturer in the UQ Business School at the University of Queensland, Brisbane. Her research interests include understanding the interactive process of sharing of know-how and its impact on the innovation process and firm growth; developing an understanding of the processes of leadership and learning in teams; change management; entrepreneurial learning and business development; and developing a fuller understanding of the dynamics of clusters within networks. She has published a number of book chapters and refereed journal articles and has presented her work at premier international and national management conferences.

E-mail: p.rowe@business.uq.edu.au

Olukemi O. Sawyerr is Assistant Professor in the Department of Management and Human Resources at California State Polytechnic University, Pomona. Her research interests include environmental volatility, corporate intelligence gathering and the process of entrepreneurship in developing countries; personal social networks as sources of entrepreneurial intelligence; and the processes of knowledge management in entrepreneurial organizations. Her work has appeared in such journals as *Strategic Management Journal, Journal of Small Business Management, International Small Business Journal, International Journal of Cross Cultural Management* and others.

E-mail: oosawyerr@csupomona.edu

David Smallbone is Professor of Small Business and Entrepreneurship in the Small Business Research Centre (SBRC) at Kingston University and Visiting Professor in Entrepreneurship at the China University of Geosciences in Wuhan, China. His research interests include: high-growth SMEs; enterprise development in rural areas; innovation and innovation policy; ethnic minority and entrepreneurship; entrepreneurship and small business development in transition economies; and small business policy issues. He has extensive experience of research-based consultancy for a range of national and international clients, including the European Commission, the UNDP and the OECD.

E-mail: d.smallbone@kingston.ac.uk

Robert Smith is a MA doctoral student at the Centre for Entrepreneurship at Aberdeen Business School, Robert Gordon University, Scotland. His research interests include the social construction of entrepreneurship, dyslexia and entrepreneurship, rural entrepreneurship, criminal entrepreneurship and criminology, and he has published widely on these topics.

E-mail: Robertnval@aol.com

Joakim Tell is an Assistant Professor at the School of Business and Engineering at Halmstad University, Sweden. His research interests concerns the development of different action technologies, such as learning networks, to connect the university with organizations in the region; managerial behaviour in small enterprises; and leadership and learning issues in general.

E-mail: joakim.tell@set.hh.se

Jan Waalkens was born in 1965. His career as an academic started in 1992 when he finished his study in Human Geography with a specialization in Economic Geography. He started as researcher at the Human Geography Faculty of the University of Groningen and later worked as product developer of post-graduate courses at the Business School of the University of Groningen. In 1999 he started as assistant professor and PhD researcher at the Faculty of Management and Organization of the University of Groningen. His dissertation *Building capabilities in the construction sector, Absorptive Capacity of architectural and engineering medium-sized enterprises* was published in 2006. Currently he is Director of the Planning Expertise and Innovation Centre (www.peic.nl). PEIC research focuses on planning in relation to issues of organizational design.

E-mail: j.waalkens@peic.nl

Acknowledgements

This volume has its origins in a Special Issue of *Entrepreneurship Theory and Practice* (July 2005) that we guest edited on the subject of entrepreneurial learning. Such was the level of interest in that issue that we were encouraged to develop the project into the current volume. This volume collects together papers drawn from three sources: papers originally published in the journal Special Issue; papers submitted for consideration for the Special Issue that, although positively reviewed, could not be published because of space constraints; and papers specifically invited for this volume to reflect the range of research currently being undertaken on the topic of entrepreneurial learning. We are grateful for the enormous amount of effort put into the review process by an extensive panel of anonymous reviewers.

We are grateful to Blackwell Publishing for permission to reprint Chapters 3, 5 and 6 from the Special Issue of *Entrepreneurship Theory and Practice*, vol. 29, no. 4, (July 2005) on entrepreneurial learning. These were originally published as: Diamanto Politis, The process of entrepreneurial learning: a conceptual framework, *Entrepreneurship Theory and Practice* vol. 29, no. 4 (July 2005), pp 399–424; G. T. Lumpkin and Benyamin B. Lichtenstein, The role of organizational learning in the opportunity-recognition process, *Entrepreneurship Theory and Practice*, vol. 29, no. 4 (July 2005), pp 451–72; and Andrew C. Corbett, Experiential learning within the process of opportunity identification and exploitation, *Entrepreneurship Theory and Practice*, vol. 29, no. 4 (July 2005), pp 473–91.

Preface

A conversation between entrepreneurship and organizational learning

Mark Easterby-Smith

Two critical skills for the successful entrepreneur are being able to solve novel problems within real time, and learning how best to draw from the expertise of others. These two skills are often conceived as the property of individuals and are explained by theories of experiential learning, and education and training, respectively. But the entrepreneur, however heroic, is not an isolated individual, and is part of the organization that he or she may have played a key part in creating. It is therefore important to consider the extent to which there are ideas from *organizational learning* that are relevant to understanding the role and performance of entrepreneurship. In this short preface I will make some comments primarily about organizational learning and how some key ideas in the field are relevant to entrepreneurship.

There are very many different frameworks for understanding the field of organizational learning – almost as many as there are academics writing about it – and so here is a relatively simple one to get us started on the topic. It starts by dividing the field according to the sources of learning: whether the organization learns from its own internal processes (endogenous), or whether it learns from things that take place outside its organizational boundaries (exogenous). With regard to *endogenous* learning, the organization can learn horizontally, vertically or in sequence. Horizontal learning takes place when useful ideas move from one department to another, or between different business units or projects. More often than not this kind of learning is problematic because people do not want to share their ideas with others and resent being told that they should learn from their colleagues. Hence we have common expressions like 'silo mentality', and the 'not invented here' syndrome. There are various ways of tackling the problem of horizontal learning, including the development of knowledge management systems, the structuring of reward systems to encourage sharing, the circulation of staff between departments, and the creation of cross-departmental project teams.

Vertical learning involves, for example, senior managers learning from the salespeople who are in direct contact with customers or employees, or operatives becoming sufficiently well informed about the strategic direction and context of the organization. This kind of learning is facilitated formally by mechanisms such as management information systems, or by cascade briefing procedures. But it can be equally problematic due to issues such as power differentials and the different agendas that people at different levels of the organization will have. In some respects, knowledge and information is similar to water: it flows down the hierarchy with moderate ease, but it flows up the political hierarchy with considerable difficulty.

The third kind of endogenous learning is sequential, and depends on how far organizations are capable of learning from their past successes and failures. Stereotypically, they tend to repeat their successes and obliterate their failures, whereas some of the most significant learning ought to come from understanding why things have gone wrong. Association with failed projects or events is unlikely to help anybody's career, and even when organizations try to make a virtue of failure – as in the case of 'no blame' reviews – there needs to be very active top management support for this kind of behaviour.

If we turn to *exogenous* forms of organization learning we can look either at absorptive capacity, which is the ability of an organization to gather useful information from its environment, or the learning that takes place between organizations as part of alliances or networks. There are many ways for a single organization to learn from the outside. Individuals can develop their own networks of business and professional contacts, and this is often a key contribution made by the entrepreneur or by other senior managers at the top of an organization. But others at lower levels may learn what is going on elsewhere, again through personal or professional contacts; or a decision may be taken to recruit new managers and employees who can bring their experiences from other companies to the benefit of the organization itself. There are also an increasing array of public sources of information including the press, databases, trade journals and the Internet. In general it is assumed that a virtuous cycle operates here: the more knowledge and skills that are already contained within the organization, the more it is likely to be able to appreciate the value of knowledge and skills from outside.

The second form of exogenous learning involves transfer of knowledge and information between two or more organizations that have relationships through supply chains, trading partnerships, alliances or joint ventures. This has become an increasingly hot area for research between large organizations because of the increasing complexity of business relationships and the increasing internationalization or globalization of many business enterprises. The rapid growth of global service industries within India, and of manufacturing capabilities within China, mean that most large organizations have to enter into relationships that span national and cultural boundaries, and no business of any size can ignore the impact of global competitive factors and the need to seek alliances. Many alliances start off with differentiated contributions from each partner: the Japanese company designs the cassette recorder, the Chinese company manufactures it, and the British company distributes it. But increasingly this is leading to what researchers call the 'learning race' where each company attempts to learn or acquire the expertise of its partners through their mutual interactions; and the partner that is most successful in this respect over time then moves into a position where they are able to dominate the relationships when contracts come up for renewal. In such cases the origins and identity of each organization can play a major role in determining which one learns best. Typically, it is the organization from the less developed country that starts out by trying to learn the technology and the processes of the organization from the more developed country, and this openness to learning tends to persist as the relationship evolves, which eventually leads to a reversal of roles with the (stereotypically) Asian company starting to dominate over the Western company.

I will now comment briefly on some of the current trends and debates within the field of organizational learning, although the three that I identify – performance, process and innovation – might be seen as illustrative rather than a comprehensive mapping of the issues currently under debate. First, there is a concern among researchers to establish that there are measurable links between learning processes and organizational performance. Some have been cross-organizational surveys that have taken a quantitative approach to establishing these links; others have looked at case studies over time; and still others have simply gathered the observations of experienced observers as proxy evidence. Although there is no single definitive study that has finally established the relationship, most observers still believe that there is a good linkage, all other things being equal, and this position is neatly encapsulated by the comment that, 'if you think learning is expensive, try ignorance'.

The second stream of research takes a process view of organizational learning. This concentrates on studies that look at how groups and teams learn over time, and one of the most popular concepts here is the idea of 'communities of practice'. These involve groups of peers or professional networks across an organization who agree to share their experiences and insights at a practical level – often in contrast to the formal organizational view of how things should be done. There is therefore a slightly radical, or revolutionary, flavour to some of the literature on communities of practice. But it is also an idea that has been 'captured' by managers who see the potential to gain the benefits of communities that provide fast transmission of knowledge and insights, and who therefore construct them as part of the formal organizational structure. Although this may be seen to contradict the radical origins of communities of practice, there are many organizations and examples where they have been structured by management and yet appear to work quite well; but there are also examples where they don't work well, either.

The third area of current interest in organizational learning concerns creativity and innovation. Here there have been a large number of studies conducted on new product development procedures, especially in semiconductors and the biotechnology industry. There are many factors that appear to aid new product development, including structured mechanisms for internal learning and project reviews, the proximity of related organizations, the day-to-day management of work practice, and the wider cultural and political context within which innovative activities are embedded. This kind of research has the most obvious relevance to entrepreneurship since many entrepreneurial organizations make their living through being more creative and faster-moving than their rivals, and the fluidity of knowledge and the mobility of personnel in many areas of a new technology mean that entrepreneurship, innovation and learning become intertwined.

This brings us full circle because it is clear that both the field of organizational learning and entrepreneurship have much to gain from a mutual conversation. In terms of direct exchanges, organizational learning research can gain better insights of the whole process of organizational learning, and access to larger populations of organizations since small business are far more numerous than large ones. The field of entrepreneurship can gain more fully developed theories from organizational learning because of the investment already made by researchers into larger organizations; and it can also gain directly from some of the insights into processes that take place within large organizations but which are generalizable to smaller organizations. Finally, there are common agendas, such as innovation, where it seems imperative for research on organizational learning and entrepreneurship to proceed hand in hand. I also hope that, as a result of the debates and discussions in the remainder of this book, further areas of potential trade-off and synergy will be identified and steps will be taken to initiate further research in these areas.

Section I

Introduction

1 Entrepreneurial learning

A review and research agenda

Claire M. Leitch and Richard T. Harrison

Introduction

There is a burgeoning interest in organizational learning (the acquisition by an organization or any of its units of knowledge that it recognizes as potentially useful for the organization) and the learning organization in the organizational and managerial literatures (Starkey 1996a; Easterby-Smith *et al.* 1999; Dierkes *et al.* 2001; Easterby-Smith and Lyles 2003). Although the link between learning and organizational effectiveness is far from proven, logically or empirically, the interest in organizational learning has been underpinned by a set of beliefs about the importance of learning in organizational adaptation and flexibility in conditions of change and uncertainty (Moingeon and Edmundson 1996). According to Easterby-Smith and Lyles (2003), the fields of organizational learning and knowledge management have developed rapidly over the past decade or so, in terms of both the volume and the diversity of the research being undertaken. In particular, they highlight four characteristics of the field. First, it is characterized by both novelty and diversity: much of the research has been undertaken since 1990, even 1995, and this makes it problematic to satisfactorily discern trends and a cumulative sense of development. Second, the field is increasingly diverse and specialized, with the consequence that much research is being undertaken in parallel traditions without cross-reference or cross-fertilization. Third, this diversity in research has stimulated debates and arguments around definitions and terminology, the meanings of concepts, methodological issues, applications and influences on organizational learning processes, and the purposes to which new knowledge of organizational learning and knowledge management should be put. Finally, despite the diversity of the research, there are a relatively small number of core references and citations, which suggest an underlying commonality in the field to which the majority of current scholars refer.

Relatively little of this research has been explored within the entrepreneurship tradition, nor has the entrepreneurial context informed much of the organizational learning literature. The first substantive integrated approach to the discussion of entrepreneurial learning is a special issue of *Entrepreneurship Theory and Practice* (Harrison and Leitch 2005a, 2005b). The papers in this issue cover a relatively restricted range of topics including conceptual overviews of the relevance of learning for understanding and thinking about entrepreneurial phenomena (Cope 2005; Politis 2005); the identification and elaboration of concepts of intra-organizational learning in the context of entrepreneurial opportunity recognition (Corbett 2005; Dutta and Crossan 2005; Lumpkin and Lichtenstein 2005); and detailed empirical investigations of aspects of learning in inter-organizational contexts (De Clercq and Sapienza 2005; Schildt *et al.* 2005). In this book we extend the discussion of learning in entrepreneurial contexts to a wider range of conceptual and empirical perspectives and bring together a collection of chapters which deal with a variety of entrepreneurship issues and draw on the diverse range of literature on organizational learning, to contribute to both theory development and practice within the field of entrepreneurship.

It has been argued, in the context of the evolution of entrepreneurship as a field of study, that 'the conscious and critical transfer and application of theories and methodologies from one research area to another may stimulate creative advances in both, and may provide the basis for the resolution of old problems in new ways' (Harrison and Leitch 1994: 112). Although ideas of organizational learning have gained currency within the field of management, their application to entrepreneurship has been limited. More specifically, 'entrepreneurship is a process of learning, and a theory of entrepreneurship requires a theory of learning' (Minniti and Bygrave 2001: 7).

Both the discourse of entrepreneurial management and the discourse of learning in organizations occur within the contemporary 'experimentally organized economy' (Eliasson 1996a, 1998), which is fundamentally entrepreneurial (rather than managerial), and requires entrepreneurs (construed in this context by Eliasson as 'experimenter managers') to continually engage in learning. Specifically, in order to be successful, these experimenter managers – at both the individual firm level and the economic system level—have to bundle together a number of interrelated competences into a 'competence bloc'. This has been defined as the total infrastructure needed to *create* (innovation), *recognize* (risk capital provision), *diffuse* (spillovers) and successfully *exploit* (receiver competence) new ideas in clusters of firms (Eliasson 1996b, 1996c). The non-technical competences of such a 'competence bloc' must be: first, entrepreneurial awareness, the realization of the marketability of a new product or technology; second, acquiring risk capital to finance the start-up and growth of firms to exploit these opportunities; and third, the capability to manage the enterprise from start-up through expansion into maturity. Each of these domains (awareness, resource acquisition and management) requires that entrepreneurs engage in learning. For Smilor (1997: 344), learning is not an optional extra, but is central to the entrepreneurial process:

> effective entrepreneurs are exceptional learners. They learn from everything. They learn from customers, suppliers, and especially competitors. They learn from employees and associates. They learn from other entrepreneurs. They learn from experience. They learn by doing. They learn from what works, and more importantly, from what doesn't work.

Senge (1995) has captured both the importance of understanding the entrepreneurial context and the recoupling of theory and practice. The link between entrepreneurship and learning is not as unequivocal as Smilor (1997) implies. This reflects the nature of the entrepreneurial firm and the people who lead them. In Senge's (1995) words:

> the organization and culture of entrepreneurial firms can foster organizational learning . . . Entrepreneurial ventures frequently lack the kind of traditional authoritarian, hierarchical structures that inhibit collaborative learning . . . . Also, the entrepreneurial challenge often attracts individuals motivated by a strong desire to pursue their own personal visions. This can result in a business culture committed to both continuous individual improvement and collective innovation.

However, the organizational culture of entrepreneurial firms can also impede learning, specifically, the ability of entrepreneurs

> to actually succeed in continually renewing their organizations is often limited by what [they] often don't do well. In particular, they very often do not create an environment for reflection. They are often very action oriented. This can be a great strength, but it can also mean that people get caught up in a 'ready, fire, aim' mentality. Consequently, while they may have a strong personal vision, entrepreneurs often are not as skilful at fostering shared visions, and entrepreneurial firms can easily become dominated by one or two strong personalities. This tends to be particularly problematic when the firm reaches a size where power needs to be shared and more orderly management systems established.

In other words, while entrepreneurial firms may in effect be learning organizations (Pedler *et al.* 1997), this is not necessarily the case, and the widely-recognized need for a learning culture (to underpin innovation, development and competitive advantage) is not always matched by the presence of effective learning processes and culture.

Given this, progress in research on entrepreneurial learning will be achieved better through a robust focus on context-of-application-based problems than attempts to develop grandiose integrative theories within a single powerful paradigm, which in any case does not yet exist in the organizational learning field (Easterby-Smith 1997). In this book, our starting point is that the process of organizational learning is a context-of-application research problem relevant to entrepreneurship:

> virtually every aspect of organizational learning has relevance either directly or indirectly for entrepreneurial management . . . [and] . . . issues in organizational learning [relevant for entrepreneurship] include structures and processes which encourage learning, differences in learning across the levels of the organization and . . . transfer mechanisms and learning.
>
> (Day 1992: 137–40)

Over the last decade there have been a number of explorations of 'learning' in the context of entrepreneurship and small and medium-sized enterprise (SME) development. Among these are attempts to model the learning process (Minniti and Bygrave 2001), and discussions of learning in new venture creation (Lichtenstein *et al.* 2000; Erikson 2003), in SME growth and development (Watts *et al.* 1998; Wyer *et al.* 2000), in innovation (Sweeney 1987/88; Ravasi and Turati 2005), in new-technology-based firm formation (Fontes and Coombs 1996), in venture capital (Busenitz *et al.* 2004), in enterprise training and learning capability (Ulrich 1997; Chaston *et al.* 1999, 2001; Rae 2000, 2004; Rae and Carswell 2000, 2001; Taylor and Thorpe 2004) and in applications of the learning organization construct in SMEs (Leitch *et al.* 1996; Choueke and Armstrong 1998; Harrison and Leitch 2000; Leitch 2007). However, despite this fragmented research effort, it remains the case that 'research on learning processes in entrepreneurial ventures' is still in an early stage (Ravasi and Turati 2005: 139). In other words, the field does not appear to have progressed significantly beyond the point where 'our limited knowledge and understanding of the interaction of learning and the entrepreneurial process remains one of the most neglected areas of entrepreneurial research, and thus, understanding' (Deakins 1999: 23).

Knowledge and learning[1]

As Prange (1999) has recently pointed out, ideas such as 'organizational learning' and the 'learning organization' have been discussed in the literature as ways of increasing the knowledge intensity of companies. This in turn has focused attention on issues of 'knowledge management' and, in a neat reversion, to a renewed focus on the essence of the learning process through which that knowledge is generated (Berthoin Antal *et al.* 2001). Driving this interest is the recognition that 'organizations are reeling from discontinuities created by a growing level of globalization, heightened volatility, hypercompetition, demographic changes, and the explosion of knowledge' (Prange 1999: 23). More recently, Easterby-Smith and Lyles (2003) have provided a framework for mapping the field of organizational learning and knowledge management based on two dichotomies. The first dichotomy is the distinction between theory (the concerns of academics) and practice (the concerns of practitioners). The second dichotomy separates content (the knowledge that the organization possesses) from the process (learning) by which it acquires this knowledge (Figure 1.1).

It is important to recognize that there is a fundamental distinction to be drawn between knowledge (that which is known) and learning (the process by which knowledge is generated). Dixon (1994, 1999) has stated that 'we have entered the knowledge age and the new currency is learning – it is learning, not knowledge itself which is critical' (Dixon 1994: xx). This is because learning is a process that leads to the production of knowledge, and as knowledge is ephemeral it constantly needs to be revised and updated. Starkey (1996b: 1) concurs with this and observes, 'learning is the creation of useful meaning, individual or shared.

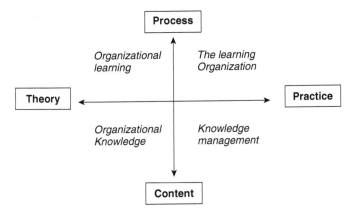

Figure 1.1 Mapping the organizational learning landscape (from Easterby–Smith and Lyles 2003: 3).

Learning generates knowledge which serves to reduce uncertainty' and continues by noting that 'learning and knowledge are major strategic resources, crucial to competitive advantage'.

This is a point that has been made by Castells (1996: 32) in his discussion of changes in the way knowledge is produced:

> what characterizes the current technological revolution is not the centrality of knowledge and information but the application of such knowledge and information to knowledge generation and information processing/communication devices, in a cumulative feedback loop between innovation and the uses of innovation. . . . New information technologies are not simply tools to be applied but processes to be developed. Users and doers may become the same. . . . For the first time in history the human mind is a direct productive force, not just a decisive element of a production system.

It is in this context that it becomes important to identify the extent to which organizations in Eliasson's (1976, 1996a, 1998) experimentally organized economy (or knowledge-based firms) 'learn' or approach their learning differently to other, more traditionally organized firms. Eliasson's work refers both to changes in the 'old' economy (i.e. traditional manufacturing sectors) and to the emergence of 'new economy' organizations. Indeed, as Prusak (1997: xx) has argued, changes in the scope of knowledge production are not confined to sectors conventionally referred to as knowledge-intensive:

> This shift is more apparent in research labs, consulting firms and software vendors, but as all products are increasingly 'smart' and as flexible production processes need to process higher levels of information about changing

customer requirements, delivery times, and so on it arguably applies right across the board.

The 'learning construct' has not, of course, been immune from critique. The available literatures on the concepts of the learning organization and knowledge management have been critically evaluated by Scarborough and Swann (2003) in an attempt to identify the key features of both concepts and what these implications might be for people management. They believe that the literature on the learning organization has to date been theory-driven, with abstract thinking shaping much of the research conducted. As a result they conclude that the implications for management practice are at times unclear. However, a more detailed review of the literature would suggest that while the field of organizational learning is indeed theory-driven, much of the research and writing on the learning organization/company has, in fact, been driven by the concerns of practitioners (Coopey 1995; Snell and Chak 1998; Easterby-Smith and Araujo 1999; Leitch *et al.* 1999; Coopey and Burgoyne 2000). As Easterby-Smith *et al.* (2000: 737) have observed, these two communities mainly operate independently, and 'where boundary crossing takes place, it is largely one-way'. As a result, practitioners who wish to implement more prescriptive models of the learning organization often draw on the more academic literature so that they might better understand the challenges they potentially face. However, it is rarer for academics to draw on the more prescriptive literature developed by the practitioner community. In turn, this is consistent with a view that the ontology of learning is different in different cultural contexts (Easterby-Smith and Araujo 1999). Learning cannot and should not be divorced from the specific context, including organizational context, within which it takes place: it is the product of a community (of practice), not of individuals within it, and so may be organizationally-bound as well as culturally, socially and economically contextualized (Brown and Duguid 1991, 2000; Wenger 1998).

In essence, we see the emergence of entrepreneurial learning as the embodiment of the 'decoupled realities' (Astley 1984) of organizational learning and organizational practice. While theory development in this area is valuable in its own right (Prange 1999), for the field of entrepreneurial learning to build on the platform represented by the chapters in this book it will be necessary to recouple the 'realities' of theory and practice and of content and process. Future work, therefore, should develop an agenda for examining how existing knowledge is shared, used and stored in entrepreneurial organizations, and for exploring the process of learning in the context of entrepreneurial practice.

Structure of the book

In this book we have collected together a set of chapters which focus on the development and application of learning concepts in a wide range of entrepreneurial and small business contexts. These have been grouped under four themes: conceptual approaches; intra-organizational learning; inter-organizational learning; and learning, education and development.

Conceptual approaches

It is widely recognized that the field of organizational learning is characterized by conceptual diversity and a lack of intellectual maturity (Easterby-Smith 1997; Prange 1999; Easterby-Smith and Lyles 2003), to the extent that Prange (1999: 24) describes it as 'an organizational learning jungle' in which 'the scientific community devoted to organizational learning has not produced discernible intellectual progress' (Mackenzie 1994: 251). There is, therefore, no clearly identifiable and agreed corpus of theory, constructs, methodologies and results on which to build a theory of entrepreneurial learning. However, if the growing interest in entrepreneurial learning in a wide range of contexts is to be consolidated as a major field within the discipline, it will be necessary to engage in conceptual argument and development on a broader scale than is required to ground particular studies in specific contexts. In this section we include three chapters which engage with the wider intellectual context in which the field of entrepreneurial learning will evolve.

In the opening chapter, Robert Chia explores the significance and importance of peripheral vision for enhancing entrepreneurial learning. He argues that the capacity for peripheral vision is a vital feature of all entrepreneurial ventures. Building in part on the argument of Day and Shoemaker (2004), Chia suggests that peripheral vision involves the ability to see from the 'corners-of-the-eye' what is going on around our main object of focus. Unlike the clarity that focal vision brings with it, peripheral vision is necessarily vague, ill-defined and 'blurry'. Yet it accounts for an entrepreneur's acute awareness and comprehension of emerging entrepreneurial situations. Chia suggests that our understanding of the phenomenon and process of entrepreneurial learning will be deepened by taking a much broader view than is typical. In particular, he argues that art and literature with their long-established tradition of attending to the vague, the ephemeral and the illusive elements of social phenomena have much to say about entrepreneurial learning, which is clearly more analogous to artistic endeavour than to the practice of normal science. Successful entrepreneurial ventures may be likened to a good literary work, a crime novel or a piece of art in that they show how oftentimes seemingly irrelevant developments occurring at the periphery of the public's awareness become vital to the unfolding of a story, an image or an outcome. For Chia, this is not just a theoretical argument but has important practical consequences. Peripheral vision can be systematically cultivated through educational strategies that deliberately direct attention away from the visible gestalt figures of comprehension to the unformed and invisible background against which figure, identity and meaning emerge.

This emphasis on the conceptual and theoretical underpinnings of research on entrepreneurial learning is continued in the chapter by Diamanto Politis. Her starting point is to review and synthesize the available research on learning in entrepreneurial contexts into a conceptual framework that explains the process of entrepreneurial learning as an experiential process. In so doing, the chapter makes a number of contributions to the development of the field. In particular, Politis highlights the role of experience in developing entrepreneurial knowledge through reference to a number of theories of experiential learning. Specifically, Politis argues that there is a need to move beyond an understanding of experience in terms only of prior involvement in start-ups. Taking a broader view of the career experience of the entrepreneur in turn leads to a distinction between the experience of an entrepreneur and the knowledge acquired as a result of that experience. Although the potential learning effects of entrepreneurs' past experience have been discussed in the literature, Politis is among the first to formally distinguish between learning as a process and knowledge as the outcome of the process. A final element in Politis' framework is the embracing of a dynamic perspective on the process of entrepreneurial learning, which draws attention to the intermediate processes through which experiences are transformed into knowledge and which represents a major focus for further research.

In her chapter, Joyce McHenry uses evidence from a detailed longitudinal case study to explore how learning from experience is managed in an entrepreneurial context. Taking a cue from Politis' emphasis on the experiential basis for organizational learning, McHenry argues that the matter of learning from experience has become a vital part of entrepreneurial practice and research in that entrepreneurs are considered to be action-oriented, seek opportunity and learn continuously from experience. While many of the elements of the entrepreneurial context are clear, McHenry draws on work from other fields of research to demonstrate that learning can be explained and managed in many ways. Building on theories of adult learning and knowledge management, her chapter discusses the impact of different learning views on the management of experiential learning in an entrepreneurial context. The chapter draws upon some results from a longitudinal field study in a Norwegian medium-sized entrepreneurial venture, where the management actively aims to administer the experiential learning with the assistance of a competence management model in order to facilitate the growth of the organization. This study allows for new conversations about the role and management of experiential learning (competence), recognizing that it is not a simple activity. Managing learning in self-motivated entrepreneurial settings involves profound discussions on learning assumptions that shape the management of learning from experience.

Intra-organizational learning

Fundamentally, at the core of most definitions of organizational learning is the view that learning, to a greater or lesser degree, involves the acquisition, processing and exploitation of new knowledge by the organization (Argyris and Schön 1978; Cohen and Levinthal 1990; Nonaka and Takeuchi 1995). In the intra-organizational context, learning is viewed in two ways. First, as a technical process, learning is seen as the 'effective processing, interpretation of, and response to information both inside and outside the organization' (Argyris and Schön 1978; Zuboff 1988; see Huber 1991; Easterby-Smith and Araujo 1999: 3). Second, when looked at as a social process, learning is seen as an outcome of and grounded in social inter-actions around the tacit and explicit processing of information (Brown and Duguid 1991; Lave and Wenger 1991; Nonaka and Takeuchi 1995). While there are concerns about the extent to which it makes sense to talk about learning at the level of the work group or the organization rather than the individual (Crossan *et al.* 1999; Dutta and Crossan 2005), this domain has been a longstanding and fruitful research area, although it remains true that 'rarely are there any attempts to define precisely what collective learning means at this level' (Pawlowski 2001: 76).

The first two chapters in this section of the book begin the exploration of some of these issues in the context of a focus on opportunity recognition as a key locus for entrepreneurial learning, and in so doing pick up the theme of opportunity recognition as central to entrepreneurial action which was introduced by both Politis and McHenry in Section I. Tom Lumpkin and Benyamin Bergmann Lichtenstein argue that organizational learning can strengthen a firm's ability to recognize opportunities and help equip them to effectively pursue new ventures. They identify three approaches to organizational learning: behavioural learning, based on the assumption that organizations are goal-oriented, routine-based systems that learn by experience by repeating behaviours that have been successful and avoiding those that are not; cognitive learning, which focuses on the cognitive content of organizational learning and how changes in individuals' cognitive maps are aggregated and translated into changes in an organization's cognitive schema; and action learning, which focuses on the moment-to-moment practice of correcting misalignments between espoused theory and theory-in-use. They then relate this to a creativity-based model of opportunity recognition, which depicts this as a staged process involving both discovery (preparation, incubation and insight) and formation (evaluation and elaboration). On the basis of a comparison between the organizational learning framework and the opportunity recognition model, Lumpkin and Lichtenstein develop a number of propositions for further research to empirically test how learning methods might best be integrated into venture creation and growth processes.

In his chapter, Andrew Corbett takes as his point of departure the same creativity-based opportunity recognition model and develops this explicitly in the context of a cognitive perspective on entrepreneurship. He argues that cognitive mechanisms and heuristics, and an individual's existing stocks of knowledge, are not synony-mous with learning. Rather, learning is identified as a social process by which learning is created through the transformation of experience. Specifically, Corbett relies on experiential learning theory, archetypically represented in Kolb's (1973) work, to emphasize that the acquisition and transformation experience is central to the learning process. He concludes that part of the variance in behaviour and knowledge that affects the opportunity identification and exploitation process is based on the existence of learning asymmetries, which reflect the fact that indi-viduals acquire and transform their experiences (i.e. learn) in different ways. By integrating a learning perspective with the literature on opportunity identification and exploitation, Corbett demonstrates that differences in learning matter, with respect both to the ability of an individual to identify opportunities and to the ability of the entrepreneur to adapt and learn as he or she progresses through the process of entrepreneurship.

Olukemi Sawyerr and Jeanette Gilsdorf take a rather different perspective on intra-organizational learning in an entrepreneurial context. Specifically, they focus on a knowledge-based view of the firm which identifies firm heterogeneity in creating, storing and leveraging knowledge as the primary basis for generating above-normal returns and sustained competitive advantage. In particular, they argue for a process-based understanding of knowledge creation, management and integration and argue that tacit knowledge is central to these processes. Using detailed case study information from five small firms, they focus on three core research questions. How do entrepreneurial firms generate new knowledge? How do they diffuse new knowledge throughout the organization? How do they absorb and exploit new knowledge competitive advantage? They conclude that success-ful small firms do manage knowledge deliberately but that this is most commonly through informal rather than formal means and they remain deliberately oppor-tunistic. Furthermore, it appears that entrepreneurial firms invested greater time and resources in building the context for knowledge creation and use than in developing an elaborate knowledge management infrastructure. In this respect, Sawyerr and Gilsdorf follow von Krogh *et al.* (2000) in arguing that perhaps knowledge cannot be managed per se but can be enabled. The firms in their study appear to have engendered innovativeness by creating an organizational context with internal and external knowledge enablers where ideas can germinate, percolate, develop, be evaluated and eventually turned into a product or service.

The chapter by Ignatius Ekanem and David Smallbone pursues the discussion of intra-organizational entrepreneurial learning in the context of a detailed analy-sis of the learning processes involved in the making of investment decisions in small manufacturing enterprises. The starting point for their analysis is that while there has been a growing recognition of the role of organizational learning in the survival and growth of small firms, there are limited empirical studies to demon-strate the link between learning and organizational effectiveness. The chapter reports on a study using insider accounts involving in-depth semi-structured interviews and direct observation, conducted longitudinally in eight case study companies. They adopt a perspective on learning as the acquisition, storage and interpretation of knowledge previously generated by others and incorporate Polanyi's (1967) distinction between tacit (non-codified) and explicit (codified) knowledge, and Nelson and Winter's (1982) emphasis on the embedding of group learning in organizational routines. Their overall conclusion is the key role of experiential learning rather than more formalized methods in the investment decision-making process. This emphasis on the importance of experience in entrepreneurial learning reinforces the arguments of many of the other contribu-tors to this volume. However, Ekanem and Smallbone also raise the issue of how individuals and firms can learn in the absence of experience relevant to the learning context.

In the final chapter in this section, Patricia Rowe and Michael Christie continue the theme of tacit knowledge as a key element in entrepreneurial learning. They do so, however, in the context of a very different entrepreneurial domain. Their concern is with the sharing of tacit knowledge within organizational entrepreneurship, and they move beyond the more common discussion of corporate entrepreneurship to consider civic entrepreneurship as the means by which public administration is recognized for being entrepreneurial and innovative. Furthermore, Rowe and Christie focus specifically on learning within the top management team as in the civic entrepreneurship context this role is critically defined by the management of non-routine (unexpected) situations. Based on the analysis of data collected from a sample of local government authorities in Queensland, Australia, Rowe and Christie conclude that leadership support – the degree of support and consideration a person receives from his or her supervisor – has a direct and positive effect on the explication of tacit knowledge, and they suggest that greater consideration be given to the selection of top management teams, to the way managers are integrated into organizational decision-making processes, and to the behaviours that are valued and rewarded in such teams. In so doing, the link between civic entrepreneurship, learning and the development of tacit knowledge and organizational performance will be enhanced.

Inter-organisational learning

Concern with the processes by which knowledge is acquired and exploited leads to a primary concern with learning processes in an inter-organizational context. This has perhaps been most clearly articulated in the focus on absorptive capacity as a constraint on the extent to which organizations can realize their learning objectives (Cohen and Levinthal 1990) and is reflected in a wide-ranging discussion of learning processes and outcomes in diverse national, international and inter-organizational contexts, where the roles of boundary-spanning activities, alliances and other forms of inter-organizational collaboration are identified as important requirements for and drivers of learning (Child and Heavens 2001; Macharzina *et al.* 2001; Muthusamy and White 2005). As Van den Bosch *et al.* (2003; 279) point out, there is still a significant gap between 'the speed of proliferation of theoretical and empirical contributions [on absorptive capacity] and the speed of accumulation of the acquired scientific knowledge regarding [it]', which is reinforced by the multilevel and transdisciplinary characteristics of the construct.

Four chapters fall within this theme. Paul Friga addresses gaps in the literature relating to the nature of investigations on the topics of entrepreneurial learning and knowledge. Specifically, he highlights weaknesses in the methodological approaches predominately employed in research studies to date, including a reliance on small sample sizes, unclear and varying performance measures, and a lack of control for moderating variables. Furthermore, Friga argues that there is a need to study entrepreneurship earlier in the process and especially the pre-venture phase. He also suggests that more attention should be paid to the backgrounds and traits of entrepreneurs, with particular focus on an entrepreneur's prior experience and education which constitute knowledge of past learning. These comprise the 'stocks' (Dierickx and Cool 1989) of an entrepreneurial organization, while 'flows' refer to the acquisition of additional knowledge resources (learning) through entrepreneurship initiatives and training. Friga's research represents an initial attempt at understanding the role and impact that a nascent entrepreneur's pre-venture learning activities and antecedents play during the pre-venture stage of the process. Using a multivariate analysis of data from 492 entrepreneurs, Friga concludes that general education and experience as well as attendance on entrepreneurial courses do not significantly impact the likelihood of an individual engaging in new venture creation. However, formal assistance through attendance on entrepreneurship programmes was significantly related to new venture creation. This is pertinent given the increasing emphasis at policy level on the need to promote entrepreneurial activity through education initiatives (Rae and Carswell 2001; Henry *et al.* 2004). Friga concludes that determining the impact of social networks with respect to the generation of general or past learning and specific knowledge which has been more recently acquired might provide a fruitful avenue for future research.

The focus of Edward Gonsalves and Colin Gray's chapter takes a more strategic perspective on organizational learning and entrepreneurship, and they suggest that the organizational learning concept can contribute to the understanding of entrepreneurial success. In particular, they argue that a multidimensional approach to theorizing organizational learning will provide a more robust basis from which to deliver both normative and diagnostic models of learning within entrepreneurship. They propose a process-based approach to describing the relationships between the constructs of SME strategy making, organizational learning and environmental uncertainty and performance, which they argue are vital in advancing understanding of the process of organizational learning within an entrepreneurial SME context. By adopting a 'meta-theoretic' and integrative perspective, they argue that it will be possible to conceptualize learning and strategy making as a multidimensional and temporal phenomena. Specifically, strategy making and organizational learning are conceived as potentially firm-specific endowments, a perspective that is underpinned by the resource-based view of the firm (Penrose 1959; Wernerfelt 1984). They argue in an entrepreneurial context that the resource-based view accords greater weight to the positive role of entrepreneurial managerial discernment in explaining the sustainable competitive advantage of firms. Furthermore, they suggest that this perspective posits a positive role for entrepreneurial management action and the possibility of viewing organizational learning processes as firm-specific, differential resources. As in Friga's chapter, Gonsalves and Gray conceptualize organizational learning as both a resource stock and a flow (Dierickx and Cool 1989). Finally, this chapter contributes to the methodological debate within entrepreneurship by emphasizing the structure—agency debate as duality rather than dualism. In particular, Gonsalves and Gray emphasize that research conducted under the auspices of a entrepreneurial learning resources perspective will need to complement the conceptual gains and arguments already made in the field with rigorous, exploratory measurement-based support.

One of the conceptual contributions in Politis' chapter in this volume is the attention that is drawn to the process of the entrepreneurial transformation of knowledge as both an explorative and exploitative process (March 1991). Jan Waalkens, René Jorna and Theo Postma expand on this to consider innovation and absorptive capacity in knowledge-intensive firms (Cohen and Levinthal 1990). This chapter builds on the work of Lane *et al.* (2002), who have identified three major shortcomings in the area of absorptive capacity: first, there are limited attempts to revise the definition of absorptive capacity; second, little attention is paid to the actual process underlying absorptive capacity; and third, few attempts are made to measure it outside the R&D context. In addressing these issues, Waalkens *et al.* argue that individual learning and knowledge capabilities should be considered in terms of variables contributing to the absorptive capacity of the firm and, thus, they adopt a knowledge-based view of the firm (Grant 1996) which focuses on a firm's domain of knowledge use, transfer and development to inform their research. They have employed a refined definition of absorptive capacity (Zahra and George 2002) whereby the construct is divided into two elements, potential absorptive capacity and realized absorptive capacity. The former refers to the search for knowledge through exploration of the internal and external environment, while the latter focuses on the effective exploitation and implementation of knowledge. The research study reported in this chapter focuses on attempting to determine the absorptive capacity of architectural and engineering SME firms in the construction sector, which tend to be knowledge-intensive. While the classic indicator of absorptive capacity is R&D expenditure, Waalkens *et al.* argue that this moderates knowledge-gathering behaviour. Furthermore, as these types of firms often lack R&D investment, they suggest alternative indicators to measuring absorptive capacity, which include measuring prior related knowledge, formal collaboration with parties, the network of informal relationships and the locus of absorptive capacity in a firm.

The final chapter in this section by Joakim Tell discusses the use of a university-led approach to facilitated learning through organized networks of SME managers and researchers. In particular, it examines if networks between small enterprises can be facilitated by the active involvement of a regional university. In an attempt to determine this he employs a learning network perspective to explore the relationship between individuals within a network, with a specific focus on trust and commitment. The approach has similarities with an action learning perspective (Revans 1971; Leitch 2007), which is based on 'the straightforward pedagogical notion that people learn most effectively when working on real-time problems occurring in their own work setting' (Raelin 1999: 117). In such an approach, managers or entrepreneurs learn by reflecting on actions being taken in solving a real organizational problem with peers of similar position who are also experiencing challenging situations. The empirical part of this chapter explores various collaborative approaches developed by two networks comprising representatives from the university and small enterprises in the region of

Halmstad in Sweden. Tell found that organizing a university-led learning network provided a means of establishing a systematic and formalized interaction between the SME managers. In addition, it also provided a platform for dialogue for researchers and managers to come together to discuss and reflect upon opportunities and issues faced on a daily basis. From a learning perspective it was possible over time to identify a shift from a focus on primarily single-loop or adaptive learning to one that incorporated double-loop or generative learning also (Argyris and Schön 1978). A vital element of the process was the establishment of trust between all the players resulting in a long-term commitment to the network. This element in association with the process of dialogue resulted in the development of 'an open-hearted and questioning milieu' which increased the possibilities of exploiting the potential for double-loop learning over time.

Learning, education and development

Building on the emphasis in Tell's chapter, there is a need to consider entrepreneurial learning in a context beyond the concepts and categories adopted in the study of learning in intra- and inter-organizational contexts. In particular, as the entrepreneurial learning field develops, there is an opportunity to explore some wider aspects of learning in the context of the entrepreneurial process.

Robert Smith focuses on the implications of one specific issue in our emerging understanding of some aspects of the entrepreneurial process. Specifically, he explores the impact that experiencing dyslexia or other learning difficulties may have for the many highly successful entrepreneurs who have self-reported on this issue. As he acknowledges, learning difficulties can be a hidden, taboo subject associated with failure, and Smith suggests this may lead entrepreneurs with dyslexia to develop a different conceptual framework in learning and practising entrepreneurship than non-dyslexic entrepreneurs. This is important, he argues, as learning plays a crucial role in the development of entrepreneurial propensity and is closely allied with communication. Furthermore, those who have dyslexia often develop highly strategic and creative cognitive abilities. Indeed, many individuals who have dyslexia are often referred to as 'visual thinkers' who can be world leaders in technological and creative developments (West 2001). Based on the experiences of over fifty entrepreneurs, chief executive officers and inventors who have self-reported experiencing learning difficulties, Smith focuses on the impact of dyslexia and other learning difficulties on the communication ability and styles of these individuals. He concludes that there are specific communication techniques, which have been adopted by these entrepreneurs to overcome their communication difficulties. These techniques include looking at the bigger picture, learning from pictures, relying on one's memory, a preference for talking, avoiding the written word and refusing to work from a script. Possessing a distinctly different way of processing information can provide those with dyslexia an edge in a volatile, rapidly moving environment (Morris 2002); they are better placed to turn a perceived disadvantage into a competitive advantage. The implications of this exploratory research are far-reaching and suggest that as specific learning difficulties can be screened for, those people with the physiological gift of thinking pictorially could be encouraged to consider an entrepreneurial career path. Furthermore, from a pedagogical perspective it becomes clear that academics will need to adopt different approaches to teaching and learning so that differently-abled individuals are given an opportunity to excel alongside their counterparts.

A more traditional context of entrepreneurship education provides the focus for the final chapter by Sandra Fisher, Mary Graham and Marc Compeau, who attempt to determine the effectiveness of entrepreneurship education. Little detailed evaluative research has been conducted in this area and thus the authors argue that it is necessary to review the existing literature on entrepreneurial learning outcomes in an attempt to organize it within a common framework. In so doing they hope to facilitate continuous improvement efforts in the field and, by acknowledging the contributions of both academics and practitioners, to improve communication between both constituencies. They highlight that one of the limitations of the literature in this area is that learning outcomes tend to be presented in the form of relatively unorganized lists that are not grounded either in theory or on a well-defined conceptual foundation. Furthermore, they note that it is unclear how academics should integrate entrepreneurship learning outcomes into courses or other learning experiences. Thus, they adopted the typological framework proposed by Kraiger *et al.* (1993), which emphasizes three broad learning outcomes: cognitive or knowledge-based outcomes, skills-based or behavioural outcomes, and affective outcomes that comprise attitudinal and motivational outcomes. They argue that this typology is ideal for understanding learning outcomes in entrepreneurial education for two reasons: first, it permits a coherent specification of desired learning outcomes; and second, for purposes of continuous improvement because the three elements are related to different types of improvement interventions. Thus, it allows teachers and lecturers to address both learning content and learning type deficiencies by re-designing the curriculum or adopting different pedagogical approaches. Learning outcomes were further categorized on the basis of content – business-specific and interpersonal/personal content – which they suggest further enhances definition of the appropriate learning outcomes by emphasizing that there are multiple types of outcomes in a given area. The advantage of adopting this framework is that it can potentially assist in the design of experientially based entrepreneurship courses which aim to provide students with a solid foundation in the knowledge, skills and attitudes necessary to act entrepreneurially or to apply entrepreneurial principles within organizations.

Conclusion

The chapters in this volume represent one of the first attempts to provide a systematic treatment of the interface between the entrepreneurship and organizational learning literatures. They demonstrate that in terms of both conceptual development and empirical application there is a very diverse range of perspectives and approaches that can guide the development of this area. As with other areas of entrepreneurship research, the newness of the domain as a context of application for theories, models and constructs derived from other established domains makes it difficult to identify or establish a single integrative perspective on entrepreneurial learning. This is reinforced by the lack of conceptual and theoretical consensus in the wider organizational learning literature itself. Further research on entrepreneurial learning will have to recognize this diversity and seek to build on it.

In this book we have demonstrated the application of learning concepts in the opportunity recognition and exploitation process, the role of experience and experiential learning, the distinction between learning as a process and knowledge as the outcome of that process, the dynamics of learning processes and outcomes within and between organizations, and, to some extent, the relationship between learning and organizational effectiveness in entrepreneurial contexts. In addition to further wok on these topics, future research could also usefully focus on a number of other themes, including the nature of learning at individual and group level within organizations, the nature of inter-organizational learning in entrepreneurial networks, learning as problem-solving and experimentation, cross-cultural dimensions of (and differences in) entrepreneurial learning, and the process of unlearning and the role of organizational memory. In developing this field, and addressing some of these issues, there will be an ongoing requirement that scholars engage with the latest thinking in individual and organizational learning theory and commit to the development and application of alternative quantitative and qualitative methodologies to access learning processes and outcomes in entrepreneurial contexts.

Notes

1 This section is based in part on material in Harrison and Leitch (2005b).

References

Argyris, C. and Schön, D. (1978) *Organizational Learning: A Theory in Action Perspective* New York: Addison-Wesley.
Astley, W. G. (1984) Subjectivity, sophistry and symbolism in management science. *Journal of Management Studies*, 21: 259–72.
Berthoin Antal, A., Dierkes, M., Child, J. and Nonaka, I. (2001) Introduction: finding paths through the handbook. In M. Dierkes, A. Berthoin Antal, J. Child, and I. Nonaka, (eds), *Handbook of Organizational Learning and Knowledge*. Oxford: Oxford University Press, pp. 1–7.
Brown, J. S. and Duguid, P. (1991) Organizational learning and communities of practice: toward a unified view of working, learning and innovation; *Organization Science*, 2(1) 40–57.
Brown, J. S. and Duguid, P. (2000) *The Social Life of Information*, Cambridge, MA: Harvard Business School Press.

Busenitz, L. W., Fiet, J. O. and Moesel, D. D. (2004) Reconsidering the venture capitalists' 'value added' proposition: an interorganizational learning perspective. *Journal of Business Venturing*, 19: 787–807.

Castells, M. (1996) *The Rise of the Network Society*. Oxford: Blackwell.

Chaston, I., Badger, B. and Sadler-Smith, E. (1999) Organizational learning: research issues and application in SME sector firms. *International Journal of Entrepreneurial Behaviour and Research*, 5: 191–203

Chaston, I., Badger, B., Mangles. T. and Sadler-Smith, E. (2001) The internet and e-commerce: an opportunity to examine organizational learning in progress in small manufacturing firms. *International Small Business Journal*, 19(2): 1417–32.

Child, J. and Heavens, J. S. (2001) The social constitution of organizations and its implications for organizational learning. In M. Dierkes, A. Berthoin Antal, J. Child and I. Nonaka (eds), *Handbook of Organizational Learning and Knowledge*. Oxford: Oxford University Press pp. 308-26.

Choueke, R. and Armstrong, R. (1998) The learning organization in small and medium-sized enterprises: a destination or a journey? *International Journal of Entrepreneurial Behaviour and Research*, 4(2): 129–40.

Cohen, W. M. and Levinthal, D. A. (1990) Absorptive capacity: a new perspective on learning and innovation. *Administrative Science Quarterly*, 35: 128–52.

Coopey, J. C. (1995) The learning organization: power, politics and ideology. *Management Learning*, 26: 193–213.

Coopey, J. C. and Burgoyne, J. (2000) Politics and organizational learning. *Journal of Management Studies*, 37: 869–85.

Cope, J. (2005) Towards a dynamic learning perspective of entrepreneurship. *Entrepreneurship Theory and Practice*, 29(4): 373–98.

Corbett, A. C. (2005) Experiential learning within the process of opportunity identification and exploitation. *Entrepreneurship Theory and Practice*, 29(4) 473–92.

Crossan, M. M., Lane, H. W. and White, R. E. (1999) An organizational learning framework: from intuition to institution. *Academy of Management Review*, 24(3): 522–37.

Day, D. L. (1992) Research linkages between entrepreneurship and strategic management or general management. In D. L. Sexton and J. D. Kasarda (eds), *The State of the Art of Entrepreneurship*. Boston: PWS-Kent.

Day, G. S. and Shoemaker, P. H. J. (2004) Driving through the fog: managing at the edge. *Long Range Planning*, 37: 127–42.

Deakins, D. (1999) *Entrepreneurship and Small Firms*, 2nd ed., London McGraw-Hill.

De Clercq, D. and Sapienza, H. J. (2005) When do venture capital firms learn from their portfolio companies? *Entrepreneurship Theory and Practice*, July: 517–35.

Dierickx, I. and Cool, K. (1989) Asset stock, accumulation and sustainability of competitive advantage. *Management Science*, 35: 1504–11.

Dierkes, M., Berthoin Antal, A., Child, J. and Nonaka, I. (2001) *Handbook of Organizational Learning and Knowledge*. Oxford: Oxford University Press.

Dixon, N. (1994) *The Organizational Learning Cycle: How Can We Learn Collectively?* Maidenhead: McGraw-Hill.

Dixon, N. (1999) *The Organizational Learning Cycle: How Can We Learn Collectively?*, 2nd ed. Aldershot: Gower.

Dutta, D. K. and Crossan, M. M. (2005) The nature of entrepreneurial opportunities: understanding the process using the 4I organizational learning framework. *Entrepreneurship Theory and Practice*, 29(4): 425–50.

Easterby-Smith, M. (1997) Disciplines of organizational learning: contributions and critiques. *Human Relations*, 50: 1085–113.

Easterby-Smith, M. and Araujo, L. (1999) Current debates and opportunities in M. Easterby-Smith, J. Burgoyne and L. Arajuo (eds), *Organizational Learning and the Learning Organization*. London: Sage.

Easterby-Smith, M. and Lyles, M. (2003) *The Blackwell Handbook of Organizational Learning and Knowledge Management*. Oxford: Blackwell.

Easterby-Smith, M., Burgoyne, J. and Araujo, A. (eds) (1999) *Organizational Learning and the Learning Organization*. London: Sage.

Easterby-Smith, M., Crossan, M. and Nicolini, D. (2000) Organizational learning: debates past, present and future. *Journal of Management Studies*, 37(6) 783–96.

Eliasson, G. (1976) *Business Economic Planning: Theory, Practice and Comparison*. London: Wiley.

Eliasson, G. (1996a) *Firm Objectives, Controls and Organization*. Boston: Kluwer.

Eliasson, G. (1996b) Spillover, integrated production and the theory of the firm. *Journal of Evolutionary Economics*, 6: 125–40.

Eliasson, G. (1996c) *The Pharmaceutical and Biotechnological Competence Bloc*. Occasional Paper of the Royal Institute of Technology, Department of Industrial Economics and Management, Stockholm.

Eliasson, G. (1998) *The Nature of Economic Change and Management in the Knowledge-Based Information Economy*. Working Paper, Department of Industrial Economics and Management, KTH Stockholm.

Erikson, T. (2003) Towards a taxonomy of entrepreneurial learning experiences among potential entrepreneurs. *Journal of Small Business and Enterprise Development*, 10: 106–12.

Fontes, M. and Coombs, R. (1996) New technology-based firm formation in a less advanced country: a learning process. *International Journal of Entrepreneurial Behaviour and Research*, 2(2): 82–101.

Grant, R. M. (1996) Toward a knowledge-based theory of the firm. *Strategic Management Journal*, 17 (Winter Special Issue): 109–22.

Harrison, R. T. and Leitch, C. M. (1994) Entrepreneurship and leadership: the implications for education and development. *Entrepreneurship and Regional Development*, 6: 111–25.

Harrison, R. T. and Leitch, C. M. (2000) Learning and organization in the knowledge-based information economy: initial findings from a participatory action research case study. *British Journal of Management*, 11(2): 103–19.

Harrison, R. T. and Leitch, C. M. (eds) (2005a) Special issue on Entrepreneurial Learning. *Entrepreneurship Theory and Practice*, 29(4): 351–535.

Harrison, R. T. and Leitch, C. M. (2005b) Entrepreneurial learning: researching the interface between learning and the entrepreneurial context. *Entrepreneurship Theory and Practice*, 29(4): 351–72.

Henry, C., Hill, F. and Leitch, C. (2004) The effectiveness of training for new business creation: a longitudinal study. *International Small Business Journal*, 22(3): 249–72.

Huber, G. P. (1991) Organizational learning: the contributing processes and the literatures. *Organization Science*, 2(1): 88–115.

Kolb, D. A. (1973) *Organizational Psychology*. Eaglewood Cliffs, NJ: Prentice-Hall.

Kraiger, K., Ford, J. K. and Salas, E. (1993). Application of cognitive, skill-based, and affective theories of learning outcomes to new methods of training evaluation. *Journal of Applied Psychology*, 78: 311–28.

Lane, J. L., Koka, B. and Pathak, S. (2002) A thematic analysis and critical assessment of absorptive capacity. *Academy of Management Proceedings* MA, 6 pp.

Lave, J. and Wenger, E. (1991) *Situated Learning: Legitimate Peripheral Participation*. Cambridge: Cambridge University Press.

Leitch, C. M. (2007) An action research approach to entrepreneurship, in H. Neergaard and J.P. Ulhøi (eds), *Handbook for Qualitative Research Methods in Entrepreneurship*. Cheltenham: Edward Elgar.

Leitch, C. M., Harrison, R. T., Burgoyne, J. and Blantern, C. (1996) Learning organizations: the measurement of company performance. *European Journal of Industrial Training,* 20(1): 16–25.

Leitch, C. M., Harrison, R. T. and Burgoyne, J. (1999) *Understanding the Learning Company: A Constructivist Approach*. Working Paper, School of Management and Economics, Queen's University of Belfast/School of Management, University of Edinburgh.

Lichtenstein, B. B., Lumpkin, G. T. and Walton, J. W. (2000) Organizational learning in new ventures: enhancing entrepreneurial success in the new millennium. http://www.sbaer. uca.edu/Research/2000/USABE-SBIDA/Lichtenstein.pdf

Lumpkin, G. T. and Lichtenstein, B. B. (2005) The role of organizational learning in the opportunity recognition process. *Entrepreneurship Theory and Practice*, 29(4): 451–72.

Macharzina, K., Oesterle, M.-J. and Brodel, D. (2001), Learning in multinationals. In M. Dierkes, A. Berthoin Antal, J. Child and I. Nonaka. (eds), *Handbook of Organizational Learning and Knowledge*. Oxford: Oxford University Press, pp. 631–56.

Mackenzie, K. D. (1994) The science of an organization. Part I: A new model of organizational learning. *Human Systems Management*, 13(4): 248–58.

March, J. (1991) Exploration and exploitation in organizational learning. *Organization Science*, 2: 71–87.

Minniti, M. and Bygrave, W. (2001) A dynamic model of entrepreneurial learning. *Entrepreneurship Theory and Practice,* 25(3): 5–16.

Moingeon, B. and Edmundson, A. (eds) (1996) *Organizational Learning and Competitive Advantage*. London: Sage.

Morris, B. (2002) Overcoming dyslexia. *Fortune Magazine*, 28 April.

Muthusamy, S. K. and White M. A. (2005) Learning and knowledge transfer in strategic alliances: a social exchange view. *Organization Studies*, 26(3): 415–41.

Nelson, R. R. and Winter, S. G. (1982) *An Evolutionary Theory of Economic Change*. Cambridge, MA: Belknap Press.

Nonaka, I. and Takeuchi, H. (1995) *The Knowledge Creating Company: How Japanese Companies Create the Dynamics of Innovation*. Oxford: Oxford University Press.

Pawlowski, P. (2001) The treatment of organizational learning in management science. In M. Dierkes, A. Berthoin Antal, J. Child, and I. Nonaka. (eds), *Handbook of Organizational Learning and Knowledge*. Oxford: Oxford University Press, pp. 61–88.

Pedler, M., Burgoyne, J. and Boydell, T. (1997) *The Learning Company: A Strategy for Sustainable Development*, 2nd ed. London: McGraw-Hill.

Penrose, E. (1959) *The Theory of the Growth of the Firm*. New York: Wiley.

Polanyi, M. (1967) *The Tacit Dimension*. Garden City, NY: Anchor Books.

Politis, D. (2005) The process of entrepreneurial learning: a conceptual framework. *Entrepreneurship Theory and Practice*, 29(4): 399–424.

Prange, C. (1999) Organizational learning – desperately seeking theory? In M. Easterby-Smith, J. Burgoyne and L. Arajuo (eds), *Organizational Learning and the Learning Organization*. London: Sage, pp. 24–43.

Prusak, L. (1997) *Knowledge in Organizations*. Oxford: Butterworth-Heinemann.

Rae, D. (2000) Understanding entrepreneurial learning: a question of how? *International Journal of Entrepreneurial Behaviour and Research*, 6(3): 145–59.

Rae, D. (2004) Practical theories from entrepreneurs' stories: discursive approaches to entrepreneurial learning. *Journal of Small Business and Enterprise Development*, 11: 195–202.

Rae, D. and Carswell, M. (2000) Using a life-story approach in researching entrepreneurial learning: the development of a conceptual model and its implications in the design of learning experiences. *Education and Training*, 42: 220–7.

Rae, D. and Carswell, M. (2001) Towards a conceptual understanding of entrepreneurial learning. *Journal of Small Business and Enterprise Development*, 8: 150–8.

Raelin, J. (1999) Preface to special issue: The action dimension in management: diverse approaches to research, teaching and development. *Management Learning*, 30(2): 115–26.

Ravasi, D. and Turati, C. (2005) Exploring entrepreneurial learning: a comparative study of technology development projects. *Journal of Business Venturing*, 20: 137–64.

Revans, R. (1971) *Developing Effective Managers* London: Longman.

Scarborough, H. and Swann, J. (2003) Discourses of knowledge management and the learning organization: their production and consumption. In M. Easterby-Smith and M. Lyles (eds), *The Blackwell Handbook of Organizational Learning and Knowledge Management*. Oxford: Blackwell pp. 495–512.

Schildt, H., Maula, M. and Keil, T. (2005) Explorative and exploitative learning from external corporate ventures. *Entrepreneurship Theory and Practice*, 29(4): 493–516.

Senge, P. (1995) What does 'learning organization' mean for entrepreneurial firms? http://web.mit.edu/entforum/www/focus_online/Fall95/ask_mit/AskMITa95.html, accessed 21 March 2001.

Smilor, R. W. (1997) Entrepreneurship: reflections on a subversive activity. *Journal of Business Venturing*, 12(5): 341–421.

Snell, R. and Chak, A. M.-K. (1998) The learning organization: learning and empowerment for whom? *Management Learning*, 29: 337–64.

Starkey, K. (ed.)(1996a) *How Organizations Learn*. London: International Thomson Business Press.

Starkey, K. (1996b) Introduction. In K. Starkey (ed.), *How Organizations Learn*. International London: Thomson Business Press, pp. 7–17.

Sweeney, G. P. (1987/88) The entrepreneurial firm as a learning system in the information economy. *The Information Society*, 5(2).

Taylor, D. W. and Thorpe, R. (2004) Entrepreneurial learning: a process of co-participation. *Journal of Small Business and Enterprise Development*, 11: 203–11.

Ulrich, T. A. (1997) An empirical approach to entrepreneurial-learning styles. Paper to the Conference—Internationalizing Entrepreneurship Education and Training, IntEnt97, Monterey Bay, California, 25–27 June.

Van den Bosch, F. A. J., Van Wijk, R. A. and Volberda, H. W. (2003) Absorptive capacity: antecedents, models and outcomes. In M. Easterby-Smith, and M. Lyles, (eds), *Handbook of Organizational Learning and Knowledge Management*. Oxford: Blackwell, pp. 278–302.

von Krogh, G., Ichijo, K. and Nonaka, I. (2000) *Enabling Knowledge Creation*. New York: Oxford University Press.

Watts, G., Cope, J. and Hulme, M. (1998) Ansoff's matrix, pain and gain: growth strategies and adaptive learning among small food producers. *International Journal of Entrepreneurial Behaviour and Research*, 4: 101–11.

Wenger, E. (1998) *Communities of Practice.* Cambridge: Cambridge University Press.

Wernerfelt, B. (1984) A resource based view of the firm. *Strategic Management Journal,* 5: 171–80

West, T. G. (2001) Images and reversals: visual thinkers and Nobel Prizes. *ACMSIGGRAPH Computer Graphics Quarterly,* 35(1): 14–15.

Wyer, P., Mason, J. and Theodorakopoulos, N. (2000) Small business development and the 'learning organization'. *International Journal of Entrepreneurial Behaviour and Research,* 6: 239–59.

Zahra, S. A. and George, G. (2002) Absorptive capacity: a review, re-conceptualisation, and extension. *Academy of Management Review,* 27(2): 185–203.

Zuboff, S. (1988) *In the Age of the Smart Machine: The Future of Work and Power*, New York: Basic Books.

Section II

Conceptual approaches

2 Enhancing entrepreneurial learning through peripheral vision

Robert Chia

Introduction

> Business art is the step that comes after Art. . . . Being good at business . . .
> is the most fascinating kind of art.
>
> (Andy Warhol 1977: 91)

Entrepreneurial learning may be characterised by creative search, incessant experimentation, the regular transgression of social norms and institutional boundaries, and the imaginative reconfiguring of sources of potentialities into resources and productive outcomes. It is about 'learning along the way' (Bateson 1994). The term 'entrepreneur' derives from two etymologically related Latin words: *intrare*, meaning to enter or to 'penetrate in between', and *prendere* or *prehendere* meaning to 'grasp' or 'seize hold of'. The entrepreneur is therefore one who *penetrates* and *transgresses* established boundaries and seizes the opportunities otherwise overlooked by others. This is the essence of enterprise and the entrepreneurial venture: to enter and prise open that which would otherwise remains hidden, overlooked, inaccessible or unexploited.

The entrepreneurial mentality is inextricably linked to what we call here the capacity for 'peripheral' vision (Ehrenzweig 1967; Bateson 1994; Chia 1998; Day and Shoemaker 2004a). Peripheral vision is a cultivated disposition for attending to the hidden, the obscured and the overlooked. It involves a *re-education of attention* one that redirects attention and awareness away from focal objects and events to the marginal activities, the cognitively repressed, the discarded, the seemingly incidental events surrounding them. Peripheral vision entails a kind of seeing from the 'corner-of-the-eye', so to speak. It can be systematically cultivated through educational strategies that deliberately direct attention away from the visible gestalt figures of comprehension to the unformed and the seemingly invisible background against which figure, identity and meaning emerge. These educational strategies amount to a kind of *negative pedagogy* that instils a sustained resistance to the attractions of the immediate, the visible and the formed. Such a cultivated resistance to conceptual closure has been called 'negative capability': 'when a man is capable of being in uncertainties, mysteries, doubts, without any irritable reaching after fact and reason' (John Keats, letter to G. and T. Keats, Dec. 1817).

Negative capability describes the capacity to be at ease with an inherently vague, unformed, ambiguous and changing world.

In this regard, art and literature with their long-established tradition of attending to the vague, the ephemeral, the uncertain and the illusive elements of social phenomena have much to say about entrepreneurial learning that has been overlooked in entrepreneurial research. This is unfortunate since entrepreneurial ventures are clearly more analogous to artistic exploits than to the practice of normal science. The structure of an entrepreneurial venture, for instance, can be likened to the hidden structure of a good literary work, a crime novel or a piece of art. By examining what we now know about the hidden order of art and its capacity and power to evoke our deeper awareness, sympathy and understanding, we can achieve a better understanding of the hidden structure of the entrepreneurial mentality.

In this chapter, we take peripheral vision as the key focus of analysis and attempt to show how the study of the arts can help throw fresh light on the nature of entrepreneurship and entrepreneurial learning. By entrepreneurship, we do not, however, just mean the narrow *economic* form that pervades the business entrepreneurship literature. Rather, we mean the generic process of disclosing new and novel way of living and being to a community at large. The social activist and reformer, the intellectual who trades in revolutionary ideas and ideals, the crime novelist who tantalises us with his or her hidden schemas, the journalist and commentator who plays with evocative images and the scientist who initiates new lines of discovery are as much entrepreneurs in this generic sense as the archetypal business entrepreneur. We argue here that entrepreneurship is best conceived as a generic and progressive social transformational activity, one that is characterised by a refined sensitivity for detecting and disclosing inarticulate or unconscious societal aspirations and preferences, and of articulating them in such a way as to create novel possibilities hitherto unthought and hence unavailable to the society at large. Genuine entrepreneurs are the antennas of society. They redirect and re-educate our attention to new possibilities and ways of living and being that were previously unthinkable. Entrepreneurial learning entails a sustained transgression of the 'unconscious metaphysics' (Whitehead 1933: 180) shaping a society's dominant habits of thought. Like the air we breathe, these habits of thought are so translucent, so pervasive and so seemingly necessary that they often blind us to the possibilities existing outwith. Entrepreneurial opportunities often go unrecognised precisely because they do not fit into traditionally held assumptions about the nature of social progress or of value creation. Paradoxically, blindness and insight are inextricably linked. Every way of seeing is also a way of not seeing. Learning to see what we do not normally see, therefore, constitutes a major breakthrough in cultural and corporate renewal. This is what we mean here by saying that entrepreneurial learning involves a 're-education of attention'.

Our purpose in this chapter is to elaborate on the basic claim that entrepreneurial learning is essentially characterised by the refined capacity for *peripheral vision*. Such peripheral vision can be systematically cultivated through visual and cognitive strategies that elevate *subsidiary* rather than *focal awareness* (Polanyi 1962) as the basis of human comprehension. It involves internalising a cognitive strategy that directs attention away from precise outcomes, self-evident facts and clear identities to emergent processes, the contextual circumstances and the relational nexus that contribute to surfacing social phenomena. A heightened sensitivity to the unexpressed, the unrealised, the ephemeral and the hidden is a primary condition for the entrepreneurial mind. As the ancient Greek philosopher Heraclitus reminds us: '*Harmonié aphanés phranerés kreittôn. . . .*' ('The hidden order is deeper, the invisible connection stronger, the inconspicuous correspondence more interesting that the apparent') (Heraclitus, in Parkes 1987: 106). We learn more fundamentally from immersion in ambiguity than from attending to already-formed gestalts figures, from *glancing* rather than from *gazing* from *scanning* and *browsing* than from *looking at*, from *noticing* than from focal *seeing*.

This is partly because, physiologically, the retina of the human eye contains twenty times more peripheral rod cells located at the corners of the eye than it does the cone cells found at the centre of the eye. The rod cells are low-level weak signal detectors more sensitive to movement than to shape or colour. Because of this the quality of information gathered through peripheral vision is ill-defined compared to the cone cells found at the centre of the eye which enable us to see with detailed clarity shapes and colour in good light. But because there are twenty times more rod cells than cone cells, much of what we visually register comes by way of the rod cells and thus lacks the kind of clarity and definition that allows it to be passed as formal knowledge. As a result we pay less attention to data gleaned from this peripheral process. This lower-definition knowing, what the social philosopher Michael Polanyi (1962) calls 'tacit knowledge', derives from a subsidiary awareness and it is this subsidiary awareness which accounts for the importance of peripheral vision. But to truly appreciate how we have been culturally shaped to ignore the importance of peripheral vision for so long and to understand why focal vision has dominated the process of knowledge creation, we need to go back to the historical roots of the Western epistemological tradition.

Vision and focal knowledge

> . . . sight is the sense that especially produces cognition in us and reveals many distinguishing features of things.
>
> (Aristotle, *Metaphysics*, Book Alpha 1, trans. Lawson-Tancred 1998: 4)

In a provocative caricaturing of the modern Western mentality, the Belgian surrealist René Magritte created a sculpture that is now displayed at the Museum of Modern Art in Brussels entitled 'The White Race'. The piece of art depicts the human senses with the eye mounted atop the ear below which is located the mouth and which is in turn supported by two noses. Magritte is ostensibly alluding to the implicit hierarchy of senses installed over a period of two millennia by the Western world as the founding basis for the production of knowledge. In this hierarchy, sight rules over all the other senses as the most precise and reliable form of knowledge. This is because the eyes are considered the sharpest and hence most reliable of all the senses, possessing a finely honed ability to differentiate between the minutiae of contrasts, colours and tones. Next in the hierarchy comes the ear, which as the sensor of sounds is the basis for a less exacting form of aural/oral discrimination and communication. The mouth and nose with their even lesser degree of precision are situated at the bottom of the hierarchy in Magritte's work of art, suggesting their inferiority in terms of the accuracy and reliability of knowledge associated with them.

In this simple and yet profound masterpiece Magritte captures succinctly the essence of the Western (hence The White Race!!!) obsession with vision and especially focal vision as the crowning basis of proper learning and knowledge. Thus, even when we have to resort to our other senses, we nevertheless still use the ocular metaphor as the basis of our linguistic expression: 'See how that tastes'; 'See how that smells'; 'See how hard that is'; 'Do you see what I mean?' Seeing belongs properly to the eyes, but because it is deemed the sole reliable basis for proper knowledge we use the word 'see' even for the other senses when we are thinking in cognitive terms. In consequence, our everyday language is infused with this language of visual presence. 'Observation' privileges visual data; 'definition' comes from *definire*, meaning to draw a line around; and sight is internalised into our vocabulary of knowledge – insight, idea, illuminate, enlighten, reflect, survey, point of view, perspective, etc.

Such an obsession with vision and visibility as the founding basis of knowledge creation in the West is a legacy that owes its debt to the Aristotelian privileging of sight over all the other senses. For Aristotle, as for much of the modern West, seeing is regarded as the most potent of the senses because it is the most powerful way of *presenting* (i.e. making appear) things before us. The word 'phenomenon', for instance, owes its origin in Greek to the notion of 'showing itself'. Learning and knowledge are thus construed in terms of the *bringing to presence* of things that are otherwise inaccessible, obscure, obdurate or intractable to our cognitive grasp. By definition, that which *cannot* be brought to presence, either because it is too ephemeral, vague, intractable or obdurate or because of its essentially hidden nature, is denied an epistemological status. A 'metaphysics of presence' (Derrida 1981) prevails.

One major consequence of this elevating of visibility as the basis of learning and knowledge is that much of current business practices are driven by the security of 'hard tangible facts'; only facts that can be visually identified, verified and quantified count. 'Bottom-line' measures are the be-all and end-all of effective business performance. The implicit, the intangible, the nuanced and the inarticulated such as employee morale, loyalty or customer goodwill etc. are overlooked or undervalued. This same attitude prevails in much of social science research in general and entrepreneurial research in particular. Our theories of entrepreneurship, like much of the social sciences, have been driven by an emphasis on the importance of tangible, quantifiable factor variables. In entrepreneurial studies, for example, there is a widespread reliance on a variance model of explanation in which entrepreneurial success is couched primarily in terms of identifiable dependent and independent variables (Miller 1983; Lumpkin and Dess 1996;

Dess *et al.* 1999; Stetz *et al.* 2000). Dess and Lumpkin (2001, 2005), for instance, postulate the existence of an 'entrepreneurial orientation' consisting of five dimensions: innovativeness, risk-taking, proactiveness, aggressiveness and autonomy. From this they propose a 'multivariate contingency framework' (2001: 9) for investigating the entrepreneurial orientation–performance relationship.

Entrepreneurial studies of this sort may identify the visible characteristics associated with entrepreneurship, but they do not begin to unravel what processes for instance are involved in becoming 'innovative' or what leads to a tendency towards 'risk-taking' as perceived by the researcher. Much of the psychologically driven literature on entrepreneurship, leadership and creativity follows these lines of analysis. There has been an overwhelming preoccupation with personality attributes and properties of individuals who are ostensibly 'leaders' and/or 'entrepreneurs'. The literature in entrepreneurial studies is replete with terminologies, typologies and determinant variables that purport to explain entrepreneurial behaviour. Such studies are often 'outcome-oriented' (in that they are retrospective analyses), based upon empirical investigations of already identifiable 'successful' entrepreneurs. What is overlooked in entrepreneurial research is the far more messy micro-learning processes and activities through which would-be entrepreneurs (both the successful and the unsuccessful) come to enact themselves into what they are.

In other words, in the 'haste-of-wanting-to-know' entrepreneurship researchers have, in their explanatory schemas, tended to overlook the deeper and hence more invisible social and epistemological structures that shape the learning and perception of entrepreneurs. Because they are often unaware of the epistemological biases inherent in the knowledge-creation process, their research attention is directed only to those visible and manifest aspects of entrepreneurship that readily lend themselves to systematic investigation. This is an epistemological asymmetry that this chapter seeks to correct.

The *gaze* and the *glance*: from focal to peripheral awareness

In a book entitled *Ways of Seeing*, John Berger (1972) makes the important observation that prior to the Renaissance in Western Europe, paintings were often expressed in a story-like form and it was not therefore uncommon to have several scenes painted onto a canvas depicting a sequence of events. For instance, the story of Adam and Eve was often depicted in a sequel leading up from the Garden of Eden to the moment of temptation and to the eventual expulsion of Adam and Eve from the Garden. Subsequent paintings after the Renaissance, however, tended to depict only that moment of shame when Adam and Eve became painfully aware of their nakedness. For Berger this shift in attention was caused by the advent of the Renaissance, which precipitated an awareness and mentality that directed focal attention solely to the consequential 'moment of revelation' – in this case the moment of 'shame' when both Adam and Eve tried to cover themselves: 'During the renaissance the narrative sequence disappeared, and the single moment depicted became the moment of shame . . . their shame is not so much in relation to each other as to the spectator' (Berger 1972: 49).

In other words, Adam and Eve are now not naked as they are but naked to an *observing eye*. Through a series of reflections on a range of other paintings, including especially nude paintings of the various periods, Berger concludes that what had developed in the Renaissance was a *logic of Gaze* in which focal attention and observation became privileged. The Gaze is associated with a desire to fix, arrest and take possession of. Subjects of painting such as the 'nudes' portrayed became 'objects' of desire rather than 'innocent' representations. They were subjected to the Gaze of another. Now, the 'subject (a woman) is aware of being seen by a spectator. She is not naked as she is!! She is naked as the spectator sees her' (ibid.). The woman has been objectified into an object of desire by an observing eye that seeks to possess her.

This logic of the Gaze underpins the Western epistemological attitude towards phenomena in the world (Chia 1998). In a fascinating study of the methods of Western painting and Chinese art, the art theorist Norman Bryson observes that many Western paintings are predicated on the 'disavowal of deictic reference' whilst painting in China is predicated on the 'acknowledgement and indeed the cultivation of deictic markers' (Bryson 1982: 89). What Bryson means by this is that in Western paintings, the individual history of a work of art, in the course of its transformation into a completed piece, is largely irretrievable because at various points there have been concerted attempts to cover up previous imperfections. Thus, although a trained artistic eye can tell that the visible surface of a particular piece of work may have been worked over and over again, the viewer is unable to ascertain what other images lie concealed beneath the surface display. The final image presented suppresses *deixis* and has 'no interest in its own genesis or past, except to bury it in a palimpsest of which only the final version shows through, above an interminable debris of revisions' (Bryson 1982: 92). The work of erasure stops only when the first image is totally obliterated and the viewer cannot ever work out how the final image has come to be what it is.

In the art of Chinese painting, on the other hand, the mastery of the stroke lies in the subliminal ability to paint out the traces that have brought the strokes into being. Chinese painting has always selected a form which

> permits a maximum of integrity and visibility to the constitutive strokes of the brush: foliage, bamboo, the ridges of boulder . . . and forms whose lack of outline (mist, aerial distance, the themes of still and moving water, of the pool and the waterfall) allows the brush to express to the full the liquidity and immediate flow of the ink.
>
> (Bryson 1982: 89)

In other words, Chinese paintings appear to openly and transparently display the uncertainties, hesitations, imperfections and improvisations that have gone into the production of the final effect. The work involved in the production of a piece of art is constantly displayed in the wake of its traces 'just as it . . . would apply . . . to a *performing* art' (Bryson 1982: 92, emphasis in original). In one case the process of becoming is incorporated into the painting whilst in the other process has been eliminated. The painting is placed outside duration. Easel paintings of the West are 'autochthonous, self-created, parthenogeneses, virgin-births' (Bryson 1982: 95).

Bryson uses this distinction to reveal two alternative logics of ordering and hence the forms of learning and cognition associated with them: the Gaze, which is fixing, prolonged and contemplative, and the Glance, which is 'a furtive or sideways look whose attention is always elsewhere' (Bryson 1982: 94). The Gaze attempts to arrest and extract form from fleeting temporal process. It is a vision disembodied, a vision decarnalised. In the Gaze the observer 'arrests the flux of the phenomena, contemplates the visual field from a vantage-point outside the mobility of duration, in an eternal moment of disclosed presence' (ibid.: 94). The Gaze is penetrating, piercing, fixing, objectifying. It is a violent act of focusing that forcibly extracts figure from ground. The Glance, on the other hand, 'addresses vision in the durational temporality of the viewing subject . . . [Chinese] calligraphic work cannot be taken in all at once . . . since it has itself unfolded within the *durée* of process' (Bryson 1982: 94).

What Bryson (1982) is getting at in this penetrating analysis of the two forms of art is the fundamental distinction between two contrasting approaches in visual observation: the Gaze with its emphasis on frontal focus and the Glance where vision is necessarily peripheral. Although Bryson used a comparison of Western and Chinese paintings to illustrate his point, it is the pervasiveness of each of these contrasting perspectives which differentiates the East from the West. The Gaze with its clarity of focus and its capacity for achieving clear distinct outlines is highly valorised within Western culture. It provides the foundational basis for legitimising formal learning and knowledge. On the other hand, the importance of the Glance, the quick subconscious seizing-up of situations, has been surreptitiously underestimated and/or overlooked and it is this very feature which defines entrepreneurial learning.

Peripheral vision in strategic thinking

> Peripheral vision entails the ability to pay attention to the part of the world you are not paying attention to.
>
> (Day and Shoemaker 2004b: 131)

In a recent special issue of *Long Range Planing* (Vol. 37, 2004) devoted to 'Peripheral Vision', the guest editors George Day and Paul Shoemaker, both from the Wharton Business School, emphasised the importance of sensing and acting on weak signals in the practice of business. For them this is a strategic necessity for remaining ahead of the competition and this, in turn, requires the vital capacity for peripheral vision. The special issue represents the tangible outcome of a conference held a year earlier during which 'It became clear to us, during the conference, that managing the periphery has not yet become a focal area of management' (Day and Shoemaker 2004a: 118). Because the dominant mantra in strategy-speak has traditionally been 'focus, focus, focus', there has been a tendency to ignore events and things occurring at the periphery of our attention. A paper by Sidney Winter

(2004) in the special issue convincingly argues that, like moths and bees, organisations evolve by adapting their sensors to specific focal purposes. Because of the demands of the environment, both organisms and organisations develop special-purpose sensors that are particularly attuned to certain aspects of the environment and that enable the organism/organisation to respond effectively to these elements. This process of evolution is generally termed 'selection, adaptation, learning' (SAL). However, whilst this process enables the organism/organisation to deal with the future from past experience, it cannot prepare the latter for unexpected events. A moth, for instance, can detect a bat and take effective evasive action, but it has no warning system to alert it to an impending blow from a rolled-up newspaper. Likewise, an organisation that learns from past experiences and develops a 'dominant logic' (Prahalad 2004) may be blinded by the latter and hence be ill-prepared for the future. As several authors in the special issue rightly point out, many things of crucial import take place at the periphery, just as snow melts first at the edges and then gradually moves to the centre. For that reason there is every need to be alert to changes taking place on the periphery of our attention. Yet, as Day and Shoemaker point out, the periphery is 'ever elusive' and always a 'bit blurry', and this is especially why there is a need to 'master the art of peripheral vision'.

Despite this appreciation of the importance of peripheral vision, Day and Shoemaker together with many of the other contributors to the special issue in *Long Range Planning* underestimate the true elusiveness of the periphery and hence the form of awareness required for dealing with it. This is clearly demonstrated by the rather disappointing remedies offered in the collection of articles that Day and Shoemaker usefully summarise. These include: (a) expand your focus; (b) ask the right questions; (c) experimentation and immersion in the periphery; (d) use technology to become more agile. We can deal with each of these and show how grossly inadequate they are in addressing the problem of the periphery. To begin with, as Day and Shoemaker rightly point out, 'Each time you turn your head to look at it, you create a new "periphery"' (Day and Shoemaker 2004a: 117). This is precisely the case so that shifting focus or even expansion of the latter will not help in engaging with the problem of the periphery. The periphery is not a definable or locatable space. It is that which lies beyond the bounds of our focal vision. Expanding the focus only shifts the periphery further back. The periphery is a receding horizon of awareness and as we will show can only be approached elliptically, not through expansion of the focus but through the cultivation of the Glance. The Glance is associated with scattered attention, subsidiary awareness and unconscious scanning. We will examine these aspects in greater detail in the next section.

Second, asking the 'right' questions presupposes that we can know what is 'right' when the questions are asked. The paradox is that if we knew what is right *a priori*, it must presuppose a clear distinction that we have already been able to establish between what is right and what is wrong, what is relevant and what is not relevant. This is only possible through focused attention and evaluation. But the whole point about peripheral vision is that it is 'blurry' so that we cannot as yet establish what constitutes right or wrong until we turn our focus towards it.

If we are to genuinely reflect on the form of these searching questions, we will realise that we can only know if we have asked the right questions if the outcomes turn out to be favourable to us. Right and wrong are judgements made *post hoc* on outcomes of action. What is needed is not to think in terms of premature evaluation but to remain open to possibilities.

Third, experimentation and immersion in the periphery is indeed a promising start, but how do we make ourselves aware of what is the 'potentially productive' periphery in the first place? The periphery is everywhere and nowhere. It can be inconsequential or consequential. Again we cannot know until after the fact, so do we then invest time and energy by scattering our attention and expanding our focus? In that case, as one contribution to the special issue rightly points out, there is a tendency towards diminishing returns when you begin to scan and explore the periphery. Thus, 'as more resources are devoted, information overload can be a serious problem' (Day and Shoemaker 2004b: 127). The challenge of peripheral vision, therefore, is to 'fly reconnaissance missions over these areas *without* devoting the full attention of the organisation to them' (Day and Shoemaker 2004b: 132). Yes, indeed, but this is not the same thing as immersion in the periphery. Flying 'reconnaissance missions' is tantamount to oscillating between focal and peripheral vision, between the Gaze and the Glance, and this, we argue, is what is needed to heighten our subsidiary awareness of things going on at the periphery of our attention. We will argue that this perceptual strategy of oscillation is well understood and deployed by artists and musicians and something much explored and emphasised in the arts.

Finally, contrary to the common presumption that technology will facilitate agility and enable better quality decision-making, technology in fact is predicated upon a need for focal selection. Technology is effective precisely because it aids our focus and hence enables us to concentrate our energies and to extract maximum gain from minimum efforts. The word technology derives from the Greek word *techné* meaning to 'negate' touch: technology is that which negates the human *senses*. It substitutes and replaces direct human interventions. For instance, the television enables us to watch a football game taking place several thousand of miles away in the comfort of our living room. But it does so at a price: we can only see and follow what the camera-person wants us to see or follow. He or she has already pre-selected (in other words given a focus) to what is to be seen and what is not to be seen. For that very reason we cannot truly participate in the rising sense of anticipation of the crowds occurring outside the televisual frame – what is sometimes called 'the movement off the ball' – something that we only experience by being physically present in the football stadium. All technologies including the technology of 'writing', the internet, etc., are fundamentally defined by locatability, framing, fixity, selectivity and abstraction; these processes presuppose the focusing of attention, the creation of division and boundaries and the marginalising of the periphery. As such technology, in and of itself, cannot help improve our peripheral vision. What is really needed is an entirely different visual strategy which is steeped in temporality and process and which thus takes into account the processual *forming* of in-form-ation.

Focal and subsidiary awareness

> When we are relying on our awareness of something (A) for attending to
> something else (B), we are but subsidiarily aware of A. The thing B to which
> we are thus focally attending, is then the meaning of A . . . The two kinds
> of awareness are mutually exclusive.
>
> (Michael Polanyi, *Personal Knowledge*, 1962: xiii)

In a series of powerfully argued seminal works, the social philosopher Michael
Polanyi (1962, 1967, 1969) drew attention to a crucial missing element in our
understanding of the structure of knowledge and of human experience –
subsidiary awareness and the *tacit dimension* associated with it. Polanyi believed
that throughout most of Western philosophy from Plato and Aristotle onwards,
what constituted proper knowledge had been defined far too narrowly in terms of
the explicit and the visible, so much so that the invisible and tacit aspects underlying our epistemological endeavours have been surreptitiously ignored. Polanyi
distinguishes between a *focal awareness* that underpins explicit and articulatable
knowledge and a more elusive *subsidiary awareness* that generates tacit understanding. Focal awareness and subsidiary awareness are complementary but
mutually exclusive forms of comprehension. This distinction between focal
awareness and subsidiary awareness is formulated in recognition of the essentially *vectorial* character of human comprehension. Awareness is, of necessity,
directional. Polanyi, who is Hungarian by birth, tells the story of a regular break-
fast routine in which he reads his mail and then occasionally passes it on to his
son, who can only understand English, to read, often unaware that the letter had
not been written in English at all:

> My correspondence arrives at my breakfast table in various languages, but
> my son understands only English. Having just finished reading a letter I may
> wish to pass it on to him, but must check myself and look again to see in what
> language it was written. I am vividly aware of the meaning conveyed by the
> letter, yet know nothing whatever of its words.
>
> (Polanyi 1962: 57)

Although having read and understood the contents of the letter, he had not
consciously noted that it was written in a language other than English. *Focal* and
subsidiary awarenesses are mutually exclusive in the sense that one cannot focus on
what is presently functioning subsidiarily since awareness is, as we have maintained,
always vectorial. The relationship is one of gestalt figure and ground.

This idea that we can sometimes be only subsidiarily or vaguely aware of things
around us that are nevertheless registered in our comprehension suggests that
perception and cognition takes place not just at the conscious surface level but
also concurrently at a much deeper unconscious level. In studies conducted in the
area of psychoanalysis, depth perception and unconscious scanning and cognition
(Freud [1913] 1976; Varendonck 1923; Ehrenzweig 1965, 1967), it has been
shown that a great deal of information is registered in the subconscious which is

not conscious to the individual experiencing it. Much of our daily life proceeds in this manner. Freud, in his *Interpretation of Dreams*, discusses a patient of his who dreamt that he ordered a 'Kontuszówka' in a café. The patient was puzzled by the specificity of his order since he had never come across the term before. Freud was, however, able to inform him that it was the name of a Polish liquor which was freely advertised, so that the term was not a mere figment of his imagination. His patient did not believe him initially but some days later noticed hoardings carrying the advertisement at a street corner that he had been passing at least twice a day for several months. It appeared that he had unconsciously absorbed this information without being aware of it at all. No matter how hard we try, subsidiary awareness and the tacit knowledge associated with it can not be accessed directly or focally. It will always remain a kind of 'corner-of-the-eye' form of knowing. Yet, it nonetheless has a profound impact on our sense of comprehension and on our actions and decisions. It is what we would mean by an entrepreneurial intuition. Such an intuition, however, has a deep structure that can be systematically cultivated.

Unconscious scanning and scattered attention

> There are other forms in a painting unseen . . . but which nevertheless exert great influence. I refer to the minute, almost microscopic, scribbles which make up the technique of a great draftsman or the brushwork of a great painter.
>
> (Ehrenzweig 1965: 29)

We are socialised and educated to notice simple, discrete, compact and precise forms and to generally ignore vague, incoherent and inarticulate forms in our perceptual apprehension. Because of our deep cultural programming, our eyes are always eager to perceive a good gestalt: a clear picture, form or shape, the familiar features of someone we know, the distinct outlines of a building, etc. We are often guilty of oversimplifying our complex experiences into familiar stereotypical forms in our haste-of-wanting-to-know. We are impatient with vagueness, ambiguity and formlessness. As a result of this irresistible urge for clarity and coherence, we inevitably gloss over and overlook those inarticulate micro-forms or emergent formations that cumulatively make for recognition and comprehension. Conscious perception is purposeful focal awareness which, because of its gestalt bias, actively seeks out clearly formed end-states and excludes inarticulate form elements from our attention. Because of this impatience for achieving coherence we tend to gloss over the hesitancies, detours, digressions and false starts that better characterise the precarious emergence of a phenomenon. We become concerned only with outcomes and functional instrumentality governs our cognitive concerns. In the more concept-friendly terms that James March (1991) uses, we become more intent on *exploitation* rather than on *exploration*. This exploitative orientation is so entrenched within much of the modern psyche that when we apprehend a piece of art, the seemingly chaotic and random scribbles of an artist that go a long way towards producing the artistic effect is surreptitiously glossed over and overlooked by our gestalt perception. Our focally biased attention melts those 'little strokes and arabesques down to the same grey shading or to the continuous outline of real objects' (Ehrenzweig 1965: 30). Much of the richness of the form deriving from these invisible and seemingly random strokes and scribbles is generally treated as an aberration or imperfection and is not considered important enough to warrant our scrutiny and attention. We do not as a rule encourage our attention to wander away from the gestalt figure imposing itself onto our consciousness.

Unconscious scanning, however, does take place at a subsidiary level alongside our dominant instrumentality, notwithstanding our concerted attempts to deny its legitimacy. But we are often unaware that that is occurring. Sir Herbert Read calls this unconscious activity 'eye-wander' (Read, *Art and Industry*, in Ehrenzweig 1965: 22), where the eyes occasionally de-focus and our attention is then scattered to the periphery of things. Eye-wander is typically exemplified by our occasional experience of absent-minded browsing in the retail shops and bookstores whilst waiting for someone or something to happen. It is undirected, scattered attention that subconsciously glides over familiar outlines and details and it is during these moments of non-purposeful attention that we, in fact, become much more observant and 'in tune' with our surroundings. There is a certain uncontaminated 'purity' in our seeing in which we appear to lose ourselves amongst our objects of attention. The art critic John Ruskin calls this momentary unevaluative directness of vision the *innocence of the eye*: 'a sort of childish perception of these flat stains of colour, merely as such, without consciousness of what they signify, – as a blind man would see them if suddenly gifted with sight' (Ruskin 1927, Vol. 15: 27).

Anton Ehrenzweig (1965, 1967) calls this kind of subconscious awareness 'unconscious scanning' or 'scattered attention'. Contrary to Polanyi's insistence on the mutual exclusivity of focal and subsidiary awareness, what Ehrenzweig maintains is that it is actually possible through disciplined application and training to equip ourselves with the capacity to hold both figure and ground together in a unitary act of comprehension. This is what marks out the truly accomplished artists. For instance, in the case of music, the surface gestalt figure is typically represented by the melody. The melody draws our conscious awareness and keeps it as the focus of attention. The accompanying voices serve only as a background and are not as pregnant and 'ear-catching' as the main melody itself. The serious music student, however, gradually realises that what is called the 'accompaniment' really consists of several voices that 'form more or less continuous melodies in their own right' (Ehrenzweig 1965: 41). The pupil's attention is thus directed away from an exclusive concentration on the main melody and made to simultaneously follow the several competing melodies unfolding at the same time in order to truly begin to appreciate the rich polyphonic character of music. Instead of focusing singularly on the melody, the student is now able to scatter his or her attention and concurrently follow multiple potential lines of development.

The same thing applies in art. Here, like the student of music, the student of art learns to deliberately work *against* the gestalt principle by actively resisting the familiarity of form: 'When the art-school student takes up drawing he is made to watch not only the outline of the object he draws (the figure of the gestalt), but also the negative forms which the figure cuts out from the background' (Ehrenzweig 1965: 28). In other words, art students are taught to observe, simultaneously, the unfolding of the negative form as its outline emerges at the tip of the pencil. They are taught to attend to the varied minute combination of these invisible negative strokes that will make for a great improvement in the general impression of the formed figure. Unconscious scanning involves a subliminal sensitivity to the hesitant details of emergence that is generally overlooked by the untrained eye. In both the instances, of music and art training, what is developed is the capacity for a kind of 'scattered' or dispersed attention that is able to follow multiple lines of possibilities of development without the compulsion to prematurely achieve closure.

Extending entrepreneurial learning through peripheral vision

The classical rational mind with its focus on immediate, local causality, visible material outcomes and end-states finds it difficult to understand how it is possible that major transformations can be brought about by sometimes seemingly insignificant events occurring remotely or peripherally both in space and time. Chaos and complexity theories now, however, reveal the possibilities of what is popularly called the 'butterfly effect', where small, seemingly inconsequential events occurring often unnoticed at a periphery can trigger off major catastrophes. The possibilities of *non-local causality* are forcing us to re-evaluate our understanding of the traditional relationship between cause and effect. It forces us to expand our awareness and to look further afield for causal connections. Yet the wider our scan, the more uncertain and ambivalent the causal possibilities appear. What we have argued for in this chapter is the value of a peripheral vision that enables us to resist the urge to prematurely seek closure and to allow us to see how it is possible for seemingly inconsequential events to substantially influence central outcomes in the fullness of time.

In art, as we have seen, this insight is well understood. The art student is taught to scrupulously attend to the microscopic scribbles or the individual strokes of brushwork instead of attending to the dominant form figure that emerges. The good artist knows from a hundredfold experience how important it is to be aware of these 'invisible' chaotic scribbles because of the eventual cumulative impact they will have on the general impression of the picture. In music, the pupil's attention is similarly turned away from an exclusive concentration on the surface gestalt (which in this case is the melody) and made to observe the polyphonic character of the accompanying voices. In both instances it is the seemingly inconsequential details and peripheral micro-movements that are observed at the 'corner-of-the-eye' so to speak that turn out to be crucial for achieving the final effect. In both instances it is the subsidiary awareness that is cultivated and a scattering of attention through 'eye-wander' encouraged.

However, the learning of this form of *subsidiary awareness* or *unconscious scanning* is not just restricted to music and the arts. It can also be cultivated in a number of ways, including the playing and mastery of a variety of combination games like crosswords, chess, bridge (or even mahjong) and in the reading of crime novels. In all such instances the player, much like the entrepreneur, has to make a decision based on changing circumstances and inadequate information and hence to rely on his or her subsidiary awareness and unconscious scanning to grasp what is going on. There are, however, significant differences in degrees of opportunistic search beginning from crossword puzzles, combination games like chess and bridge, and much more open-ended ones like the Chinese game Go (or Wei Chi). Go is far more open-ended than chess, for instance, and much more akin to a crime novel as we shall see in a moment.

In crossword puzzles the search is limited to a relatively narrow range of combinational possibilities. It is a puzzle with a fixed final outcome. You either get it right or not at all. In some ways a crossword puzzle represents an appropriate metaphor for the kind of traditional business planning mode that is appropriate in relatively stable business circumstances, where the influencing factors are fixed and elements of variability are relatively unchanging, limited and definable. There is an in-built assumption that situations, and the significance and value of each puzzle piece (in this case the letters, or in the case of business planning the factor variables), do not materially change during the period of analysis. The playing of chess, however, is far more complex in that it can have a large number of final outcomes depending on the interaction of both players and on how the game progresses. Chess is about the arrangement, coding and decoding of a restrictive space in order to achieve overall mastery and control. There are clear rules of engagement and the status of each piece is well defined hierarchically. The object is conquest and subjugation of the opponent. Chess is the ultimate example of strategic positioning in business environmental manoeuvres. It is linear, focused and mission-led. It relies upon a precise logic of focused attention, clear judgement, structured reasoning and controlled action. Yet, as we now well know, it is possible to program a computer to learn sufficiently about these logical combinations to actually pose a real threat to the chess masters and even to beat them convincingly. Deep Blue is one example of this triumph of the power of information processing. Given a large enough processing capability, a computer can become better than a human being at the game of chess.

The playing of Go, on the other hand, is much more open-ended and does not, as of the present, lend itself to the kind of programming attainable in chess. It is closer to that of a crime novel. Like chess, Go is also played on a board but its units are simple pellets or discs, anonymous arithmetic units without any privileged status and that only have a collective function. Whilst chess pieces entertain bi/univocal relations with one another, and with their adversary's pieces, Go pieces have only extrinsic relationships and only exist within a nebula or constellation where they fulfil their function of 'insertion or situation, such as bordering, encircling, shattering' (Deleuze and Guattari 1988: 353). Playing Go is like going to war without battle lines, with neither direct confrontations nor decisive retreats.

Go is more like terrorism and guerrilla warfare, the enemy is often unknown or invisible and the attacks are sporadic and can come from any direction. In Go small, seemingly insignificant moves can have massive repercussions. Playing Go is a matter of 'arraying oneself in an open space, of holding space, of maintaining the possibility of springing up at any point: the movement is not from one point to another, but becomes perpetual without aim or destination, without departure or arrival' (Deleuze and Guattari 1988: 353). In chess you win by defeating the opponent and when you win you know it. The victory is decisive. It is all or nothing. In Go you win by occupying more territory and hence have a greater leverage than your opposition. Your adversary may be weakened but not totally destroyed. Go is the logic of entrepreneurs who celebrate the possibilities that come with the vagueness, ambiguity and fluidity of experience.

In the case of a good crime novel, the reader is often left in suspense right until the end of the novel, or sometimes even then the culprit is not identified. The crime novel appeals more through the skill of its construction than by its content or outcome. Suspense and intrigue are built into the plot. Its technique can be called one of *deliberate ambiguity*. A good crime novelist never allows the clues he or she surreptitiously inserts ever so discretely to narrow down prematurely so that the culprit can be identified early on. Instead he or she keeps these clues as discrete, disconnected and as ambiguous as possible. As this chaotic complex of information mounts in the reader's mind, the reader has to bear the tension and suspense only because he or she assumes that, in the end, all will fall into an orderly and logical pattern. The final twist comes when the reader is invariably surprised or taken aback by whoever the culprit turns out to be. A few odd bits that are smuggled unnoticed under a dazzling camouflage of insignificant details are triumphantly dragged out and delivered as the logical outcome of the unfolding story.

Writing a really good crime novel is no mean achievement since it requires several sub-themes and hence several series of accompanying clues to be kept running simultaneously, much like the polyphonic character of music. The reader is not allowed to concentrate on the development of a singular plot. Instead there are multiple possible lines of development and the reader's attention is constantly diverted from one possibility to another. He or she follows the 'unfolding of the whole intentionally incoherent and ambiguous story in a state of diffused attention with one or the other possibility dimly flickering and extinguishing again, but never attracting attention exclusively' (Ehrenzweig 1965: 44). The crime novel technique is a supreme example of a peripheral logic and a valuable guide as to how we should be re-educating our attention so as to achieve a deeper insight into the situations in which we find ourselves.

Entrepreneurial learning entails a shift in attention away from focal awareness to the concerns of *subsidiary awareness*, from conscious apprehension to unconscious scanning. Learning to develop peripheral vision is learning to resist the seductions of premature closure. The experience of art, music and drama, the playing of increasingly more open-ended combination games, helps develop the kind of scattered attention and the cultivating of the 'negative capability' required for achieving a deeper resonance with the material events taking place around us. This is a vital quality for successful entrepreneurship and novel value creation.

Conclusion

What we have argued in this chapter is that entrepreneurial learning is inextricably linked to the capacity for peripheral vision and that this quality can be cultivated through a *re-education of attention*. Because we are culturally programmed to Gaze and not to Glance, to develop our focal vision and not our peripheral vision, we often miss significant goings-on that take place on the margins of our consciousness. The Glance is much more sensitive to event-happenings at the periphery of vision and hence more able to grasp the unfolding minutiae of event-situations. To shift our attention away from focal awareness we must attend to the emerging 'negative' form generated by focal attention and the deep unconscious structure associated with it. Sensitivity to such deep structures can be systematically cultivated through a variety of ways. Crosswords and the playing of combination games such as chess go some way to helping us to be more sensitised to the alternative possibilities confronting any given situation. Go and crime novels represent a much more radical extension of this kind of dispersive activity, a scattering of attention that blurs lines of confrontation, levels out hierarchical differences and confuses simple cause-and-effect thinking. The exemplary case is in great works of art, poetry and music which plumb the depths of human consciousness and provide us with magnificent glimpses of the inherently open-ended and creative nature of the human imagination.

References

Bateson, M. C. (1994) *Peripheral Visions: Learning Along the Way*. New York: Harper Collins.
Berger, J. (1972) *Ways of Seeing*. Harmondsworth: Penguin.
Bryson, N. (1982) *Vision and Painting: The Logic of the Gaze*. London: Methuen.
Chia, R. (1998) From complexity science to complex thinking: organization as simple location. *Organization*, 5(3): 341–69.
Day, G. S. and Shoemaker P. J. H. (2004a) Peripheral vision: sensing and acting on weak signals. *Long Range Planning*, 37: 117–21.
Day, G. S. and Shoemaker, P. H. J. (2004b) Driving through the fog: managing at the edge *Long Range Planning*, 37: 127–42.
Deleuze, G. and Guattari, F. (1988) *A Thousand Plateaus*. London: Athlone Press.
Derrida, J. (1981) *Positions*, trans. A. Bass Chicago: University of Chicago Press.
Dess, G. G. and Lumpkin G. T. (2001) Emerging issues in strategy process research. In M. A. Hitt, R. E. Freeman and J. S. Harrison (eds), *Handbook of Strategic Management*. Oxford: Blackwell, pp. 3–34.
Dess, G. G. and Lumpkin, G. T. (2005) The role of entrepreneurial orientation in stimulating effective corporate entrepreneurship. *Academy of Management Executive*, 19(1): 147–56.
Dess, G. G., Lumpkin, G. T. and McGhee J. E. (1999), Linking corporate entrepreneurship to strategy, structure, and process: suggested research directions *Entrepreneurship Theory and Practice*, 23(3): 85–102.

Ehrensweig, A. (1965) *The Psychoanalysis of Artistic Vision and Hearing*. New York: George Braziller.

Ehrenzweig, A. (1967) *The Hidden Order of Art* Berkeley: University of California Press.

Freud, S. ([1913] 1976) *The Interpretation of Dreams*, trans. J. Strachey. Harmondsworth: Penguin.

Keats, J. (1817) Letters to G. and T. Keats, 21st December 1817, in *The Oxford Library of Words and Phrases*. London: Guild Publishing.

Lawson-Tancred, H. (1998) *Aristotle: The Metaphysics*. London: Penguin.

Lumpkin, G. T. and Dess, G. G. (1996) Clarifying the entrepreneurial orientation construct and linking it to performance. *Academy of Management Review*, 21(1): 135–72.

March, J. G. (1991) Exploration and exploitation in organizational learning *Organization Science*, 2: 71–87.

Miller, D. (1983) The correlates of entrepreneurship in three types of firms. *Management Science*, 29: 770–91.

Parkes, G. (1987) *Heidegger and Asian Thought*. Honolulu: University of Hawaii Press.

Polanyi, M. (1962) *Personal Knowledge*. New York: Harper & Row.

Polanyi, M. (1967) *The Tacit Dimension*. London: Routledge & Kegan Paul.

Polanyi, M. (1969) *Knowing and Being* (edited by M. Grene). Chicago: University of Chicago Press.

Prahalad, C. K. (2004) The blinders of dominant logic. *Long Range Planning*, 37: 171–80.

Ruskin, J. (1927) *The Complete Works*. London: Weidenfeld & Nicholson.

Stetz, P. E., Howell, R., Stewart, A., Blair, J. D. and Fottler, M. D. (2000) Multidimensionality of entrepreneurial firm-level processes: do the dimensions covary? Paper presented at the 2000 Babson-Kaufmann Entrepreneurship Research Conference, Wellesley, MA.

Varendonck, J. (1923) *The Evolution of the Conscious Faculties*. London: Allen & Unwin.

Warhol, A. (1977) *The Philosophy of Andy Warhol: From A to B and Back Again*. New York: Harcourt Brace Jovanovich.

Whitehead, A. N. (1933) *Adventures of Ideas*. Harmondsworth: Penguin.

Winter, S. G. (2004) Specialised perception, selection and strategic surprise: learning from the moths and bees. *Long Range Planning*, 37: 163–9.

3 The process of entrepreneurial learning

A conceptual framework

Diamanto Politis

Introduction

Extant research suggests that entrepreneurs who have been involved in starting up a new venture also seem to be more successful and effective in starting up and managing their second and third organization (see e.g. Lamont 1972; Vesper 1980; Ronstadt 1988; Starr and Bygrave 1992; Wright *et al.* 1998). If this is true, what expertise and special knowledge do these entrepreneurs gain from doing their first start-up, and how do entrepreneurs develop their personal experiences into such expertise and special knowledge? Considering that entrepreneurship is a field of research that has not been particularly well studied in relation to the process of learning (Agnedal 1999; Rae and Carswell 2001; Ravasi *et al.* 2004), it is not surprising that these and similar questions have remained largely unanswered within this field.

Literature and research suggest that much of the learning that takes place within an entrepreneurial context is experiential in nature (e.g. Collins and Moore 1970; Reuber and Fischer 1993; Deakins and Freel 1998; Sullivan 2000; Minniti and Bygrave 2001; Sarasvathy 2001). This implies that the complex process by which entrepreneurs learn from past experience is of great importance to consider if we are to increase our understanding of entrepreneurial learning. Previous research has frequently pointed out the role of experience, and in particular prior start-up experience, as a proxy for entrepreneurial learning (e.g. Lamont 1972; Ronstadt 1988; Box *et al.* 1993; Sapienza and Grimm 1997). Despite this recognition, the current knowledge of how entrepreneurs learn from past experience is rather fragmented (Starr *et al.* 1993; Reuber and Fischer 1999).

A reason for this is probably the way in which entrepreneurial learning has been approached. Studying entrepreneurial learning has primarily been equal to comparing the relative difference between entrepreneurs' 'total stock' of experience at a given point of time, and researchers have then related this stock of experience to variations in new venture performance (e.g. Lamont 1972; Bailey 1986; Box *et al.* 1993; Sapienza and Grimm 1997). A major critique that can be directed towards these previous approaches to understand the role of experience in entrepreneurial learning are findings from literature and research on new venture growth, which have shown that it is very hard to sort out the effects of single endogenous and exogenous factors that ultimately may influence firm perform-ance (Sandberg and Hofer 1987; Keeley and Roure 1990; Storey 1994; Wiklund 1998). Many things could be argued to have an impact on the performance of new ventures, such as the firm location, the choice of sector or market where the firm operates, market positioning, etc., which makes the assumed direct relationship between entrepreneurs' experience and new venture performance very hard to establish. It could also be argued that the knowledge derived from past experience first and foremost has an influence on the strategic choices made by entrepreneurs in their subsequent ventures, which *then* influences firm performance. This means that it may be more plausible to study the influence of entrepreneurs' expe-rience on the development of relevant knowledge that may indirectly have an impact on subsequent new venture performance, rather than its direct influence on firm-level performance.

Another critique that can be directed towards previous approaches to under-stand the role of learning in entrepreneurship research is that it takes a rather static perspective on the process of entrepreneurial learning, where 'process' merely refers to the logic of explaining the causal relationship between entrepre-neurs' previous experience and the performance of the subsequent venture. Little attention is hence devoted to how entrepreneurs, through experience, develop entrepreneurial knowledge that enables them to recognize and act on entrepre-neurial opportunities and to organize and manage new ventures. What still remains largely unanswered in the literature is consequently the question of *how* entrepreneurs develop entrepreneurial knowledge that may indirectly have a positive impact on subsequent venture performance.

Based on this background, the aim of this chapter is to review and synthesize available research into a conceptual framework that explains the process of entre-preneurial learning as an experiential process. By achieving this aim, the chapter will contribute to existing literature on entrepreneurial learning in several ways. First, the study emphasizes the role of experience in developing entrepreneurial knowledge by integrating theories of experiential learning (e.g. Kolb 1984; March 1991) into the entrepreneurship field. The study consequently highlights entrepreneurial learning as an experiential process where enterprising individuals continuously develop their entrepreneurial knowledge throughout their profes-sional lives. Second, the study draws a distinction between the experience of an entrepreneur and the knowledge acquired thereby (Reuber and Fischer 1994). Despite the extensive efforts in investigating the potential learning effects of entrepreneurs' past experience, there has been very little effort to distinguish between these two important, yet distinct, concepts. Third, the study moves away from previous static approaches and develops a more dynamic perspective on the process of entrepreneurial learning (Reuber and Fischer 1999; Minniti and Bygrave 2001), as it does not solely focus on the relationship between entrepreneurs' experience and the development of entrepreneurial knowledge, but also on the intermediate process where their experiences are transformed into such knowledge. Hence, the study puts its focus on the transformation process of entrepreneurs' experience (Reuber and Fischer 1999; Minniti and Bygrave 2001) rather than the direct link between a particular experience and the knowledge gained from this experience.

The rest of the chapter will proceed as follows. First, a review of literature and research on entrepreneurial learning is conducted in which a number of central concepts and ideas derived from experiential learning theory are discussed and elaborated on. Based on this review, the chapter presents a conceptual framework and develops five major propositions to refine our understanding of how entrepreneurs learn from experience and pave the way for future empirical research. The chapter ends with conclusions and implications for practice and future research.

Entrepreneurial learning

Entrepreneurial learning is often described as a continuous process that facilitates the development of necessary knowledge for being effective in starting up and managing new ventures. However, although there have been extensive efforts in investigating the potential learning effects of entrepreneurs' experience, there has been very little effort to distinguish between 'entrepreneurial experience' and 'entrepreneurial knowledge' (or what Reuber *et al.* (1990) refer to as 'experientially acquired knowledge'). A starting point for studying the process of entrepreneurial learning could hence be to draw a distinction between the experience of an entrepreneur and the knowledge acquired thereby (Reuber and Fischer 1994). One way to distinguish between these two concepts is to consider entrepreneurs' experience as a direct observation of, or participation in, events associated with new venture creation, while the practical wisdom resulting from what an entrepreneur has encountered represents the knowledge derived from this particular experience (Reuber *et al.* 1990). This line of reasoning can be related to Kolb (1984), who emphasizes two basic dimensions of experiential learning – acquisition (grasping) and transformation. The former can be argued to correspond to 'experience' (hereafter referred to as entrepreneurs' experience), while the latter is considered equivalent to 'experientially acquired knowledge' (hereafter referred to as entrepreneurial knowledge).

Having thereby distinguished between the experience of an entrepreneur and the knowledge, we can start to investigate the experiential process where the personal experience of the entrepreneur is continuously transformed into knowledge. In order to organize the various arguments and reflections on the process of entrepreneurial learning that have been found in the literature, a conceptual framework was developed. The term 'conceptual framework' is used in the study as the goal at this initial stage is mainly to advance our understanding of entrepreneurial learning as an experiential process by exploring antecedents and outcomes of the transformation process of entrepreneurs' experience, rather than to fully specify a model or test strong causal propositions. The conceptual framework is illustrated in Figure 3.1. The framework illustrates that, in addition to investigating the direct link between entrepreneurs' career experience and the development of entrepreneurial knowledge (A), we also need a better understanding of how the entrepreneurs' predominant mode of transforming experience into knowledge influences the specific type of knowledge developed (B) and, additionally, also the factors that influence the entrepreneurs' predominant mode of transforming experience into knowledge (C). The rest of this chapter will continue to develop these arguments.

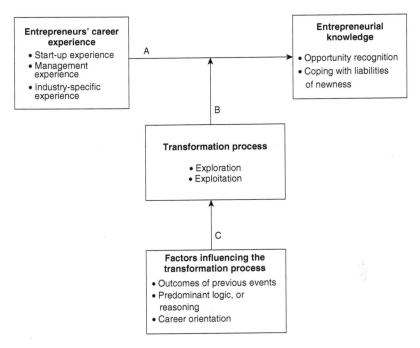

Figure 3.1 A conceptual framework of entrepreneurial learning as an experiential process.

Entrepreneurial knowledge

Any discussion of learning is confronted with the somewhat difficult task of trying to describe or define what 'learning' involves. One way to accomplish this task is to elaborate on the key outcomes related to the process of learning that have been identified in recent research represented in the particular field of study. When learning is applied to the concept of entrepreneurship, it has often been concerned with learning how to recognize and act on opportunities (Ronstadt 1988; Shane and Venkataraman 2000; Corbett 2002), and learning how to overcome traditional obstacles when organizing and managing new ventures, i.e. handling liabilities of newness (Stinchcombe 1965; Starr and Bygrave 1992; Aldrich 1999; Shepherd *et al.* 2000). In reality most entrepreneurs engage in both activities simultaneously, as they often are involved in several concurrent projects that are at different stages of development (Johannisson 2000; Shane 2003). However, the organizing of a new venture centers on an entrepreneurial opportunity that must have been recognized and acted upon at some earlier time.

Thus, from a theoretical point of view, handling liabilities of newness cannot take place without prior opportunity recognition. This point of departure implies in particular two distinct learning outcomes related to entrepreneurial learning: (i) increased effectiveness in opportunity recognition, and (ii) increased effectiveness in coping with the liabilities of newness.

Opportunity recognition

The ability to discover and develop business opportunities is often considered to be among the most important abilities of a successful entrepreneur, and this has consequently also been a key issue to investigate and explain in literature and research on entrepreneurship (Ronstadt 1988; Shane and Venkataraman 2000; Ardichvili *et al.* 2003). Several scholars have pointed out that experienced entrepreneurs have acquired valuable knowledge about relevant contacts, reliable suppliers, viable markets, product availability, competitive resources and response, which enhance their ability to seize and spot entrepreneurial opportunities (Ronstadt 1988; Starr and Bygrave 1992; Hudson and McArthur 1994; Shepherd *et al.* 2000). Experienced entrepreneurs may also be more likely than novice entrepreneurs to pursue ventures as a means of gaining access to a wider range of 'shadow options', i.e. opportunities that have not been recognized (McGrath 1999). Over time, valuable information regarding the real option can be made available, or suitable entrepreneurial opportunities emerge. For example, McGrath and MacMillan (2000) suggest that entrepreneurs with prior start-up experience have developed an 'entrepreneurial mindset' that drives them to seek and pursue entrepreneurial opportunities with enormous discipline, and hence, they can be expected to pursue only the very best opportunities. This argument also corresponds to Carroll and Mosakowski (1987), who assert that prior start-up experience increases the probability of exploitation of entrepreneurial opportunities since learning reduces the costs related to this endeavor. The lessons learned from prior experience might consequently enhance entrepreneurs' ability to recognize and act on entrepreneurial opportunities effectively (Ronstadt 1988; Ucbasaran *et al.* 2003).

However, considering increased effectiveness in the opportunity recognition process as an outcome of entrepreneurial learning raises the question of why some individuals have the ability to discover entrepreneurial opportunities, and others do not. Previous research has identified at least two factors that influence the probability that particular individuals will enhance their likelihood to discover entrepreneurial opportunities: (i) the possession of the prior information necessary to identify an opportunity, and (ii) the cognitive properties necessary to value it (Shane and Venkataraman 2000; Ardichvili *et al.* 2003). The possession of the prior information necessary to identify an opportunity has to do with an individual's total stock of information that influences his or her ability to recognize particular opportunities. The cognitive properties necessary to value it refers to an individual's ability to identify new means–ends relationships in response to a particular change (Shane and Venkataraman 2000).

Even if both factors describe quite different things, they are nevertheless necessary to be able to recognize and act on entrepreneurial opportunities. This means that even if an individual possesses the prior information necessary to identify or create an opportunity, he or she could fail in actually doing so because of the individual's inability to see potential new means–ends relationships. Hence, the cognitive properties of an individual, i.e. the ability to combine existing concepts and information into new ideas, can be argued to play a central role in the process of entrepreneurial learning (Kaish and Gilad 1991; Busenitz and Barney 1997). An increased effectiveness in opportunity recognition consequently means that the entrepreneur has picked up more relevant information necessary to identify entrepreneurial opportunities, as well as having developed his or her cognitive properties necessary to value it (Shane and Venkataraman 2000). Hence, prior experience gives rise to further creativity, permitting the sorts of associations and linkages that may never have been considered before. This argument also fits theories that argue that the level of prior experience is a key factor for the ability to evaluate and utilize outside knowledge and exploit new market opportunities (Cohen and Levinthal 1990; Gatewood *et al.* 1995; Zahra and George 2002; Shane 2003). Prior experience consequently confers an ability to recognize the value of new information, to learn, and to apply it to new commercial ends (Cohen and Levinthal 1990). Experienced entrepreneurs are in this respect more likely to search information within a more specific domain of business ideas based on their past experience in terms of routines and information sources that have worked well in the past (Cyert and March 1963; Fiet *et al.* 2000; Shane 2003), while novice entrepreneurs with no prior experience may have fewer benchmarks to access whether the information they have gathered is appropriate to identify an entrepreneurial opportunity (Cooper *et al.* 1995). The amount of prior experience seems in this respect to be highly associated with an entrepreneur's effectiveness in recognizing and acting on entrepreneurial opportunities.

Coping with the liabilities of newness

Another learning outcome that is assumed to be an important ability of a successful entrepreneur is the ability to cope with the liabilities of newness (Stinchcombe 1965; Starr and Bygrave 1992; Aldrich 1999; Shepherd *et al.* 2000). It is a well-known fact that the rate of mortality among newly founded firms is very high (Laitinen 1992; Timmons 1999). The main reasons for this rather sad statistic have been found to be inadequate funding and inefficient marketing (Storey 1994; Sullivan *et al.* 1999). Potential customers have for example little basis for trusting newcomers without a sufficient track record because of their short operating histories, and buyers can hence be hesitant to place orders. The shortfall in cash flow can moreover reduce the ability of the new firm to adequately respond to outside problems and threats. Entrepreneurs must consequently earn the recognition that they are a legitimate business person by reliably providing goods and services in a timely manner. Financial problems as well as marketing problems seem consequently to be common reasons for the high failure rates among new ventures, and the average first-time entrepreneur seems to be ill equipped to handle the traditional obstacles and uncertainties related to setting up a new venture.

Previous experience could, however, lead to a greater likelihood of a customized set of benefits, such as relevant business skills, well-developed networks and a business reputation, that can be leveraged into subsequent ventures (Starr and Bygrave 1992; Hudson and McArthur 1994; Wright *et al.* 1997; Shepherd *et al.* 2000; Shane and Khurana 2003). The ability to better cope with liabilities of newness could in this respect involve several aspect related to the various ways entrepreneurs reduce the traditional obstacles and uncertainties related to setting up a new venture (Aldrich and Auster 1986; Starr and Bygrave 1992; Shepherd *et al.* 2000), such as finding financial start-up capital, legitimacy building, adaptation to changes, having access to social and business networks, etc. There can also be certain knowledge-based barriers to entry, meaning that a certain level of production technology or managerial capability is a prerequisite to meet the contextual constrains that new ventures face and the difficulties that managers have in overcoming them (Cohen and Levinthal 1990; Shepherd *et al.* 2000). A diverse background may in this respect stimulate creativity by associating to more linkages, which in turn provides a more robust basis for learning and development in new uncertain situations (Cohen and Levinthal 1990). Hence, it can be argued that previous experience provides entrepreneurs the opportunity to increase their ability to cope with the liabilities of newness, and learn new knowledge that can be readily redeployed in other ventures, thereby providing them with the ability to enter into new markets, products, or technologies with greater success (MacMillan 1986; Kolvereid and Bullvåg 1993; Starr *et al.* 1993; McGrath 1999). An increased effectiveness to cope with the liabilities of newness seems in this respect to be manifested through the 'wealth' that entrepreneurs have created in terms of financial facilities, the 'power' they possess by exploiting their social networks, and the 'legitimacy' they have acquired by developing a business reputation, which can help the entrepreneur to secure financial resources and develop a market for their products or services (Starr and Bygrave 1992).

Entrepreneurs' career experience and entrepreneurial knowledge

If prior experience can explain why certain entrepreneurs are more successful than others (e.g. Lamont 1972; Kolvereid and Bullvåg 1993; Reuber and Fischer 1993; Wright *et al.* 1997), which type of career experience can then be considered to have an impact on entrepreneurs' learning in terms of developing their effectiveness in opportunity recognition and in coping with the liabilities of newness? A widely used measure in studies of entrepreneurial learning is prior start-up experience (e.g. Box *et al.* 1993; Kolvereid and Bullvåg 1993; Sapienza and Grimm 1997; Westhead and Wright 1998; Reynolds *et al.* 2000). Previous research indicates that prior start-up experience provides tacit knowledge that facilitates decision making about entrepreneurial opportunities under uncertainty and time pressure (Johannisson *et al.* 1998; Sarasvathy 2001). As a result, individuals with more start-up experience should see a given opportunity as more desirable than other individuals see it, and therefore be more likely to exploit it (Shane 2003). Several empirical studies provide support for this 'learning by doing' argument. For example, Gimeno *et al.* (1997) showed that prior start-up experience enhances the profitability of new ventures, suggesting that new ventures whose founders had more previous start-up experience took more income out of their businesses. Previous start-up experience is in addition often considered to provide knowledge that helps an entrepreneur to overcome the liabilities of newness that new ventures face (Starr and Bygrave 1992; Reuber and Fischer 1993; Shane and Khurana 2003). Moreover, Cooper *et al.* (1989) showed that entrepreneurs' prior start-up experience had a significant and positive relationship with firm performance (for similar results see also Stuart and Abetti 1990 and Dyke *et al.* 1992). Several authors also point out that even if some of the information and knowledge can be learned through education, much of the necessary information about exploiting opportunities and in coping with the liabilities of newness can only be learned by doing (Cope and Watts 2000; Rae 2000; Shane 2003). For example, the routines to form organizations may only be learned by creating organizations (Bruderl *et al.* 1992; Shepherd *et al.* 2000), and gathering the right information and making effective decisions about opportunities may be something that can only be understood by undertaking those activities (Ronstadt 1988; Duchesneau and Gartner 1990).

Another type of experience that has been highlighted in the literature on entrepreneurial learning is the entrepreneurs' amount of management experience. For example, Bruderl and Preisendorfer (1998) showed that entrepreneurs' years of work experience increased their ventures' three-year survival rates, and thereby reduced the likelihood of new venture failure. Similarly, Taylor (1999) examined the duration of self-employment of individuals responding to the British Household Panel Survey, and found that having prior paid employment reduced the rate of exit from self-employment. Also, Duchnesneau and Gartner (1990) indicated a positive relationship between founders' management experience and new venture survival, pointing out that founders of failed ventures had narrower managerial experience than the founders of successful ventures. Moreover, several studies suggest that prior management experience increases an individual's intention to start a new venture, thereby facilitating opportunity recognition process (e.g. Vesalainen and Pihkala 1999; Delmar and Davidsson 2000; and Davidsson and Honig 2003). Hence, general management experience seems to provide individuals with information about many of the basic aspects of business that are relevant to recognizing and acting on entrepreneurial opportunities, such as finance, sales, technology, logistics, marketing and organization (Shepherd *et al.* 2000; Romanelli and Schoonhoven 2001). Moreover, having prior management experience provides the entrepreneurs training in many of the skills needed for coping with the liabilities of newness, such as selling, negotiating, leading, planning, decision-making, problem-solving, organizing and communicating (Lorrain and Dussault 1988; Shane 2003).

Considering that entrepreneurs often face uncertainty about the value of the goods and services that they plan to produce, it seems fair to assume that industry-specific experience can also have a strong influence on their development of entrepreneurial knowledge (Shepherd *et al.* 2000; Shane 2003). This implies that individuals with prior experience as a customer or supplier in an industry often have a better understanding of how to meet demand conditions in that market-place, as industry experience provides information that outsiders cannot gather (Johnson 1986). For example, Aldrich (1999) showed that founders tend to start businesses in industries in which they were previously employed, because their employment experience allows them to take advantage of information of the exploitation of opportunities gathered from their previous employment. Similarly, Cooper *et al.* (1988) shows that the products, services, customers and suppliers of surviving ventures were more closely related to the products, services, customers and suppliers of the entrepreneurs' previous employer, than were those of failing ventures (for similar results see also Bates and Servon 2000). Consequently, it seems fair to assume that the number of previous start-ups alone cannot be a satisfactory measure of entrepreneurs' prior experience. Rather, it can be argued that entrepreneurs' experience can include various entrepreneurial events, and even if these events usually are connected to the start-up of a new independent business, some of these events can be related to experiences of business venturing in existing organizations as well (e.g. Drucker 1985; Pinchot 1985), and as such also provide managers with inputs to develop entrepreneurial knowledge.

Taken together, the events that are antecedent to entrepreneurial knowledge are not always readily apparent in the case of a new venture due to the presence of ambiguity and continuous changes that is usually evident in an entrepreneurial context (Sarasvathy 2001; Ravasi *et al.* 2004). This means that prior experience from similar situations often serves as the base for expertise and knowledge in entrepreneurial contexts (Reuber *et al.* 1990; Johannisson *et al.* 1998; Shook *et al.* 2003). The literature seems to suggest at least three types of career experience that are associated with entrepreneurial learning: start-up experience, management experience, and industry-specific experience. Each of these types of experiences does seem likely to expose individuals to problems, which they might encounter in running a new venture, and hence facilitates acquiring knowledge that would help to solve similar problems in the future. The following proposition summarizes our predictions regarding the development of entrepreneurial knowledge derived from the entrepreneur's career experience:

P1: The entrepreneur's career experience, in terms of start-up, management and industry-specific experience, is positively related to the development of entrepreneurial knowledge.

1a: The more career experience, the more effective is the entrepreneur in recognizing and acting on entrepreneurial opportunities.

1b: The more career experience, the more effective is the entrepreneur in coping with the liabilities of newness.

The transformation process of entrepreneurial learning

Entrepreneurial learning has been presented as an experiential process where the personal experience of the entrepreneur is transformed into knowledge, which in turn can be used to guide the choice of new experiences. When investigating entrepreneurial learning, it is, however, necessary to acknowledge that entrepreneurs' career experience does not directly lead to that entrepreneurial knowledge is acquired. Instead the gaining of new experiences and the development of new knowledge can rather be described as a process where experiences are *transformed* into experientially acquired knowledge (Kolb 1984). Hence, the simple perception of prior experience is not sufficient for entrepreneurial learning to happen, but requires that something must be done with it. Similarly, transformation alone cannot represent learning, for there must be something to be transformed, some state or experience that is being acted upon. What still remains unanswered is consequently the fundamental question of *how* entrepreneurs transform their career experiences into entrepreneurial knowledge.

To develop our theoretical knowledge of the transformation of entrepreneurs' career experience into entrepreneurial knowledge, it seems fruitful to integrate concepts and ideas derived from experiential learning theory into the field of entrepreneurship (see e.g. Bailey 1986; Deakins and Freel 1998; Johannisson *et al.* 1998; Cope and Watts 2000; Rae 2000; Minniti and Bygrave 2001). The chapter initially suggested that both dimensions of experiential learning (i.e. both the grasping and transformation dimensions) are essential to include when understanding the process of entrepreneurial learning. Experiential learning can hence be described as 'the process whereby knowledge is created through the transformation of experience' (Kolb 1984: 41). The central idea of experiential learning is that learning (or knowing) requires a grasp or figurative representation of experience, and then some transformation of that representation (Kolb 1984). This point of view regards learning as a transformation process of experiences being continuously created and recreated, and not as an independent entity to be acquired or transmitted (Holmqvist 2000). Relating this standpoint to an entrepreneurial setting, it can be argued that entrepreneurs often are confronted with immediate and concrete experiences (Gartner 1989; Johannisson 1992b), implying that they have a great variety of experiences that provides them with opportunities to develop entrepreneurial knowledge. Entrepreneurial knowledge can hence be regarded as the results from the combination of both grasping experience as well as transforming this experience.

Kolb's (1984) model of experiential learning proposes four learning phases that individuals need to carry out in order to develop effective learning (i.e. complete the learning cycle). Based on Kolb's ideas, entrepreneurial learning can be regarded as an experiential process in which entrepreneurs develop knowledge through four distinctive learning abilities: experiencing, reflecting, thinking and acting (Bailey 1986; Johannisson *et al.* 1998). Although Kolb's experiential learning theory continues to be one of the most influential theories of individual learning, it has also been the target of much scrutiny. Such criticisms generally argue that Kolb's theory of experiential learning decontextualizes the learning process and provides only a limited account of the many factors that influence learning (for more extensive reviews see e.g. Reynolds 1998, Vince 1998 and Kayes 2002). When studying the process of entrepreneurial learning, it is important to recognize that Kolb's cyclical model is not fully adequate to understand the complex uncertainties that entrepreneurs have to deal with. For instance, Johannisson *et al.* (1998) found that entrepreneurs have a rich source of concrete experiences, which is formed into an intuitive capacity, ready to use as a base for analogies when challenged by surprising 'critical' events (for similar arguments see also Busenitz and Barney 1997 and Baron 1998). This more or less conscious use of analogies may be reinforced by the fact that entrepreneurs seldom have time for explicit conceptualization, or for theorizing beyond individual choices. Consequently, it can be argued that the process of entrepreneurial learning does not necessarily follow a predetermined sequence of steps according to Kolb's (1984) four-stage learning cycle, but rather can be conceived as a complex process where entrepreneurs transform experience into knowledge in disparate ways. Here, the alternative modes of transforming entrepreneurs' experience into knowledge become an essential part of the process of entrepreneurial learning.

Modes of transforming experience into knowledge

The transformation process of experience is suggested to have two distinctive courses depending on how entrepreneurs transform their experience into knowledge (Minniti and Bygrave 2001). The role of experience may in this respect be twofold, implying that entrepreneurs can rely on one of two possible strategies when making decisions: exploitation or exploration. In the first case, entrepreneurs may choose actions that replicate or are closely related to the ones they have already taken, thereby exploiting their pre-existing knowledge. In the second case, entrepreneurs can choose new actions that are distinct from the ones that they have already taken.

This line of reasoning is in accordance with March's (1991) ideas on the trade-offs between exploitation and exploration in organizational learning. March argues that organizations or individuals are confronted with a set of experiences that force them to make choices. These choices are usually reflected in two inter-related, yet disparate, ways to transform experience into knowledge, namely exploitation and exploration. Exploitation concerns the exploitation of what is already known, implying that individuals learn from experience by exploiting old certainties. This includes such things as refinement, routine, and implementation of knowledge. Exploitation is thus about creating reliability in experience, which means that stable behavior becomes the dominant state of the learner (Holmqvist 2000). This way of transforming experience into knowledge is in contrast to exploration, which is about creating variety in experience resulting in that change in behavior becomes the dominant state. Exploration means that individuals learn from experiences by exploring new possibilities, including issues such as variation, experimentation, discovery and innovation. This line of reasoning also fits Cohen and Levinthal's (1990) arguments that there is a tradeoff between standardization and diversity of knowledge. Getting too specialized will consequently lead to increased expertise in one area at the cost of reduced experimentation and alternative ideas, and vice versa (for similar arguments see also Cyert and March 1963; Ghemawat and Costa 1993; Levinthal and March 1993).

It should be explicitly noted that none of these two different courses of transforming experience into knowledge is automatically better than the other. March (1991) argues that both these ways of transforming experience into knowledge are essential to sustain learning, but that they compete for scarce resources. For instance, individuals who are engaged in exploration to the exclusion of exploitation are likely to find that they suffer the cost of experimentation without gaining many of its benefits. This focus on exploration may result in too many underdeveloped new ideas and too little distinctive competence. Conversely, individuals engaging in exploitation to the exclusion of exploration are likely to find themselves trapped in suboptimal stable equilibrium. The returns to exploitation are hence generally more certain, closer in time and closer in space than are the returns to exploration (March 1991). In contrast, exploration is associated with substantial success as well as failure, implying a larger performance variation. Based on this argument, it can be concluded that maintaining an appropriate balance between exploration and exploitation is a primary concern for survival and prosperity (March 1991), as the exploitation of commercially successful new ideas provides the resources to support new exploration (Mintzberg and Waters 1982). However, the optimal mix of exploration and exploitation is complex and hard to specify, because it is easy to become trapped into the dynamics of accelerating exploration or exploitation (Levinthal and March 1993).

Exploration and exploitation and entrepreneurial knowledge

In the discussion on the development of entrepreneurial knowledge it was argued, all else being equal, that prior experience is positively related both to the entrepreneur's effectiveness in recognizing and acting on opportunities, and in coping with liabilities of newness. However, although this can be regarded as likely when comparing individuals with significantly different amounts of experience, it can be argued that two entrepreneurs with about the similar amount of experience may have developed different kinds of entrepreneurial knowledge depending on their predominant mode of transformation. Research on the opportunity recognition process has for example suggested that opportunity-seeking entrepreneurs who are continuously involved in new venture creation, so-called habitual entrepreneurs, often strive for variation and new challenges (e.g. Hall 1995; Westhead and Wright 1998). Moreover they often start new ventures with the aim of learning something new and, as such, consider their habitual entrepreneurship as an exciting and challenging career option (MacMillan 1986; Katz 1994). This line of reasoning suggests that entrepreneurs who are highly explorative and alert, taking a broad intuitive perspective that incorporates many different inputs at once, also tend to become more effective in recognizing and acting on business opportunities (Hills *et al.* 1997;

Zietsma 1999; Corbett 2002). On the other hand, it is often pointed out that effective handling of the liabilities of newness requires the use of analogous reasoning and routinized behavior in order to handle conflicts with new roles, delegate responsibility, and develop stable links with important stakeholders (Stinchcombe 1965; Starr and Bygrave 1992; Shepherd *et al.* 2000). This suggests that entrepreneurs who put their prime focus on the exploitation of pre-existing knowledge, including such things as refinement, habit and implementation, seem to become more effective in coping with liabilities of newness and overcoming the traditional obstacles facing new ventures. Hence, the predominant mode of transformation can have consequences for which specific type of entrepreneurial knowledge is developed.

Based on the above discussion, it seems fair to suggest that the entrepreneurs' predominant mode of transformation can moderate the relationship between entrepreneurs' career experience and the development of entrepreneurial knowledge. Entrepreneurs who primarily rely on exploration as the predominant mode of transformation seem to favor the development of their effectiveness in opportunity recognition, while entrepreneurs who primarily rely on exploitation as the predominant mode of transformation seems to favor developing their effectiveness in coping with the liabilities of newness.

This leads to the following proposition:

P2:   The entrepreneur's predominant mode of transformation moderates the relationship between the entrepreneur's career experience and entrepreneurial knowledge.

2a: The more overall reliance on exploration as the predominant mode of transformation, the more effective is the entrepreneur in recognizing and acting on entrepreneurial opportunities.

2b: The more overall reliance on exploitation as the predominant mode of transformation, the more effective is the entrepreneur in coping with the liabilities of newness.

Factors influencing the transformation process

Based on the discussion above, it seems fair to argue that the mode of transforming experience into entrepreneurial knowledge is made either through the exploitation of pre-existent knowledge where entrepreneurs focus their attention and activity on what has been working well in the past, or through the exploration of new possibilities where experimentation serves as an important learning technique (Sitkin 1992; Minniti and Bygrave 2001). How, then, can we predict entrepreneurs' predominant mode of transforming experience into entrepreneurial knowledge? Previous literature and research on entrepreneurship highlights at least three aspects that can be of importance to consider in order to better understand the entrepreneur's predominant mode of transforming experience into entrepreneurial knowledge: the outcome of previous entrepreneurial events

(Sitkin 1992; Johannisson and Madsén 1997; Cardon and McGrath 1999; Minniti and Bygrave 2001), the predominant logic, or reasoning, of the entrepreneur (Sarasvathy 2001; Ravasi *et al.* 2004), and the entrepreneur's career orientation (Dyer 1994; Katz 1994). These aspects will be dealt with in the following sections.

The outcome of previous entrepreneurial events

One particular aspect that can be expected to have an impact on the entrepreneur's predominant mode of transforming experience is the outcomes of previous entrepreneurial events in the entrepreneur's past (i.e. if the events turned out to be a success or a failure). Minniti and Bygrave (2001) argue that many successful entrepreneurs tend to choose actions that replicate, or are closely related to, the ones they have already taken, thereby exploiting their pre-existing knowledge (see also Sitkin 1992; Starr and Bygrave 1992; Wright *et al.* 1998; McGrath 1999). Successful experiences from prior business venturing can, for example, create a perceived 'path' for successful business venturing where the entrepreneur has moved from his or her specific observations to make broader generalizations and theories of how to achieve success in subsequent new ventures.

It can further be suggested that successful experiences are likely to have long-lasting effects on strategies in subsequent business venturing due to tendencies towards path dependence and lock-in. Path dependence in relation to entrepreneurial learning means that although the entrepreneur was initially successful in adjusting his or her strategies in response to, for example, competition, regulations and technology, the old successful strategies may not always reflect the current situation (Wright *et al.* 1998). Hence, even if the needs of the current situation have significantly changed from the time of the founding the path dependence of previous entrepreneurial events can make an entrepreneur unable to respond to changing customer composition, changing regulations, changing technology, etc., through the exploration of new possibilities. This implies that previous success leads to persistence, at the expense of adaptability (Sitkin 1992; Levinthal and March 1993).

This line of reasoning can also be related to Cyert and March (1963), who assert that the changing of goals and procedures is primarily a function of previous experiences. For instance, when an entrepreneur discovers a solution to a problem by searching in a particular way, he or she will be more likely to search in that way when approaching future problems of the same type. On the other hand, when an entrepreneur fails to find a solution by searching in a particular way, it will be less likely that he or she searches in that way in future problems of the same type. It can moreover be argued that organizations develop, stabilize and follow routines that are fairly difficult to change in the short run since they function as carriers of knowledge and experience (e.g. Nelson and Winter 1982). This line of reasoning consequently implies that past success primarily stimulates entrepreneurs to focus their attention and activity on what has been working well in the past, involving the use of an iterative and exploitative mode of transforming experience into knowledge (Sitkin 1992).

Entrepreneurs' experience may, however, not only originate from prior success, but from prior failures as well (Johannisson and Madsén 1997; Ripsas 1998; McGrath 1999; Minniti and Bygrave 2001; Stokes and Blackburn 2002). Recent research suggests that many successful entrepreneurs credit learning from past failures as a crucial aspect of their experience base (Sitkin 1992; Johannisson and Madsén 1997; Cardon and McGrath 1999; Minniti and Bygrave 2001). For instance, Sitkin (1992) argues that failure is an essential prerequisite for learning since it provides the opportunity to pinpoint why a failure has occurred. Failures provide entrepreneurs the opportunity to discover uncertainties that were previously unpredictable (Sitkin 1992; McGrath 1999; Sarasvathy 2001), which implies that failure analysis can serve as a powerful mechanism to resolve uncertainty. This line of reasoning is in accordance with McGrath's (1999) arguments. She stresses that prior failure can have positive effects on entrepreneurs' knowledge base as it helps them in reducing uncertainty, increasing variety, and expanding the search for new opportunities. It can moreover be argued that failure stimulates entrepreneurs to pursue an explorative search for new possibilities where learning through experimentation becomes a central learning technique (Sitkin 1992; Sarasvathy 2001). Entrepreneurial failure can consequently stimulate entrepreneurs to choose new actions that are distinct from the ones they have already taken (Minniti and Bygrave 2001), which intensifies their search for variance through exploring new possibilities as a coping strategy to reduce uncertainties (March 1991; McGrath 1999; Minniti and Bygrave 2001; Sarasvathy 2001).

However, not all failures are equally adept at facilitating learning. Those failures that are most effective at fostering learning are referred as 'intelligent failures,' which means failures that provide a basis for altering future behavior through new information from which to learn (Sitkin 1992). The goal of experiencing failure is consequently to obtain information that would not be available without the experience. Intelligent failures are those of modest outcome scale, which means that they have large enough outcomes to attract attention, but small enough outcomes to avoid negative responses (Lounamaa and March 1987). Another prerequisite to consider a failure as intelligent is that the outcome of action must be uncertain (and not highly predictable) in order to provide new information from which to learn (Sitkin 1992). This means that failure facilitates for entrepreneurs to pursue new ways of doing things when the current ways are relatively successful and, as such, stimulates them to learn by experimentation (Johannisson and Madsén 1997; Sarasvathy 2001). Modest levels of failure can consequently promote a willingness to take risks and foster resilience-enhancing experimentation.

From the above discussion it seems fair to assume that failure fuels learning through experimentation – a learning technique that facilitates for entrepreneurs to increase variety, reduce uncertainty and expand the search for new opportunities (Sitkin 1992; McGrath 1999; Sarasvathy 2001). Past success may on the other hand stimulate confidence and persistence because individuals are rewarded for success (Sitkin 1992), but also because success provides a secure and stable basis for the launching of future activity (Weick 1984). Hence, routines and procedures are not strictly invariant, but will change as a result of the search for new solutions when old ones fail to work (Cyert and March 1963; Nelson and Winter 1982). This implies that the way in which entrepreneurs' experience becomes transformed into knowledge can be expected to be influenced by the entrepreneur's previous experience of success or failure.

The above discussion leads to the following proposition:

P3: The outcome of the entrepreneur's previous entrepreneurial events is related to his or her mode of transforming experience into knowledge.

3a: The higher the degree of past entrepreneurial failures, the higher the degree of an explorative mode of transforming experience into knowledge.

3b: The higher the degree of past entrepreneurial success, the higher the degree of an exploitative mode of transforming experience into knowledge.

The predominant logic, or reasoning, of the entrepreneur

An additional aspect that can be expected to have an impact on entrepreneurs' mode of transforming experience to knowledge is the predominant logic, or reasoning, in their present situation. Sarasvathy (2001) describes two kinds of predominant logics, or reasoning, in economic theories: causation and effectuation. Causal reasoning uses techniques of analysis and estimation to explore and exploit existing and latent markets. Effectual reasoning calls on the other hand for synthesis and imagination to create new markets that do not already exist. Causation consequently focuses on what ought to be done given predetermined goals and possible means, while effectuation emphasizes the question of what can be done given possible means and imagined ends (Sarasvathy 2001). Effectual reasoning is hence a process that rests on logic of control while causal reasoning primarily relies on logic of prediction. However, despite the differences, both causation and effectuation are integral parts of human reasoning that can occur simultaneously, overlapping and intertwining over different contexts of decisions and actions (Sarasvathy 2001).

Entrepreneurs rely on causation as the predominant logic when they focus on the predictable aspects of an uncertain future. The market is hence assumed to exist independently of the entrepreneur and the main task is to grasp as much of that market as possible by being involved in planning and then gathering necessary information to see how strategies materialize according to plan and to identify possible reasons why plan and outcome differ. Entrepreneurs who rely on causation consequently take a particular effect as given, and the center of attention is on selecting between various means to create that effect. Hence, the choice of means is driven by the entrepreneur's knowledge of possible means, as well as the characteristics of the effect the entrepreneur wants to create (Sarasvathy 2001). This means that who entrepreneurs rely on causation as the predominant logic are primarily involved in exploiting pre-existent knowledge to come up with efficient competitive strategies in existing markets.

The reason for entrepreneurs to rely on effectuation as the predominant logic is when they choose to focus more on the controllable aspects of an unpredictable future rather than on the predictable aspects of an uncertain future (Sarasvathy 2001). Entrepreneurs involved in the exploration of new possibilities often make decisions in the absence of pre-existent goals, which implies the need to rely on effectual reasoning rather than conventional causation models (Sarasvathy 2001). It can hence be argued that entrepreneurs who operate in highly ambiguous settings have to rely to a larger extent on an exploration of new business domains (Sarasvathy 2001; Ravasi *et al.* 2004). This means that entrepreneurs who rely on effectuation as the predominant logic are primarily involved in exploiting contingencies around them to explore new environments and create markets that do not yet exist.

Taken together, the use of effectuation processes can be considered as preferable when the entrepreneur explores new possibilities and contingencies that arise unexpectedly over time. Entrepreneurs who use effectuation will hence prefer an experimental and iterative mode of transforming experience when gathering information to discover the underlying distribution of future events (Johannisson and Madsén 1997; Sarasvathy 2001). The use of causational processes might on the other hand be preferable in situations when pre-existing knowledge forms the source of competitive advantage, such as expertise in a particular new technology (Minniti and Bygrave 2001; Sarasvathy 2001). Entrepreneurs who use causation will in this respect prefer an exploitative mode of transforming experience.

The above discussion leads to the following proposition:

P4: The entrepreneur's predominant reasoning is related to his or her mode of transforming experience into knowledge.

  4a: The more reliance on effectuation as the predominant reasoning, the higher the degree of an explorative mode of transforming experience into knowledge.

  4b: The more reliance on causation as the predominant reasoning, the higher the degree of an exploitative mode of transforming experience into knowledge.

The career orientation of the entrepreneur

A third aspect that can be expected to have an impact on entrepreneurs' predominant mode of transforming experience into knowledge is the career orientation that influences their future actions. The basic premise of this argument is that most individuals develop diverse concepts of what career means to them, which greatly influence their choice of career path and experience at work

(Larsson *et al.* 2001). Extant research has shown that entrepreneurs are a heterogeneous group of individuals who differ in terms of characteristics and career motivations (e.g. Kolvereid and Bullvåg 1993; Katz 1994; Rosa 1998; Westhead and Wright 1998). Hence, it seems reasonable to suggest that entrepreneurs with different kind of career motivations can be expected to seek different types of entrepreneurial events and learning situations (Ronstadt 1988; Starr and Bygrave 1992; Minniti and Bygrave 2001), which in turn influence their predominant mode of transforming experience into knowledge.

Based on the assumption that individuals have different conceptions of careers, Schein (1987) argues that individuals differ regarding their career motivations and hence possess distinctive 'career anchors,' which he refers to as . . . 'the self-image that a person develops around his or her career, which both guides and constrains career decisions' (Schein, 1987: 155). Similar arguments are also pointed out by Brousseau *et al.* (1996), who have developed a model that differentiates between four basic career concepts held by individuals in terms of direction (of career movement or change) and frequency of movement within and across different kinds of work over time (durability in a given field of work). The model developed by Brousseau *et al.* (1996) identified four distinctive career concepts; linear, expert, spiral and transitory[1]. These four patterns of career preferences are based on distinctly different sets of motives that underlie each of these career orientations. This means that individuals who differ in their particular career orientations also differ predictably in their underlying work and career-related motives (Brousseau *et al.* 1996).

The ideal linear career consists of a progressive series of steps upward in a hierarchy (such as a managerial hierarchy) with infrequent changes in career field, while upward promotions to positions of increasing authority and responsibility are desired as frequently as possible (Larsson *et al.* 2001). Entrepreneurs with a linear career orientation are hence motivated by opportunities to make important things, implying that power and achievement become key motives to their career choice. It is consequently the prospect of achievement satisfaction, not personal wealth, that drives the entrepreneur, although wealth and status is an important measure of how well one is doing (McClelland 1961; Katz 1994). The ideal expert career is on the other hand characterized by the lifelong commitment to a specific occupation, in which the individual strives for further development and refinement of his or her knowledge within that specialty. This career orientation can hence be compared to the professional small business 'craftsman' who develops praxis in terms of genuine (often tacit) knowledge within the specific profession (Schön 1983; Dreyfus and Dreyfus 1986; Molander 1993). Both entrepreneurs who favor linear and expert career orientations can be expected to be less inclined to explore new possibilities and domains since this may divert them from the achievement, prestige or specialist knowledge that they so highly strive for. Rather, the literature suggests that these kinds of entrepreneurs are likely to have a higher degree of exploitation of pre-existent knowledge since they mainly strive to refine their pre-existent knowledge to become experts within their specific profession (Schön 1983; Johannisson 1992a; Molander 1993).

Individuals with a spiral career orientation prefer to explore new activities related to previous ones in which creativity and personal development becomes key motives (Larsson *et al.* 2001). Entrepreneurs favoring the spiral career can thus be characterized by periodic major moves across occupational areas, specialties or disciplines that are closely related to previous ones. This means that the new field draws on knowledge developed in the previous field and at the same time provides opportunities to develop an entirely new set of knowledge. Lastly, individuals with a transitory career profile make frequent changes of fields, organizations and jobs in which variety and independence are key motives to their career choices. Individuals who intentionally pursue transitory careers rarely consider themselves as actually having careers. Instead they are likely to treat themselves to a fascinating smorgasbord of work experiences, seeking variety and independence (Brousseau *et al.* 1996). Entrepreneurs who have either a transitory or a spiral career orientation can be expected to favor new entrepreneurial projects in order to search for new challenges and to learn something new (MacMillan 1986; Westhead and Wright 1998; McGrath 1999). The career patterns of these entrepreneurs can be described as project-oriented and 'episodic' implying that the competence developed consists of skill diversity, networking, speediness and adaptation (Brousseau *et al.* 1996). Hence, the literature suggests that these kinds of entrepreneurs are likely to have a higher degree of exploration of new possibilities compared to the focus they put on the exploitation of pre-existent knowledge.

The discussion above leads to the following proposition:

P5: The career orientation of the entrepreneur is related to his or her mode of transforming experience into knowledge.

    5a: Entrepreneurs with a transitory or spiral career orientation may to a larger extent focus on an explorative mode of transforming experience into knowledge.

    5b: Entrepreneurs with a linear or expert career orientation may to a larger extent focus on an exploitative mode of transforming experience into knowledge.

Conclusions

This chapter has reviewed and synthesized available research into a conceptual framework to enhance our understanding of entrepreneurial learning as an experiential process. In the review, the role of experience is highlighted as central as it provides entrepreneurs the possibility to improve their ability to discover and exploit entrepreneurial opportunities and to learn how to overcome traditional obstacles when organizing and managing new ventures (i.e. the liabilities of newness). It is also argued that there is a need to reconsider the predominant static view on entrepreneurial learning, which presumes a direct link between a particular experience and the knowledge gained from this experience. Hence, even if experience is conceived as an important source of entrepreneurial learning, it is necessary to acknowledge the experiential process where experience is transformed into entrepreneurial knowledge.

The conceptual framework provides a theoretical platform from which to explore further the dynamics of entrepreneurial learning as an experiential process. The framework does not solely focus on the relationship between entrepreneurs' experience and the development of entrepreneurial knowledge, but is also directed towards the intermediate process where their experiences are transformed into such knowledge. Based on these arguments are the processes of entrepreneurial knowledge, suggested to consist of three main components: entrepreneurs' career experience, the transformation process, and entrepreneurial knowledge in terms of increased effectiveness in opportunity recognition and in coping with the liabilities of newness. These components are then discussed in order to develop the arguments on how experience is transformed into knowledge, through the exploration of new possibilities and exploitation of pre-existent knowledge, which in turn influences the development of the entrepreneur's ability to discover and exploit entrepreneurial opportunities as well as coping with the traditional obstacles facing new ventures. The framework consequently suggests a need to draw a distinction between the events experienced by an entrepreneur and the knowledge acquired thereby when studying the process of entrepreneurial learning (Reuber *et al.* 1990).

Implications for future research

The conceptual framework presented in this chapter may serve as a point of departure for future empirical research on entrepreneurial learning. The chapter has developed several propositions of how entrepreneur's career experiences are transformed into knowledge, through the exploration of new possibilities and exploitation of pre-existent knowledge, which in turn influences the development of the entrepreneur's ability to discover and exploit entrepreneurial opportunities as well as coping with the traditional obstacles facing new ventures. An avenue for future research could then be used to address and develop operationalizations of the constructs in the framework, and empirically test the propositions to confirm or reject the theoretical assumptions in this study. In assessing entrepreneurs' career experience, researchers could for example draw on measures similar to previous work in the area (e.g. Lamont 1972; Vesper 1980; Stuart and Abetti 1990; Sandberg and Hofer 1987; Cooper *et al.* 1989; Dyke *et al.* 1992; Reuber and Fischer 1994). Based on this stream of literature, it is suggested that entrepreneur's career experience can be broadly divided into prior start-up experience, prior management experience, and prior industry-specific experience. With regard to the two proposed learning outcomes, researchers could assess the entrepreneur's ability to recognize and act on opportunities by drawing on measures similar to those developed by Hills *et al.* (1997) and Ucbasaran *et al.* (2003) on opportunity recognition behaviors. Researchers could furthermore measure an entrepreneur's ability to cope with the liabilities of newness by asking respondents to assess the validity of statements that have been linked to the liability of newness in the literature, such as for example the cost of learning new tasks, conflicts regarding new organizational roles, the absence of informal organizational structures, and lack of organizational stability to ensure customer trust (Shepherd *et al.* 2000; Shane and Khurana 2003).

Another main feature in the developed framework is the transformation of experience to knowledge through either the exploration of new possibilities or the exploitation of pre-existent knowledge. The respondents' reliance on exploration or exploitation as their predominant mode of transforming experience into knowledge could, for example, be measured by drawing on the theoretical work of March (1991) and Levinthal and March (1993). Specifically, the researchers could ask the respondent to assess the validity of statements connected to exploration (including terms such as variation, experimentation, discovery and playfulness) and exploitation (including terms such as refinement, efficiency, implementation and execution) respectively.

The literature review has also elaborated on three major factors that are expected to have an influence on how entrepreneurs' experience is transformed into experientially acquired knowledge: the outcome of previous entrepreneurial events, the entrepreneur's predominant logic or reasoning, and the entrepreneur's career orientation. Regarding the first of the three main determinants of the transformation process, researchers could operationalize the outcomes of previous entrepreneurial events based on arguments in the work of Sitkin (1992), Starr and Bygrave (1992) and McGrath (1999), where previous success/failure with both business ideas as well as firms should be included. Moreover, researchers could operationalize the entrepreneur's predominant logic or reasoning based on the arguments proposed by Sarasvathy (2001). Specifically, the researcher could ask the respondent to assess the validity of relevant statements connected to the reliance on the logic of control and the logic of prediction respectively. Finally, one recent example of a reliable operationalization of the career orientation of individuals has been developed and empirically tested by Brousseau *et al.* (1996). Using this developed scale, researchers can ask respondents to gauge their choice of career path and experience at work in terms of direction (career movement or change) and frequency of movement within and across different kinds of work over time (durability in a given field of work).

Another avenue for future research could be to investigate the link between individual and organizational-level learning in order to increase our understanding of the role of social relations and the embedding of learning techniques that can develop the adoption of new ideas and technologies, and empower innovation in new and small ventures (Deakins *et al.* 2000). In new and small firms, entrepreneurial learning can be expected to influence and closely mirror organizational learning, as the entrepreneur often has a dominant position as the central actor within the organization, and is the one who develops routines that encourage flexibility and the ability to respond to continuous change (Johannisson 2000). It can hence be expected that the development of an entrepreneurial culture will be strongly influenced by individual efforts towards innovation and growth in emerging organizations. However, the literature on organizational learning is primarily focused on large organizations, while the role of individual learning for successful enterprise development in small firms has been largely neglected (Deakins *et al.* 2000). Much consequently remains unknown regarding the drivers of entrepreneurial learning in new and small firms, and there is a lack of theoretical knowledge of how successful entrepreneurs develop their strategic learning to decrease the degree of novelty (ignorance) associated with these ventures (Gibb 1997; Shepherd *et al.* 2000).

Implications for practice

The present study may finally provide some implications for practice. The review and synthesis of the literature suggests that entrepreneurship is learned primarily by experience and discovery, and that entrepreneurial learning should be conceived as a lifelong process, where knowledge is continuously shaped and revised as new experience takes place (Sullivan 2000). Hence, the development of entrepreneurial knowledge of individuals is a slow and incremental process that evolves throughout their professional lives. This means that attempts to stimulate entrepreneurial activities through formal training and education is not likely to have any strong and direct impact on the development of entrepreneurial knowledge. Rather, educational policy efforts aimed at stimulating entrepreneurial activities should primarily focus on developing creativity, critical thinking and reflection among individuals, which in turn can have a profound influence on both their motivation and ability to develop entrepreneurial knowledge throughout their professional lives. Moreover, these educational efforts should start early in the system, and not only at its very end (Johannisson and Madsén 1997).

Furthermore, the review of literature and research indicates that the experience relevant for developing entrepreneurial knowledge not only involves the actual start-up of a new venture, but also the preparatory activities that enables the initial venture to be started (Reuber and Fischer 1993; Rae and Carswell 2001) as well as the subsequent career events that entrepreneurs encounter throughout their professional lives (Deakins and Freel 1998; McGrath 1999). This means that attention should be directed also to the issue of how potential entrepreneurs can progress throughout their careers, and then start a venture when timing is right. Hence, policy efforts aimed at stimulating individuals to undertake entrepreneurial activities should focus on efforts to make entrepreneurship more attractive as a potential career, such as for example support for reconciliation of family life and entrepreneurship, and incentives in the form of social security for entrepreneurs.

Taken together, it seems fair to argue that studies into the learning process of entrepreneurs so far have lacked a common framework, and many questions regarding entrepreneurs' learning still remain unanswered. Studying only the learning outcomes of entrepreneurs' prior experience is of little relevance to the entrepreneurship research field. What is needed is the inclusion of concepts and theories that explore entrepreneurial learning as an experiential process, and how this process evolves throughout the entrepreneurial career. Moreover, attention should be paid to the fact that different groups of entrepreneurs have different characteristics and career motivations (Kolvereid and Bullvåg 1993; Katz 1994; Rosa 1998; Westhead and Wright 1998), which lead them to focus on distinctive learning aspects and processes when transforming their experience into knowledge. This calls for further and intensified studies on the process of entrepreneurial learning, and future research to develop this important field of study within the entrepreneurship domain is consequently warranted.

Acknowledgements

This research has been supported by the Scandinavian Institute for Research in Entrepreneurship (SIRE), Halmstad University. The author is grateful for the helpful contributions of Jonas Gabrielsson, Hans Landström, Rikard Larsson and two anonymous reviewers.

Notes

1 The four career concepts are not necessarily pure in nature but can also be combined in various ways to form 'hybrid' concepts, which means that they can be used to describe various patterns of career preferences (Larsson *et al.* 2003).

References

Agnedal, H. (1999) Individual learning among entrepreneurs – towards a research agenda. In C. Salvato, P. Davidsson and A. Persson (eds), *Entrepreneurial Knowledge and Learning: Conceptual Advances and Direction for Future Research*. JIBS Research Report, No. 1999-6, pp. 48–63.
Aldrich, H. (1999) *Organizations Evolving*. London: Sage.
Aldrich, H. and Auster, E. (1986) Even dwarfs started small: liabilities of age and size and their strategic implications. *Research in Organizational Behavior*, 8: 165–98.
Ardichvili, A., Cardozo, R. and Ray, S. (2003) A theory of entrepreneurial opportunity identification and development. *Journal of Business Venturing*, 18(1): 105–23.
Bailey, J. (1986) Learning styles of successful entrepreneurs. In R. Ronstadt, J. Hornaday, J. R. Peterson. and K. Vesper (eds), *Frontiers of Entrepreneurship Research*. Wellesley, MA: Babson College, pp. 199–210.
Baron, R. A. (1998) Cognitive mechanisms in entrepreneurship: why and when entrepreneurs think differently than other people. *Journal of Business Venturing,* 13(4): 275–94.
Bates, T. and Servon, L. (2000) Viewing self employment as a response to lack of suitable opportunities for wage work. *National Journal of Sociology*, 12(2): 25–53.
Box, T. M., White, M. A. and Barr, S. H. (1993) A contingency model of new manufacturing firm performance. *Entrepreneurship Theory and Practice*, 18(2): 31–45.
Brousseau, K. R., Driver, M. J., Eneroth, K. and Larsson, R. (1996) Career pandemonium: realigning organizations and individuals. *Academy of Management Executive,* 10(4): 52–66.
Bruderl, J. and Preisendorfer, P. (1998) Network support and the success of newly founded businesses. *Small Business Economics,* 10(1): 213–25.

Bruderl, J., Preisendorfer, P. and Ziegler, R. (1992) Survival chances of newly founded business organizations. *American Sociological Review,* 57: 227–302.

Busenitz, L. and Barney, J. (1997) Differences between entrepreneurs and managers in large organizations: biases and heuristics in strategic decision-making. *Journal of Business Venturing,* 12(1): 9–30.

Cardon, M. S. and McGrath, R. G. (1999) When the going gets though . . . toward a psychology of entrepreneurial failure and re-motivation. In P. Reynolds *et al.* (eds), *Frontiers of Entrepreneurship Research.* Wellesley, MA: Babson College, pp. 58–72.

Carroll, G. and Mosakowski, E. (1987) The career dynamics of self-employment. *Administrative Science Quarterly,* 32: 570–89.

Cohen, W. M. and Levinthal, D. A. (1990) Absorptive capacity: a new perspective on learnng and innovation. *Administrative Science Quarterly,* 35: 128–52.

Collins, O. and Moore, D. G. (1970) *The Organization Makers: A Behavioral Study of Independent Entrepreneurs.* New York: Appleton-Century-Crofts.

Cooper, A. C., Dunkelberg, W. C. and Woo, C. Y. (1988) Survival and failure: a longitudinal study. In B. Kirchhoff *et al.* (eds), *Frontiers of Entrepreneurship Research.* Wellesley, MA: Babson College, pp. 225–37.

Cooper, A. C., Woo, C. Y. and Dunkelberg, W. C. (1989) Entrepreneurship and the initial size of firms, *Journal of Business Venturing,* 4(5): 317–32.

Cooper, A. C., Folta, T. B. and Woo, C. Y. (1995) Entrepreneurial information search. *Journal of Business Venturing,* 10(2): 107–20.

Cope, J. and Watts, G. (2000) Learning by doing. An exploration of experience, critical incidents and reflection in entrepreneurial learning. *International Journal of Entrepreneurial Behaviour and Research,* 6(3): 104–24.

Corbett, A. C. (2002) Recognizing high-tech opportunities: a learning and cognitive approach. In W. D. Bygrave *et al.* (eds), *Frontiers of Entrepreneurship Research.* Wellesley, MA: Babson College, pp. 49–60.

Cyert, R. M. and March, J. G. (1963) *A Behavioral Theory of the Firm.* Englewood Cliffs, NJ: Prentice Hall.

Davidsson, P. and Honing, B. (2003) The role of social and human capital among nascent entrepreneurs. *Journal of Business Venturing,* 18(3): 301–33.

Deakins, D. and Freel, M. (1998) Entrepreneurial learning and the growth process in SMEs. *The Learning Organization,* 5(3): 144–55.

Deakins, D., O'Neill, E. and Mileham, P. (2000) Executive learning in entrepreneurial firms and the role of external directors. *Education + Training,* 42(4/5): 317–25.

Delmar, F. and Davidsson, P. (2000) Where do they come from? Prevalence and characteristics of nascent entrepreneurs. *Entrepreneurship and Regional Development,* 12(1): 1–23.

Dreyfus, H. and Dreyfus, S. (1986) *Mind over Machine: The Power of Human Intuition and Expertise in the Era of the Computer.* New York: The Free Press.

Drucker, P. (1985) *Innovation and Entrepreneurship: Practice and Principles.* London: Heinemann.

Duchesneau, D. A. and Gartner, W. B. (1990) A profile of new venture success and failure in an emerging industry. *Journal of Business Venturing,* 5(5): 297–312.

Dyer, W. G. (1994) Towards a theory of entrepreneurial careers. *Entrepreneurship Theory and Practice,* 19: 7–21.

Dyke, L. S., Fischer, E. M. and Reuber, A. R. (1992) An inter-industry examination of the impact of owner experience on firm performance. *Journal of Small Business Management,* 30(4): 72–87.

Fiet, J. O., Piskounov, A. and Gustavsson, V. (2000) How to decide how to search for entrepreneurial opportunities. Paper presented at the 20th annual Babson College-Kauffman Foundation Entrepreneurship Research Conference, Boston, USA.

Gartner, W. B. (1989) 'Who is an entrepreneur?' is the wrong question. *Entrepreneurship Theory and Practice,* 13(4): 47–68.

Gatewood, E. J., Shaver, K. G. and Gartner, W. B. (1995) A longitudinal study of cognitive factors influencing start-up behaviors and success at venture creation. *Journal of Business Venturing,* 10(5): 371–91.

Ghemawat, P. and Costa, J. (1993) The organizational tension between static and dynamic efficiency. *Strategic Management Journal,* 14: 59–73.

Gibb, A. (1997) Small firms' training and competitiveness. Building upon the small business as a learning organisation. *International Small Business Journal,* 15(3): 13–29.

Gimeno, J., Folta, T., Cooper, A. and Woo, C. (1997) Survival of the fittest? Entrepreneurial human capital and the persistence of underperforming firms. *Administrative Science Quarterly,* 42: 750–83.

Hall, P. J. (1995) Habitual owners of small businesses. In F. Chittenden, M. Robertson and I. Marshall (eds), *Small Firms: Partnership for Growth.* London: Paul Chapman, pp. 217–30.

Hills, G. E., Lumpkin, G. T. and Singh, R. P. (1997) Opportunity recognition: perceptions and behaviors of entrepreneurs. In P. D. Reynolds *et al.* (eds), *Frontiers of Entrepreneurship Research.* Wellesley, MA: Babson College, pp. 168–82.

Holmqvist, M. (2000) The dynamics of experiential learning: balancing exploitation and exploration within and between organisations. Doctoral dissertation, Stockholm: School of Business.

Hudson, R. L. and McArthur, A. (1994) Contracting strategies in entrepreneurial and established firms. *Entrepreneurship Theory and Practice,* 18(4): 43–59.

Johannisson, B. (1992a) Entrepreneurship – the management of ambiguity. In T. Polesie and I.L. Johansson (eds), *Responsibility and Accounting – the Organizational Regulation of Boundary Conditions.* Lund: Studentlitteratur, pp. 155–79.

Johannisson, B. (1992b) Entrepreneurs as learners – beyond education and training. Paper presented at the Conference on Internationalizing Entrepreneurship Education and Training, Dortmund, Germany.

Johannisson, B. (2000) Modernizing the industrial district: rejuvenation or managerial colonisation? In E. Vatne and M. Taylor (eds), *The Networked Firm in a Global World: Small Firms in New Environment.* Aldershot: Ashgate, pp. 283–307.

Johannisson, B. and Madsén, T. (1997) *I entreprenörskapets tecken – en studie av skolning i förnyelse In the sign of entrepreneurship – a study of training and renewal.* Närings-och handelsdepartementet, Ds 1997:3. Stockholm: Regeringskansliets förvaltningskontor.

Johannisson, B., Landström, H. and Rosenberg, J. (1998) University training for entrepreneurship – an action frame of reference. *European Journal of Engineering Education,* 23(4): 477–96.

Johnson, P. (1986) *New Firms: An Economic Perspective.* London: Allen & Unwin.

Kaish, S. and Gilad, B. (1991) Characteristics of opportunities search of entrepreneurs versus executives: sources, interests, and general alertness. *Journal of Business Venturing,* 6(1): 45–61.

Katz, J. A. (1994) Modeling entrepreneurial career progressions: concepts and considerations *Entrepreneurship Theory and Practice,* 19(2): 23–39.

Kayes, D. C. (2002) Experiential learning and its critics: preserving the role of experience in management learning and education. *Academy of Management Learning and Education,* 1(2): 137–49.

Keeley, R. H. and Roure, J. B. (1990) Management, strategy, and industry structure as influences on the success of new firms. *Management Science*, 36(10): 1256–67.

Kolb, D. A. (1984) *Experiential Learning: Experience as the Source of Learning and Development*. Englewood Cliffs, NJ: Prentice Hall.

Kolvereid, L. and Bullvåg, E. (1993) Novices versus experienced business founders: an exploratory investigation. In S. Birley and I. C. MacMillan (eds), *Entrepreneurship Research: Global Perspectives*. Amsterdam: Elsevier Science, pp. 275–85.

Laitinen, E. K. (1992) Prediction of failure of a newly founded firm. *Journal of Business Venturing*, 7(4): 323–40.

Lamont, L. (1972) What entrepreneurs learn from experience. *Journal of Small Business Management*, 10(3): 36–41.

Larsson, R., Driver, M., Holmqvist, M. and Sweet, P. (2001) Career dis-integration and re-integration in mergers and acquisitions: managing competence and motivational intangibles. *European Management Journal*, 19(6): 609–18.

Larsson, R., Brousseau, K. R., Driver, M. J., Holmqvist, M. and Tarnovskaya, V. (2003) International growth through cooperation: brand-driven strategies, leadership, and career development in Sweden. *Academy of Management Executive*, 17(1): 7–24.

Levinthal, D. A. and March, J. (1993) The myopia of learning. *Strategic Management Journal*, 14: 95–112.

Lorrain, J. and Dussault, L. (1988) Relation between psychological characteristics, administrative behaviors and success of founder entrepreneurs at the start-up stage. In B. Kirchhoff *et al.* (eds), *Frontiers of Entrepreneurship Research*. Wellesley, MA: Babson College, pp. 150–64.

Lounamaa, P. H. and March, J. G. (1987) Adaptive coordination of a learning team. *Management Science*, 33: 107–23.

MacMillan, I. C. (1986) To really learn about entrepreneurship, let's study habitual entrepreneurs. *Journal of Business Venturing*, 1(3): 241–3.

March, J. G. (1991) Exploration and exploitation in organizational learning. *Organization Science*, 2(1): 71–87.

McClelland, D. C. (1961) *The Achieving Society*. Princeton, NJ: Van Norstrand.

McGrath, R. G. (1999) Falling forward: real options reasoning and entrepreneurial failure. *Academy of Management Review*, 24(1): 13–30.

McGrath, R. G. and MacMillan, I. C. (2000) The entrepreneurial mindset. Boston: Harvard Business School Press.

Minniti, M. and Bygrave, W. (2001) A dynamic model of entrepreneurial learning. *Entrepreneurship Theory and Practice*, 25(3): 5–16.

Mintzberg, H. and Waters, J. A. (1982) Tracking strategy in an entrepreneurial firm. *Academy of Management Journal*, 25(3): 465–99.

Molander, B. (1993) *Kunskap i handling* [*Knowledge in action*]. Göteborg: Bokförlaget Daidalos AB.

Nelson, R. R. and Winter, S. G. (1982) *An Evolutionary Theory of Economic Change*. Cambridge, MA: Harvard University Press.

Pinchot, G. (1985) *Intrapreneuring: Why You Don't Have to Leave the Corporation to Become an Entrepreneur*. New York: Harper & Row.

Rae, D. (2000) Understanding entrepreneurial learning: a question of how? *International Journal of Entrepreneurial Behaviour and Research*, 6(3): 146–59.

Rae, D. and Carswell, M. (2001) Towards a conceptual understanding of entrepreneurial learning. *Journal of Small Business and Enterprise Development*, 8(2): 150–8.

Ravasi, D., Turati, C., Marchisio, G. and Ruta, C. D. (2004) Learning in entrepreneurial firms: an exploratory study. In G. Corbetta, M. Huse and D. Ravasi (eds), *Crossroads of Entrepreneurship*. Boston: Kluwer Academic, pp. 165–84.

Reuber, R. A. and Fischer, E. M. (1993) The learning experiences of entrepreneurs. In N. C. Churchill *et al.* (eds), *Frontiers of Entrepreneurship Research*, Wellesley, MA: Babson College, pp. 234–45.

Reuber, R. A. and Fischer, E. M. (1994) Entrepreneurs' experience, expertise, and the performance of technology-based firms. *IEEE Transactions of Engineering Management,* 41(4): 365–74.

Reuber, R. A. and Fischer, E. M. (1999) Understanding the consequences of founders' experience. *Journal of Small Business Management,* 37(2): 30–45.

Reuber, R. A., Dyke, L. S. and Fischer, E. M. (1990) Experiential acquired knowledge and entrepreneurial venture success. *Academy of Management Best Paper Proceedings,* 69–73.

Reynolds, M. (1998) Reflection and critical reflection in management learning. *Management Learning,* 29(2): 183–200.

Reynolds, P. D., Hay, M., Bygrave, W. D., Camp, S. M. and Autio, E. (2000) *Global Entrepreneurship Monitor 2000 Executive Report*. Wellesley, MA/Kansas City: Babson College, London Business School and Kauffman Center for Entrepreneurship Leadership.

Ripsas, S. (1998) Towards an interdisciplinary theory of entrepreneurship. *Small Business Economics,* 10: 103–15.

Romanelli, E. and Schoonhoven, K. (2001) The local origins of new firms. In K. Schoonhoven and E. Romanelli (eds), *The Entrepreneurial Dynamic*. Stanford, CA: Stanford University Press, pp. 40–67.

Ronstadt, R. (1988) The corridor principle. *Journal of Business Venturing,* 3(1): 31–40.

Rosa, P. (1998) Entrepreneurial process of business cluster formation and growth by 'habitual entrepreneurs'. *Entrepreneurship Theory and Practice,* 22(4): 43–61.

Sandberg, W. R. and Hofer, C. W. (1987) Improving new venture performance: the role of strategy, industry structure and the entrepreneur. *Journal of Business Venturing*, 2(1): 5–28.

Sapienza, H. J. and Grimm, C. M. (1997) Founder characteristics, start-up process, and strategy/structure variables as predictors of shortline railroad performance. *Entrepreneurship Theory and Practice*, 23(1): 5–24.

Sarasvathy, S. D. (2001) Causation and effectuation: toward a theoretical shift from economic inevitability to entrepreneurial contingency. *Academy of Management Review,* 26(2): 243–63.

Schein, E. H. (1987) Individuals and careers. In J. W. Lorsch (ed.), *Handbook of Organizational Behavior*. Englewood Cliffs, NJ: Prentice Hall, pp. 155–71.

Schön, D. (1983) *The Reflective Practitioner*. New York: Basic Books.

Shane, S. (2003) *A General Theory of Entrepreneurship: The Individual–Opportunity Nexus*. Cheltenham, UK: Edward Elgar.

Shane, S. and Khurana, R. (2003) Bringing individuals back in: the effects of career experience on new firm founding, *Industrial and Corporate Change*, 12(3): 519–43.

Shane, S. and Venkataraman, S. (2000) The promise of entrepreneurship as a field of research. *Academy of Management Review*, 25(1): 217–26.

Shepherd, D. A., Douglas, E. J. and Shanley, M. (2000) New venture survival: ignorance, external shocks, and risk reduction strategies. *Journal of Business Venturing,* 15(5–6) 393–410.

Shook, C. L., Priem, R. L. and McGee, J. E. (2003) Venture creation and the enterprising individual: a review and synthesis. *Journal of Management*, 29(3): 379–99.

Sitkin, S. B. (1992) Learning trough failure: the strategy of small losses. *Research in Organizational Behavior*, 14: 231–66.

Starr, J. A. and Bygrave, W. D. (1992) The second time around: the outcomes, assets, and liabilities of prior start-up experience. In S. Birley and I. C. MacMillan (eds), *International Perspectives on Entrepreneurship Research 1991: Proceedings of the First Annual Global Conference on Entrepreneurship Research.* Amsterdam: North Holland, pp. 340–63.

Starr, J. A., Bygrave, W. D. and Tercanli, D. (1993) Does experience pay? Methodological issues in the study of entrepreneurial experience. In S. Birley and I. C. MacMillan (eds), *Entrepreneurship Research Global Perspectives.* Amsterdam: Elsevier Science, pp. 125–55.

Stinchcombe, A. (1965) social structure and organizations. In J. March (ed.), *Handbook of Organizations.* Chicago: Rand McNally.

Stokes, D. and Blackburn, R. (2002) Learning the hard way: the lessons of owner-managers who have closed their businesses. *Journal of Small Business and Enterprise Development,* 9(1): 17–27.

Storey, D. (1994) Understanding the Small Business Sector. London: Routledge.

Stuart, R. W. and Abetti, P. A. (1990) Impact of entrepreneurial and management experience on early performance. *Journal of Business Venturing,* 5(3): 151–62.

Sullivan, R. (2000) Entrepreneurial learning and mentoring. *International Journal of Entrepreneurial Behaviour and Research,* 6(3): 160–75.

Sullivan, T., Warren, E. and Westbrook, J. (1999) *Financial Difficulties of Small Businesses and Reasons for Their Failure.* Small Business Research Summary, No. 188, US Small Business Administration, Office of Advocacy.

Taylor, M. (1999) The survival of the fittest: an analysis of self-employment duration in Britain. *Economic Journal,* 109: C140–55.

Timmons, J. A. (1999) *New Venture Creation: Entrepreneurship for the 21st Century.* Boston: Irwin/McGraw-Hill.

Ucbasaran, D., Westhead, P. and Wright, M. (2003) Business ownership experience, information search and opportunity identification: a research note. Paper presented at the Academy of Management Meeting in Seattle, USA.

Vesalainen, J. and Pihkala, T. (1999) Motivation structure and entrepreneurial intentions. In P. Reynolds *et al.* (eds), *Frontiers of Entrepreneurship Research.* Wellesley, MA: Babson College, pp. 73–87.

Vesper, K. H. (1980) *New Venture Strategies.* Englewood Cliffs, NJ: Prentice Hall.

Vince, R. (1998) Behind and beyond Kolb's learning cycle. *Journal of Management Education,* 22(3): 304–19.

Weick, K. E. (1984) Small wins: redefining the scale of social problems. *American Psychologist,* 39(1): 40–9.

Westhead, P. and Wright, M. (1998) Novice, portfolio, and serial founders: are they different? *Journal of Business Venturing,* 13(3): 173–204.

Wiklund, J. (1998) Small firm growth and performance: entrepreneurship and beyond. Doctoral dissertation, No. 003, Jönköping: Jönköping International Business School.

Wright, M., Robbie, K. and Ennew, C. (1997) Serial entrepreneurs. *British Journal of Management,* 8(3): 251–68.

Wright, M., Westhead, P. and Sohl, J. (1998) Editors' Introduction: Habitual entrepreneurs and angel investors. *Entrepreneurship Theory and Practice,* 22(4): 5–21.

Zahra, S. A. and George, G. (2002) Absorptive capacity: a review, reconceptualization, and extension. *Academy of Management Review,* 27(2): 185–203.

Zietsma, C. (1999) Opportunity knocks – or does it hide? In P. D. Reynolds *et al.* (eds), *Frontiers of Entrepreneurship Research.* Wellesley, MA: Babson College, pp. 242–56.

4 The role and management of learning from experience in an entrepreneurial context

Joyce McHenry

Introduction

In organisation studies it is now common to consider that we live and work in a 'knowledge society' with faster technological change, greater international competition and an increasing demand for skilled, flexible and creative employees (Drucker 1992). Rigid forms of managing and organising whereby employees are instructed about how and where they should perform in accordance with a pre-defined task cannot survive and need to be abandoned (Nonaka and Takeuchi 1995). Such a viewpoint encourages employees or rather 'knowledge workers' at all levels to be self-driven, to learn from their experiences, to develop competences, to be innovative and to actively engage in order to survive in the new high-performance workplaces (Prahalad and Hamel 1990; Nordhaug 1993; Moingeon and Edmondson 1996).

Worldwide, organisations have responded to the increased uncertainty and volatility in the environment and the trend, or at least the rhetoric, is towards flatter (Galbraith 1995), flexible (Volberda 1996), learning (Senge 1990; Pedler *et al*. 1997), knowledge-creating (Nonaka and Takeuchi 1995) and innovative organisations (Drucker 1993). This trend is also apparent in the Nordic countries and has contributed to a focus on competence, learning, knowledge creation, balanced scorecards, teamwork, and improved interpersonal and inter-company relations (Brewster and Holt Larsen 2000), as well as an increased focus by Nordic policy-makers (Nordic Industrial Fund 2002) on, creative and innovative SMEs. In order to achieve this, it has been suggested that entrepreneurship in the education system should be promoted and that innovation and entrepreneurship policies should encourage companies' abilities to develop new competences, including efficient learning processes and networking. Accordingly there is a call for the promotion of an entrepreneurial approach to managing in organisations (Morris 1998; Sharma and Chrisman 1999; Deakins *et al*. 2002; Matlay and Mitra 2002) as well as a growing focus on the dynamic process of entrepreneurial learning (Gartner 1988; Reuber and Fischer 1993; Rae 2000; Nordic Industrial Fund 2002; Cope 2003).

The aim of this chapter is to create a deeper understanding about the role and management of entrepreneurial learning. The research reported here was conducted in a medium-sized entrepreneurial IT consultancy firm that faces continuous change and development. In this sector, mergers and acquisitions are common in order to facilitate the growth of the organisation, which potentially increases the uncertainty faced by the managers and executives of such organisations. One means of addressing this is to introduce the idea of entrepreneurial learning whereby employees are encouraged to handle problems and issues and learn from them (Deakins and Freel 1998) as well as to adjust to unpredictable critical incidents (Cope and Watts 2000). The focus in this chapter is consequently on a processual study of learning in an entrepreneurial context. Thus, the starting point for this research is the fact that entrepreneurs are excellent learners (Smilor 1997) who are action-oriented with a preference for experientially based learning (Dalley and Hamilton 2000; Minniti and Bygrave 2001; Rae and Carswell 2001; Cope 2003). Such learning is mainly contextual as entrepreneurs learn from peers, learn by doing, learn by opportunity taking, and learn by experimenting (Gibb 1997). Such an approach has strong ties to pragmatist and experiential learning theories (Revans 1982; Kolb 1984). In addition, it has been suggested that it is from this action-oriented position that research on entrepreneurial learning needs to be designed (Leitch 2007). It is therefore appropriate to place this dynamic action-oriented entrepreneurial learning in perspective and discuss how it relates to other learning theories as well as assessing the implications for facilitating growth in entrepreneurial contexts.

The remainder of this chapter explores the dominant views on learning and discusses how multiple meanings of learning have had an influence on the management of entrepreneurial learning. This is followed by a discussion on the research methodology adopted. Reflecting upon the case study presented leads to a deeper appreciation about the role of learning perspectives and how these relate to the challenges of managing learning from experience in an entrepreneurial context. Finally, the implications of this study are examined with particular emphasis on the significance of giving space to the dynamic and social aspects of entrepreneurial learning.

Theoretical overview: a consideration of individual approaches to learning

Although the meaning of the term 'learning' is mostly taken for granted in our daily language and practice, the social science literatures have for the last two centuries struggled to find an answer to the question 'What is learning?'. This has resulted in a multitude of definitions and learning perspectives, each claiming to provide an accurate description of learning. Traditionally the dominant Western view on learning and knowledge has been inspired by the behaviourist theories with their emphasis on sensory experience and laws of association (Bower and Hilgard 1981). Most behaviourist theories have their roots in the work of classical behaviourists such as Thorndike (1874–1949) and Pavlov (1849–1936) and the more recent work of Skinner (1904–1990), who developed operant behaviourism. The behaviourists portray human beings as being relatively passive individuals who respond to the environment without actively involving their own thoughts and will. Learning occurs through stimulus-response whereby an individual acquires knowledge about a stimulus (event) through sensory experiences from the environment with which the stimulus is associated. Continual reinforcement of a response leads to the development of habitual behaviour (Skinner 1953).

Towards the end of the 1950s an alternative approach, in the work of cognitivist researchers, appeared. Cognitivist researchers claimed that the approach adopted by behaviourists could not address the issues of how perceptual processes and memory development (i.e. the process of encoding, storing and retrieving) could function. Under the auspices of cognitive psychology such researchers are interested in how organisms gain knowledge about the world and how they use that knowledge to guide decisions and perform effective actions (Bower and Hilgard 1981). This perspective builds upon the assumption that the mind is a representational system and the unit of thinking is known as a schema, and these, along with scripts, allow symbols and meanings to be interpreted (Schank 1975). The ideas of Piaget (1970) about intellectual development have been a major influence in the development of cognitive learning theories. According to Piaget (1970), humans learn through formal reasoning and move through various stages known as sensorimotor, preoperational, operational and formal operational. His main claim rests on the assumption that cognitive development consists of a constant effort to adapt to the environment in terms of assimilation and accommodation. Assimilation occurs when a new sense impression is incorporated into already existing cognitive structures. Accommodation is the process of restructuring cognitive structures when the input does not fit the already- existing structure. If the input does not fit, an imbalance known as cognitive conflict occurs. However, balance can be restored through equilibration, that is, by an interplay between assimilation and accommodation.

Piaget (1970) further specifies that a human's abstracting properties of the process of knowing occurs through a process of projection and reflection. The first phase, termed projection, involves extrapolating a structure from a lower developmental level onto a higher level so that it can be understood consciously or explicitly. This process is known as empirical abstraction and it has to be in place before the next phase can start. The second phase, reflection, reorganises the structure at a higher level. Understanding is not merely a copy of the initial structure, but involves integration into other cognitive structures – this process is termed reflecting abstraction. An application of Piaget's genetic epistemology can be found in the work of Helmersson (1984), where he illustrates how knowledge is developed with a basis in the field of experience and how existing cognitive structures influence the field of action (see Figure 4.1).

At the same time that the cognitivists rejected behaviourism, the views of other groups of learning theorists anchored in the pragmatist and social-cultural traditions became more apparent. These approaches developed as a reaction against the static and mechanical approaches of the behaviourist and cognitivist learning theories. The pragmatist philosophy of learning is founded on the premise that, by reflecting on experiences, understanding of the world we live in is constructed.

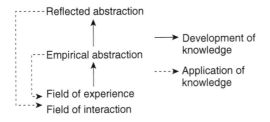

Figure 4.1 Constructive development cycle (Helmersson 1984).

In this approach the emphasis is that all learning starts in practice and results from unhampered participation in a meaningful situation (Illich 1971). 'Pragma', meaning 'action', indicates that action, instead of belief, is the point of departure in the definition of knowledge and learning. The human being is seen as a holistic, generative and creative individual, who acts or responds towards things or items on the basis of the meanings that those things or items have for him or her (Blumer 1969). This view of learning has its roots in the ideas of both Piaget (1970), who proposed that knowledge has its basis in experience, as well as those of Dewey (1938/1963), who suggested that all learning is embedded in social practice. For Piaget (1970) abstraction from actions is an active construction from the knowing subject and does not already exist in the subject's consciousness. Such reflecting is considered to be constructive and leads to a generalisation that is a novel composition which involves a new scheme that has been developed by means of elements borrowed from prior schemes by differentiation.

Although Piaget considered that knowledge depends on experience, he is clearly not a stimulus-response theorist, who claims that knowledge is represented as a 'copy' of conditions that exist in the physical world. Instead, he connects knowledge with cognitive structures that offer the potential to deal with the environment. These cognitive structures are thus projected on the physical environment and thereby create or construct the environment. In common with other cognitive theorists, he believes that learning involves both the acquisition and cognitive representation of information. However, such schemes, according to Piaget, are dynamic representations of mental actions, while schemata or elemental theories are static representations of dynamic events. Von Glaserfield (1990) argues that Piaget's perspective is different from other cognitive theories due to his use of organic language, his focus on active constructivism and his attempt to understand the epistemological status of the mind's products. For Piaget an 'object' is never a thing-in-itself, but something that the cognising subject has constructed by making distinctions and co-ordinations in his or her perceptual field. Therefore, understanding cannot be imposed, but instead it evolves as the learner actively tries to make sense of the world (Von Glaserfield 1990). A gap between a learner's existing knowledge and a formal abstract may, however, cause learning difficulties, as it may be too abstract to assimilate (Helmersson 1984). As a result, learning has to take as a starting point the existence of experience-based knowledge.

Dewey (1916/1966), on the other hand, places more emphasis on social practice. He claims that every idea, value and social institution has its origin in the practical circumstances of human life. Experience is an active and social process and knowing is primarily a matter of knowing how. Dewey defines learning as a continuous reorganisation and reconstruction of experience that is embedded in social practice, thereby indicating that:

> To learn from experience is to make a backward and forward connection between what we do to things and what we enjoy or suffer from things in consequence. Under such conditions doing becomes a trying; an experiment with the world to find out what it is like . . . . 1) Experience is primarily an active-passive affair; it is not primarily cognitive. But 2) the measure of the value of an experience lies in the perception of relationships or continuities to which it leads up. It includes cognition in the degree in which it is cumulative or amounts to something, or has meaning.
>
> (Dewey 1916/1966: 140)

Dewey's contribution to this area is his emphasis on a non-dualist understanding of action and thinking as well as his belief that learning is active, intentional and social (Elkjaer 1999). He views learning as a natural process and not something that needs to be forced, which is also reflected in emancipatory adult learning theories (Rogers 1969; Freire 1975; Knowles 1980). These experiential approaches to learning value the autonomy and participation of the learner, emphasise connected ways of knowing, recognise the personal and subjective and acknowledge the ways in which power relations influence practice.

The social-cultural view distinguishes itself with its focus on learning as interaction in a socio-cultural practice, rather than as an individual cognitive activity. The roots of this perspective lie in the writings of Vygotsky (1886–1934) and more recently those of Bruner (1990) and Lave (1993). Instead of taking an individualistic approach, these writers emphasise that human beings are socially interactive and thus, by nature, engage in social activity with their contemporaries and learn from their predecessors. Such an approach considers the actual lived, emotional experiences of interacting human beings to be more important than excessively rational, individual cognitive theories of human behaviour. For instance, Wertsch (1985) points to this in Vygotsky's theoretical framework, where social interaction and socio-cultural history play a fundamental role in the development of cognition. Indicating that the social and cultural aspects of thinking are mediated by language and other products of culture, i.e. mental functioning in the individual has its origins in social activity, Vygotsky (1978) states:

> Every function in the child's cultural development appears twice: first, on the social level, and later, on the individual level; first, between people (interpsychological) and then inside the child (intrapsychological). This applies equally to voluntary attention, to logical memory, and to the formation of concepts. All the higher functions originate as actual relationships between individuals. (p.57)

Vygotsky characterises the relationship of humans to their environment as mediated by tools, such as concepts, logics, signs and words, that enable humans to make a view of the world they occupy together with others. Language is, however, viewed as the supreme human psychological tool that makes other forms of learning possible. In this, Vygotsky (1978), like Dewey, believes that language is a means of communication that is transmitted and acquired in a social medium. Prominence is, thus, given to the key factor in social learning, namely learning by imitation and interaction with adults and peers in a co-operative social setting so that through observation and imitation higher mental functions can develop. The social-cultural view emphasises that learning is a natural activity that is a by-product of a learner's participation in social practices. It is argued that learning as it normally occurs is a function of the activity, context and culture in which it occurs (i.e. it is situated). Indeed, learning is an implicit and emergent sense-making activity where meaning is constructed from experience through conversations (Bruner 1990).

The implications of these four individual learning views will be further examined in the next section, and it will become clear that they are also significant in relation to debates about learning, knowledge, competence development and organisational learning in organisations.

Implications of individual learning views on learning in organisations

Within organisation studies the learning theories discussed above have also informed the debate about learning, competence development and knowledge creation as well as organisational and entrepreneurial learning (Sandberg 1994; Blackler 1995; Fox 1997; Easterby-Smith *et al.* 2000; Gherardi 2000; Rae and Carswell 2001). These have commonly been divided into two major groups each with a different epistemological stance, the positivist (reductionist) orientation and the interpretative (situated) perspective (McHenry 2003) (see Figure 4.2). Figure 4.2 demonstrates that as each orientation explores the concepts from a specific assumption base, there will be associated implications for the specific research focus, rhetoric, definitions and recommendations for learning in organisations.

For instance, the behaviourist view has contributed to the conviction that people learn in a pre-described way and that an individual's learning path can be programmed. Taylor (1911) introduced the idea of measuring and managing learning through a rigid scientific method of reducing knowledge and skill to laws, rules and even mathematical formulas. This codification of human skills made it possible to educate people faster, as well as matching a worker's competences to the tools and tasks in a much more efficient way. In this approach, organisational learning was prompted by incentives for individuals to act as rationally as possible as well as being enhanced through the design and implementation of formal management systems for information, planning, and control (Shrivastava 1983). Given the static and pre-defined way of explaining learning through external

	Positivist, functionalist, reductionist		Interpretative, phenomenological, situated	
Theoretical views	Behaviourism	Cognitivism	Pragmatism	Social – cultural
	Stimulus-response	Information processing	Action learning	Situated learning
Reality	Concrete	Adaptive	Participative	Socially constructed
Human nature	Responding mechanism	Rational information processor	Active transformer	Social actor
Learning view	Change of behaviour	Individual cognitive process	Continuous process- action and reflection	Enculturation Identity creation
Focus	Reward-punishment	Feedback and memorising	Dialogue and reflection on experience	Participation in community of practice
Knowledge view	Objective and true facts	Facts, objective and true until falsified	Common knowledge, justified knowing	Social creation of meaning
Focus	Explicit	Explicit	Tacit and explicit	Tacit-tacit
Competence	Individual trait	Individual trait	Knowing-in-action Contextual	Relational, contextual and social
Described as	Scientific descriptions of skills	Detached list describing knowledge + skills + attitude (KSA)	Reflection on own development	Narrative
Organisational learning	Bureaucratic mechanistic learning system	Acquire, store, retrieve (share) systems	Knowledge creation systems	Shared meaning-making, travelling of ideas
Entrepreneurial learning	Not relevant	Acquisition, storage and use of entrepreneurial knowledge in the long-term memory	Continuous process of exploration and reflection on and in entrepreneurial experience to inform further action	Contextual process of becoming: making meaning and developing the self from acting upon opportunities and managing new ventures

Figure 4.2 Four views on learning, knowledge and competence (McHenry 2003).

reinforcement, the behaviouristic view cannot offer much insight in the dynamic process of entrepreneurial learning, where people are seen to be proactive, seek opportunities and are engaged in the learning process (Cope 2003).

In organisation studies the contribution of the cognitive approach to learning has been to explain the mental processes by which people acquire, store and retrieve information in a rational way (Fox 1997). It is based on the belief that learning is a logical and goal-oriented process that occurs independently from a specific context (Tolman 1948). There is a strong belief that human learning at work is best represented through indirect descriptions of competences (Woodruffe 1990/1993). In this way the worker becomes separated from the work and, thus, work activities are described independently of the worker. This has resulted in the development of a variety of competence lists. Those who subscribe to such a perspective claim that such lists of required competence (in the form of knowledge, skill and attitude–KSAs) are amenable to quantitative measurement and objective assessment and, furthermore, have predictive value across diverse domains of functioning (Boyatzis 1982). This view has also contributed to the insight that organisations are adaptive organisms that survive because of their information-processing abilities (Huber 1991). Within entrepreneurship this has led to the generation of cognitive studies that seek to determine how entrepreneurs select and process information in order to make sense of the external environment, resulting in the belief that opportunity recognition is influenced by prior knowledge (Shane 2000). Such an approach also explains how an entrepreneur's cognitive schema contributes to framing an opportunity as favourable (Palich and Bagby 1995). Other studies have focused on how entrepreneurs differ in their learning style (see e.g. Bailey 1986; Baron 1998). Yet, given that entrepreneurial learning is action-oriented, these cognitive theories can give only a limited explanation about entrepreneurial learning (Rae and Carswell 2001).

The pragmatic learning view has stimulated a focus on the active and social nature of experience and reflection in workplace settings (Boud *et al.* 1993). Learning is described as a participative, natural and continuous process where experience is transformed into knowledge (Rogers 1969; Freire 1975; Knowles 1980; Revans 1980), thereby, making learning from one's own experiences, i.e. reflection in and on action, important in order to allow development (Schön 1983). Action in this context should not to be equated with a simple response to a stimulus, with observable behaviour or with goal attainment, as this may result in missing the subtle ways in which action creates meaning (Weick 1995). Within management studies, Revans (1980) uses the term action learning to describe the 'learning by doing' approach and states that 'managers learn most effectively to manage with and from other managers, in the course of attacking the management problems-opportunities they are under contract to attack' (Revans 1982: 18). Learning thus embraces both know-how (tacit knowledge) and know-that (explicit knowledge). Action learning, therefore, takes place through grappling not with puzzles, but with real work, and such an approach carries a significant risk of penalty or failure. Dreyfus and Dreyfus (1986) have captured this learning from experience as a skill development process whereby individuals develop through five stages from novice, advanced beginner, competent, proficient to expert. Their model draws from the work of philosophers like Polanyi (1958) and Kuhn (1962/1970), who have observed that people have many skills (know-how) that have been acquired without explicit knowledge (knowing-that). This implies that much learning is tacit and hard to verbalise and, therefore, not all of the knowledge embedded in expertise can be captured in theoretical propositions. Benner (1984) asserts that the development stages of know-how can only be captured by interpretative descriptions of actual practices and visualised as 'exemplars' in narrative form.

According to Docherty and Marking (1997), the individual as an interpreting, acting and problem-solving being will express their learning in a given situation, with a certain meaning being created in a particular context in a given environment. They suggest that competence in this context consists of overlapping components of knowledge (facts, data, theory), experience (combine, formulate, integrate, reconstruct) and application (act and react in a given context). In this approach learning is considered to be experiential. Indeed, such a perspective has had a major impact on entrepreneurial learning research, and has, for example, stimulated studies on how entrepreneurs transform experience into entrepreneurial knowledge (Minniti and Bygrave 2001) as well as attempting to explain how people develop entrepreneurial capability through learning (Rae and Carswell 2001).

The social-cultural perspective of learning differs from the individualistic approach as it emphasises that human beings are social, interactive individuals and that learning is embedded in practice. Humans by nature engage in social activity with their contemporaries and learn from their predecessors. Learning is a natural activity that is a by-product of the learner's participation in social practices. It is argued that learning as it normally occurs is a function of the activity, context and culture in which it occurs (i.e. it is situated). All learning is therefore situated as no task or activity exists independently of a learner's contextualisation, which is determined from an individual's experience. Learning how to be, or to become, is motivated by desire, goals and needs, to be accepted, to emulate a desired person or to join a group. This is further described in Lave and Wenger's (1991: 50) account of learning in workplace situations where they present a theory of learning as becoming and describe learning as 'an aspect of participation in socially situated practices'. Learning as a process of enculturation in which an individual becomes a legitimate member of a community takes place within a community of practice (COP). This has been defined by Lave and Wenger (1991: 51) as 'a set of relations among persons, activities, and world, over time and in relation with other tangential and overlapping communities of practice. A community is an intrinsic condition for the existence of knowledge, not least because it provides the interpretive support necessary for making sense of its heritage'.

Communities of practice are not only a central theme in the work of Lave and Wenger (1991) and Wenger (1998, 2000), but also in the work of Schön (1983), and others who value culturally and symbolically sensitive theories (Mead 1934/1956; Blumer 1969). Such approaches focus on the fact that as humans cannot be separated from their social context, the creation of knowledge is more related to communities of practice than individuals and, thus, learning is described as guided participation that involves interpersonal communication. Moreover, the concept of competence in this context relates to 'knowing how to be competent' in a usable environment. As such it is considered to be relational and social and thus, can only be understood in relation to a community of practice (Sandberg 1994; Gherardi and Nicolini 2000). Further, such knowing is continually reproduced and negotiated and therefore it is dynamic and provisional (Gherardi and Nicolini 2000).

Bramming and Holt Larsen (2000) have described this concept as competence-in-practice and as it is socially created and recreated in a particular context it has a fluid status. Assessment of such competences, they believe, has to occur in the actual community of practice where the meaning of being competent (a shared notion of the standard) is jointly created through dialogue and an emerging understanding of what knowledge/skill/attitude is necessary to do the work. Each individual can then form an opinion about his or her own level of expertise, leaving the assessment grounded in the social practice. Assessment is made on the understanding that to be considered as competent in a particular skill is a symbolic and political tool that only partly captures an individual's full competence.

Researchers who work from this perspective have commonly looked upon organisations as social worlds where people create meaning and identity through the efforts of competing individuals and coalitions of interests. Organisations are portrayed as being composed of multiple interacting communities (Lave and Wenger 1991), where people share stories for entertainment, for instruction and for managing the relationships with others, i.e. learning is seen as a social process involving social relations. Focus is then on how learning is accomplished in practice and on the mutual creation of compatible and shared meanings (Cook and Yanow 1993). Organisations are, thus, defined in terms of shared meaning. From this situated and cultural approach to learning, Cook and Yanow (1993) and Yanow (2000) have challenged the more cognitive-oriented accounts that emphasise behaviour change as well as systems-oriented accounts that focus on error detection and correction as well as adaptation to environment. Instead they value the embodied and the aesthetic, as well as the cognitive dimensions of learning activity. Inquiry into organisational learning from this perspective emphasises how meaning is created, communicated and imposed through stories, myths, rhetorical devices and the use of formal and informal power. The recognition that diverse communities may share similar words and concepts at the surface level, but may actually be using them in entirely different ways resulting in communication and co-ordination problems, is acknowledged. This view has contributed to the understanding that entrepreneurial learning not only is about learning from experience, but that it also has to encompass the personal and contextual part of the development of the self (Rae and Carswell 2001). Entrepreneurial learning is about learning to become an entrepreneur and is expressed through stories with focus placed on the emotional aspects of learning and the community in which the entrepreneur is working (Rae 2000).

In summary, the four learning views discussed above have influenced workplace learning, knowledge and competence as well as entrepreneurial and organisational learning in their own particular way. While the behaviourist and rational-cognitive accounts have dominated in the Western world, the pragmatist and social-cultural accounts have contributed with a critical and situated perspective to the traditional, detached and scientific orientation. This means that focus has shifted from a predominantly 'episteme orientation' and 'learning from explicit instructions and in pre-defined ways' to exploring 'common knowledge as embedded in situated practices' and learning as 'a process where concepts are derived from and continuously modified by experience' (McHenry 2003). It is from the latter approach, i.e. from a pragmatist and social understanding of learning, that those working in entrepreneurial learning have started to develop their insights. This is because it was felt that the cognitive and behaviourist theories have given limited support in explaining action (Rae and Carswell 2001). For instance, Deakins and Freel (1998) suggest that the entrepreneur is not only encouraged to alter his or her behaviour through experiential learning, but also has to make sense of the experience while being engaged in a social context (Rae and Carswell 2001). In the next section, a case study will illustrate how particular learning assumptions have had an impact on the management of learning from experience in an entrepreneurial context.

Research method

This research is based on a longitudinal case study of an entrepreneurial venture in which the firm's managers aspired to manage the experiential learning (competence) of employees in order to contribute to the organisation's growth. As the aim of the study was to develop a deeper understanding about the role and management of experiential learning, this work explores in depth how a competence management tool has been employed in an entrepreneurial context. This study is based on an interpretative research design (Lincoln and Guba 1985), which emphasises research in a natural setting as a dynamic emerging process. In addition, the research approach incorporated the assumptions of practice-based inquiry (Gherardi 2000) and reflexive insight construction (Alvesson and Skjöldberg 2000). Furthermore, the study has been guided by Blumer's (1969: 50) four central conceptions of symbolic interactionism as described below:

- People, individually and collectively, are prepared to act on the basis of the meanings of the objects that comprise their world.
- The association of people is necessarily in the form of a process in which they make indications to one another and interpret each other's indications.
- Social acts, whether individual or collective, are constructed through a process in which actors note, interpret and assess the situations confronting them.
- The complex interlinkages of acts that comprise organisations, institutions, division of labour and networks of interdependency are dynamic and not static affairs.

The intention of the study is not to try to objectify and quantify human experience, but rather to investigate how organisational participants interpreted the competence management tool on the basis of their own self-image, the artefact encountered, and the influences of other social forces on these images.

Such a methodological approach implies that the researcher cannot be detached from the research setting and, thus, that the research cannot be value-free. The results of the research are therefore a co-creation between the people being studied and the researcher. The research method is based on the hermeneutic process of translating interactions into texts which are then examined in detail for their context and meaning with the aim of providing relevant theoretical insights that might be useful in understanding similar and related organisational situations. Data has been derived from historical data, unstructured interviews and participative observations in a variety of contexts across the organisation over two years which aimed to capture the meaning-making of top managers, line managers, competence project manager, developers of the competence model and the employees of the organisation (IT consultants, project managers, personnel and marketing persons) in everyday life. The researcher conducted this research over a two-year period. She was granted free access to the organisation and was permitted to observe activities related directly or indirectly to the management of experiential learning. The unit of analysis in this study centred around how the new competence model was given meaning by the individuals in their practices rather than one particular group of individuals or one management level.

The case study: how learning views influence managing learning from experience

The case study firm was a medium-sized Norwegian computer consultancy that was established as a government agency in 1972. In 1986, the company's status changed and it became a state-owned company. At the time this research was conducted in 1998 to 2000 the company was being reorganised again into a holding company. Since 1997, when the company consisted of six divisions, Infrastructure, Electronical Services, Professional Services, as well as Development, Postal Services and Sales/Market, it has rapidly developed and grown, and at the time of this study employed approximately 1,200 employees. This has occurred mainly through acquisitions and mergers with other IT companies or IT divisions. In 2000, the organisation was restructured and the six divisions were divided into a holding organisation with 12 limited companies. Increasingly the organisation operates in a global environment of rapid technological developments and thus, according to the HR Manager, it is vital that the company is as highly flexible as possible with competent and self-driven people, capable of learning new skills. As the Human Resources Manager has observed:

> Sharing of knowledge and the ability to learn are the critical resources for survival. As change will be a normal setting, individuals need to feel secure in themselves and not because they hold a particular position. They are themselves responsible for development and remaining attractive in the new organisational form as well as to update themselves with the latest information. Nobody can expect to be looked after. You need to be proactive. This is the new reality.

Owing to the history of mergers and acquisitions as well as of structural reorganisation, the management has traditionally relied heavily on their own experiences of these processes as well as on the previous experiences of the firm's employees to shorten the work process, to improve the chances for success of any new projects that have been implemented, and to accelerate the development and creation of innovative business units.

The research began in the autumn of 1998, after top management decided to implement an integrated competence model based on the belief that such a model, which visualises competence (learning from experience), would support their learning capacity. Furthermore, it was felt that it would give the option to manage the learning potential across organisational boundaries and to facilitate the planning for future resources. The top management team, consisting of the General Manager, the Human Resources Manager and Division managers, expressed that as a knowledge organisation the competence of the employees was one of the most critical factors the firm had and thus managing this competence effectively across the organisation's boundaries was crucial for survival. Indeed, as a top manager noted: 'Through the competence system as a governance tool that computes what and how many competencies there are in stock, we can visualise the gap between the desired, and existing competencies and make superior strategic decisions'.

In this context, the term 'competence' relates to the ability to perform in relation to a given level of experience. In short, the computer-based competence model allowed an individual to assess and visualise their personal professional competence from a beginner to an expert level in a pre-defined competence area that was linked to the role that that person occupied. The assessment was conducted through an individual self-appraisal on the company intranet with an explanatory text indicating what each competence level meant. The model and system were designed in-house and the specific text and the ideal competence profiles per role were created by the competence project manager assisted by a forum of ICT experts. The outcome of the registration of competence was a personal competence profile that illustrated how far an individual's existing competence deviated from the ideal competence profile for the chosen role. The individual scores were aggregated to unit and company level and transformed into unit and company competence gap analysis reports.

After this scheme had been in operation for two years, the competence project manager claimed to have succeeded in implementing the model. However, the employees and middle managers were more cautious. Through listening and observing it was noticed that there was a group of employees who claimed that the competence management tool was not rigid and objective enough in its measurement. On the other hand, other employees believed that the model did not take into account an individual's learning needs and, further, felt that it was not possible to make a measurement system out of such a loose mapping of individual experience levels. When these apparent anomalies were questioned, it was discovered that nobody had thought of or investigated the learning assumptions of the competence model and, consequently, the validity of the results may be questioned. The confusion that arose resulted from the fact that difficult and deep disagreements about how to visualise learning from experience were held by employees and managers within the organisation.

In analysing the competence model, it appears that the framework was mainly based on functional learning and knowledge assumptions in that it conceptualises decontextualised individual skills. In addition, the assessment of competence was conducted in relation to a pre-defined model. The exception to this was that the competence descriptions were not described in an extensive and atomistic detailed way with clear behaviour indicators, assessment criteria and extensive guidelines being provided. Instead a general description of the competence domain and what it entailed on an increasing level of experience had been developed. Furthermore, the 'teachers', i.e. the implementers, indicated that the assessments were subjective and that each manager had to create their own meaning about how to interpret the different levels. At the same time the intention of the implementers seems to have been to steer the socially created world with the competence tool: they interfered in what was recognised as a socially constructed transaction by the introduction of the tool. This is because the tool took the form of an externally specified objective reality, where people performed pre-ordained roles and 'action routines'. In this way the implementers tried to institutionalise the meaning of competence and learning and to make it a measurable unit. It seems that the implementers were trying to balance the desire for objective measurement with the realisation that competence is a concept anchored in practice and relations. In other words, they have created a hybrid model in the sense that it contains aspects of analytical thinking and rational learning assumptions with the detached criteria of objectivity and generalisability, as well as aspects of interpreative and situated learning assumptions that adhere to a contextual and dynamic understanding of learning processes with alternative criteria of trustworthiness, social legitimacy and usability.

The competence descriptions are also a combination of detached and pre-defined descriptions of knowledge, skills and attitude with more narrative and community-constructed approaches of describing competence. The pre-defined and standardised text as well as the adherence to an ideal competence profile relates to the detached approach to learning. The narrative aspect is apparent in the loosely described levels of experience based on the understanding that the text is an approximation that has to be interpreted in context. However, as the descriptions are not very rich, the model is weighted in the direction of a detached knowledge/skill/attitude framework. With reference to the four views on learning, it becomes possible to notice that the model is based on both detached and situated assumptions of learning and competence management. This implies that the outcome of the competence assessments is both objective and valid and can be used to make strategic decisions. In addition, they can be used as dialogue tools for improving and speeding up the process of learning from experience. The fact that the model is a hybrid has, however, never been discussed in these terms and the management has shown a tendency to apply the detached view on learning when using the competence model for creating organisation competence profiles. This detached perspective resembles a quest for control and belief in quantitative measurement and has left many users of the competence model wondering about the purpose and role of managing experiential learning.

Conclusion

As a result of conducting this research it was discovered that the management in the case study organisation value an entrepreneurial culture and encourage employees to adopt active and self-motivated learning and meaning-making from experience in order that they may adapt in the continuously changing and challenging environment in which they operate. Employees' work is not pre-defined and, thus, they have to develop themselves through learning from interesting projects where they are exposed to new experiences, so that they can take advantage of new opportunities that emerge. However, within the organisation a tension exists as management need to make strategic decisions with respect to resource planning, ensuring that the right competences are available in-house, while at the same finding ways to manage the experiential learning needs of their employees in the optimum way. This study explored how learning from experience is managed with the assistance of a competence management model. It demonstrates how managing learning in entrepreneurial settings, where people are self-motivated and action-oriented, should involve profound discussions about the learning assumptions underpinning the tools developed to assess and develop each individual's ability to manage their learning from experience. It should also be noted that it is not only necessary to develop a model to classify experiential learning but also that important decisions about assessment and the value of the competence profiles have to be made.

Thus, the design of an appropriate competence model should be influenced by the assumptions about how people learn (see Figure 4.2), and the following issues should therefore be taken into consideration:

- Are people capable of being developed in a proactive and self-motivated way or do they need to be steered against a pre-defined goal?
- Is learning from experience an emerging and social phenomenon or does it need to be pre-defined in a career plan?
- Is learning best evaluated through personal reflections on experience or can it be assessed in a detached and objective way?

In this study the competence model was founded on the management team's assumption that in order for experiential learning to occur, it is necessary for an individual to diagnose him- or herself against an ideal or goal. Such a diagnosis will trigger a process of reflection as the next step in the process emphasises the need to improve and close any potential gap that may exist between current competence and optimum competence. As a result of this process each person should commence a journey of self-development. Such a perspective, with its focus on self-development, resembles the action-oriented learning theories of, for instance, Kolb (1984). Yet, in the model developed in this organisation, the pre-defined learning goal resembles more the rational-cognitive learning view (see Figure 4.2). Even though there was a degree of self-involvement in this approach, there was still very much an emphasis on providing the correct competence profile. Further, the pre-defined assessment scheme provided little opportunity for experimentation in another direction or to engage in experimentation, at all. This was because the given goal of development was felt to comprise an 'ideal profile'. The competence model that was developed was, therefore, a combination of company-directed (the goal set by the dominant force) and individualised learning (the individual decides what learning activities to undertake). Even though the learner's experience and insight was acknowledged, the model was in fact instrumental as it only permitted improvement of pre-defined competence areas. This has raised concern in the organisation as to the fact that the competence model was based on a technicised pedagogy (Schön 1983; Boydell 1999) and thus was employed merely as a way of enhancing a learner's motivation because it gives the impression of involvement and self-determination. Further, a degree of confusion exists in the organisation about the role of the model; for instance, is it a diagnostic measurement that has a summative purpose, or is it a dialogue tool with a formative purpose that allows individuals to discover and achieve their own development goals?

The case study also demonstrated the challenges of employing a hybrid competence model due to that nobody in the organisation had been aware of the epistemological assumptions of the competence model and the consequences of this for managing learning from experience. The management had assumed that the competence profiles that were generated after application of the model would have predictive value for making strategic decisions. However, this was not the case. While the theoretical overview of learning perspectives (see Figure 4.2) suggests that it might be possible for such a detached approach to assist in prediction, it is likely to be difficult to achieve due to the fact that such an approach requires employing objective assessments and rigorous competence descriptions in order to allow for comparisons across boundaries. On the other hand, a situated approach may more fully capture how competence is defined in local contexts and, indeed, may support emerging individual learning needs through reflection. However, such an approach is constrained by the need to collate information for shared use. Without understanding and acknowledging these differences, the competence model employed by the company resulted in confusion about its value and use.

This study also raised the question whether it was beneficial in an entrepreneurial context to visualise competence in a pre-defined scheme with an ideal competence profile and also whether it was appropriate to use the results as a steering tool in an aggregated and objective way. It is not surprising that this way of managing learning from experience in an entrepreneurial setting did not survive. This is because each individual learner continued to explore opportunities even if they were outside the pre-defined development model. A situated and pragmatic way of describing competence through stories that focus on reflection and dialogue may subsequently be the most promising approach to adopt in an entrepreneurial context, as it facilitates a further understanding of the self and one's own learning needs and how these fit in relation to the development of the organisation. It also allows for insight into each individual's learning while at the same time empowering one with being in charge of one's own development.

The case also illustrates that without reflecting on the learning assumptions underpinning particular learning approaches, it is possible to create a hybrid model without realising it, which can be problematic to employ due to the fact that using such a model demands clear insight in how to communicate and balance the contradictory values of the competence assessment profiles that have been developed. For this reason, reflections on learning assumptions are vital in order to make informed choices about the design and value of tools for managing learning from experience. Even though this study has contributed to a deeper understanding about the complexity of managing learning from experience by highlighting how the theoretical framework on learning views can be used as a dialogue tool to reveal the multiple learning assumptions and to make their consequences apparent, further research needs to be undertaken in this area.

Acknowledgements

The author is grateful for the helpful contributions of Fred Strønen and Claire Leitch.

References

Alvesson, M. and Skjöldberg, K. (2000) *Reflexive Methodology, New Vistas for Qualitative Research*. London: Sage.

Bailey, J. B. (1986) Learning styles of successful entrepreneurs. In R. Rastadt *et al.* (eds), *Frontiers of Entrepreneurship Research* Wellesley, MA: Babson College pp. 199–210.

Baron, R. A. (1998) Cognitive mechanisms in entrepreneurship: why and when entrepreneurs think differently than other people *Journal of Business Venturing*, 13(4): 275–94.

Benner, P. (1984) *From Novice to Expert: Excellence and Power in Clinical Nursing Practice*. Reading, MA: Addison-Wesley.

Blackler, F. (1995) Knowledge, knowledge work and organizations: an overview and interpretation. *Organization Studies*, 16(6): 1021–46.

Blumer, H. (1969) *Symbolic Interactionism: Perspective and Method*. Englewood Cliffs, NJ: Prentice Hall.

Bower, G. H. and Hilgard, E. R. (1981) *Theories of Learning*. Englewood Cliffs, NJ Prentice Hall.

Boud, D., Cohen, R. and Walker, D. (1993) *Using Experience for Learning*. Buckingham: SRHE and Open University Press.

Boyatzis, R. E. (1982) *The Competent Manager: A Model for Effective Performance*. New York; Wiley.

Boydell, T. H. (1999) *Module 1 Unit 3 The Learning Organisation* Inter-logics, UK.

Bramming, P. and Holt Larsen, H. (2000) Making sense of the drive for competence. In C. Brewster and H. Holt Larsen (eds) *Human Resource Management in Northern Europe: Trends, Dilemmas and Strategy* Malden, MA: Blackwell.

Brewster, C. and Holt Larsen, H. (eds) (2000) *Human Resource Management in Northern Europe: Trends, Dilemmas and Strategy*, Malden, MA: Blackwell.

Bruner, J. (1990) *Acts of Meaning*. Cambridge, MA: Harvard University Press.

Cook, S. D. N. and Yanow, D. (1993), Culture and organizational learning, *Journal of Management Inquiry*, (4): 373–90.

Cope, J. (2003), Entrepreneurial learning and critical reflection: discontinuous events as triggers for higher-level learning, *Management Learning*, 34(4): 429–50.

Cope, J. and Watts, G. (2000) Learning by doing: an exploration of experience, critical incidents and reflection in entrepreneurial learning. *International Journal of Entrepreneurial Behaviour and Research*, 6(3): 104–24.

Dalley, J. and Hamilton, B. (2000) Knowledge, context and learning in the small business. *International Small Business Journal*, 18(3): 51–9.

Deakins, D. and Freel, M. (1998), *Entrepreneurial learning and the growth process in SMEs*. The Learning Organisation, 5(3): 144–55.

Deakins, D., Sullivan, R. and Whittam, G. (2002) Developing support for entrepreneurial learning: evidence from start-up support programs *International Journal of Entrepreneurship and Innovation Management*, 2(4/5): 323–38.

Dewey, J. (1916/1966) *Democracy and Education*. New York: The Free Press.

Dewey, J. (1938/1963) *Experience and Education*. New York: Collier Books.

Docherty, P. and Marking, C. (1997) Understanding changing competence demands. In P. Docherty and B. Nyhan (eds), *Human Competence and Business Development Emerging Patterns in European Companies*, London: Springer-Verlag.

Dreyfus, H. L. and Dreyfus, S. E. (1986) *Mind over Machine The Power of Human Intuition and Expertise in the Era of the Computer*. New York: The Free Press.

Drucker, P. F. (1992) The new society of organizations. *Harvard Business Review*, September–October 95–104.

Drucker, P. F. (1993) *Innovation and Entrepreneurship*. New York: HarperBusiness.

Easterby-Smith, M., Crossan, M. and Nicolini, D. (2000) Organizational learning: debates past, present and future, *Journal of Management Studies* 37(6): 783–96.

Elkjaer, B. (1999) In search of a social learning theory, In M. Easterby-Smith *et al.* (eds), *Organizational Learning and the Learning Organization Developments in Theory and Practice*. London: Sage.

Fox, S. (1997) Situated learning theory versus traditional cognitive learning theory: why management education should not ignore management learning. *Systems Practice*, 10(6): 727–47.

Freire, P. (1975) *Pedagogy of the Oppressed*. Rio de Janeiro: Paz e Terra.

Galbraith, J. (1995) *Designing Organizations*. San Francisco: Jossey-Bass.

Gartner, W. B. (1988) Who is an entrepreneur? is the wrong question. *American Journal of Small Business*, 13(1): 11–32.

Gherardi, S. (2000) Practice-based theorizing on learning and knowing in organizations *Organization*, 7(2): 211–23.

Gherardi, S. and Nicolini, D. (2000) To transfer is to transform: the circulation of safety knowledge *Organization*, 7(2): 329–48.

Gibb, A. A. (1997) Small firms' training and competitiveness: building on the small business as a learning organisation. *International Small Business Journal*, 15(3): 13–29.

Helmersson, H. (1984) *Kognitive betingelser för implementering av formelle planer-ingsmodeller- datorbaserad skolschemalägging med tolkning enligt Piagets genetiska epistemologi*. Akademisk avhandling, Lund Universitet.

Huber, G. P. (1991) Organizational learning: the contributing processes and the literatures. *Organization Science*, 2(1): 88–115.

Illich, I. (1971) *Deschooling Society*. New York: Harper & Row.

Knowles, M. S. (1980) *The Modern Practice of Adult Education: From Pedagogy to Andragogy*. New York: Cambridge University Press.

Kolb, D. A. (1984) *Experiential Learning: Experience as the Source of Learning and Development,* Englewood Cliffs, NJ: Prentice Hall.

Kuhn, T. S. (1962/1970) *The Structure of Scientific Revolutions*. (1st ed. 1962). Chicago: University of Chicago Press.

Lave, J. (1993) The practice of learning In S. Chaiklin and J. Lave (eds), *Understanding Practice: Perspectives on Activity and Context.* Cambridge: Cambridge University Press.

Lave, J. and Wenger, E. (1991) *Situated Learning Legitimate Peripheral Participation*. Cambridge: Cambridge University Press.

Leitch, C. M. (2007) An action research approach to entrepreneurship. In H. Neergard and J. P. Ulhøi (eds), *Handbook for Qualitative Research Methods in Entrepreneurship*. Cheltenham: Edward Elgar.

Lincoln, Y. S. and Guba, E. G. (1985) *Naturalistic Inquiry*. Beverly Hills, CA: Sage.

Matlay, H. and Mitra, J. (2002) Entrepreneurship and learning: the double act in the triple helix, *Entrepreneurship and Innovation*, 3(1): 7–16.

McHenry, J. E. H. (2003) Management of Knowledge in Practice, learning to visualise competence. Doctoral dissertation, series of dissertations 1/2003, Norwegian School of Management, BI, Department of Leadership and Organisational Management, Norli, Norway.

Mead, G. H. (1934/1956) *Mind, Self, and Society.* Chicago: University of Chicago Press.

Minniti, M. and Bygrave, W. (2001) A dynamic model of entrepreneurial learning *Entrepreneurship: Theory and Practice*, 25(3): 5–16.

Moingeon, B. and Edmondson, A. (1996) *Organizational Learning and Competitive Advantage*. London: Sage.

Morris, M. H. (1998) *Entrepreneurial intensity: Sustainable Advantages for Individuals, Organizations, and Societies*. Westport, CT: Quorum Books.

Nonaka, I. and Takeuchi, H. (1995) *The Knowledge-Creating Company.* Oxford: Oxford University Press.

Nordhaug, O. (1993) *Human Capital in Organizations – Competence, Training and Learning*. Oslo: Scandinavian University Press.

Nordic Industrial Fund (2002) *Recommendations and Report from the Conference: Small Innovative Companies and Entrepreneurship in the Nordic Countries*. Center for Innovation and Commercial Development, Oslo, 15–16, Oct. www.nordicinnovation.net

Palich, L. E. and Bagby, D. R. (1995) Using cognitive theory to explain entrepreneurial risk-taking: challenging convential wisdom. *Journal of Business Venturing*, 10(6): 425–38.

Pedler, M. Burgoyne, J. and Boydell, T. (1997) *The Learning Company: A Strategy for Sustainable Development* (1st ed. 1991) New York: McGraw-Hill International.

Piaget, J. (1970) *Genetic Epistemology*. New York: Columbia University Press.

Polanyi, M. (1958) *Personal Knowledge*, London: Routledge & Kegan Paul.

Prahalad, C. K. and Hamel, G. (1990) The core competence of the corporation, *Harvard Busienss Review*, May–June, 79–91.

Rae, D. (2000) Understanding entrepreneurial learning: a question of how. *International Journal of Entrepreneurial Behaviour and Research*, 6(3): 145–9.

Rae, D. and Carswell, M. (2001) Towards a conceptual understanding of entrepreneurial learning. *Journal of Small Business and Enterprise Development* 8(2): 150–8.

Reuber, A. R. and Fischer, E. M. (1993) The learning experiences of entrepreneurs. In *Frontiers of Entrepreneurship Research*: Wellesy, MA: N. C. Churchill *et al.* (eds) Babson Centre for Entrepreneurial Studies.

Revans, R. W. (1980) *Action Learning, New Techniques for Managers*. London: Blond & Briggs.

Revans, R. W. (1982) *The Origins and Growth of Action Learning*. Bromley: Chartwell-Bratt.

Rogers, C. R. (1969) *Freedom to Learn* Columbus, OH: Merrill.

Sandberg, J. (1994) Human competence at work, an interpretative approach. Doctoral dissertation, Business School of the University of Gøteborg, Sweden.

Schank, R. C. (1975) *Conceptual Information Processing*. New York: Elsevier.

Schön, D. A. (1983) *The Reflective Practitioner: How Professionals Think in Action*. New York: Basic Books.

Shane, S. (2000) Prior knowledge and the discovery of entrepreneurial opportunities. *Organization Science*, 11: 448–69.

Senge, P. M. (1990) *The Fifth Discipline*. New York: Doubleday.

Sharma, P. and Chrisman, J. J. (1999) Towards a reconciliation of the definitional issues in the field of corporate entrepreneurship. *Entrepreneurship: Theory and Practice*, Spring: 11–27.

Shrivastava, P. (1983) A typology of organizational learning systems. *Journal of Management Studies*, 20(1): 7–28.

Skinner, B. F. (1953) *Science and Human Behavior*. New York: Macmillan.

Smilor, R. W. (1997) Entrepreneurship: reflections on a subversive activity. *Journal of Business Venturing*, 12(5): 341–6.

Taylor, F. (1911) *Principles of Scientific Management*. New York: Norton & Co. reprinted in 1967.

Tolman, E. C. (1948) Cognitive maps in rats and men. *Psychological Review*, 55: 189–208.

Volberda, H. (1996) Towards the flexible form: how to remain vital in hyper-competitive environments. *Organization Science*, 7(4): 359–74.

Von Glaserfield, E. (1990) An exposition of constructivism: why some like it radical. In R. B. Davis, C. A. Maher and N. Noddings, *Journal for Research in Mathematics Education,* Monograph No. 4: *Constructivist Views on the Teaching and Learning of Mathematics*. Reston, VA: National Council of Teachers of Mathematics.

Vygotsky, L. S. (1978) *Mind in Society: The Development of Higher Psychological Processes*. Cambridge, MA: Harvard University Press.

Weick, K. E. (1995) *Sensemaking in Organisations*. London: Sage.

Wenger, E. (1998) *Communities of Practice, Learning, Meaning, and Identity*. Cambridge: Cambridge University Press.

Wenger, E. (2000) Communities of practice and social learning systems. *Organization*, 7(2): 225–56.

Wertsch, J. V. (ed.) (1985) *Culture, Communication and Cognition*. New York: Cambridge University Press.

Woodruffe, C. (1990/1993) *Assessment Centres, Identifying and Developing Competence*, 2nd ed. London: Institute of Personnel Management.

Yanow, D. (2000) Seeing organizational learning: a 'cultural view'. *Organization*, 7(2): 247–68.

Section III

Intra-organizational learning

5 The role of organizational learning in the opportunity recognition process

Benyamin B. Lichtenstein and G. T. Lumpkin

Introduction

Firms often engage in entrepreneurship to strengthen performance and further growth through strategic renewal and the creation of new venture opportunities (Guth and Ginsberg 1990; Stevenson and Jarillo 1990). Recently, many firms have found that organizational learning (OL) can provide a major impetus for such efforts. That is, firms that implement organizational learning practices by configuring themselves to capitalize on the knowledge gained during the course of business have been able to leverage this newly learned knowledge to their strategic advantage (Lei *et al.* 1999). Organizational learning, in some firms, has become a central component of strategic renewal (Davis and Botkin 1994).

But what of the creation of new venture opportunities – can organizational learning further that aspect of entrepreneurship? The discovery, evaluation and exploitation of opportunities is a defining feature of entrepreneurship (Shane and Venkataraman 2000; Shane 2003), and the degree to which firms act entrepreneurially correlates with their ability to generate new products and services (Lumpkin and Dess 1996). Although few have explored the links between organizational learning and opportunity recognition, we believe that making those links can support the theory and practice of both fields. Organizational learning, for example, emphasizes improving practices and expanding into new arenas by creating new knowledge (Senge 1990), building new understandings (Fiol and Lyles 1985) and detecting and correcting misalignments (Argyris 1990). These qualities may strengthen efforts to be more entrepreneurial. Moreover, the same attributes used to distinguish a learning organization – 'an organization skilled at creating, acquiring, and transferring knowledge, and at modifying its behavior to reflect new knowledge and insights' (Garvin 1993: 81) – are among the qualities needed to effectively recognize and pursue new venture opportunities.

This chapter argues that organizational learning can enhance a firm's ability to recognize opportunities and equip it to effectively pursue new ventures. We begin by highlighting three distinct approaches to organizational learning – behavioral learning, cognitive learning and action learning – and we provide examples of firms that are using each of these learning approaches to be more entrepreneurial. Then, drawing on a model of opportunity recognition (OpR) that was developed from the literatures of entrepreneurship (e.g. Shane and Venkataraman 2000) and creativity (e.g. Csikszentmihalyi 1996), we show how the processes of discovery and formation of new venture opportunities can be enhanced through organizational learning. Each of the three types of learning links to a specific aspect of the opportunity recognition process. Finally, we provide practical guidelines for how firms might promote new venture creation by implementing organizational learning practices and procedures.

Organizational learning: three related themes

Organizational learning continues to be an important issue for all types of firms. Studies exploring the nature of knowledge creation, intellectual capital and knowledge management have been on the rise, with recent papers being published for academics (e.g. Nonaka 1994; Matusik and Hill 1998; Nahapiet and Ghoshal 1998) and for practitioners (e.g. Brown and Duguid 1998; Fryer 1999). Multiple frameworks and typologies have been used to define and describe organizational learning (e.g. Shrivastava 1983; Huber 1991). Rather than re-invent these categorizations, we orient our discussion around two of the most common categories of OL – behavioral learning and cognitive learning. To these we add a third mode – action learning – which, although an aspect of cognitive learning, plays a particularly important role in the learning processes of new ventures (Lichtenstein *et al.* 2003). These three modes of learning correspond to the broad categories of learning theories identified by Greeno *et al.* (1996) – behavioral, cognitive, and situative or action learning. In the three subsections that follow, behavioral, cognitive and action modes of learning will be briefly described.

Before proceeding, it is important to acknowledge that the processes that contribute to learning outcomes are complex, and they occur on multiple levels of analysis (Argyris and Schön 1978; Low and MacMillan 1988). Some scholars have distinguished between individual-, group- and organizational-level qualities of organizational learning and suggested how they might interact (Nonaka 1994; Crossan *et al.* 1999). Different aspects of the opportunity recognition process may also involve both individual and team-related activities (Singh *et al.* 1999). In the context of OpR and OL, one can imagine numerous types of cross-level phenomena. For example, a firm's efforts to integrate new knowledge might influence an individual's opportunity recognition process or an individual's entrepreneurial insights might evoke new learning at the team level.

We concur with entrepreneurship scholars who note that entrepreneurial processes are emergent and iterative, usually changing over time and often involving multiple layers of analysis (Davidsson and Wiklund 2001). The relationships that we propose are very likely to involve cross-level interactions as well as multiple time frames and such issues should be addressed when developing research questions and study designs. Although it is beyond the scope of this chapter, we acknowledge the importance of multiple levels of analysis in presenting our integration of the OL and OpR literature (e.g. Kim 1993), but focus more directly on the relationship between organizational learning and entrepreneurial opportunity recognition.

Behavioral learning

Many of the classic ideas about organizational learning are based on the assumption that organizations are goal-oriented, routine-based systems that respond to experience by repeating behaviors that have been successful and avoiding those that are not (Lundberg 1995). This learning approach describes the acquisition, distribution and storage of information and knowledge in a firm (Leavitt and March 1988; Huber 1991; Walsh and Ungson 1991). In addition, it focuses on the adaptive learning concept that trial-and-error learning leads to routines and processes that confer selective advantage to the firm (Herriott *et al.* 1985; Levinthal 1991; Van de Ven and Polley 1991). Because of the emphasis on learning from repeated behaviors, this perspective is often referred to as behavioral learning.

Behavioral learning focuses on the 'antecedents and changes in organizational structures, technologies, routines and systems as the organization responds to their own experience and that of other organizations' (Lundberg 1995: 7). These theories argue that organizational learning is an adaptive process and thus is triggered only by performance gaps or other signals of poor market performance (Cyert and March 1963). In a similar way, because trial-and-error learning generates routines that tend to make an organization stable, it is only possible to spark major organizational change through significant externally generated structural events. As such, behavioral learning is primarily incremental (Levinthal 1991).

One good example of behavioral learning occurred in the entrepreneurial development of the Vanguard Group, a leading-edge mutual fund management firm (Siggelkow 2002). The founder of the company had, based on his research of the fledgling industry (in 1951), concluded that a low-cost strategy could pay off in the long term. This cost-cutting approach was a driving force for a variety of experiments that John Bogle enacted in his tenure as CEO of the organization. For example, Bogle had learned from entrepreneurial experience that it is better to borrow than to buy resources (Stevenson and Gumpert 1985). Prodded by unpredictable spikes in the volume of telephone calls, Bogle initiated a routine involving 'borrowing' employees in which all employees could be made available to handle client telephone calls at any point. The program was called the 'Swiss Army' because, like its namesake, it involved every existing employee, from clerical workers to the CEO. Bogle learned from experience that in order to ensure that employees inexperienced in handling client issues would be well prepared for potential emergency situations, 'each employee, from clerical workers to the CEO, had to perform several hours of phone service every month to stay in practice' (Siggelkow 2002: 148). The program paid off during the stock market crash of 1987, during which virtually all Vanguard clients were able to be served without a major glitch.

The Swiss Army was also adapted in a different form to the deployment of an updated IT system, in which an enhanced version of Vanguard.com's enterprise database program became the basis for external *and* internal communications and business processes throughout the company (Dragoon 2003). This unique approach simplified internal operations, increased customer service, and cut maintenance and upgrade costs for what were previously ten separate client/server systems. Further, through their repeated interactions with the Vanguard.com system, employees became experts in their own company website, sparking learning that enhanced future versions. For example, although seemingly automated, the initial version of Vanguard.com required that on-line customer actions had to be printed out, processed by hand, and re-entered by other employees. The problems that employees identified with this approach led them to develop new software objects which ensured that information entered on-line by customers or employees went directly into the back-end system with no employee intervention. This behavioral learning has dramatically reduced re-keying errors and cut costs; presently over 98 percent of all on-line customer interactions require no support from Vanguard employees (Dragoon 2003).

Cognitive learning

More recently, a perspective has emerged that focuses on the cognitive content of organizational learning and how changes in individuals' cognitive maps are aggregated and translated into changes in an organization's cognitive schema (Bartunek 1984; Brown and Duguid 1991; Kim 1993; Weick and Roberts 1993; Nonaka 1994). Here, the focus is on the content of learning rather than on its behavioral outcomes, on processes that improve the creation of knowledge in a firm, and the utilization of knowledge to improve creativity, quality of interaction and other types of performance (Fryer 1999). By putting the right processes in place a learning organization can, in essence, transform data into information, and information into knowledge, which can then be leveraged to generate organizational knowledge (Kim 1993; Davis and Botkin 1994). Organizational learning in this sense includes the process of exploiting externally generated knowledge (Cohen and Levinthal 1990) or transforming internally stored knowledge (Garud and Nayyar 1994) to increase the strategic assets of the firm. The assets in question are knowledge or 'thought process' assets, so this perspective is referred to as cognitive learning.

Cognitive learning is related to the resource-based view of strategy because it holds that the very process of knowledge creation can generate unique organizational competencies and potential sources of competitive advantage. 'Knowledge assets underpin competencies. . . . The firm's capacity to sense and seize opportunities, to reconfigure its knowledge assets, competencies, and complementary assets. . . . all constitute its dynamic capabilities' (Teece 1998: 64). As such, organizational learning leads to an increase in the 'organization's capacity to take effective action' (Kim 1993: 43) as well as to the 'mobilization of tacit knowledge held by individuals [that can] provide the forum for a "spiral of knowledge" creation' (Nonaka 1994: 34). Such learning, in turn, leads to greater firm effectiveness (Barney 1991).

Examples of cognitive learning are evident at the origins of Starbucks corporation, which was originated through a re-conceptualization of the US coffee industry by founder Howard Schultz. Based on his 1983 trip to Milan, Schultz recognized 'an enormous opportunity for Starbucks to recreate the Italian coffee bar culture in the US' (Koehn 2001: 8). The opportunity was to re-frame coffee drinking into a social experience in America, by providing a high-end product in a personalized environment to consumers wanting 'affordable luxury' (Koehn 2001). In this way, Schultz re-defined the coffee industry in America, which for the past 40-plus years had been led by a few large companies competing on price and delivering a low-quality commodity that was meant to be made and consumed at home. By importing into his company the knowledge he gained from his (external) sources in Italy, Schultz developed a new framework for entrepreneurial action that was composed of several strategic assets gained through cognitive learning.

One of the most important strategic assets at Starbucks involves Schultz's re-thinking of the human resource side of the consumer-driven stores. Whereas servers are traditionally the lowest-paid employees in the restaurant industry, Schultz had learned that a 'high-touch' personalized experience was the biggest motivator for customers, and this was only possible if all the front-end employees were able to learn the names and preferences of their frequent customers. Thus, Schultz re-conceived Human Resources as a core component of his overall strategy, leading to a set of HR benefits that were previously unheard of in the industry. Not only are Starbucks' front-end employees the highest paid in the restaurant industry, Starbucks was the first to institute a benefits package for part-time employees, provide stock options for most of their workers and offer a full-week of paid training for every new member. The result: turnover at Starbucks is the lowest of any similar organization and the high-touch experience translates into the strongest form of word-of-mouth publicity, thus obviating the need (and expense!) for local or national advertising. Further, as front-line employees are empowered to constantly suggest and implement new improvements, knowledge creation has been institutionalized as an active and ongoing process within the company.

Action learning

In contrast to the other two frameworks, action learning focuses on the moment-to-moment practice of correcting misalignments between 'espoused theory' (what individuals or organization say they do) and its 'theory-in-use' (what individuals or organizations actually do), to produce more effective action in real time (Argyris 1990; Torbert 1991; Senge *et al.* 1994). Action learning is primarily concerned with the patterns of belief and qualities of interaction between organizational members that facilitate (or constrain) the capabilities of the firm. Such learning is simultaneously personal and organizational, as it is built through a commitment to improve the integrity of individual action, as well as the alignment of activities within the organization (Torbert 1973, 1991, 2000; Schön 1983). When a group of individuals commit to an action learning approach, a community of learning practice can be generated that may significantly impact the quality of communication, innovation and team performance in a firm (Senge *et al.* 1994).

According to this approach, learning happens in 'real time,' through a nearly simultaneous re-framing of personal belief and action that can transform the individual as well as the organization (Torbert 1991). Thus, this perspective is referred to as action learning.

Among the insights that have arisen through the research practice of action learning is the distinction between single-loop incremental learning and 'double-loop' transformative learning (Bateson 1972; Argyris and Schön 1978; Bartunek 1984). In single-loop learning, incremental modifications are made to organizational behaviors that improve the *efficiency* of organizing. Double-loop learning, by contrast, challenges the context within which such actions are being done, by continuously asking whether the organization and its members are pursuing the right actions that might lead to the appropriate goals (Torbert 1991). Asking this type of reflective question requires a willingness to uncover hidden assumptions and face uncomfortable feelings (Argyris 1990). Developing this awareness is a key goal of action learning, for it allows individuals and organizations to break through defensive routines that keep people from producing their best work, which can impact all areas of organizational life (Argyris and Schön 1978).

The on-line re-framing activity of action learning is often focused on operating beliefs and interaction patterns that refer to cognitive schemata of organizational leaders, which explains why action learning is a type of cognitive learning. However, rather than the external focus of cognitive learning, toward the creation of firm-level resources and organizational knowledge, action learning has a more inward focus, on the patterns of belief and action of key organizational members and their interpersonal relationships. In this way, action learning is 'situative' in nature (see Corbett's analysis of experiential learning theory, Chapter 6, this volume), for its foundations are individuals' situated (e.g. personal and contextual) experiences with others. A key outcome of action learning can be a mutual commitment to new 'rules of engagement' in an organization, thus creating a culture of more transparency, openness and decisiveness.

A good example of action learning occurred in a start-up software company that was struggling to gain a second round of venture capital (Torbert and Associates 2004 Chap.: 9). Although successful in releasing innovative products, the executives recognized that without a breakthrough in sales the organization would never receive more capital and would soon collapse. Knowing that a transformation was necessary, they hired a consultant, who was himself experienced in the action learning method, to lead a one-day management retreat, ostensibly to frame a new company strategy and handle some persistent organizational problems.

After interviewing the two founders and the other two executive team members, the consultant recognized that the underlying problem was an entrenched pattern of interaction between the two founders, caused by a misalignment between the 'equality' they both espoused versus the differences in power they actually enacted on a day-to-day basis. Seeking to disrupt this pattern, the consultant persuaded the founders – the CEO and Vice President of Development – to switch roles for the day. He further altered the firm's 'rules of engagement' by limiting the retreat to just the two founders, pushing them to re-define their roles and carefully examine their ongoing patterns of interaction.

These unexpected and risky moves triggered significant shifts in the founders' perceptions, communications and interactions. The next day they reached written agreement on six major organizational changes, including a significant strategic decision to focus on only one of their multiple products, and the demotion of the Vice President of Sales to a role subordinate to the Vice President of Marketing – a shift that the Sales Vice President unexpectedly welcomed with relief. Within a month all six changes were implemented; two months later the company introduced – six months ahead of schedule – their newest product, which was designed to capitalize on a major untapped market opportunity. Sales revenues quickly outpaced costs for the first time in the company's history. Moreover, several months after the initial experiment the two founders decide to switch positions permanently and in so doing triggered even more openness within the company culture, as well as improved strategic capabilities overall. In these ways, action learning transformed the perceptions and actions of both founders, who enacted their learning through an entirely new operating approach that transformed the company as a whole.

These three modes – behavioral learning, cognitive learning and action learning – provide a framework for understanding how entrepreneurial organizations may learn. We recognize that these three modes are not permanent within individuals, groups or ventures; indeed, much of the action learning perspective is dedicated to supporting entrepreneurs, venture teams and whole organizations to become more adept at cognitive and behavioral learning (Senge *et al*. 1994). Thus, over time an individual or a venture may become more adept at cognitive, behavioral or action learning. The evidence showing increases over time of behavioral and cognitive learning is mainly based on simulations (e.g. Carley 1999) or case studies (e.g. Lichtenstein and Brush 2001). Empirical research also shows that individuals and organizations can successfully gain expertise in action learning (Torbert 1991; Torbert and Associates 2004).

Moreover, these modes are not strictly independent; we have presented them as 'ideal types' for the sake of clarity only. Learning theorists have shown that the presence of one mode can support the presence of the other modes. In addition, the theoretical separation of behavioral and cognitive learning may only be an artifact of the empirical research process that requires operational distinctions between these closely related concepts. Indeed, as we suggested in the section on action learning, some theorists argue that these two qualities of learning are deeply intertwined and cannot be practically separated (e.g. Sarasvathy 2001; McElroy 2002). As one of our reviewers put it, 'Common sense suggests that learning is a continual reflexive cycle of action–cognition–behavior.'

Indeed, it is the interconnectedness of these learning approaches that helps explain how organizational learning supports the key entrepreneurial process of opportunity recognition. As the model that we will introduce in the next section suggests, opportunity recognition is a recursive process that involves different types of activity over multiple levels of analysis. Learning in a given context is also likely to involve more than one type of process. As a result, firms and individuals that are sincerely attempting to learn – as we suggest they are when engaged in an OpR process – are likely to use different learning styles. Therefore it is our general contention that individuals and firms engaged in behavioral learning are more likely to practice cognitive learning as well, and vice versa. This may be particularly true with action learning as mentioned above, which can create the context within which the other modes of learning are encouraged.

To make the link between organizational learning and opportunity recognition, we turn next to a model for understanding the process by which individuals and organizations recognize and capitalize on entrepreneurial opportunities.

A creativity-based model of entrepreneurial opportunity recognition

Opportunity recognition – one of the central ideas of entrepreneurship – is the ability to identify a good idea and transform it into a business concept that adds value and generates revenues. Bygrave and Hofer (1991) define an entrepreneur as 'one who recognizes an opportunity and creates an organization to pursue it.' Shane and Venkataraman (2000) argued that the discovery, evaluation and exploitation of opportunities is a defining feature of the field of entrepreneurship.

Recently, a model of the OpR process has been proposed that builds on the idea of discovery and evaluation (Hills *et al.* 1999; Lumpkin *et al.* 2004). Based on a classic psychological theory of creativity (Wallas 1926; Csikszentmihalyi 1996), the model depicts opportunity recognition as a staged process that involves a Discovery phase consisting of preparation, incubation and insight, and a Formation phase of evaluation and elaboration (see Figure 5.1). A key feature of this general model of OpR is its recursive nature. Opportunity recognition is not limited to a singular 'Aha' experience; it is an iterative process through which insights are contemplated, new information is collected and considered, and knowledge is created over time. In this way an idea for a business must be formed into an opportunity that adds value to the firm (Timmons 1994).

A creativity-based model of OpR is well suited for entrepreneurial opportunity recognition for several reasons. First, entrepreneurship is an emergent process, especially at its earliest stages. The recursive nature of creativity parallels the back-and-forth activities that entrepreneurs often engage in when trying to grasp an emerging business concept (Gartner *et al.* 1992; Sarasvathy 2001). Second, the model is distinguished from other models of creativity in the organization literature because it is used principally to describe an individual-level activity whereas other creativity-based approaches typically address the use of group-level creativity techniques in the context of established organizations (e.g. Amabile 1988; Woodman *et al.* 1993).

After a brief summary of the five stages of opportunity recognition, we show how the three modes of OL – behavioral, cognitive and action – are linked to the Discovery and Formation phases of the OpR process.

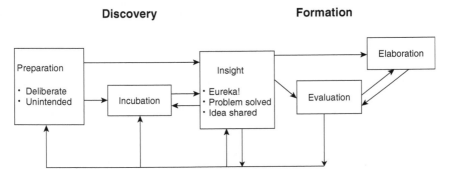

Figure 5.1 Creativity-based model of entrepreneurial opportunity recognition (based on Hills *et al.* 1999; Lumpkin *et al.* 2004).

Five stages of opportunity recognition

Several scholars have endeavored to characterize the OpR process (e.g. Shane 2000, 2003; Fiet 2002). Some OpR models depict opportunity recognition as a staged process (e.g. Bhave 1994) where the outcome of the process is defined as 'recognition' (Christensen *et al.* 1989). Most scholarly attempts to model opportunity recognition have characterized it as the confluence of many factors such as the background of the entrepreneur and the influence of the business and general environment (Long and McMullan 1984; Gaglio and Taub 1992). In a synthesis of these perspectives, Hills *et al.* (1999) and Lumpkin *et al.* (2004) proposed a model suggesting that a 'stages of creativity' framework (Wallas 1926; Csikszentmihalyi 1996) provides the necessary elements for modeling opportunity recognition. These stages include (1) preparation, (2) incubation and (3) insight, which form the Discovery phase, and (4) evaluation and (5) elaboration, which constitute the Formation phase. In the subsections that follow, each of these five elements is discussed in terms of how it relates to the opportunity recognition process.

Preparation

Previous research suggests that preparation and prior knowledge are essential to the opportunity recognition process (e.g. Shane 2000). Preparation refers to the experience and knowledge that precedes the opportunity discovery process (Kao 1989). Such preparation is typically a conscious effort to develop expertise in a domain and develop a sensitivity to the issues and problems in a field of interest (Csikszentmihalyi 1996). But preparation also includes knowledge and experience that is gathered unintentionally, that is, without aiming to discover opportunities. In an organizational setting, the ideas that result in successful venturing often emerge incrementally from the firm's background, current line of product or services, or technological knowledge. However, individuals may bring new ideas and skills to a firm that result in new ventures.

Incubation

Incubation refers to the part of the opportunity recognition process in which entrepreneurs or an entrepreneurial team contemplates an idea or a specific problem. It does not, however, refer to conscious problem-solving or systematic analysis. Rather, Csikszentmihalyi argues that during incubation, 'ideas churn around below the threshold of consciousness' (1996: 79). Thus, incubation is typically an intuitive, non-directional style of considering various possibilities or options. Gaglio and Taub (1992) described incubation as the period when the 'pre-recognition stew' is 'simmering.' It is the part of the OpR process in which the new combinations that Schumpeter (1934/1959) envisioned might emerge (Ward 2004).

Insight

Insight refers to the 'Eureka' moment or 'Aha' experience. Whereas incubation refers to an ongoing process, insight refers to a moment of recognition (Csikszentmihalyi 1996). In many cases, it is the point at which a whole answer or core solution springs into awareness suddenly and unexpectedly. This sudden convergence is the result of a cognitive shift that breaks existing means–ends relationships (Gaglio and Katz 2001). Insights may provide sweeping catalysts to new venture creation or uncover incremental knowledge that advances an ongoing discovery process. It is unlikely that an insight is a singular 'event'; insights often occur recursively throughout the OpR process (de Koning 1999). Entrepreneurial insights typically consist of either the sudden recognition of a business opportunity, the solution to a well-considered problem, or the acquisition and revisioning of an idea from colleagues, friends or other associates.

Evaluation

Evaluation signals the start of the second phase of the opportunity recognition process – Formation. It involves analyzing whether concepts developed in the discovery phase are workable, whether the entrepreneur/team has the necessary skills to accomplish it, and whether it is truly a novel enough idea to pursue. In the context of entrepreneurial OpR, evaluation may involve feasibility analysis wherein ideas are put to the test via various forms of investigation such as preliminary market testing, financial viability analysis and/or feedback from business associates and others in one's social network (Bhave 1994; Singh *et al.* 1999). Evaluation also involves an internal process in which the entrepreneur(s) must question the prospects for the new insight and ask, 'Is the business concept sufficiently valuable and worthwhile to pursue?' (Csikszentmihalyi 1996).

Elaboration

In the context of entrepreneurial creativity, elaboration involves 'capturing value from the creative act' (Kao 1989: 17). In contrast to the confidence-seeking aspects of evaluation, elaboration involves legitimacy-seeking: forming the business into a viable opportunity by subjecting it to external scrutiny and building its support system. Elaboration is typically the most time-consuming part of the process since it represents the relatively more tedious work of selecting options, finalizing choices and organizing resources (Csikszentmihalyi 1996). Assuming the business idea is still considered viable after the evaluation process, elaboration may involve detailed planning activities to reduce uncertainty. The elaboration process itself, however, often reveals aspects of the business concept that need attention or more careful analysis and thus may result in further evaluation (Aldrich 1999).

The process of opportunity recognition outlined by these five stages can be advanced by applying the principles and practices of organizational learning. In the remainder of the chapter, we describe how that might be achieved. Next, we turn to how organizational learning can enhance the opportunity recognition process.

Three modes of organizational learning in entrepreneurial opportunity recognition

A quote from the organizational learning literature (Garvin 1993) suggests the close link between opportunity recognition and organizational learning:

> New ideas are essential if learning is to take place. Sometimes they are created de novo through flashes of insight or creativity; at other times they arrive from outside the organization or are communicated by knowledgeable insiders. Whatever their source, they are a trigger for organizational improvement. (1993: 81)

Garvin's statement is one of many that demonstrates how the qualities valued by learning organizations are similar to the elements of the opportunity recognition process. In particular, opportunity recognition involves the conversion of information into knowledge: new business ideas are generated and evaluated for their quality and viability in the same way that information is analyzed and combined to create knowledge (Nonaka 1994). Framed in this way, the opportunity recognition process is a type of organizational learning. In a formal sense, organizational learning is the ongoing process of acquiring and interpreting information that leads to the creation of new knowledge (Huber 1991; Van de Ven and Polley 1991; Davis and Botkin 1994; Brown and Duguid 1998; Galunic and Rodan 1998). In the same way, the activity of acquiring and interpreting information is at the heart of the opportunity recognition process, and the result of both endeavors is an increase in knowledge and value to the firm. Just as the creative process involves the generation of new knowledge and new forms of expression, entrepreneurial opportunity recognition is a learning process that initiates the creation of new wealth (Corbett 2002; Dimov 2003).

This perspective leads to the primary argument in this chapter – that the principles and practices of organizational learning can strengthen the opportunity recognition process. Given this premise, we now extend our argument by showing how the three related approaches to learning (behavioral, cognitive and action) link to the two phases of the OpR process (Discovery and Formation) (Lumpkin *et al.* 2004). Specifically, the shifts in mental constructs that occur in Cognitive learning are indicative of the Discovery phase of OpR; behavioral learning is expressed in the evaluation and elaboration aspects of Formation in OpR; and action learning, in its ability to challenge underlying assumptions in a recursive way, creates a contextual openness that supports both the Discovery and Formation phases of OpR.

Cognitive learning in the Discovery phase

As described above, cognitive learning focuses on one's internal frameworks for knowing – what have been called 'cognitive schemata' – and in how those frameworks can be transferred to others and leveraged to improve personal and organizational action (Kim 1993). Through these mental processes and the creativity they can engender, new information and knowledge is created; this is the essence of cognitive learning (Nonaka 1988, 1994). This mode of organizational learning is dependent on individuals' ability to identify and change their pattern of cognitive associations, and share those changes with others (Brown and Duguid 1991).

The transformation of mental models that occurs in cognitive learning is roughly analogous to the Discovery phase of opportunity recognition. Cognitive learning happens in OpR when acquired knowledge shifts an entrepreneur's cognitive map such that their understanding or interpretation of events changes (Daft and Weick 1984). Essentially, cognitive learning enhances an individual's or an organization's ability to (re)create information and knowledge, opening new opportunities for interpretation and action (Nonaka 1994). Sometimes involving 'entrepreneurial intuition' (Crossan *et al.* 1999), this process is likely to exist in a climate of opportunity search and problem-solving such as may be found in the Discovery phase of opportunity recognition. In this phase, innovative new combinations may occur because of a heightened need to discover new ideas (Schumpeter 1934/1959; March 1991). Such conditions invoke entrepreneurs 'to make these novel connections, perceive new or emergent relationships, and discern possibilities that have not been identified previously' (Crossan *et al.* 1999: 526). Cognitive insight may involve a re-framing or synthesizing of resources already accessible to the individual or company, resulting in a transformation of pre-existing ideas or assets that generates new knowledge (Garud and Nayyar 1994) and creates new firms (Petzinger 1999).

Just as cognitive learning can enhance strategic assets (Teece 1998), the Discovery phase of opportunity recognition can be the basis for new strategic options and avenues for competition, or recombinations of resources that result in the creation of new ventures (Brush *et al.* 2001; Fiet 2002) or that expand the value of existing firms (Galunic and Rodan 1998). As an entrepreneur draws on his or her experience and expertise, letting the problem or issue at hand incubate and develop internally, the emergent concept – whether a new product idea or an expanded service offering – can become the basis for an entirely new strategic direction in the firm (Quinn 1992; Mintzberg 1994). For these reasons, we make the following proposal:

P1: The more that entrepreneurial firms engage in cognitive learning processes, the more effective they will be in the Discovery phase of opportunity recognition.

Behavioral learning in the Formation phase

As mentioned above, the behavioral mode of organizational learning focuses on the tangible outcomes of learning-by-doing, which learning theorists have addressed from two perspectives. One describes how organizations use existing information in order to compare current situations with situations from the past and situations in other environments (Leavitt and March 1988; Walsh and Ungson 1991). In this approach, knowledge resources can be utilized only to the extent that they can be classified and stored in the organization (Huber 1991). Thus, many of the recent forms of 'knowledge management' are driven by the utilization of information technology, which becomes a driver of behavioral learning modes (KPMG 1998; IBM Group 1999). The second approach in behavioral learning focuses on trial-and-error adaptability, through which learning-by-experience becomes embodied in the form of specific routines, systems and processes (Feldman and Pentland 2003) as well as unexpected advances in organizing new ventures (Gartner *et al.* 1992; Sarasvathy 2001). Theoretically, behavioral routines provide consistency and replicability to the firm, increasing its chances for long-term survival (Nelson and Winter 1982). At the same time, the performance and improvement of routines can lead to organizational change, expanding the potential for learning (Feldman 2000).

These two perspectives highlight how behavioral learning is essential to the Formation phase of OpR. In the Formation phase, evaluation and elaboration processes help develop a business concept into an opportunity. First, evaluation involves distributing information to stakeholders, in order to determine if the business concept is feasible (Fryer 1999). This leads to a series of analyses and experiments that formally explore whether and how the opportunity is viable for this specific entrepreneur and/or venture. As the new opportunity is organized and elaborated, a side result is a more responsive entrepreneurial process (Sarasvathy 2001) and/or a more adaptive, evolutionarily adept organization (Aldrich 1999). The adaptive quality of learning is initiated primarily by specific, tangible incidents within the firm, such as performance gaps or other signals of poor market performance (Cyert and March 1963).

Opportunity recognition often has similar causes – a desire to generate something new or the need to solve a problem that is affecting the competitive quality of the firm. Additionally, the process of behavioral learning is usually incremental and iterative, involving a constant cycling between the internal development of routines and their preliminary effectiveness in the environment, often generating innovation and entrepreneurial change (Feldman and Pentland 2003). Likewise, entrepreneurial opportunity recognition is an iterative process, and because each stage can feed back on the others, the overall framework occurs in an incremental way. Thus, we propose:

P2: The more that entrepreneurial firms engage in behavioral learning processes, the more effective they will be in the Formation phase of opportunity recognition.

Action learning across both phases of opportunity recognition

Action learning approaches involve the practice of correcting misalignments between expectations and reality in order to generate more effective organizational behavior in real time (Argyris 1990; Senge *et al.* 1994). The reflective and personal nature of action learning makes it less common than the other two forms; at the same time, by challenging long-held patterns of belief and behavior it can rapidly transform an executive's ability to communicate and to develop effective strategic competencies, Such competencies include the ability to engage in double-loop learning (Argyris and Schön 1978; Roach and Bednar 1997), which goes beyond the single-loop improvements in efficiency to transformative explorations about the very nature of an organization's design and strategy (Senge *et al.* 1994).

Action learning creates a context for both the Discovery and Formation phases of entrepreneurial opportunity recognition in combination. Asking the reflective questions that are at the heart of action learning requires a personal willingness to uncover one's hidden assumptions, and thus face the discomfort of recognizing that one's espoused theory may be different than one's theory-in-use in the organization (Argyris 1990). Developing such an awareness, which leads to a re-alignment of belief and behavior, allows entrepreneurs and their teams to break through defensive routines that keep people from producing their best work (Argyris and Schön 1978; Torbert and Associates 2004). As such, the openness that action learning offers can itself become a competitive advantage by creating more opportunities for creative thinking, innovation and productive interaction.

This context of openness also connects the two phases of opportunity recognition. In the first place, the generative nature of action learning operates at a cognitive level, offering tools for questioning and re-framing longstanding beliefs and attitudes. When calling these cognitive models into question un-blocks the emergence of a new insight or recombination, action learning supports the Discovery phase of OpR. In the second place, action learning happens during the process of enacting ongoing activities, solving conflicts and adapting to new circumstances in an ongoing way. 'This kind of cooperative inquiry occurs in real time with partners also committed to integrating action and inquiry' (Torbert 2000: 79). As such, double-loop learning becomes an essential tool for successfully implementing a new insight, and thus it supports the Formation phase of OpR.

Finally, action learning is based on an ongoing iterative process of reflection and action which can be used to tie together and create synergies between both the Discovery and the Formation phases of OpR. Therefore:

P3: The more that entrepreneurial firms engage in action learning processes, the more effective they will be in encouraging both the Discovery and Formation phases of opportunity recognition.

In the next section we provide tangible suggestions and examples of how entrepreneurial firms can use each of these three modes of organizational learning in order to improve their efforts at opportunity recognition.

The role of organizational learning in opportunity recognition

The OpR model describes opportunity recognition as a form of creativity that can result in organizational innovation and the identification of new venture opportunities. In the previous section, we proposed that these outcomes can be strengthened by organizational learning. Although the way we have linked venture creation and organizational learning is unique, our approach is in some ways parallel to the literature that has connected individual creativity with organizational innovation through the rubric of learning and action (e.g. Dougherty 1992; Glynn *et al.* 1994; Nonaka 1994; Nonaka and Takeuchi 1995; Amabile *et al.* 1996; Crossan *et al.* 1999; Feldman and Pentland 2003). We now draw on that literature to extend our argument, by proposing that the more elements of creativity and innovation a venture or firm expresses – that is, the higher or more intense its capacity for organizational innovation – the more opportunities it may identify (Petzinger 1999; cf. Barringer and Bluedorn 1999). Thus, in a practical way, the more of the three modes of learning that a firm or an entrepreneur can enact, the more likely that new opportunities will be recognized that can be leveraged for strategic advantage. Following our threefold categorization of learning, we next provide examples that show how each mode of learning can increase innovation, creativity and the identification of new opportunities.

Recognizing opportunities through cognitive learning

As described above, cognitive learning involves changes in individual and/or organizational patterns of cognition, and shifts in the way knowledge is transferred within the organizational system (Glynn *et al.* 1994). To the extent that these changes generate new products or open up new markets, cognitive learning is a source of opportunity recognition for new venture creation. In most cases, cognitive learning in entrepreneurial companies occurs as a type of transformational capacity (Garud and Nayyar 1994), that is, the ability to re-define the meaning or value of currently existing ideas or resources into a new economic opportunity for the firm. This re-definition can occur in at least two ways: through a transformation of currently existing resources into new products, or through a re-interpretation of internal processes such that more information and knowledge can be generated.

Cognitive learning is exemplified by two employees at Patterson Fan Company who created an unusual-looking grill out of spare parts from the industrial fans being manufactured in the South Carolina plant (Rosenwein 2001). By cognitively re-framing the use (meaning) of the flared fan parts, these industrious employees developed a unique design that allowed for greater heat circulation while maintaining cooler unit temperatures than standard grills. CEO Vance Patterson patented the grill in his name and the names of the two inventors, and the spin-off company – Down South Inc. – represents a new opportunity in the form of a unique product in a new market for the corporation. In this way, cognitive learning in product design and the creation of a new organization led to new opportunities for the venture.

Recognizing opportunities through behavioral learning

Behavioral learning is primarily adaptive, focusing on the modification of routines and structures in the face of experience. 'The classic prediction is that success yields stability in routine functioning, while failure produces change' (Glynn *et al.* 1994: 46). Yet as Feldman (2000) shows, routines may be more mutable than previously thought. Similarly, one of the benefits of newness is flexibility, the capacity to change direction by altering even core properties of the organization (Lichtenstein 2000). In this sense, behavioral learning can spark new opportunities for new ventures in at least two ways – through modifications of routines that create unexpected extensions to a firm's offerings, and through an ongoing stream of organization-wide adaptations that can lead to unexpected synergies and marketable solutions.

The story of Philadelphia Pharmacy exemplifies how a serendipitous change in routines can generate unexpected strategic opportunities (Petzinger 1999: 11–14). One day its founder, Leon Ost, found an assistant writing out a prescription by hand, rather than using the computer-generated labeling system. To his surprise, Ost found that the assistant was writing the personalized label in Spanish, as she often did for the neighborhood's Hispanic population. Rather than berating her for circumventing standard operating procedures, Ost leveraged this knowledge into a change in routines by translating every computer-generated prescription into Spanish, thus opening up the market for a huge local clientele. Then, following a rapid influx of Vietnamese residents into the neighborhood, he added a third language to the computer program. These adaptive actions brought him even more recognition and within a few years Philadelphia Pharmacy was doing four times more business per square foot than the average American drugstore. In this way, incremental adaptations can result in the creation of new opportunities through expanded markets and more valuable product offerings.

Recognizing opportunities through action learning

The third mode of change, action learning, creates the potential for new opportunities by transforming the context within which new ideas can emerge. By focusing on the underlying norms of the organization and questioning whether the rules of engagement are appropriate, action learning can create a culture of openness, effectiveness and creativity (Argyris 1990). This broadening awareness can increase individuals' connection between espoused theory and theory-in-use (Schön 1983), setting up conditions for increased discovery and more refined evaluation and enactment of ideas.

The first outcome of action learning – agreeing to new rules of engagement that free individuals to speak honestly and act with fewer defenses – can transform an organization's ability to innovate and excel. Such a second-order transformation was enacted in The Natural Step, an entrepreneurial organization that has significantly advanced the movement toward environmental sustainability in Sweden, and more recently in the United States (Bradbury and Clair 1999). The organization's CEO wanted to develop scientific guidelines for sustainability that could be understood by non-scientists and applied in business. However, given the prevailing industrial-age assumption that environmental and economic gains are mutually exclusive (Hawken 1993; Shrivastava 1995), he recognized that conventional decision-making approaches would be inappropriate. Instead he enacted a double-loop action learning model, 'a form of thinking that goes beyond solution-seeking to reconceive the very foundation of one's problem, such that entirely new solutions may emerge' (Bradbury and Clair 1999: 72n17).

Through a highly iterative process of collaborative dialogue, a consensus document emerged that was endorsed by 50 of the top scientists in Sweden, and at the same time was clearly understandable to public figures in education, politics and business. Soon a network of business leaders and others, encouraged by the king of Sweden, provided funding to disseminate the colorful booklet and audiotape to the entire population of Sweden (7 million households). In addition, several of the supporting businesses, including IKEA, Scandic Hotels and Electrolux, have led the country in developing highly innovative products that are ecologically sustainable and commercially successful (Bradbury and Clair 1999). By shifting the rules of engagement, a learning-based context was generated that secured the organizational success of The Natural Step and, at the same time, transformed the society in which the organization exists.

In summary, each of these modes of learning – cognitive, behavioral and action – have been successfully utilized to create new and unexpected opportunities with great success. Table 5.1 summarizes the ways in which these modes can be integrated into venture creation activities and how each one can open up the potential for opportunity recognition. In these ways, organizational learning can increase the capacity for entrepreneurial firms to discover and form new economic opportunities.

Table 5.1 Modes of learning that generate opportunities in entrepreneurial firms

	Nature of entrepreneurial learning	*Elements affected by entrepreneurial learning processes*	*Potential opportunities for entrepreneurial learning*
Cognitive	Identify and alter cognitive patterns, generating new opportunities for knowledge and action (Nonaka 1994; Crossan *et al.* 1999)	Existing and potential knowledge Existing and potential resources Systemic processes	Design new products/services Develop new ways of doing business Attract/retain customers Apply proprietary knowledge in unique/ innovative ways
Behavioral	Alter tangible processes through experience (Feldman and Pentland 2003) Determine feasibility through trial-and-error learning (Sarasvathy 2001)	Existing and emerging routines Adaptive processes	Streamline processes to achieve new efficiencies Integrate learned experience to improve tangible processes
Action	Transform the context by questioning assumptions and aligning espoused belief with actual practice (Argyris 1990; Torbert 1991)	Underlying norms and beliefs Interaction 'rules of engagement'	Accelerate innovation processes Generate highly productive and creative organizations and collaborations

Conclusion

A firm's learning processes include its commitment to learning, the structural processes that contribute to or detract from learning, the quality of learning processes, and the rate at which new learning is applied to organizational processes. Each of these has important strategic implications in terms of how effectively a firm can add value and thus achieve or sustain a competitive advantage (Moingeon and Edmonson 1996; Teece 1998). Similarly, entrepreneurial firms can be successful to the degree that they identify, evaluate and enact strategic opportunities. Thus, opportunity recognition, like organizational learning, has important implications for how firms create wealth by converting entrepreneurial insights into strategic advantage. In this chapter, we have argued that organizational learning can enhance the opportunity recognition process.

We have attempted to show the presence of organizational learning can enhance the opportunity recognition process. First, like cognitive learning, OpR is advanced through the conversion of information into knowledge, such that what starts as tacit knowing can be re-framed into a realizable possibility in the market. Second, like behavioral learning, OpR involves adaptation and change. That is, once an insight has emerged out of an entrepreneur's 'pre-recognition' stew, that idea undergoes a great deal of analysis and testing, each aspect of which changes (and hopefully improves) the original conception. Finally, like action learning, OpR relies on a willingness to suspend assumptions and re-frame current expectations, while at the same time submitting one's emerging conceptualization (mental model) to a series of tests to see how well aligned it is to the reality of the situation.

In a sense, then, the success of an OpR process will depend on the ability of individuals and organizations to learn through all phases of the process. If this is true, then each mode of learning should be useful for increasing the viability of opportunity recognition, and for improving the results of creative problem-solving in the creation of new ventures – whether new firms or new products/services. This logic leads to our final set of propositions:

P4a: The more organizational learning practices that are enacted by entrepreneurs, the higher the likelihood that new opportunities will be recognized.

P4b: The more organizational learning practices that are enacted by entrepreneurial firms, the higher the likelihood that new opportunities will be recognized.

It is important to note that in proposing these relationships, we make no assumptions about an individual or firm's alertness (Kirzner 1979) or entrepreneurial 'competence' (Fiet 2002) as some prior research has emphasized. Such factors may affect the type of learning processes that are used or the likelihood that entrepreneurial opportunities will be recognized. Similarly, an entrepreneur's biases (Busenitz and Barney 1997) or path-dependent routines (Gavetti and Levinthal 2000; Siggelkow 2002) may also influence the relationship between learning activities and opportunity recognition. We view these potentially important influences as primarily contextual – elements to be specified or controlled for in future research into the role of organization learning in the opportunity recognition process.

Indeed, the concepts presented here and the limitations of the present study have important implications that can fruitfully be addressed in future research. First, the wealth of scholarship and research that has been pursued in order to understand the organizational learning process can be brought to bear on the opportunity recognition process. That is, insights from learning research may provide new insights into opportunity recognition.

The converse may also be true. The opportunity recognition process provides an ideal context for studying organizational learning. In fact, opportunity recognition can be thought of as a situation where learning occurs in a heightened state. As mentioned above, the entrepreneur or the entrepreneurial team seeking to identify and enact new business opportunities is likely to want to learn what is valid and useful as quickly as possible. Thus, it can be argued that the OpR process is an 'extreme' example of learning. This presents a particularly salient area for research, in the same way that Karl Weick and his colleagues have expanded our knowledge of organizational learning through the study of critical situations like fighting forest fires and being on the flight deck of an active aircraft carrier (Weick and Roberts 1993). In a similar way, the opportunity recognition process may represent a heightened state of learning where researchers may be able to observe a 'fully engaged' learning process.

Linking organizational learning to an OpR model that is creativity-based suggests another avenue for future research, namely, the relationship between organizational learning and creativity. For example, research by Getzels and Csikszentmihalyi (1976) indicates that 'problem finding' abilities may be more important to understanding creativity than problem solving. Problem finding involves the way problems are formulated when a gap or deficiency in knowledge is detected. Entrepreneurs with a strong urge to find problems as they evaluate ideas and form them into opportunities may have a greater ability to discern which opportunities are valid. Creativity research also suggests that question-asking and information-obtaining behaviors affect creative outcomes (Glover 1979). Gathering information and posing questions is also central to the learning process and future research may find that studying opportunity recognition provides a means to understand the creative dimensions of learning.

Finally, new ventures offer fertile ground for the best practices that are emerging from the organization learning and opportunity recognition research to take root and grow. Chances for both short-term survival and long-term success, we believe, will be enhanced if entrepreneurial firms adopt organizational learning practices. The ability to recognize opportunities may provide a key advantage by which established firms can remain viable and competitive in ever-changing environments. Future research should expand on these insights and endeavor to empirically test how learning methods might best be integrated into venture creation and growth processes so that opportunity recognition and other learning processes become essential elements of an organization's strategy and culture. Our hope is that by providing these perceptions we will support entrepreneurs and their firms to generate more opportunities and enact them in ways that expand the capabilities of their organizations and themselves.

References

Aldrich, H. (1999) *Organizations Evolving*. Newbury Park, CA: Sage.

Amabile, T. (1988) A model of creativity and innovation in organizations. In B. M. Staw and L. L. Cummings (eds), *Research in Organizational Behavior*, 10: 123–67.

Amabile, T., Conti, R., Coon, H., Lazenby, J. and Herron, H. (1996). Assessing the work environment for creativity. *Academy of Management Journal*, 39: 1154–84.

Argyris, C. (1990) Overcoming Organizational Defenses. Boston, MA: Allyn 2 Bacon.

Argyris, C. and Schön, D. (1978) *Organizational Learning: A Theory of Action Perspective*. Reading, MA: Addison-Wesley.

Barney, J. (1991) Firm resources and sustained competitive advantage. *Journal of Management*, 17(1): 99–120.

Barringer, B. R. and Bluedorn, A. C. (1999) The relationship between corporate entrepreneurship and strategic management. *Strategic Management Journal*, 20: 421–44.

Bartunek, J. (1984) Changing interpretive schemes and organizational restructuring: the example of a religious order. *Administrative Science Quarterly*, 29: 224–41.

Bateson, G. (1972) *Steps to an Ecology of Mind*. New York: Ballantine Books.

Bhave, M. P. (1994) A process model of entrepreneurial venture creation. *Journal of Business Venturing*, 9: 223–42.

Bradbury, H. and Clair, J. (1999) Promoting sustainable organizations with Sweden's Natural Step. *Academy of Management Executive*, 13(4): 63–73.

Brown, J. S. and Duguid, P. (1991) Organizational learning and communities-of-practice: toward a unified view of working, learning, and innovation. *Organization Science*, 2: 40–57.

Brown, J. S. and Duguid, P. (1998) Organizing knowledge. *California Management Review*, 40(3): 90–111.

Brush, C., Greene, P. and Hart, M. (2001) From initial idea to unique advantage: the entrepreneurial challenge of constructing a resource base. *Academy of Management Executive*, 15(1): 64–78.

Busenitz, L. and Barney, J. (1997) Biases and heuristics in strategic decision making: differences between entrepreneurs and managers in large organizations. *Journal of Business Venturing*, 12: 9–30.

Bygrave, W. and Hofer, C. (1991) Theorizing about entrepreneurship. *Entrepreneurship Theory and Practice*, 16(2): 13–23.

Carley, K. (1999) Learning within and among organizations. *Advances in Strategic Management*, 16: 33–53.

Christensen, P. S., Masden, O. and Peterson, R. (1989) *Opportunity Identification: The Contribution of entrepreneurship to Strategic Management*. Aarhus, Denmark: Aarhus University Institute of Management.

Cohen, W. and Levinthal, D. (1990) Absorptive capacity: a new perspective on learning and innovation. *Administrative Science Quarterly*, 35: 128–52.

Corbett, A. C. (2002) Recognizing high tech opportunities: a learning and cognitive approach. In *Frontiers of Entrepreneurship Research* Wellesley, MA: Babson College pp. 49–61.

Crossan, M., Lane, H. and White, R. (1999) An organizational learning framework: from intuition to institution. *Academy of Management Review*, 24: 522–37.

Csikszentmihalyi, M. (1996) *Creativity*. NY: HarperCollins.

Cyert, R. and March, J. (1963) *A Behavioral Theory of the Firm*. Englewood Cliffs, NJ: Prentice Hall.

Daft, R. and Weick, K. (1984) Toward a model of organizations as interpretation systems. *Academy of Management Review*, 9: 284–95.

Davidsson, P. and Wiklund, J. (2001) Levels of analysis in entrepreneurship research: current practice and suggestions for the future. *Entrepreneurship Theory and Practice*, 25(4): 81–99.

Davis, S. and Botkin, J. (1994) The coming of knowledge-based business. *Harvard Business Review*, September–October: 165–70.

de Koning, A. (1999) Opportunity formation from a socio-cognitive perspective. Paper presented at the UIC/AMA Research Symposium on the Interface of Marketing and Entrepreneurship, Nice, France.

Dimov, D. P. (2003) The nexus of individual and opportunity: opportunity recognition as a learning process. Paper presented at the 2003 Babson-Kauffman Entrepreneurship Research Conference, Wellesley, MA.

Dougherty, D. (1992) A practice-centered model of organizational renewal through product innovation. *Strategic Management Journal*, 13: 77–92.

Dragoon, A. (2003) All for one view. CIO New Zealand, July 1: http://cio.co.nz/cio.nsf/0/7CC8C00869E0766FCC256D86006333A7?OpenDocument

Feldman, M. (2000) Organizational routines as a source of continuous change. *Organization Science*, 11: 611–29.

Feldman, M. and Pentland, B. (2003) Reconceptualizing organizational routines and a source of flexibility and change. *Administrative Science Quarterly*, 48: 94–118.

Fiet, J. O. (2002) *The Systematic Search for Entrepreneurial Discoveries*. Westport, CT: Quorum Books.

Fiol, C. M. and Lyles, M. A. (1985) Organizational learning. *Academy of Management Review*, 10: 803–13.

Fryer, B. (1999) Get smart: Profit from knowledge management. *Inc. Magazine*, 3: 61–9.

Gaglio, C. M. and Katz, J. A. (2001) The psychological basis of opportunity identification: entrepreneurial alertness. *Journal of Small Business Economics*, 16: 95–111.

Gaglio, C. M. and Taub, P. (1992) Entrepreneurship and opportunity recognition. In *Frontiers of Entrepreneurship Research* Wellesley, MA: Babson College, pp. 136–47.

Galunic, C. and Rodan, S. (1998) Resource recombinations in the firm: knowledge structures and the potential for Schumpeterian innovation. *Strategic Management Journal*, 19: 1193–1201.

Gartner, W., Bird, B. and Starr, J. (1992) Acting as if: differentiating entrepreneurial from organizational behavior. *Entrepreneurship Theory and Practice*, 16(3): 13–30.

Garud, R. and Nayyar, P. (1994) Transformative capacity: continual structuring by intertemporal technology transfer. *Strategic Management Journal*, 15: 365–85.

Garvin, D. (1993) Building a learning organization. *Harvard Business Review*, July–August: 78–91.

Gavetti, G. and Levinthal, D. (2000) Looking forward and looking backward: cognitive and experiential search. *Administrative Science Quarterly*, 45: 113–37.

Getzels, J. W. and Csikszentmihalyi, M. (1976) *The Creative Vision: A Longitudinal study of Problem Finding in Art*. New York: Wiley.

Glover, J. A. (1979) Levels of questions asked in interview and reading sessions by creative and relatively noncreative college students. *Journal of Genetic Psychology*, 135: 103–8.

Glynn, M. A., Lant, T. and Milliken, F. (1994) Mapping learning processes in organizations: a multi-level framework linking learning and organizing. In *Advances in Managerial Cognition and Organizational Information Processing* Greenwich, CT: JAI Press pp. 43–83.

Greeno, J. G., Collins, A. M. and Resnick, L. B. (1996) Cognition and learning. In D. C. Berliner and R. C. Calfee (eds), *Handbook of Educational Psychology* New York: Macmillan, pp. 15–46.

Guth, W. and Ginsberg, A. (1990) Guest editor's introduction: Corporate entrepreneurship. *Strategic Management Journal*, 11: 5–15.

Hawken, P. (1993) *The Ecology of Commerce*. New York: HarperBusiness/HarperCollins.

Herriott, S., Levinthal, D. and March, J. (1985) Learning from experience in organizations. *American Economic Review*, 75: 298–302.

Hills, G. E., Shrader, R. C. and Lumpkin, G. T. (1999) Opportunity recognition as a creative process. *In Frontiers of Entrepreneurship Research*. Wellesley, MA: Babson College, pp. 216–27.

Huber, G. (1991) Organizational learning: the contributing processes and literatures. *Organization Science*, 2: 88–115.

IBM Group on Knowledge Management (1999) The second generation of knowledge management. *Knowledge Management*, October: 86–7.

Kao, J. (1989) *Entrepreneurship, Creativity, and Organization*. Englewood Cliffs, NJ: Prentice Hall.

Kim, D. (1993) The link between individual and organizational learning. *Sloan Management Review*, Fall: 37–50.

Kirzner, I. (1979) *Perception, Opportunity, and Entrepreneurship*. Chicago: University of Chicago Press.

Koehn, N. (2001) *Howard Schultz and Starbucks Coffee Company*. Boston: Harvard Business School.

KPMG (1998) *Knowledge Management Research Report*. New York: KPMG Management Consulting.

Leavitt, B. and March, J. (1988) Organizational learning. *Annual Review of Sociology*, 14: 319–40.

Lei, D., Slocum, J. and Pitts, R. A. (1999) Designing organizations for competitive advantage: the power of unlearning and learning. *Organizational Dynamics*, Winter: 24–38.

Levinthal, D. (1991) Organizational adaptation and environmental selection: interrelated processes of change. *Organization Science*, 2: 140–4.

Lichtenstein, B. (2000) Emergence as a process of self-organizing: new assumptions and insights from the study of nonlinear dynamic systems. *Journal of Organizational Change Management*, 13: 526–44.

Lichtenstein, B. and Brush, C. (2001) How do 'resource bundles' develop and change in new ventures? A dynamic model and longitudinal exploration. *Entrepreneurship Theory and Practice*, 25(3): 37–58.

Lichtenstein, B., Lumpkin, G. T. and Shrader, R. C. (2003) Organizational learning by new ventures: concepts, strategies, and applications. In J. A. Katz and D. A. Shepherd (eds), *Advances in Entrepreneurship, Firm Emergence, and Growth* Oxford: Elsevien Volume 6, pp. 11–36.

Long, W. and McMullan, W. E. (1984) Mapping the new venture opportunity identification process. In *Frontiers of Entrepreneurship Research*, Wellesley, MA: Babson College, pp. 567–90.

Low, M. B. and MacMillan, I. C. (1988) Entrepreneurship: past research and future challenges. *Journal of Management*, 14: 139–61.

Lumpkin, G. T. and Dess, G. G. (1996) Clarifying the entrepreneurial orientation construct and linking it to performance. *Academy of Management Review*, 21(1): 135–72.

Lumpkin, G. T., Hills, G. E. and Shrader, R. C. (2004) Opportunity recognition. In H. P. Welsch (ed.), *Entrepreneurship: The Way Ahead*. London: Routledge.

Lundberg, C. (1995) Conceptual issues in organizational learning. *International Journal of Organizational Analysis*, 3(1): 7–19.

March, J. (1991) Exploration and exploitation in organization learning. *Organization Science*, 2: 71–87.

Matusik, S. and Hill, C. (1998) The utilization of contingent work, knowledge creation, and competitive advantage. *Academy of Management Review*, 23: 680–97.

McElroy, M. (2002) Social innovation capital. *Journal of Intellectual Capital*, 3: 30–9.

Mintzberg, H. (1994) *The Rise and Fall of Strategic Planning*. New York: Free Press.

Moingeon, B. and Edmonson, A. (1996) *Organizational Learning and Competitive Advantage*. Thousand Oaks, CA: Sage.

Nahapiet, J. and Ghoshal, S. (1998) Social capital, intellectual capital, and the organizational advantage. *Academy of Management Review*, 23: 242–66.

Nelson, R. and Winter, S. (1982) *An Evolutionary Theory of Economic Theory and Capabilities*. Cambridge, MA: Harvard University Press.

Nonaka, I. (1988) Creating organizational order out of chaos: self-renewal in Japanese firms. *California Management Review*, Spring: 57–73.

Nonaka, I. (1994) A dynamic theory of organizational knowledge creation. *Organization Science*, 5: 14–37.

Nonaka, I. and Takeuchi, H. (1995) *The Knowledge-Creating Company*. New York: Oxford University Press.

Petzinger, T. (1999) *The New Pioneers*. Upper Saddle River, NJ: Prentice Hall.

Quinn, B. (1992) *Intelligent Enterprise: A Knowledge and Service Based Paradigm for Industry*. New York: Free Press.

Roach, D. and Bednar, D. (1997) The theory of logical types: a tool for understanding levels and types of change in organizations. *Human Relations*, 50: 671–99.

Rosenwein, R. (2001) Hiding in plain sight. *Inc. Magazine*, 23(1): 54–5.

Sarasvathy, S. (2001) Causation and effectuation: toward a theoretical shift from economic inevitability to entrepreneurial contingency. *Academy of Management Review*, 26: 243–63.

Schön, D. (1983) *The Reflective Practitioner*. New York: Basic Books.

Schumpeter, J. (1934/1959) *The Theory of Economic Development*. Cambridge: Harvard University Press.

Senge, P. M. (1990) *The Fifth Discipline*. New York: Currency/Doubleday.

Senge, P., Roberts, C., Ross, R., Smith, B. and Kleiner, A. (1994) *The Fifth Discipline Fieldbook*. New York: Currency/Doubleday.

Shane, S. (2000) Prior knowledge and the discovery of entrepreneurial opportunities. *Organization Science*, 11(4): 448–69.

Shane, S. (2003) *A General Theory of Entrepreneurship*. Northampton, MA: Edward Elgar.

Shane, S. and Venkataraman, S. (2000) The promise of entrepreneurship as a field of research. *Academy of Management Review*, 25(1): 217–26.

Shrivastava, P. (1983) Variations in strategic decision-making processes. In *Advances in Strategic Management* Vol. 2, Greenwich, CT: JAI Press, pp. 177–89.

Shrivastava, P. (1995) The role of corporations in achieving ecological sustainability. *Academy of Management Review*, 20(4): 936–60.

Siggelkow, N. (2002) Evolution toward fit. *Administrative Science Quarterly*, 47: 125–59.

Singh, R., Hills, G. E., Hybels, R. C. and Lumpkin, G. T. (1999) Opportunity recognition through social network characteristics of entrepreneurs. In *Frontiers of Entrepreneurship Research* Wellesley, MA: Babson College, pp. 228–41.

Stevenson, H. and Gumpert, D. (1985) The heart of entrepreneurship. *Harvard Business Review*, (2 March/April): 85–94.

Stevenson, H. H. and Jarillo, J. C. (1990) A paradigm of entrepreneurship: entrepreneurial management. *Strategic Management Journal*, 11 (Special Issue): 17–27.

Teece, D. (1998) Capturing value from knowledge assets: the new economy, markets for know-how, and intangible assets. *California Management Review*, 40(3): 55–79.

Timmons, J. (1994) *New Venture Creation,* 4th ed. Homewood, IL: Richard D. Irwin.

Torbert, W. (1973) *Learning from Experience: Toward Consciousness*. New York: Columbia University Press.

Torbert, W. (1991) *The Power of Balance*. Newbury Park, CA: Sage.

Torbert, W. (2000) A developmental approach to social science: a model for analyzing Charles Alexander's scientific contributions. *Journal of Adult Development*, 7: 255–67.

Torbert, W. and Associates (2004) *Action Inquiry: The Secret of Timely and Transforming Leadership*. San Francisco: Berrett-Koehler.

Van de Ven, A. and Polley, D. (1991) Learning while innovating. *Organization Science*, 3: 91–116.

Wallas, G. (1926) *The Art of Thought*. New York: Harcourt Brace.

Walsh, J. and Ungson, G. (1991) Organizational memory. *Academy of Management Review*, 16: 57–91.

Ward, T. B. (2004) Cognition, creativity, and entrepreneurship. *Journal of Business Venturing*, 19 (2): 173–88.

Weick, K. and Roberts, K. (1993) Collective mind in organizations: heedful interrelating on flight decks. *Administrative Science Quarterly*, 38: 357–81.

Woodman, R. W., Sawyer, J. E. and Griffin, R. (1993) Toward a theory of organizational creativity. *Academy of Management Review*, 18: 293–321.

6 Experiential learning within the process of opportunity identification and exploitation

Andrew C. Corbett

Introduction

Eckhardt and Shane (2003) argue that studying the *process* of entrepreneurship is one of the most important directions for future entrepreneurship research. Additionally, opportunity is seen as the linchpin around which the promise of entrepreneurship research is to be built (Shane and Venkataraman 2000). In fact, it has been suggested that a better understanding of how individuals identify and exploit opportunities may provide the field with a distinct domain that separates it from strategic management, economics, and other social science disciplines (Venkataraman 1997). In this chapter, I examine experiential learning within the context of opportunity identification and exploitation in order to better understand the process of entrepreneurship.

Shane and Venkataraman tell us that individuals must possess prior knowledge and the cognitive properties necessary to value such knowledge in order to identify new means–ends relationships. The warm reception that the work of Venkataraman and Shane has received has helped generate a great deal of interest in examining the entrepreneurship process from a cognitive perspective (Krueger 2000; McCline *et al.* 2000; Gaglio and Katz 2001; Keh *et al.* 2002; Ardichvili *et al.* 2003; Brigham and DeCastro 2003). Together with the work of other leading 'cognitive perspective' researchers (Baron, Mitchell, Busenitz and Gaglio), Shane and Venkataraman's 2000 *AMR* article helped carve out a fruitful line of inquiry examining the concomitance of an individual's cognitive properties and their ability to identify, develop and exploit opportunities.

The cognitive body of research contributes to our understanding of entrepreneurship by helping to explain how each individual's mental make-up is related to his or her ability to identify and exploit an entrepreneurial opportunity. The extant research suggests that recognition abilities differ because each of us has different pieces of the world's totality of information (Hayek 1945) and we each rely on different cognitive mechanisms or heuristics (Busenitz and Barney 1997; Baron 1998). Related research supports the hypothesis that creativity, cognition, and the opportunity identification process are correlated (Lumpkin *et al.* 2004; Ward 2004). Taken together, this research provides an understanding of what attributes (prior knowledge, cognitive mechanisms, heuristics, creative abilities) a budding entrepreneur needs to have however, it speaks less to the process of acquiring such attributes (i.e. learning). Research suggests that differences in our knowledge stocks and the various manners in which we each might process information are related to opportunity identification (Shane 2000). However, what about the manner in which we each learn – the acquisition of new information? A search of the primary management and entrepreneurship journals shows no work directly addresses the role that the process of learning plays in opportunity identification and exploitation.

The cognitive perspective on entrepreneurship is valuable and has helped us understand a great deal about how individuals identify and exploit opportunities. However, it needs to be fortified by investigations of the process of learning. Cognitive mechanisms and heuristics (for instance, overconfidence, counterfactual thinking, representation, small numbers) and an individual's existing stocks of knowledge are not synonymous with learning. Knowledge is a static concept that is activated when we put it into use. Cognitive mechanisms and heuristics are two ways in which we put our knowledge into action. In contrast, learning is a social process by which knowledge is created through the transformation of experience (Kolb 1984). This chapter proposes that to better understand opportunity identification, exploitation, and the entrepreneurship process in general, current research must be augmented by a more fine-grained examination of learning.

Previous models (Long and McMullen 1984; Timmons *et al.* 1987; Teach *et al.* 1989) that attempted to define different aspects of the entrepreneurial process were developed prior to the 're-birth' of opportunity research that was sparked by Venkataraman (1997). None of these earlier discussions, nor more current articles on the opportunity process (McCline *et al.* 2000; Keh *et al.* 2002; Ardichvili *et al.* 2003; Brigham and DeCastro 2003) examine the effects of learning.

This chapter relies on experiential learning to fill the void. Experiential learning theory (ELT) tells us that the acquisition and transformation experience is central to the learning process (Kolb 1984). ELT is an integrative perspective that combines the constructs of previous knowledge, perception, cognition, and experience (Kolb 1984). As such, it provides us with the opportunity to uncover why some individuals acquire and transform information in different manners, how they combine it with existing knowledge stocks, and why these behaviors result in different opportunity recognition and exploitation abilities. By mapping the learning modes of ELT onto the process of recognition and exploitation, we begin to better understand linkages between attributes, process and entrepreneurial activity.

When brought to bear on the opportunity recognition process, ELT can provide some clarification for why entrepreneurs develop certain cognitive behaviors and knowledge structures that have such a positive impact on their ability to recognize opportunity. This chapter explains that part of the variance in behavior and knowledge that affects the opportunity identification and exploitation process is based on the existence of *learning asymmetries* – that is, individuals acquire and transform their experiences (learn) in different ways. By providing this connection, this chapter will (1) enhance the richness of scholarly conversation, by enabling a heightened understanding of the nuances between learning, cognition and knowledge; (2) provide a more detailed understanding of the process of opportunity recognition and exploitation; and (3) facilitate entrepreneurship empirics by developing specific, testable hypotheses regarding learning effects and opportunity recognition.

The chapter proceeds by first providing a review of the pertinent opportunity identification work on cognition, knowledge and creativity. This is followed by a detailed explanation of ELT that shows how this perspective can inform and further extend the body of research on entrepreneurial process and opportunity identification and exploitation. Testable propositions based upon experiential learning and the process of opportunity identification and exploitation are then provided. Finally, the implications of an experiential learning perspective for entrepreneurship research and practice are discussed.

Opportunity: knowledge, cognition and creativity

So, why do some people recognize opportunities while others do not? Why do individuals recognize different opportunities from the same stimuli (Shane 2000)? Current theoretical conjecture and empirical investigations suggest that the answer to this question may be found by examining three broad concepts: knowledge, cognition and creativity. The extant literature suggests that differences between individuals' stocks of knowledge (Shane 2000; Ardichvili *et al.* 2003) and their behavior is based upon their cognitive processing (Baron 1998) and that these constructs are contributing factors to why some people recognize opportunities while others do not. Additionally, a burgeoning stream of literature is examining the links between creativity, cognition, opportunity and entrepreneurship (Hills *et al.* 1999; Lumpkin *et al.* 2004; Ward 2004). An overview of the contributions of each of these streams is provided below. Then, based upon this foundation, I can provide an argument for an investigation of opportunity recognition from an experiential learning perspective.

Knowledge, opportunity and entrepreneurship

While advocating for the importance of individuals within the evolution of economic markets, Hayek (1945) stated that knowledge is not given to anyone in totality. Hayek asserted that the 'economic problem' was not one of allocating resources, but instead is a problem of dispersion of knowledge and utilization of information. His assertion has provided the basis for entrepreneurship scholars (Venkataraman 1997; Shane 2000; Shane and Venkataraman 2000; Ardichvili *et al.* 2003; Eckhardt and Shane 2003) to investigate differences in knowledge as a cornerstone of their theoretical discussions of opportunity and the process of entrepreneurship.

Ardichvili *et al.* (2003) developed four specific propositions positing a relationship between knowledge and opportunity recognition. These authors theorize that individuals who have certain types of existing knowledge have a better likelihood of recognizing opportunities than those who do not have such knowledge. Specifically, Ardichvili, *et al.* propose that (1) special interest knowledge and general industry knowledge, (2) prior knowledge of markets, (3) prior knowledge of customer problems and (4) prior knowledge of ways to serve markets will all increase the likelihood of successful entrepreneurial opportunity recognition.

Shane's (2000) empirical investigation of the discovery of entrepreneurial opportunities examined the last three propositions put forth by Ardichvili and his colleagues. By investigating a newly patented process that was exploited by a number of individuals each with different 'stocks of prior knowledge,' Shane provides evidence for Ardichvili *et al.*'s propositions. Essentially, Shane showed that when presented with the same technological breakthrough, different individuals will recognize different opportunities due to their prior knowledge.

Knowledge, in the form of experience, has also been investigated as a primary factor in one's ability to identify opportunity. In a study of nearly one hundred founders, Vesper (1980) noted out of these individuals serendipity is the main reason they found the opportunity that eventually became their business. However, Vesper went on to show that work experience was the true factor in why these founders recognized business opportunities. Gilad *et al.* (1988) supported Vesper's findings and stated that experience is a significant factor that allows individuals to recognize potentially successful ventures. Ronstadt (1988) developed this work further and from his findings suggested the concept of the 'corridor principle' – the fact that experience and knowledge gained from starting one business allows an individual to see opportunities for other businesses in a similar arena.

In summary, the literature on knowledge and opportunity provides us with evidence that knowledge asymmetries are important distinguishing factors with regard to who recognizes what opportunities and who does not. However, we are not 'given' the knowledge to identify opportunities.

Venkataraman (1997) states that individuals must shape the information they are 'given' to discover opportunities because opportunities are rarely presented in prepackaged form. He suggests that investigations of opportunity should revolve around the information individuals possess *and* how they process it. Shane and Venkataraman (2000) reaffirm this position by stating that the reason why some people will discover opportunities while others may not hinges on two issues: '(1) the possession of the prior information necessary to identify an opportunity and (2) the cognitive properties necessary to value it.' (2000: 222). Essentially, while we all possess different pieces of information (Hayek 1945), we also all reason with it differently.

Cognition, opportunity and entrepreneurship

Taking this cue, Baron (1998) states that entrepreneurs are more likely than non-entrepreneurs to think and reason using various cognitive heuristics and biases (self-serving bias, counterfactual thinking, etc.) due to the conditions that entrepreneurs are likely to encounter (high uncertainty, novelty, time pressure and stress). Krueger (2000) argues that opportunities emerge based on the intentions of the individual and that intentions are derived from how people think. In summarizing the explosion of recent research on cognition and entrepreneurship, Mitchell *et al.* (2002) concur and propose a theory of entrepreneurial cognition that states that the mental processes that occur within the individual have a relationship with the process of entrepreneurship.

Mitchell *et al.* (2002) explain that cognitive psychology explores mental processes and how these processes evolve and change as an individual interacts with other people and the environment. Putting these concepts in the context of entrepreneurship, their theory states that 'entrepreneurial cognitions are the knowledge structures that people use to make assessments, judgments, or decisions involving opportunity evaluation, venture creation, and growth' (2002: 97).

Empirical studies support the theory of entrepreneurial cognition. Busenitz and Barney (1997) demonstrated that, in contrast to managers, entrepreneurs use heuristics (mental shortcuts) and biases in their decision-making. The authors suggested that these shortcuts in the cognitive processes of entrepreneurs were important in allowing entrepreneurs to seize opportunity. Mitchell *et al.* (2000) demonstrate that entrepreneurial cognitive scripts are consistent across cultures. Corbett (2002) explored the concept of cognitive style and found that the more an individual's cognitive processing style tended toward 'intuitive' and away from 'analytical,' the more opportunities an individual would identify. Brigham and DeCastro (2003) also examined cognitive style; they investigated how an individual's cognitive make-up fits with his or her venture over time. They found that while an individual's cognitive style may work well during the initial identification of an opportunity, the entrepreneur may experience burnout or misfit as the venture matures and goes though the exploitation phase. Keh *et al.* (2002) argue that cognitive biases have a direct impact on how entrepreneurs evaluate opportunities. Their study suggests that entrepreneurs tend to rely on potentially flawed small samples (law of small numbers) and an ill-placed confidence in their abilities (illusion of control) when evaluating opportunities.

Knowledge, cognition and creativity

Assimilating much of the above research in knowledge and cognition, Ward (2004) explores different cognitive approaches to creativity with the intent of developing opportunities for new businesses. Ward details different creativity-based cognitive approaches – including conceptual combination, analogical reasoning, abstraction and problem formulation – in order to show how novel ideas can emerge. By making the connection between knowledge and cognition, Ward not only demonstrates their importance to opportunity recognition, but by adding the concept of creativity, he reveals their insufficiency. Ward explains that all knowledge is not created equal and that, depending on how knowledge is processed and used (cognition), knowledge will either provide a bridge to a new opportunity (creativity) or construct a fence that blocks its path.

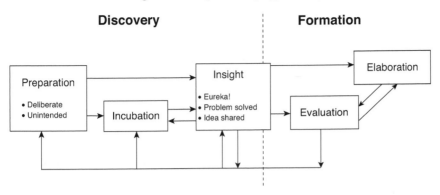

Figure 6.1 Creativity-based model of opportunity recognition (adapted from Lumpkin *et al.* 2004).

Lumpkin *et al.* (2004) argue that knocking down fences and building bridges toward new opportunities is dependent upon one's creativity. These authors argue for a creativity-based approach to opportunity recognition and build a five-stage model that details how a creativity perspective can inform the opportunity recognition process. The Lumpkin *et al.* model is replicated in Figure 6.1. Their creativity-based model of opportunity recognition is based upon Csikszentmihalyi's (1996) basic elements of creativity – preparation, incubation, insight, evaluation and elaboration. Corresponding to Shane and Venkataraman's (2000) primary components of opportunity recognition, Lumpkin *et al.* dissect their model into discovery and formation phases. The discovery phase includes preparation, incubation and insight, while the formation phase includes evaluation and elaboration. As noted by the arrows, the model is built to represent an ongoing recursive process.

Knowledge, experience and cognitive actions play primary roles during the discovery phase of this model. Lumpkin *et al.* explain that during *preparation* individuals rely on their prior knowledge (Shane 2000) but that this preparation process is neither planned nor intentional. Individuals may not yet know that they are going to start a venture, so this preparation may in fact just be activities associated with their 'normal' daily routines. During *incubation* individuals cognitively process thoughts subconsciously (Csikszentmihalyi 1996) while they are thinking about an idea or working to solve a problem. During *insight* the individual has a breakthrough, "Aha!" moment. At this time a cognitive shift takes place as the individual begins to consciously realize that he may have identified an opportunity to break an existing means–end relationship (Shane 2000; Gaglio and Katz 2001).

Lumpkin *et al.*'s formation phase includes the last two steps of the model, evaluation and elaboration. In *evaluation*, would-be entrepreneurs test the opportunity with regard to market acceptability, financial returns and resource availability. During evaluation, entrepreneurs talk to many individuals in their network and try to assess whether the concept is worthwhile to continue pursuing. Lumpkin *et al.*

state that during *elaboration* the creative insight is actually realized. It is here that true formal business planning may begin or the venture may be launched. Bhave (1994) reports that opportunity may be formally converted into a venture even though the details are not finalized; the organization will evolve and formalize over time.

A learning perspective

Baron (2004) states that everything each of us says, thinks and does is affected by how we acquire, store, transform and use information. He argues that the manner in which individuals differ with respect to these mental processes may affect entrepreneurial abilities. As shown above, the opportunity identification literature is replete with discussions of experience, creativity, knowledge and cognition, and these works address how we 'store, and use information' to pursue opportunities. There is little about how we transform information and nothing directly addresses how we acquire information, i.e. learn. Lumpkin *et al.* build a recursive model that implies learning during the evaluation step, but their focus is on the importance of creativity. To date, no one has directly addressed Hamel and Prahalad's (1996) question regarding the role that learning plays in finding and exploiting new opportunities. Using experiential learning theory, the current study augments the extant body of research by directly addressing how individuals acquire and transform information within the process of opportunity identification and exploitation.

Experiential learning theory and entrepreneurship

Experiential learning theory (ELT)

Kolb (1984) defines experiential learning as a process by which knowledge is created through the transformation of experience. Figure 6.2 is a representation of Kolb's model of experiential learning and shows that individuals learn through experience, reflection, thought and experimentation (the outside loop). This cycle involves four learning modes – concrete experience, reflective observation, abstract conceptualization and active experimentation. The inner poles refer to how one acquires and transforms information (on the vertical and horizontal axes, respectively) feeding into the process on the outer ring.

Kolb's concept of prehension, as reflected on the vertical pole in Figure 6.2, refers to the two different ways in which an individual can acquire information in the world – either through direct experience or through a recreation of experiences. Apprehension is a reliance on the tangible, felt qualities of immediate experience. Comprehension refers to a reliance on conceptual interpretation and symbolic representation. Kolb (1984) uses the example of what you are doing right now – reading – to illustrate the differences in these two concepts:

> 'If you put down this book, get up from the chair, and leave the room, your apprehensions of that situation will vanish without a trace (substituted for,

of course, by new apprehensions of the hallway or whatever new immediate situation you are in). Your comprehension of that situation, however, will allow you to create for yourself and communicate to others a model of that situation that could last forever. Further, to the extent that the model was accurately constructed from your apprehensions, it allows you to predict and recreate those apprehensions.' (1984: 43)

Similarly, Kolb explains that the dimensions of transformation of experience that are expressed on the horizontal axis in Figure 6.1 are diametrically opposed. Some people tend to transform via extension, which means that they learn through actively testing their ideas and experiences in the real world. Others transform via intention where they internally reflect upon the different attributes of their experiences and ideas.

Taken together, Kolb shows that these two dimensions of grasping and transforming information result in four ways of learning and creating knowledge. When an individual grasps experience through apprehension and transforms through intention, he or she creates divergent knowledge. Experience grasped through comprehension and transformed through intention creates assimilative knowledge. When an individual grasps through comprehension and transforms through extension, he or she creates convergent knowledge. Lastly, when one grasps experience through apprehension and transforms it through extension, accommodative knowledge results.

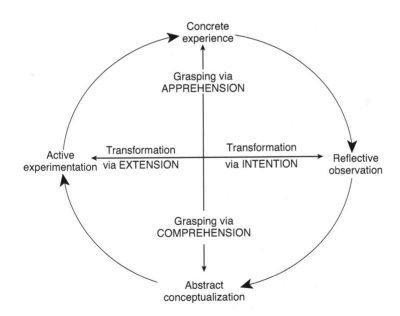

Figure 6.2 Kolb's model of experiential learning.

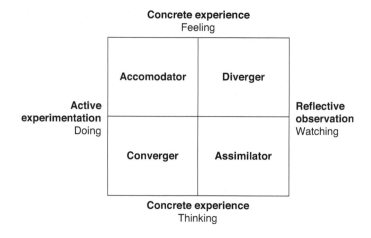

Figure 6.3 Kolb's learning styles.

Kolb and others (Kolb *et al.* 2000; Mainemelis *et al.* 2002) state that individuals learn best when they can cycle through all four forms of learning as representing by the outside curved arrows in Figure 6.2. Kolb also provides typology of learning styles – the converger, diverger, assimilator (Figure 6.3) and accommodator – and suggests that individuals have a preference for one over the others. The assimilator grasps experience by thinking and theorizing and transforms it by watching and reflecting. The converger grasps by thinking and theorizing and transforms via doing and applying. The diverger grasps by feeling and doing and transforms by watching and reflecting. The accommodator grasps experience by feeling and doing and then transforms via doing and applying.

It should be reiterated that these learning modes are relatively fixed states. Individuals may acquire and transform information in all manners, but each of us tends to rely on one mode over the others. Kolb states, 'Through their choices of experiences, people program themselves to grasp reality through varying degrees of emphasis on apprehension or comprehension' (1984: 64). Each individual also has a preference for transformation. Jung (1977) states that we all tend to have a preference for different learning mechanisms and that the complex interactions of our minds and the chaos of the environment in which we live help explain why there is great variability in the learning process. 'Outer circumstances and inner disposition frequently favor the one mechanism, and restrict or hinder the other; whereby a predominance of one mechanism naturally arises.' (1977: 12).

ELT and entrepreneurship

Greeno *et al.* (1996) report that theories of learning fall into three broad categories: behavioral, cognitive and situative. Each of these learning perspectives frames knowledge and learning in different but complementary manners. Table 6.1 details the general tasks associated with each perspective as well as the environment in which each learning theory is best suited. Experiential learning theory (ELT) can be considered a cognitive and situative learning theory because individuals transform (using cognitive properties) their experiences (situative) into new knowledge. Theories of behavior tend to overemphasize outcomes, routine and the importance of having one proper response to each stimulus. As Kolb notes, experiential learning theory is in stark contrast to behaviorist learning theories:

> When viewed from the perspective of experiential learning, the tendency to define learning in terms of outcomes can become a definition of non-learning, in the process sense that the failure to modify ideas and habits as a result of experience is maladaptive. The clearest example of this irony lies in the behaviorist axiom that the strength of a habit can be measured by its resistance to extinction. That is, the more I have 'learned' a given habit, the longer I will persists in behaving that way when it is no longer rewarded. (1984: 26).

The idea of transforming experience and not focusing on outcomes is crucially important to why ELT fits well with entrepreneurship and behavioral theories do not. Behavioral theories may prove quite useful when an organization is trying to attain operational excellence in its processes or manufacturing. However, theories of this ilk reward those who follow the routine and status quo; these theories explain well the activities in organized and defined environments with clear goals, feedback and reinforcement. This is the antithesis of entrepreneurship.

Table 6.1 Tasks and environment of different types of learning

Behavioral:	
Task	Behavioral learning involves learning to make associations and learning new skills.
Environment	Behavioral learning works best in an environment that is well organized and one where there is a routine to follow.
Note	Behavioral learning includes clear goals, feedback and reinforcement.
Cognitive:	
Task	Cognitive learning involves the tasks of reasoning, problem solving and planning. It often involves reorganization of concepts already in the individual's understanding.
Environment	Cognitive learning works best in an environment that fosters an understanding of concepts and principles, and one that makes use of reasoning and problem-solving skills.
Note	Cognitive learning is an active process of construction rather than a passive assimilation of information or rote memorization. Ability grows out of intellectual activity, not absorption.

Continued

Table 6.1 Tasks and environment of different types of learning—cont'd

Situative/Social:	
Task	Situative learning occurs through the active participation in group activities. Learning is the strengthening of those practices through interaction with others.
Environment	Situative learning occurs in an environment when individuals participate with others in social/group settings to foster confidence in their learning.
Note	Learning often occurs from people of different social or cultural backgrounds.

Source: Adapted from Greeno *et al.* (1996) and Wenger (1998).

Both start-up entrepreneurs and those in charge of strategic renewal in large organizations cannot rely on behavior and habit if they intend to survive. To succeed they must learn through their experiences and seek out new opportunities. ELT relies on the cognitive and situative concepts of thinking, feeling, doing and watching. ELT focuses on the process. By transforming experience into new knowledge, ELT allows individuals to discover *new* outcomes from their learning, which is just what entrepreneurs do when they are attempting to uncover new means–ends relationships (Shane and Venkataraman 2000).

Realizing this, we can see why ELT may shed light on the process of entrepreneurship. However, all experiential learning is not the same; Kolb illustrates that individuals tend to have a preference for one of four different experiential learning modes. Taking all of this into account, I propose that individuals with different learning modes will perform better during different parts of the entrepreneurial process. Specifically, I detail in the next section how each of these learning modes maps onto different parts of the opportunity identification and exploitation process. Lumpkin *et al.*'s model of the process of opportunity recognition details four active steps (preparation, incubation, evaluation and elaboration I do not include the insight stage because it is more of a reaction to learning, a moment in time, not an active step) and suggests that each step requires different learning and knowledge expertise. By transposing Kolb's learning modes on Lumpkin *et al.*'s model (Figure 6.4), I illustrate the importance of understanding learning as part of the process of opportunity identification and exploitation.

Experiential learning, creativity and opportunity

Lumpkin *et al.*'s model is designed to show that the process of opportunity recognition is inherently creative and that there are four sub-processes (preparation, incubation, evaluation and elaboration) and one event (insight). While the authors' focus is on creativity, the authors' imply that learning is occurring throughout the model, as evidenced by the recursive lines. In the following sections, I augment the Lumpkin model to explicitly show what type of experiential learning is best

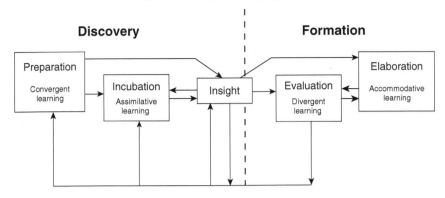

Figure 6.4 Creativity-based experiential learning model of opportunity recognition.

suited for each part of the model and develop propositions based upon these connections. Figure 6.5 illustrates how different types of learning match with the required action needed in each phase of the Lumpkin creativity model for opportunity recognition.

Preparation and convergent learning

Lumpkin *et al.* explain that preparation refers to the stocks of knowledge that an entrepreneur brings to the process of opportunity identification. As other researchers have shown, prior knowledge is an important part of the entrepreneurial process (Ronstadt 1988; Shane 2000). This knowledge can take many forms – work experience, training, knowledge of markets, knowledge of customer problems, etc. The prior explanation of Kolb's (1984) theory of experiential learning shows

Process	Action necessary during this stage	Learning style	Strengths of this learning style
Preparation	Inventorying and analysis of current stocks of knowledge and experience.	Convergent	Abstract conceptualization and analyzing existing knowledge to find solutions to problems.
Incubation	Reflecting and observing different options and possibilities.	Assimilation	Conceptualization, reflection and observation in order to bring together seemingly, separate activities.
Evaluation	Assessing ideas to test for initial feasibility.	Divergent	Use of concrete experience, observation, and imagination to gain meaning.
Elaboration	Planning, task execution, and exploitation	Accommodative	Use of experience and experimentation to carry out plans, seek opportunity, get involved and take action

Figure 6.5 Learning styles matched with action needed in each stage of opportunity identification and exploitation.

that those who tend toward a convergent learning style may be best equipped to excel during the phase of preparation.

The convergent learning style relies on the abilities of abstract conceptualization and active experimentation. On first blush, Lumpkin *et al.*'s preparation stage might appear to be relatively passive and in contradiction to this active mode. However, while convergers are continually thinking and doing, they are not necessarily acting in relation to a specific, focus idea or opportunity. The ongoing convergent learning is just preparing them to develop technical solutions and a platform for initial ideas. Convergers prefer to deal with technical tasks and technical problems as opposed to social and interpersonal issues (Hudson 1966). These individuals are happiest when they are attempting to solve problems or find the 'one correct' technical answer (Torrealba 1972). People with specific technical knowledge are generally better equipped to discover initial technical ideas (Corbett 2002). Convergers in the preparation stage will be able to find a solution that will become the idea or platform for later incubation into a true product or service opportunity.

P1: Individuals who tend toward a convergent learning preference will be more likely to develop an initial solution or idea than their counterparts who tend toward divergent, accommodative or assimilative learning.

Incubation and assimilative learning

Lumpkin's sub-process of incubation is the period when new combinations (Schumpeter 1934) emerge from the simmering pot of pre-recognition stew (Gaglio and Taub 1992). This is not a problem-solving stage but a time when options and possibilities are being considered (Lumpkin *et al.* 2004). The incubation period is marked by time when the individual is not specifically focused on the problem but reflecting, resting or observing some other unrelated activity (Campbell 1985).

Assimilators are excellent at pulling together disparate observations and building these seemingly separate activities into coherent models (Grochow 1973). The assimilators' dominant learning abilities lie in abstract conceptualization and reflective observation (Kolb 1984). In this assimilative orientation, ideas are judged less by their practical value as it is more important that the theory behind the idea is logically sound and precise. As such, this perspective matches well with the incubation phase where ideas are still being 'cooked' and the organization is still far from developing finished products that must meet the practical value of a demanding marketplace.

P2: Individuals who tend towards an assimilative learning preference will be more likely to develop more options or opportunities for products from a platform of initial ideas than their counterparts who tend toward convergent, divergent or accommodative learning.

Evaluation and divergent learning

The evaluation period is where the rubber meets the road. Csikszentmihalyi (1996) suggests that this stage is the most challenging because it requires entrepreneurs to be brutally honest with themselves; they must assess whether they have just a good idea or a truly viable business opportunity. This is the stage where ideas are often tested through feasibility analysis, initial marketing testing, financial review, and feedback from trusted advisors in your business or personal network (Gaglio and Taub 1992; Bhave 1994; Singh *et al.* 1999). Evaluation is the most explicit 'learning' stage in the Lumpkin *et al.* model. Lumpkin *et al.* 2004 suggest that entrepreneurs can learn during evaluation and this learning can tell one whether they can move forward or need to loop back to preparation and incubation.

Divergers have the opposite strengths of convergers: divergers emphasize concrete experience and reflective observation. They have strong imaginations and an ability to read people and situations through an awareness of meaning and values. Kolb (1984) tells us that divergers can take concrete situations from many perspectives and organize the many resulting relationships into a meaningful gestalt. With all of these traits and behaviors, divergers are well equipped to perform during the evaluation phase. They have 'people-orientation' and should be able to take in all of the divergent information from the market testing, financial analysis, etc., to hone in on the fit between the opportunity and the marketplace.

P3: Working from a number of different options, individuals who tend toward a divergent learning preference will be more likely to develop a workable business prototype than their counterparts who tend toward convergent, accommodative or assimilative learning.

Elaboration and accommodative learning

Business planning and tasks revolving around organizational structure are developed and modified during this stage (Lumpkin *et al.* 2004). Lumpkin *et al.* also note that the elaboration stage can be viewed as the exploitation of the opportunity. Kao (1989) states that it is during this stage that value is captured from the creative act. In this stage, final options are selected and resources are organized (Csikszentmihalyi 1996) for the going concern.

The strengths of individuals who tend toward the accommodative style are opposed to assimilators. Accommodators emphasize concrete experience and active experimentation – they are the doers! As Kolb notes, 'The greatest strength of this orientation lies in doing things, in carrying out plans and tasks and getting involved in new experiences. The adaptive emphasis of this orientation is on opportunity seeking, risk taking, and action' (1984: 78). The learning style of these individuals is a tight fit with the task of exploitation.

P4: Individuals who tend toward an accommodative learning preference will be more likely to successfully exploit working prototypes than their counterparts who tend toward divergent, convergent or assimilative learning.

In summary, it can be seen that certain learning styles can be more effective during different phases of the opportunity identification and exploitation process. The propositions put forth above illustrate, but by no means exhaust, the lines of inquiry that could be developed from applying experiential learning theory to the process of entrepreneurship. To the extent that all or any of these propositions can be verified in empirical research, they provide a foundation for more in-depth examinations of learning and the opportunity identification process.

Implications of an experiential learning perspective for entrepreneurship

Previous research has articulated the contributions of prior knowledge, creativity and cognitive mechanisms to the process of entrepreneurship. Ward (2004) emphasizes that how each individual creatively processes and uses one's knowledge affects the opportunities one can uncover. Baron (1998) and Mitchell *et al.* (2000) theorize that some people recognize opportunities where others do not due to their differences in cognitive processing. Shane (2000) tells us that people recognize different opportunities due to *knowledge asymmetries* – the fact that we each have differing stocks of knowledge. But how do these knowledge asymmetries come about in the first place? Learning. Knowledge is a function of how we learn and I argue that in addition to knowledge asymmetries and differences in cognitive abilities, the entrepreneurship literature would benefit from a further investigation of *learning asymmetries*. By bringing a learning perspective to the process of opportunity identification and exploitation, this chapter demonstrates the likelihood that differences in learning matter! They matter with respect to an individual's ability to initially identify opportunities and they matter with respect to an entrepreneurs ability to adapt and learn as he or she progresses through the process of entrepreneurship.

Specifically, the major themes of this chapter can be summarized in the following manner: (1) learning – the manner in which individuals transform their experiences, expertise and prior knowledge into new insights and new knowledge – is an important and understudied aspect of entrepreneurship research; (2) individuals learn in different ways and these differences are important with regard to who identifies what opportunities; and (3) different learning styles may be more or less effective during different stages of the opportunity identification and exploitation process. That being said, even if these assertions are true, what is the value of their worth to the future of entrepreneurship research? Practitioners? Educators?

Research implications

For researchers, the broad implication of this chapter is the need for more work examining learning and the opportunity identification process. This chapter proposes that individuals who rely on different manners of learning will be more or less effective during different stages of the opportunity identification process. Future work that attempts to validate these propositions is needed. Additionally, while the traditional view of experiential learning posits that each of us tends toward one preferred style, more recent speculation suggests a more complex approach (Kolb *et al.* 2000; Mainemelis *et al.* 2002). According to this view, individuals will tap each of the learning styles depending upon the context and content of what is being experienced. The flexibility and adaptability afforded to individuals from this perspective could provide great insights into the learning of entrepreneurs. Entrepreneurs have to wear many hats in order to be successful, and future work examining the flexibility of entrepreneurs' learning styles could help explain the variance between those who succeed and those who do not.

Additionally, while experiential learning was used in this chapter, tapping into the greater and more diverse body of learning research can provide entrepreneurship scholars with many new conceptual tools. Evidence that experiential learning and other learning perspectives may prove useful can be found by looking at other domains within the field of management. Theories from learning have previously been successfully explored and utilized in other areas within the field of management, such as organizational behavior (Cohen and Sproull 1996), knowledge transfer (Argote 1999) and corporate strategy (Quinn 1980). There is no reason to believe that more in-depth studies of learning would not benefit the field of entrepreneurship.

In fact, Busenitz *et al.* (2003) argue that future research needs to be at the intersection of individuals, opportunities and their modes of organizing. It can be argued, and I believe, it is exactly at this intersection where learning occurs! As such, there seems to be no reason to believe that a learning perspective would not also help clear some of the fog that surrounds the process of bringing new ventures to light. Encouraging this broader stream of 'entrepreneurial learning research' is one of the primary objectives of this chapter.

More specifically, the learning perspective put forth in this chapter has implications for other research domains within entrepreneurship, including teams, corporate venturing, professional service providers (financiers, vendors, suppliers and other partners) and serial entrepreneurs. Entrepreneurial teams, not individuals, drive the new venture creation process (Kamm *et al.* 1990). Experiential learning and the model developed herein can be used to further explain why this is so. As discussed, we all learn differently and different learning modes work better during different parts of the opportunity identification and exploitation process. Perhaps we need all 'types' of learners on our team to identify and successfully exploit opportunities. With regard to corporate venturing research, a learning perspective could help further research that examines selection and recruitment to internal venture teams. Empiricists could examine the use of learning scales to select members to intrapreneurial venture teams. Research that examines an entrepreneur's successful use of his or her network of service providers could examine learning to understand its contribution to this success. For example, are certain learners more equipped than others to communicate their ideas, negotiate terms, understand others' needs, or simply get things done with the help of others due to the manner in which they transform their experiences and interactions with these partners (i.e. learn)?

Lastly, cognitive style has been shown to be a contributing factor in why some entrepreneurs start more than one venture (Brigham 2001; Brigham and DeCastro 2003). The learning perspective put forth in this chapter could augment this research by examining the effect that learning has on an individual's decision to leave one venture and start another. As a venture matures and more routine practices are put in place, situative and cognitive learning may become less important than behavioral learning. A question for researchers to address could be: do serial entrepreneurs gravitate away from behavioral learning and does this contribute to why they exit one venture to begin another? In summary, by adding a learning perspective to each of these lines of inquiry (and numerous others, no doubt), scholars should be able to better understand the entrepreneurial process.

Practitioners

The model developed herein can help aspiring entrepreneurs understand that how they learn is related to their abilities during the identification and exploitation process. Since most research shows that successful ventures are started by teams, this understanding can help nascent entrepreneurs as they build their teams. The importance of entrepreneurial (and intrapreneurial) team building combined with learning cannot be understated. Convergers with their ability to develop specific technical solutions, are best suited for the preparation phase as R&D specialists. Assimilators, with their ability to pull together disparate ideas, can perform the role of product development. Divergers are superior at developing specific alternatives and could play the role of market developers on an entrepreneurial team. Finally, the action focus and people perspective of the accommodators would be best suited for the task of sales and new business development. Understanding the differing learning styles of individuals is important for all practicing entrepreneurs working in teams because matching the learning orientations of individuals to specific roles could provide optimal results.

Entrepreneurial education

This chapter demonstrates that learners of all types can find a role within the process of starting a new venture. Each of the learning styles has a fit with some particular function throughout the process of identifying and exploiting an opportunity. While it is true that some entrepreneurs do not go through all of the phases detailed here when launching their venture (Timmons 1994), this point should bolster the resolve of all nascent entrepreneurs and the educators who guide them. Since we all have a tendency toward one learning style, we are by definition less dependent upon the others. However, since all phases of the process (and all learning styles' strengths) are not always required to launch a venture (perhaps because actions in the market or other actors have fulfilled a particular role), anyone who truly wants to be involved in starting a venture should have the learning ability to do so.

With regard to a learning perspective on entrepreneurship, the role of the educator should be to first help each student uncover their learning style strengths. Armed with this knowledge, the student can then focus on not just discovering new opportunities but searching for opportunities that best fit his or her strengths as a learner. Additionally, by just providing students with information on a learning perspective for entrepreneurship, educators can help understand the need for building a team with diverse learning styles.

Lastly, a learning perspective on entrepreneurship suggests that alterations to the current manner in which educators teach entrepreneurship is warranted. In addition to the current focus on developing ideas and crafting business plans, perhaps courses should focus more on the process and how ideas morph and change shape over time. Venture capitalists and others who screen and validate entrepreneurial ideas constantly focus on the importance of the people on the team as opposed to the idea because they know that over time environmental forces will almost always change the entrepreneur's original concept. Therefore, educators might consider balancing their curriculum to align their courses with this reality. Students should learn more about how to adapt their original ideas in response to market learning. Courses that focus more on learning, improvising and adapting in reaction to changes suggested by potential customers and other actors in the marketplace may provide additional value to students. To do this, educators can test students' ability to learn in different manners by using scenarios, role-plays, and *experiences* that tap each individual's ability to grasp and transform *experiences* in each of the four manners delineated in the experiential learning model. This focus on the process – and learning from market feedback – should complement well educators' other modules on creativity, scanning, business planning, etc.

Conclusion

Many scholars have made important contributions to the understanding of the process of entrepreneurship by investigating various constructs related to knowledge, experience, cognition and creativity. The heightened understanding that was provided in this chapter of the nuances between learning and these constructs gives scholars, practitioners and educators an appreciation of the importance of learning within the entrepreneurial domain. Finally, I submit that the most important contribution of this chapter is its articulation of the concept of *learning asymmetries* and its importance to the entrepreneurial process.

References

Ardichvili, A., Cardozo, R. and Ray, S. (2003) A theory of entrepreneurial opportunity identification and development. *Journal of Business Venturing*, 18(1): 105–23.

Argote, L. (1999) *Organizational Learning: Creating, Retaining, and Transferring Knowledge.* Norwell, MA: Kluwer Academic.

Baron, R. (1998) Cognitive mechanisms in entrepreneurship: why and when entrepreneurs think differently than other people. *Journal of Business Venturing*, 13(4): 275–94.

Baron, R. (2004). The cognitive perspective: a valuable tool for answering entrepreneurship's basic 'why' questions. *Journal of Business Venturing*, 19(2): 169–72.

Bhave, M. P. (1994) A process model of entrepreneurial venture creation. *Journal of Business Venturing*, 9: 223–42.

Brigham, K. (2001) Entrepreneurship and cognitive fit. Unpublished doctoral dissertation, University of Colorado, Boulder.

Brigham, K. H. and DeCastro, J. O. (2003) Entrepreneurial fit: the role of cognitive misfit. In J. A. Katz and D. A. Shepherd (eds), *Cognitive Approaches to Entrepreneurship Research*. Oxford: Elsevier.

Busenitz, L. and Barney, J. (1997) Differences between entrepreneurs and managers in organizations: biases and heuristics in strategic decision-making. *Journal of Business Venturing* 12(1): 9–30.

Busenitz, L., West, G. P., Shepherd, D., Nelson, T., Chandler, G. and Zacharakis, A. (2003) Entrepreneurship research in emergence: past trends and future opportunities. *Journal of Management,* 29 (3): 285–308.

Campbell, D. (1985) *Take the Road to Creativity and Get off Your Dead End*. Greensboro, NC: Center for Creative Leadership.

Cohen, M. D. and Sproull, L. S. (1996) *Organizational Learning*. Thousand Oaks, CA: Sage.

Corbett, A.C. (2002) Recognizing high tech opportunities: a learning and cognitive approach. *Frontiers of Entrepreneurship Research*, Wellesley, MA: Babson College, 149–61.

Csikszentmihalyi, M. (1996) *Creativity*. New York: HarperCollins.

Eckhardt, J. T. and Shane, S. A. (2003) Opportunities and entrepreneurship. *Journal of Management*, 29(3): 333–349.

Gaglio, C. M. and Katz, J. (2001) The psychological basis of opportunity identification: entrepreneurial alertness. *Journal of Small Business Economics*. 16: 95–111.

Gaglio, C. M. and Taub, P. (1992) Entrepreneurs and opportunity recognition. *Frontiers of Entrepreneurship Research*, Wellesley, MA: Babson College,136–47.

Gilad, B., Kaish, S. and Ronen, J. (1988) The entrepreneurial way with information. In S. Maital (ed.), *Applied Behavioral Economics*, Vol. 2, pp. 481–503.

Greeno, J. G., Collins, A. M. and Resnick, L. B. (1996) Cognition and learning. In D. C. Berliner and R. C. Calfee (eds), *Handbook of Educational Psychology*. New York: Macmillan.

Grochow, J. (1973) Cognitive style as a factor in the design of interactive decision-support systems. Doctoral dissertation, Sloan School of Management, MIT.

Hamel, G. and Prahalad, C. K. (1996) Competing in the new economy: managing out of bounds. *Strategic Management Journal*, 17: 237–42.

Hayek, F. A. (1945) The use of knowledge in society. *American Economic Review*, 35(4): 519–30.

Hills, G. E., Shrader, R. C. and Lumpkin, G. T. (1999) Opportunity recognition as a creative process. *Frontiers of Entrepreneurship Research*, 216–27.

Hudson, L. (1966) *Contrary imaginations*. Harmondsworth: Penguin Books.

Jung, C. (1977) *Collected Works of Carl Jung*, Vol. 6. Princeton, NJ: Princeton University Press.

Kamm, J. B., Shuman, J. C., Seeger, J. A. and Nurick, A. J. (1990) Entrepreneurial teams in new venture creation: a research agenda. *Entrepreneurship: Theory and Practice*, Summer: 7–17.

Kao, J. J. (1989) *Entrepreneurship, Creativity, and Organization*. Englewood Cliffs, NJ: Prentice Hall.

Keh, H. T., Foo, M. D. and Lim, B. C. (2002) Opportunity evaluation under risky conditions: the cognitive processes of entrepreneurs. *Entrepreneurship: Theory and Practice*, Winter: 27(2): 124–48.

Kolb, D. A. (1984) *Experiential Learning: Experience as the Source of Learning and Development*. Englewood Cliffs, NJ: Prentice Hall.

Kolb, D. A., Boyatzis, R. E. and Mainemelis, C. (2000) Experiential learning theory: previous research and new directions. In R. J. Sternberg and L. F. Zhang (eds), *Perspectives on Cognitive, Learning and Thinking Styles*. Mahwah NJ: Lawrence Erlbaum.

Krueger, N. F. (2000) The cognitive infrastructure of opportunity recognition. *Entrepreneurship: Theory and Practice*, 24(3): 5–23.

Long, W. and McMullen, W. E. (1984) Mapping the new venture opportunity identification process. *Frontiers of Entrepreneurship Research*, Wellesley, MA: Babson College, 567–90.

Lumpkin, G. T., Hills, G. and Shrader, R. (2004) Opportunity recognition. In H. P. Welsch (ed.), *Entrepreneurship: The Way Ahead*. New York: Routledge.

Mainemelis, C., Boyatzis, R. and Kolb, D. A. (2002) Learning styles and adaptive flexibility: testing the experiential theory of development. *Management Learning*, 33(1): 5–33.

McCline, R. L. Bhat, S. and Baj, P. (2000) Opportunity recognition: an exploratory investigation of a component of the entrepreneurial process in the context of the healthcare industry. *Entrepreneurship: Theory and Practice*, Winter: 81–94.

Mitchell, R., Smith, B., Seawright, K. and Morse, E. (2000) Cross-cultural cognitions and the venture creation process. *Academy of Management Journal*, 43(5): 974–93.

Mitchell, R., Busenitz, L., Lant, T., McDougall, P., Morse, E. and Smith, E. (2002) Toward a theory of entrepreneurial cognition: rethinking the people side of entrepreneurship research. *Entrepreneurship: Theory and Practice*, Winter: 93–104.

Quinn, J. B. (1980) *Strategies for Change: Logical Incrementalism*. Homewood, IL: Richard D. Irwin.

Ronstadt, R. C. (1988) The corridor principle. *Journal of Business Venturing*, 3(1): 31–40.

Schumpeter, J. A. (1934) *The Theory of Economic Development; an Inquiry into Profits, Capital, Credit, Interest, and the Business Cycle*. Cambridge, MA: Harvard University Press.

Shane, S. (2000) Prior knowledge and the discovery of entrepreneurial opportunities. *Organization Science*, 11(4): 448–69.

Shane, S. and Venkataraman, S. (2000) The promise of entrepreneurship as a field of research. *Academy of Management Review*, 25(1): 217–26.

Singh, R., Hills, G. E., Hybels, R. C. and Lumpkin, G. T. (1999) Opportunity recognition through social network characteristics of entrepreneurs. *Frontiers in Entrepreneurship Research*, Wellesley, MA: Babson College, 228–41.

Teach, R. D., Schwartz, R. G. and Tarpley, F. A. (1989) The recognition and exploitation of opportunity in the software industry: a study of surviving firms. *Frontiers of Entrepreneurship Research*, Wellesley, MA: Babson College, 383–397.

Timmons, J. A. (1994) *New Venture Creation*, 4th ed. Homewood, IL: Richard D. Irwin.

Timmons, J. A., Muzyka, D. F., Stevenson, H. H. and Bygrave, W. D. (1987) Opportunity recognition: the core of entrepreneurship. *Frontiers of Entrepreneurship Research*.

Torrealba, D. (1972) Convergent and divergent learning styles. Master's thesis, Sloan School of Management, MIT.

Venkataraman, S. (1997) The distinctive domain of entrepreneurship research. *Advances in Entrepreneurship, Firm Emergence and Growth*, Greenwich, CT: JAI Press Vol. 3 pp. 119–38.

Vesper, K. (1980) *New Venture Strategies*. New York: Prentice Hall.

Ward, T. B. (2004) Cognition, creativity, and entrepreneurship. *Journal of Business Venturing*, 19(2): 173–88.

Wenger, E. (1998) *Communities of Practice: Learning, Meaning, and Identity*. Cambridge: Cambridge University Press.

7 An exploration of knowledge management processes in start-up firms in the high-technology sector

Olukemi O. Sawyerr and
Jeanette W. Gilsdorf

Introduction

Knowledge-based views of firm advantage consider firm heterogeneity in creating, storing and leveraging knowledge to be the primary basis for generating above-normal returns and obtaining sustained competitive advantage (Barney 1991; Kogut and Zander 1993; Grant 1996b). This has generated interest in examining the processes firms have in place for managing organizational knowledge (Spender and Grant 1996; Davenport and Prusak 1998; Simonin 1999). Davenport (1997) states that knowledge management will only succeed if there are employees devoted to gathering and editing knowledge from those who have it and setting up and managing knowledge technology infrastructures. Knowledge management (KM) described in this context would then seem to preclude small, entrepreneurial organizations without the resources for highly formalized KM processes. This study will suggest that Davenport's statement is too categorical and that knowledge is made explicit and managed in smaller firms in less formalized ways by individuals whose primary duties are manifold.

According to Grant (1996b), 'much remains to be done at both the empirical and the theoretical level, especially in relation to understanding the organizational processes through which knowledge is integrated. … Further progress is critically dependent upon closer observations of the processes through which tacit knowledge is transferred and integrated' (p. 384). This study responds to the call for greater empirical support for knowledge processes in organizations by focusing on answering three research questions (1) How do entrepreneurial firms generate new knowledge? (2) How do they diffuse new knowledge gained throughout the organization? (3) How do they absorb and exploit new knowledge to create competitive advantage? A close observation of the organizational processes in place in entrepreneurial firms may help shed additional light on KM activities.

KM research is in the nascent stage (Grant 1996a; Gupta and Govindarajan 2000) and as such would benefit greatly from the more in-depth observation possible with qualitative research methodologies (Yin 1984; Eisenhardt 1989). According to Eisenhardt (1989), 'theory-building research is begun as close as possible to the ideal of no theory under consideration and no hypotheses to test … because preordained theoretical perspectives or propositions may bias and limit the findings' (p. 536). This study contains numerous literature citations, but they are given passim, as they relate to findings that either support or seem to disconfirm them.

Methodology

Sample

Theoretical sampling, driven by a conceptual question, not by a concern for 'representativeness,' was used in sample selection (Yin 1984; Eisenhardt 1989; Miles and Huberman 1994). Small entrepreneurial firms in the software industry were targeted because of the rapid and continuous change characterizing software technologies and markets, which often means that innovations offer only temporary competitive advantage. Thus, these firms must be concerned not only with sustaining current competitive advantages, but also with renewing their advantages at a faster rate than they are being eroded (Grant 1991). Thus, it is inferred that successful firms in this competitive and turbulent industry would be forced to find ways to deal with KM issues to survive. Permission was obtained to conduct in-depth semi-structured interviews with multiple informants in five firms in the Technology Coast of Greater Los Angeles from a list of area software companies.

Early in the process the _morph_ factor was encountered. (The informants at four of the five firms used the term both as a noun and a verb.) When the market changes, as it can do rapidly in high-tech industries, the result creates a much greater change in a small firm, which often must respond with a massive directional change; it must morph (see Table 7.1).

Data sources

Data were obtained primarily through semi-structured interviews that lasted 90 minutes on average with informants in each organization over a six-month period. Company documents such as the annual report and corporate websites provided additional data. The use of multiple sources of evidence and the establishment of a chain of evidence helps to increase construct validity (Yin 1984; Miles and Huberman 1994). One of the authors recorded the responses while the other asked the questions. Interviews were conducted with the founder or a member of the founding team (at I-Mage with a high-ranking executive with some tenure in the organization), and two other individuals. In addition, the Knowledge Officer of a large IT consulting firm with an elaborate KM infrastructure was interviewed (Kochikar 2000). The data obtained from this interview were not included in the analysis, but were used to increase understanding of formal KM systems.

The interviews began by presenting to the respondents a working definition of KM (see Appendix A) and inquiring as to the presence of such a phenomenon in their organization. This was followed by open-ended questions developed from the literature (see Appendix B). A transcript of each interview was prepared and submitted to analysis.

Table 7.1 Description of sample

Firm[a]	Market	Ownership/IPO or founding	Employee size, 2000	Revenue (millions of dollars), 1999
CallMeModem	Software for major modem OEMs; retail product line; moving into the cell phone wireless industry	Public/1995	125	10
ClientBank	Data mining for e-commerce firms; moved from a focus on banking industry	Private/1997	35	7
E-Consult	E-business management consulting and IT staffing; moving from Y2K consulting	Private/1999[b]	70[c]	Not provided
I-Mage	Software development for major printer OEMs; shrinking customer base; needing to move into a new space	Public/1996	90	32[d]
Mediatrix	Mediation software for the telecommunications industry	Public/1998	140	20

[a]The names of the firms have been changed.
[b]Morphed into a completely new market, management, etc., in 1999.
[c]70 permanent employees; 30 contract employees.
[d]As the discussion will show, I-Mage does the least in terms of managing knowledge but has the highest revenues. This can be accounted for partly as a matter of scale. Note, however, that financial figures are not being offered as performance measures. Knowledge management is only one of numerous variables that affect revenue, costs and profits.

A replication strategy was utilized in the analysis of the data to strengthen external validity by enabling the researcher to achieve analytical generalization (Yin 1984). The interviews were thus staggered to enable the use of this strategy. Emerging constructs and hypotheses were confirmed, or disconfirmed, in future interviews.

Data analysis

Inductive coding techniques were utilized to develop a coding scheme (Miles and Huberman 1994). Single cases were initially analyzed in order to gain familiarity with each case as an independent entity. A line-by-line analysis of each transcript was performed to see if there were any identifiable patterns such as regularly occurring words, phrases, concepts, etc. 'In vivo' codes, the words and phrases used by the informants, were identified during the analysis (Strauss and Corbin 1990: 69) (see Appendix C). The contents of the transcripts from each firm were then compared and contrasted. There was a high level of within-firm consensus. In the two firms where one respondent's statements differed from those of a prior respondent (Mediatrix and I-Mage), subsequent interviews were used to gain an understanding as to the reasons for the differences.

Pattern codes were generated from the above process and from relevant literature. Once the pattern codes were somewhat stable, each transcript was subjected to a coding process. Codes were dropped and new ones developed as the analysis progressed from case to case. The authors coded the initial set of case transcripts separately. Intercoder reliability was in excess of 90 percent (Miles and Huberman 1994).

Following the coding process, data were examined on a case-by-case basis and then on a firm-by-firm basis in order to identify similarities and differences in the knowledge processes at each firm. A KM matrix was created with all the firm-level data presented using the pattern codes as a framework. This matrix is too long to present here, but the data presented in Tables 7.2 through 7.4 were extracted from the matrix. The conclusions drawn and verified using the KM matrix were further clarified and confirmed using the transcripts. 'In vivo' codes, emerging patterns, concepts, processes, etc., were noted. Observed patterns in the data were tested during subsequent visits to the sites to strengthen confidence in the data and in the noted patterns.

Preliminary propositions developed inductively during data analysis were examined through multiple iterations to see if they matched the data (Eisenhardt 1989; Strauss and Corbin 1990; Miles and Huberman 1994). For those that matched the data, each case was examined for deeper understanding and supporting evidence and the literature was revisited to gain additional insights into the proposed relationships between the variables of interest. Those that did not fit the data were discarded. This process resulted in the following propositions by which discussion of the results will be structured.

Some qualitative researchers have suggested the use of negative cases to increase the robustness of the findings (Miles and Huberman 1994). While the firms in the sample were not selected with a view to including negative cases, it did become apparent during data collection that there were no explicit knowledge processes in place at E-Consult and I-Mage. The five firms were classified into two groups, three with effective knowledge processes and two without. This provided the opportunity to focus on differences and similarities between the two groups of companies during data analysis.

Results and discussion

The results indicate that while the firms in the sample did *manage* knowledge, they did so in a highly informal fashion, with little or no KM infrastructure. This is supported by some of the skepticism in the literature about hard-core technocratic approaches to managing knowledge (see e.g. Scarbrough 1998; Swan *et al.* 1999). Figure 7.1 is the research model. The respondents emphasized the critical

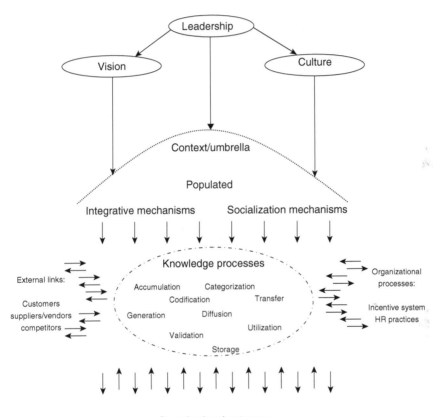

Figure 7.1 Research Model.

importance of quality leadership in setting the organizational context conducive to KM activities. In describing how KM worked in their organizations, the respondents pointed to the need for a well-articulated vision and the presence of a culture of sharing. Leadership, via vision and culture, fashioned the organizational umbrella under which new knowledge is created, diffused and leveraged. The organizational context is populated via multiple integrative and socialization mechanisms. Within this context, several activities are taking place that have been placed under knowledge processes. External organizational linkages, especially customers, suppliers/vendors and competitors, as well as internal organizational processes such as incentive systems and human resource practices, impact these activities. These knowledge processes do have outcomes, albeit expressed in non-financial terms. The respondents were able to point to specific organizational outcomes directly attributable to the KM processes in their organizations. Specific elements of the model are discussed in the following sections.

Creating the organizational context

The firms in the sample (to varying degrees) managed knowledge; however, none of them had a formalized KM system in place. The respondents maintained that this is primarily a scale issue. They are limited by financial as well as temporal constraints in implementing a formalized KM system. Rather, these firms have focused on developing a common organizational *context* to facilitate the exploitation of their intellectual capital. This common context creates organizational identification, a necessary precursor of KM activities. That is, individuals with potentially profitable ideas are likely to share them if they feel connected to, and to an extent defined by, the organization. If they feel alienated, they are unlikely to share. The degree to which this context had been developed and managed varied among the firms in the sample. In three of the firms, CallMeModem, ClientBank and Mediatrix, management had invested resources to create the context necessary for KM activities. In the other two firms, E-Consult and I-Mage, the context was not clearly discernible. The first proposition follows:

P1: In small high-tech start-ups, the more pervasive a common context to govern the knowledge processes in the firm, the greater the effectiveness of its knowledge processes.

Data analyses revealed that the firms utilized a variety of mechanisms to create the context. The critical role of top management was the development and articulation of a broad corporate vision and corporate culture, which serve as common knowledge and facilitate knowledge integration in the organization (Grant 1996b). Top management at CallMeModem, ClientBank, and Mediatrix have not only developed broad corporate visions, they have also communicated them to the whole organization with the result of a high level of commitment among organizational members. The following quotes provide support:

> The way we manage knowledge is ... we spend a lot of time making sure the core concept is understood, spend a lot of time making sure that what we're trying to do is clear–the mission is clear.
>
> (Pres. and CEO, Mediatrix)

> We use the virtual teams; we don't fly people around. It's trust – It's like the MasterCard thing in the ad–'priceless'. It's ethereal ... There are things we couldn't have done without that culture in place, and the engineers are proud to work in that environment. So the engineers had a lot of cross-pollination across locations. They had seen each other and met and thrown ideas around. It was then very easy to rely on those from other locations – be more trusting and willing to rely on them.
>
> (Sr VP and COO, CallMeModem)

Leadership displayed its commitment to the process of knowledge creation by backing the knowledge-related activities of organizational members with organizational resources. An important resource commitment made by top management was in staffing. Top management played a highly influential role in the recruitment and selection processes. The CEO at Mediatrix indicated that one of the primary objectives of the interview process was to identify the knowledge stock of the candidate. They hired for the knowledge stock that would fill the knowledge gap in the firm. This is demonstrated in the following quote:

> We're an engineering software company, and in terms of knowledge creation, [we] had the job to create the environment for the engineers ... attract bright engineers from school ... create a culture within the engineering group that would keep a person like that satisfied and happy, that they felt they could contribute and have some freedom and yet get products out the door ... We also had to change our pay structure, our bonus structure, all these others, to be competitive with what was going on in the world ... We had high turnover so we had to do things to get people to be more committed ... It takes a certain kind of management and a changed culture to have a virtual engineering team.
>
> (Sr VP and COO, CallMeModem)

E-Consult also has a clearly stated and broad new corporate mission. However, at the time of data collection, management had not communicated the new mission effectively to other members of the organization. Management had not created an organizational context to support knowledge processes in the organization. The following quote provides support:

> With the rest of the company we have not communicated the vision effectively. We are currently in transition from being a Y2K firm to this new

company. When the management team has strategy in place and a clear direction and has hired all the key players, we will formalize a vision. The strategy is fluid and changing and we have to have something more firm before we can formalize a vision.

(Founder and CEO, E-Consult)

At I-Mage, while there is a formalized corporate mission, it has not been communicated well to the employees. Actually, it appears from the comments of the informants that there is inconsistency in the vision and direction of the organization:

Our vision is to be a leading supplier of storage and imaging technology to OEM customers worldwide. It's communicated not very often and not often in writing. I think it's because we're a relatively small company with most of our people focused on small tasks relative to the mission of the company. We have a huge number of software programmers, and when we've tried to communicate the message at times, 90 percent could care less … [laughs]. But it's a great vision.

(Director of Core Technology Group, I-Mage)

[I-Mage] has undergone a lot of change in the last year or two and been through a lot of turnover at the executive level. This presented a problem with consistency of the message.

(VP Technology, I-Mage)

In addition, at I-Mage, company leadership was perceived as not providing the support necessary. This is demonstrated in the following quote:

There was a large loss of trust by engineers for the CEO because it was not uncommon for us to come up with a schedule and we're told it was not good enough. We'd ask for a 30 percent increase in headcount. The CEO would say, 'Add all the headcount you need.' We'd say we've got a pretty good product but will need more bodies, more resources – but there was no accelerator to make it happen. And then it comes down to: 'You're getting no more, but we still want everything, and on the same schedule.' That cycle repeated itself one or two times a year, certainly in every operating budget.

(Marketing Manager, I-Mage)

According to the respondents, creating a context puts everyone on the same page, making sure 'people haven't gone off the edge someplace, run off with a wild idea …' (VP R&D and CTO, CallMeModem). If organizational members are to be empowered to create new knowledge, their efforts must be fairly well orchestrated. The common context is the means by which the organization orients the knowledge-creating activities of the members of the organization. The common context is similar to what Pfeffer and Sutton (2000) refer to as 'philosophy,' a set of guidelines that convey the why of things, as opposed to the how. It is what Drucker (1998) calls a 'score' (as of an orchestral work) and Nonaka (1998) refers to as the 'conceptual umbrella' of the firm. It enables the firm to 'identify the common features linking seemingly disparate activities or businesses into a coherent whole' (Nonaka 1998: 41). To quote one of the informants:

> I think it's this business of setting context. We're interested in having ideas in a certain context. Or at least if you have one [that's outside the context] you are aware that it's outside. So one thing managers can do is make sure that the context is clear. I'm a very strong believer in giving the organization as much information about what's going as possible because none of us would have good ideas if we didn't have enough data to understand the problem, right? So it's openness, willingness to spend time educating the people on how the company works. On this [meeting] for sales strategy today, one of the things we'll be doing will be educating the team on the idea of having alternate channels and what would you use them for and what not? So at the end of that meeting all of them will be some small amount more educated about that and so I expect that over the next several weeks after the meeting people will come up to me and say, 'I've been thinking, maybe we should be doing something with retail.' They'll have ideas.
>
> (VP R&D, Mediatrix)

Integration and socialization mechanisms

Several researchers have identified the critical importance of integration and socialization mechanisms in KM activities (Kogut and Zander 1992; Nonaka 1994; Grant 1996a; Hoopes and Postrel 1999; Gupta and Govindarajan 2000). According to Grant (1996b), it is not the knowledge itself that is the critical source of competitive advantage, but rather the ability of the firm to integrate its knowledge by bringing together many areas of specialized knowledge to create new knowledge or to generate new combinations of existing knowledge that it can exploit in the marketplace. Kogut and Zander (1992) refer to this as *combinative capability*, i.e. the ability of the firm to 'synthesize and apply current and acquired knowledge' (p. 384). A firm's ability to create or recombine knowledge is embedded in social relationships constructed and facilitated by various integrative and socialization mechanisms that link organizational members to one another and to important external groups such as customers and vendors (Kogut and Zander 1992; Nonaka 1994). Thus, they increase the density of communication interface and facilitate convergence in cognitive maps that support KM activities (Edstrom and Galbraith 1977; Nonaka 1994; Gupta and Govindarajan 2000).

The common context is *populated* through the use of various integration and socialization mechanisms. The firms in the sample relied on similar integration and socialization mechanisms. However, there were differences in the degree to which these mechanisms were utilized. To help explain the differences, properties were ascribed to these mechanisms. *Frequency* is defined as how often a particular mechanism is used. The frequency with which an integrative or socialization mechanism is used increases its efficiency in integrating knowledge across multiple parts of the organization (Grant 1996a). *Variety* is defined as the number of different integrative and socialization activities in which the members of the organization engage. The use of multiple integrative and socialization mechanisms fosters knowledge integration. *Inclusiveness* refers to the extent which the activities include multiple members of the organization, multiple levels and multiple functions. Greater inclusiveness results in greater opportunities for cross-pollination among organizational units. Thus the second proposition:

P2:   In small high-tech start-ups, the greater the frequency, variety and inclusiveness of integration and socialization mechanisms in the firm, the more effective are its knowledge processes.

As displayed in Table 7.2, the frequency, variety and inclusiveness of the integration and socialization mechanisms were relatively high at CallMeModem, ClientBank and Mediatrix as compared with I-Mage and E-Consult. The following quotes provide additional evidence.

> We created a virtual engineering team. It didn't matter what city you were in. We had products from all of the locations, but almost every product we put out came from 2 or 3 offices. We put in a network to connect these people actually writing the code. The code that went into these products would cross all these offices. That gave us a lot of bright people to apply to a problem and the critical mass to solve it. And it made us fast! We're tiny – we've never had more than 50 engineers. We could do almost anything faster than anybody.
>
> (Sr VP and COO, CallMeModem)

> We have status meetings in the form of weekly conference calls with the client. We tell him what's been done to date and what is still to do. The client can ask for more things. This [client] uses an RFM scoring grade: Regency, Frequency, and Monetary value of each customer. The RFM score could be 1, 2, 3, 4, or 5. [He] can know how many customers he has in each score category, and we've also allowed him to get individual scores for just R, just F, or just M. (People who spend X dollars get an M score of 2, etc., etc.) I asked him one day during a conference call, 'Do you want to put in your assumptions?' He liked that, and thought it would be cool if he could see the exact ranges. We took the idea to the developer. I could go directly to the VP with this enhancement idea. It's being implemented with other clients also.
>
> (Client Consultant, ClientBank)

At both E-Consult and I-Mage the frequency, variety and inclusiveness of integration and socialization mechanisms were lower, as shown in Table 7.2. The following quotes provide additional evidence.

> [Do you have a process of debriefing the consultants as to what they know so that it can be available to other consultants, thus building collective knowledge?]

We don't have a good process in place. For example, when four people complete a project, they just move on to a new project. We have not built the infrastructure to support KM in the e-business part of the organization ... We are aware it is a necessity, a very high priority.

(Founder and CEO, E-Consult)

We have the all-hands meetings – today it means that the president creates a short presentation that he does and everybody is invited in one big room ... Not regular – they're as frequent as [the CEO] thinks they need to be ... At the meetings the executive staff is up front; the employees are way in the back, so it's one-way mainly. He communicates *to* employees and entertains questions.

(Dir. Core Tech Group, I-Mage)

These mechanisms perform several functions. First, they are the means through which the organizational context created by top management is populated to the entire organization. Second, in several of the firms, top management utilized these mechanisms to make company information widely available. One of the problems cited by the informants at I-Mage is that information is used for political purposes. Only those who are in the 'right' circle gain access to information. The resulting information differentials among organizational members hinder KM activities (Nonaka 1994).

Third, through these mechanisms individuals and teams are linked in multiple ways to create 'communities of interaction' (Nonaka 1994). Through these communities of interaction, a social context is created within which an individual's knowledge is amplified, developed and enlarged. Organizational members are able to advance their knowledge through a process of exchange, combination and recombination, which can lead to the creation of new knowledge and to effective knowledge transfer and use (Nonaka 1994; Grant 1996a). The customer is an important part of this community of interaction. At CallMeModem, the engineers meet regularly with the engineers of OEM customers. At ClientBank, the product implementation team meets regularly with the client. At Mediatrix, sales, engineering and architects meet with customers on a quarterly basis and as needed to develop 'a really good understanding of what the market actually looks like and understand what the customers are trying to do.' At I-Mage, while there are no regularly scheduled meetings with customers, the OEMs are often very involved in product decisions. The ideation team at I-Mage met with several of the firm's customers.

Fourth, these mechanisms enable the creation of mutual trust among organizational members (Davenport and Prusak 1998). Through a process of repeated and continual dialogue, individuals develop mutual trust that supports sharing (Nonaka 1994). At I-Mage it was evident that such mutual trust was lacking, especially between employees and management. At CallMeModem, the increased interactions among organizational members via the integration and socialization mechanism have created an atmosphere of mutual trust that has contributed to their ability to reuse code and have reusable modules in their products, factors that the informants credit for their speed to market and efficiency.

Table 7.2 Integration and socialization mechanisms

Firm	Mechanism (variety and frequency)	Participants (inclusiveness)
CallMeModem	Meetings	
	• Corporate – quarterly	All associates
	• Executive – weekly	All those who report to the CEO
	• Functional – weekly	Each division with division head
	• Cross-functional – weekly	Sales/Engineering
	• Brainstorming sessions – weekly, annually	Engineering
	• Product summit – major product development efforts	(Sr VP and COO) 'All bright people who knew those technologies'
	• Informal – daily	
	• Customers (OEMs)	
	• Ad – hoc freewheeling meetings	All associates
	Virtual teams	Sales/Engineering
	Task force	All associates
	Conference calls for problem solving – weekly	Engineering, multiple locations
	Mentoring	Cross-functional, multiple locations
	Email	Leads and managers
	Telephone	Senior engineers and new employees
		All associates
		All associates
ClientBank	Meetings	
	• Pizza lunches – weekly	All employees
	• Executive – weekly	Executives
	• Brainstorming sessions – weekly	Major actors
	• Informal – daily	
	• Clients – weekly	All employees, consultants
	Mentoring	
	• Buddy system	All employees
	E-mail	All employees
	Voicemail	All employees
E-Consult	Meetings	
	• Corporate – quarterly	All employees
	• Management – weekly	Executives
	• Informal – daily	All employees
	Project teams	Consultants
	Newsletters	Sent to all employees
	E-mail	All employees
	Voicemail	All employees

Table 7.2 Integration and socialization mechanisms—cont'd

Firm	Mechanism (variety and frequency)	Participants (inclusiveness)
I-Mage	Meeting	
	• Corporate – as needed by CEO	All employees
	• Executives – weekly	Executives
	• Functional meetings – frequency depends on manager	All employees
	Ideation team	Cross-functional special task force with the mandate to come up with new spaces within which the firm can compete
	E-mail	All employees
	Voicemail	All employees
Mediatrix	Meetings	
	• Corporate – monthly	All employees
	• Executive – weekly	Executives
	• Brainstorming sessions	Team members
	• Customers – quarterly	Sales/Marketing/R&D
	• Informal	All employees
	Teams	
	• Functional teams	Team members, Executives
	• Cross-functional teams	Engineering/Sales/Marketing
	Task forces – as needed	Sales/Marketing; Engineering/Sales/Marketing
	Orientation	All employees
	Training	All employees
	Cross-training	All employees
	Mentoring	All employees
	• Buddy system	
	Rotation	Engineering/Sales/Marketing/R&D (across locations)
	E-mail/Voicemail	All employees
	Co-location	Engineering/Sales

Incentivizing for participation in KM activities

Some researchers have suggested tying employee contributions to knowledge processes to performance evaluation and the incentive structure (Hansen *et al.* 1999; Kochikar 2000; Liebowitz 2000). The results of this study indicate that these smaller firms generally do not directly reward organizational members specifically for participation in knowledge creation activities, but rather for contributions made to firm performance.

P3: In small high-tech start-ups there is a greater reliance on soft versus hard incentives for employee participation in knowledge creation, transfer and use.

The informants made a distinction between *hard* incentives and *soft* incentives. Hard incentives are tangible rewards such as money, plaques, dinner on the town, etc. Soft incentives are less tangible and can include a pat on the back, peer recognition, intrinsic rewards, etc. These firms do not rely on direct hard incentives for employee participation in the knowledge-creating process, but rather on their culture of sharing and mutual trust. Employees are motivated to share by appreciation, public recognition, peer recognition, and the intrinsic satisfaction associated with being a part of the creative processes in the organization. Table 7.3 presents sample quotes of the respondents.

Knowledge codification

Research on managing knowledge in larger organizations indicates the necessity of documenting or writing down organizational knowledge to facilitate dissemination and transfer (Nonaka 1994; Grant 1996a; Hansen *et al.* 1999; Liebowitz 2000). Employees are expected to contribute to knowledge repositories and also to use these repositories. Codification of organizational knowledge improves the efficiency of knowledge transfer and use by allowing the organization to gain scale economies from leveraging the same knowledge multiple times (Nonaka 1994; Grant 1996a; Hansen *et al.* 1999). The data from this study support a relatively low reliance on codification. Facing a real 'crisis' such as rapid decline of performance due to changes in technologies or market can be a trigger for knowledge creation. The firms in the sample *morphed* in response to environmental fluctuations. Flexibility was of the utmost importance and the informants indicated that investing the time to document their knowledge would impede their ability to morph successfully. This, coupled with inadequate financial and temporal resources, has limited the degree of codification present in these firms. Thus, the next proposition:

P4: In small high-tech start-up firms, which tend to require organizational flexibility, exhaustive knowledge codification may be a drawback rather than an advantage.

There appeared to have been no formal attempt to develop an elaborate knowledge accumulation mechanism. This may also be a scale issue. The firms are small enough to rely primarily on face-to-face contact:

> I think it's a scale issue. As you get more people that are doing a job that's sufficiently similar that one person's experience might help the other person, it's more important to write it down. When you're still fairly small, writing it down is good, but since the guy sits next to you, you can just go over and schmooze with him. I can see that you'd be more effective if you didn't have to go over and schmooze, but you always get something else out of schmoozing.

(VP R&D, Mediatrix)

Table 7.3 Incentivizing knowledge management-related activities

Firm	Incentive systems	Sample quotes of respondents
CallMeModem	Hard incentives • Stock options • Team-based bonus • Grants Soft incentives • Product visibility • Peer pressure	(Sr VP and COO) We do bonuses. People either buy into how we do it or they don't. People who are islands of isolation don't do well in our culture and they move on. The engineers see what works and become comfortable with that. Once in a while there are bonuses. We'd rather do a rifle-shot kind of bonus. [Bonuses are] sometimes individual, usually team-based. One motivation is that the kind of software we develop is very visible. A motivation is being able to build products that are seen and used in [retail outlet]. We do bonuses but they're not routine. Employees do have stock options. Grants are generally done tied into some event of success like a product launch. In the bonus pool set-up for that team, not everybody gets same amount. [We] divvy up the pool with some guidance from the lead of the team. Once in a while a lone person gets a bonus. It's rare but it happens. I can't think of one.
ClientBank	Hard incentives • Stock options	(Founder and VP) We incentivize with stock options. We evaluate employees once a year .…. Money is nice, but most want to feel part of something exciting.
E-Consult	Hard incentives • 25% of executive evaluation depends on sales • Group incentive bonus plan ○ 50% based on corporate performance ○ 50% based on individual assessment	Founder and CEO) Incentives in place to encourage sharing. [E-Consult] is a consultant services company, employees are required to share. This is natural to a consultant services company. Our bonus plan is 50% corporate success and 50% individual assessment. If the company fails on a project, we all lose. Therefore, employees are required to share with projects and cross-sharing on projects. For example, if we get a call from the field on installing Oracle database, the employee must provide answers and may have to fly out to the field so the company can succeed on the project. (Sr VP) No, we have bonus structures but those are more based on performance rather than on new idea generation. So other than let's say reaping benefits of having a good idea come to fruition and the company be rewarded and compensated for that and then ultimately from a bonus perspective I can't say there's [incentive for knowledge creation and dissemination].

Continued

Table 7.3 Incentivizing knowledge management-related activities—cont'd

Firm	Incentive systems	Sample quotes of respondents
I-Mage	Hard incentives • Stock options • Bonus system Soft incentives • Recognition at all-hands meeting	(VP Tech) With respect to the reward aspect of it, I think reward is on an ad hoc basis. Everybody at [I-Mage] has some sort of a stock incentive. If [I-Mage] does well, they'll do well, having options they can sell or exercise. Otherwise, projects we have that are going on in the company, on completion of those projects there's typically some kind of a bonus for key contributors. (Mkt Mgr) There was a regular – although not so regular anymore – annual recognition for good deeds done by individuals – ... annual recognition, typically at a midyear kicker. If morale was not so high, engineering typically had an engineering-only kicker, where they gave out stock or bonuses for ideas not only generated but also implemented through, with a concrete result in the delivery of a product. Not only product; we have also had recognition for community service – giving blood, services to the underprivileged, children. You come up with something good, you can usually get it by to get it in. You might not get rewarded, if you pass it along and pass it up, if they think it's good, and doesn't cost too much or saves money, it'll probably get done. We don't do it necessarily for an incentive; we just do it. Sometimes there's a pat on the back.
Mediatrix	Hard incentives • Individual bonus based on team performance • Amazing Mediatrix Award Soft incentives • Appreciation • Peer pressure • Public recognition • Hearing out	(VP R&D) Also it's having an environment where having ideas is rewarded. That means that the management team and the people that own the responsibility to produce – in this case the sales strategy – need to *want* to *hear* the ideas, and when someone has one we don't instantly shut them down and tell them the five things that are the matter with the idea. If we tell them the five things that are *great* with the idea then they'll have another one, but if every time they have one we shut them down and say we're older and wiser, they'll basically stop having *ideas*.... I always have the option of giving a bonus at the quarter, but I don't really want to *buy* ideas, you know? If you think about ideas, you have to have hundreds of them to have four that are really good. So what I want to do is not say I'm going to give $5,000 if they have a hot idea. You want to create an environment where, as you would say, the soft reward is just built into the culture and then the ideas are happening; if somebody in that environment then has an extremely compelling idea then certainly we have ways of rewarding that. But we're not trying to buy ideas .... At the end of the day – people like money – *I like money* [laughs] – but the thing that charges our batteries isn't so much money as recognition and appreciation. So to create an environment where recognition and appreciation – you get the idea. I was probably just saying the same thing.

The codification that was available at both CallMeModem and ClientBank was primarily limited to software design and development – code changes, bug tracking, version control, etc. At E-Consult there were two databases, one available only to management and the other to all employees. The employee database does not contain what the consultants need to perform their jobs out in the field; as a result, they seldom use it. I-Mage has a corporate intranet with a wealth of documentation. However, according to the informants, employees seldom access the information. Mediatrix also has an intranet with a web page for each functional area containing information related to corporate strategies, new products, etc. However, there were no attempts to document knowledge gained. According to the informants, to obtain information most employees prefer face-to-face contact rather than accessing electronic sources.

According to Barney (1991), there are four empirical indicators of the potential for firm resources to generate sustained competitive advantage: value, rareness, imitability and substitutability. Codification of knowledge and its simplification increase the likelihood of imitation, thus reducing the rents that can be generated from organizational knowledge (Grant 1991; Kogut and Zander 1992). The high rate of turnover at both the executive and non-executive levels is a major problem faced by the firms in the sample relative to managing their intellectual capital. In such an environment, knowledge codification increases the likelihood of imitation. CallMeModem, ClientBank and Mediatrix have attempted to create a situation where KM takes place through person-to-person contact using the integration and socialization mechanisms described in a previous section.

External organizational linkages

The results of this study show that effective knowledge processes require the establishment of multiple links with the environment. The data revealed that the respondents had purposefully created tight links with external organizations, primarily customers, suppliers/vendors and competitors. These links served multiple functions such as sources of new knowledge, ways to validate new ideas, and sources of new talent.

P5: In small high-tech start-up firms, external organizational linkages are critical to the KM process.

By far the most important external linkage is contact with customers. Mediatrix has scheduled quarterly meetings with its customers. ClientBank has scheduled weekly meetings with its clients. Engineers at CallMeModem have regularly scheduled meetings with engineers from OEMs who are their primary customers. At I-Mage, there is frequent contact with OEM customers, but meetings do not take place on a regular schedule. At E-Consult, it was not apparent that these types of meetings occurred.

The primary goal of these meetings is to develop a deep understanding of the customers and their needs. Based on the conversations, organizational members can develop new products or services to meet needs that customers are not yet aware they have. The following quote from one of the respondents is illustrative of the value of such scheduled customer contacts:

> We frequently send architects out to talk to customers … that is a nice oppor-tunity to actually have the customer talk to you about what their business is and what they are trying to accomplish, not just 'Does your product have this feature?'…. If you can train your folks to have this conversation, it can be a very interesting way to be able to get a much better handle on how the prod-uct is going to be used and what people are really trying to accomplish with it ….And if you understand your technology then you can say, 'I could solve this customer's problem … I'll go by a few of them [customers] and see if they would be interested if I built it.'
>
> (VP R&D, Mediatrix)

An important function played by these external linkages is idea validation, or what Nonaka (1994) refers to as justification, 'the process of final convergence and screening, which determines the extent to which the knowledge created within the organization is truly worthwhile for the organization and society' (p. 26). The following quotes illustrate the importance of idea validation using external organizational links:

> Actually my original idea changed – my original vision changed – to a related area. After we got together and started to work on it we decided we weren't far enough ahead of the market. We decided to move the product farther to the right. The market's here and you've got to lead the market so by the time you've got a product ready you're not too far ahead and not too far behind. So we moved the project up. So the technology is a little more advanced than we originally planned. That came about by this process of the team getting together, going out and socializing the idea with people in the business, venture capitalists, other companies, a couple of other start-ups in the same position we're in. We shared ideas. You don't want to share your secrets, but you kind of want them to be endorsed – if you're way out on a limb, you want to know how far out you are.
>
> (Pres and CEO, Mediatrix)

External linkages proved critical also in terms of employee selection and retention. According to one of the respondents:

> The people we can't live without, we handpicked from [the founder's prior employer]. The people we've hired through a headhunter or recruiter, 75 percent don't work out and about 25 percent work out. People who know the culture. You hire the wrong element and the culture changes. We imported the right kind of culture into ClientBank.
>
> (Founder and VP, ClientBank)

Effectiveness measures of knowledge processes

The effectiveness of the knowledge processes in place in these firms was measured based on specific outcomes provided by the informants (see Table 7.4). It was difficult for the respondents to establish a direct cause–effect relationship between the knowledge processes in place and their firms' financial performance; however, they were able to identify specific outcomes attributable to the knowledge processes present (or absent) in each of their respective firms.

At CallMeModem, their speed in getting new products to the market was credited directly to the virtual engineering teams. In addition, CallMeModem engineers meet regularly with OEM engineers. This close relationship with their customers has produced competencies in partnering with OEMs. The firm is moving into wireless technology and is utilizing this competency to develop partnerships with the OEMs in this new space. This close relationship has also resulted in multiple product enhancements and innovations. The informants at CallMeModem also ascribed the firm's open culture to frequent meetings, brainstorming sessions, etc., which increase cross-pollination among the engineers. This fostered an environment of mutual trust that facilitates the sharing of code modules across teams and across products instead of reinventing the code. This has contributed to speed to market and given CallMeModem an advantage over its competitors.

At the time of data collection, ClientBank was working on a standard data model and a standard reports catalog. Both were expected to result in increased speed of product implementation, increased customer responsiveness, and increased efficiency through improvements in the sales process. Also, as a result of these documents, the learning time for consultants will be cut down since these documents would serve as mechanisms to transfer product implementation knowledge to new consultants.

Mediatrix attributes to its knowledge processes its competency in technological innovation resulting in product innovation and enhancements. They were also able to identify a new competitive space based on the core competencies of members of the founding team, identify new markets for their current products based on close linkages with their customers, and develop new competencies to compete in an ever-changing market based on the activities of corporate architects and a new product team.

At E-Consult, the firm was able to identify a new competitive space and develop new products/services during what it called the Y2K era. However, the firm was going through a morph at the time of data collection and as a result did not have any identifiable knowledge process in place.

In the case of I-Mage the outcomes were negative. In a story told by one of the informants, the CEO and the board failed to support the recommendations of the ideation team the CEO had created and given the charge to come up with a new space within which the company could compete. The team identified two new spaces within which the firm could compete and obtained a proposal from a beta client for one of those products. The lack of leadership support was demonstrated in the CEO not taking any action on the proposal. In addition, at I-Mage, the lack of coordination between organizational units has created inefficiencies such as needing to repair a bug 30 times due to 30 different code bases for the same product.

Table 7.4 Actual and expected outcomes of knowledge processes

Firm	Outcomes	Sample quotes of respondents

CallMeModem	• First mover advantages
	• Speed to market
	• Increased ability to morph
	• New competitive space
	  – wireless technology
	  (cell phone OEMs)
	• New products –
	  telemedicine
	
	• New product functionality
	• Procedural integration
	  (engineers)
	• Greater trust for sharing
	• Open culture
		(VP R&D) It was a matter of showing people what had been done, pieces that could be reused. That's key, because it's a holy grail of software – object-oriented language, reusable software. It's kind of like KM. It's much talked about, but not very many companies reuse code. We did it. People felt comfortable to trust and share what they wrote. Programming is a creative art – it's not the rote thing that you can just toss off. People who are good at it don't like to give it way. We knock down those barriers. All of our products have reusable modules in them and that's a big plus.
		
		(SrVP and COO) Idea evaluation proceeds in real time in a team implementation. The virtual engineering team dynamics that have made it work are the key to success of getting our products out. A customer walks in the door and says, 'I need this ark, so many cubits high by so many cubits wide by so many cubits long,' and we can get on it fast.

ClientBank	• Greater employee retention
	• New competitive space
	  for current product/service
	• New product functionality
	• Increased efficiency through
	  process improvement
	  ○ Standard data model
	  ○ Standard reports catalog
	• Customer responsiveness
		(Prod. Mgr) The standard data model is actually a very important document. We were in prototype mode for a while, since January, reconditioning our company and developing new functionality in the e-commerce phase. We were in shoot-from-the-hip mode. Now we need to look like we're a real company, where we can document what we're doing. Another important document is our standard reports catalog – the reports that come out of our system – we're defining what those are. The data model and the catalog will be works-in-progress for a while, but we'll at least get something that's beneficial for our new customers – not perfect, but it'll help implement quicker and answer quite a few of the questions that people have, and maybe help in the sales process. We can say to them,

	• Customer tracking • Speed – product implementation	Look: This is our standard report model; this is what you'll be getting. Selling to somebody, we're asking them for maybe $100,000 and they want to see something. The idea behind it is not only to document what we do but also to make the process easier to implement, from the time they buy to the time they use it — this could be a competitive advantage for us.
E-Consult	• New competitive space • New product/service • New product functionality	(Founder and CEO) Had intensive meetings with the board of directors and corporate offices. We knew what the market place is buying and we knew we were doing too much and we needed to niche. This brought about the new direction and vision.
		(Founder and CEO) During the Y2K era we created internal procedures to manage the Y2K efforts that worked very well for E-Consult. The employees that developed the system suggested we turn it into a product and create licenses. Therefore, we created a software product for our clients and for the market.
I-Mage	• Product innovation • Product modifications • New business development (proposed) • Inefficiencies due to lack of coordination between organizational units • Failed ideation process • Low levels of trust	(Mkt Mgr) We started up a whole group team of 7–8–10 people to look at new business, high-growth markets. We took our best thinkers, put them in a room, weeks on end, hours per day, a think-tank to come up with the next great thing. We did this. In fact, our first efforts after you talked with [VP], to share ideas and break out of the box, have failed miserably here. We've looked at storage, new high-growth areas. We haven't been able to convince the CEO and enough executives that it's the right direction. It's only partially funded – it's funded for research but not for R&D and not for marketing.
		(Mkt Mgr) Because a tech product got finished on a custom basis, it became a custom technology, which is not easily replicated. We did fix that problem but till about two and a half years ago, if you found a bug, you had 30–35 different code bases – same code but all different, so you fixed it 35 times.

Continued

Table 7.4 Actual and expected outcomes of knowledge processes—cont'd

Firm	Outcomes	Sample quotes of respondents
Mediatrix	• Technological innovation • New competitive space for current products • Product innovation – mediation software • Product enhancements • Marketing innovation • New competencies for new space	(VP R&D) We took a decision that as an overall business we needed to have something that was totally new. We then put good people onto that, which basically is an investment decision, and we give them the freedom to have *time* to have ideas. And you have no idea how long it's going to take – they've been working on it a couple of months. I'm expecting that sometime in the next six months they'll come up with something that's exciting enough that we'll want to go to market with it. Not that they'll *have* it, but they'll have thought lots of interesting things and thrown most of them away and have come down to a few ideas that they think have really good potential, okay, and then, at the [CEO] level, the VPs and the president will get together and we'll kind of pick the one we want to run with. We may sign up for more investment to cause that to come into existence. That would be the totally new thing. (Pres and CEO) But we sort of started with the core competencies of the people who built that [the initial software] and found another market for related software. What could we do? What are we able to do with our skill set? Now, where is a market around here that takes advantage of that skill set and the time we have to do it, and the money we have? Let's build something for that. Somewhat by accident and somewhat by design we came across the TMN market. The reason why it was by design was that the earlier software had some overlap with what TMN was. OSI 7-layer protocol layers that allow communications. IT is part of that; we had strengths in that.

Conclusions, limitations and directions for future research

This study has examined KM processes in entrepreneurial start-up firms in the high-technology sector. The findings indicate that successful small firms manage knowledge deliberately but via informal and less structured means than advocated in the KM literature. Some researchers have criticized the overemphasis of KM literature on information processing to the exclusion of the people who actually possess the knowledge (Scarbrough 1998; Alvesson *et al.* 2002). Scarbrough's (1998) review of KM literature found little attention being paid to the human element and an overemphasis of information technology and information systems on creating networks that link geographically dispersed individuals together. Swan *et al.* (1999) argue that the information-processing view of KM has been limiting and should be balanced by an approach that places greater emphasis on localized communities of practice and social networking. The practice of KM in these entrepreneurial start-up firms does not seem to place a great emphasis on IT and IS tools per se, even though the firms in the sample are in the high-technology sector. Rather, they have emphasized such 'localized communities of practice' connected by various integration and socialization mechanisms.

Knowledge is managed in many smaller high-tech firms, but most of them look at their options and deliberately remain opportunistic. The interviewees are well aware of the potential problems of limited knowledge management. They know, for instance, that they are ready for only certain kinds of sudden shifts. They know that tacit knowledge leaves the organization as turnover occurs. They know that reinventing something takes more time than retrieving it. They also know, however, that a great deal of knowledge is not reusable, especially in the turbulent software industry, and that managing a selection and storage process takes resources most of which are beyond their present reach. A CallMeModem sales interviewee said, 'I've worked in companies where there were more formal processes. But we're a small company .... It takes a day to figure out the smart way to save a day.' Organizational slack typically precedes formalization of knowledge management structures. Small firms do not enjoy the luxury of this slack. Successful small firms do, however, manage their knowledge using less formal structures as effectively as limited time and personnel will permit.

Knowledge management in its many forms is a subset of the larger construct of overall effective management. Some have argued that KM is not really new, but rather has been part of the conversations of organization and communication theorists (Swan *et al.* 1999; Zorn and May 2002). Perhaps the management of intellectual capital boils down to the effective implementation of good management practices enabled by advances in information technology as demonstrated by the firms in this sample. One wonders whether or not knowledge can really be managed. Perhaps knowledge cannot be managed per se, but can be enabled (Von Krough *et al.* 2000). Perhaps what the firms in the sample have done is engender innovativeness in their organizations by creating an organizational context with knowledge enablers – intense, frequent, purposeful contact with customers, suppliers, across functions, across levels, where ideas can germinate, percolate, develop, be evaluated, and eventually be turned into a product or service or process that can meet a customer's need. This was demonstrated in several of the narratives of new product/service ideas.

This exploratory study has developed some propositions that can be further examined and tested. Future studies will be needed to test these propositions to see whether or not they hold in a larger sample of small entrepreneurial firms. Additional in-depth studies of KM in small entrepreneurial firms can further increase understanding of the organizational processes through which knowledge is integrated. One of the limitations of this study is the small sample size necessitated by the qualitative nature of the research methodology (Yin 1984; Miles and Huberman 1994). The results of the study have to be viewed in light of the limitations and strengths inherent in research of this nature. Future studies can utilize a larger sample of entrepreneurial firms using more quantitative research methodologies to see whether or not the results of this study are generalizable. Studies that evaluate the effectiveness of KM in general would also add to this emerging field. Although it may be difficult to place financial value on KM processes, it is imperative that measures of organizational outcomes attributable to these processes are developed. The field is in the nascent stage and there is a need to develop a better understanding of what happens in organizations in terms of KM processes through closer observations.

References

Alvesson, M., Karreman, D. and Swan, J. (2002) Departures from knowledge and/or management in knowledge management. *Management Communication Quarterly*, 16(2): 282–91.

Barney, J. (1991) Firm resources and sustained competitive advantage. *Journal of Management*, 17(1): 99–120.

Davenport, T. (1997) Think tank: making the most of an information-rich environment. *CIO*, 10(17): 34 and 36.

Davenport, T. H. and Prusak, L. (1998) *Working Knowledge: How Organizations Manage What They Know*. Boston: Harvard Business School Press.

Drucker, P. F. (1998) The coming of the new organization. In *Harvard Business Review on Knowledge Management*. Boston: Harvard Business School Press.

Edstrom, A. and Galbraith, J. R. (1977) Transfer of managers as a coordination and control strategy in multinational organizations. *Administrative Science Quarterly*, 22: 248–63.

Eisenhardt, K. M. (1989) Building theories from case study research. *Academy of Management Review*, 14(4): 532–50.

Grant, R. M. (1991) The resource-based theory of competitive advantage: implications for strategy formulation. *California Management Review*, Spring: 114–35.

Grant, R. (1996a) Toward a knowledge-based theory of the firm. *Strategic Management Journal*, 17 (Winter Special Issue): 109–22.

Grant, R. (1996b) Prospering in dynamically-competitive environments: organizational capability as knowledge integration. *Organizational Science*, 7(4): 375–87.

Gupta, A. K. and Govindarajan, V. (2000) Knowledge flows within multinational corporations. *Strategic Management Journal*, 21: 473–96.

Hansen, M. T., Nohria, H. and Tierney, T. (1999) What's your strategy for managing knowledge? *Harvard Business Review*, March–April: 106–16.

Hoopes, D. G. and Postrel, S. (1999) Shared knowledge, 'glitches', and product development performance. *Strategic Management Journal*, 20: 837–65.

Kochikar, V. P. (2000) Personal interview.

Kogut, B. and Zander, U. (1992) Knowledge of the firm, combinative capabilities and the replication of technology. *Organizational Science*, 3(3): 383–97.

Kogut, B. and Zander, U. (1993) Knowledge of the firm and the evolutionary theory of the multinational corporation. *Journal of International Business Studies*, 4th Quarter: 625–45.

Liebowitz, J. (2000) *Building Organizational Intelligence: A Knowledge Management Primer.* Boca Raton, FL: CRC Press.

Miles, M. B. and Huberman, A. M. (1994) *Qualitative Data Analysis,* 2nd ed. Thousand Oaks, CA: Sage.

Nonaka, I. (1994) A dynamic theory of organizational knowledge creation. *Organizational Science,* 5(1): 14–37.

Nonaka, I. (1998) The knowledge creating company. In *Harvard Business Review on Knowledge Management*. Boston: Harvard Business School Press.

Pfeffer, J. and Sutton, R. I. (2000) *The Knowing-Doing Gap*. Boston: Harvard Business School Press.

Scarbrough, H. (1998) Path(ological) dependency? Core competence from an organizational perspective. *British Journal of Management*, 12: 3–12.

Simonin, B. L. (1999) Ambiguity and the process of knowledge transfer in strategic alliance. *Strategic Management Journal*, 20: 595–623.

Spender, J. C. and Grant, R. M. (1996) Knowledge and the firm: overview. *Strategic Management Journal*, 17 (Winter Special Issue): 5–9.

Strauss, A. and Corbin, J. (1990) *Basics of Qualitative Research: Grounded Theory Procedures and Techniques*. Newbury Park, CA: Sage.

Swan, J., Newell, S., Scarbrough, H. and Hislop, D. (1999) Knowledge management and innovation: networks and networking. *Journal of Knowledge Management*, 3(4): 262–75.

Von Krough, G., Ichijo, K. and Nonaka, I. (2000) *Enabling Knowledge Creation*. New York: Oxford University Press.

Yin, R. K. (1984) *Case Study Research: Design and Methods*. Beverly Hills, CA: Sage.

Zorn, T. E. and May, S. K. (2002) Forum: Knowledge management and/as organizational communication. *Management Communication Quarterly*, 16(2): 237–41.

Appendix A: Working definitions

Knowledge: 'A fluid mix of framed experience, values, contextual information, and expert insight that provides a framework for evaluating and incorporating new experiences and information. It originates and is applied in the minds of knowers. In organizations, it often becomes embedded not only in documents or repositories but also in organizational routines, processes, practices, and norms.' (Davenport and Prusak 1998: 5).

Knowledge management: Tapping the tacit knowledge of organization members making it available to organization members, and leveraging it for competitive advantage (Nonaka 1998).

Organizational intelligence: 'An organization's capability to process, interpret, encode, manipulate and access information in a purposeful, goal directed way so it can increase its adaptive potential in the environment in which it operates'. (Liebowitz 2000:11)

Learning organization: 'An organization that has an enhanced capacity to learn, adapt, and change.' (Gephart 1996 in Liebowitz 2000: 31)

'An organization in which learning processes are analyzed, monitored, developed, managed and aligned with improvement and innovation goals.' (Liebowitz 2000: 31)

Appendix B: Sample interview questions

Knowledge creation

- What is the vision of [firm name]? How is it communicated to other members of the organization?
- (Often an interviewee was a founder of the firm.) What was the source of the idea that led to or drove the founding? Is there a story?
- What are the current sources of new ideas?
- Where do people go to obtain new knowledge?
- Do you have a story about the generation of an idea?
- How many ideas generated are internal versus external?
- Does the organization have a mechanism for idea generation?
- What incentives do organizational members have to generate and share new knowledge? Are the reward systems supportive of knowledge creation and dissemination?

Capturing/Transferring knowledge

- How do you/How do members of the company know what the company knows?
- Do you have knowledge dissemination mechanisms? These could range all the way from Lotus Notes exchanges to water-cooler conversations or regular what-if brainstorming sessions.
- How does the company know what it knows? How does it identify crucial gaps in what it knows?
- Does the company have a formal knowledge management process?

Knowledge use

- How does the company exploit its intellectual capital for competitive advantage?
- Do you have a story or example?
- Are there examples where someone has been able to identify a piece of knowledge, whether tacit or explicit, and carry it all the way to product development? How was this done?
- How have you continued idea generation?

Appendix C: Glossary of 'in vivo' terms

The respondents used the following possibly unfamiliar terms as they spoke with us:

- *Context* – an understood set of ideas that enriches or gives additional meaning to a single idea or behavior existing within the set.
- *Incentivize* – to motivate employees to perform a desired behavior by providing rewards.
- *Morph* – to change shape in order to compete more successfully.
- *Populate* – to fill a construct with specific examples.
- *Space* – a market or market niche in which a business competes.

8 Investment decision-making in small manufacturing firms

A learning approach

Ignatius Ekanem and David Smallbone

Introduction

This chapter is concerned with how investment decisions are made in small manufacturing enterprises, adopting a learning approach as the most appropriate framework for analysing this behaviour. Although there has been a growing recognition of the role of organisational learning in the survival and growth of small firms, there are few empirical studies that demonstrate the link between learning and organisational effectiveness. This research explores the learning process of owner-managers in relation to their investment decision-making behaviour.

Investment is one of the keys to the success of any business organisation, contributing to competitiveness through its potential influence on innovation, productivity and quality (Storey *et al.* 1989), as well as through cost reduction and new product development (Smallbone *et al.* 1995). An understanding of investment decision-making processes in small firms requires an understanding of the motivations of owner-managers and the barriers they face. Previous authors have warned against methodological approaches that attempt to reduce the complexities of everyday life to simplistic 'mathematical' concepts, making them of limited relevance to understanding the actual behaviour of small firms (Jarvis *et al.* 1996).

In this context, the more specific aims of the chapter are to:

- identify the learning process of owner-managers in relation to investment decision-making;
- show how organisational learning provides an appropriate interpretative frame of reference for investment behaviour in small firms; and
- assess the merits of a learning-based approach, compared with alternative frameworks.

Following a review of previous literature and description of the methodology employed in the study, empirical evidence from eight case studies is analysed in a learning framework. Although the study as a whole investigates a range of types of investment decision, this chapter focuses on equipment purchases. The final section summarises the main themes emerging from the analysis, reflecting on the merits of the learning-based approach utilised in the study.

The literature context

A review of existing literature relevant to an understanding of investment decision-making in small firms suggests a division into two types of approach. The first type is essentially neo-classical in that it is based, implicitly or explicitly, on a set of normative, economic rationality assumptions. The second group may be characterised as behavioural or organisational, focusing on what firms actually do rather than what they ought to do, with some studies incorporating organisational perspectives including the influence of firm characteristics, such as size. It must be emphasised that not all of the literature considered relevant to this study is necessarily concerned with investment decision-making per se, but rather with financial management practices more generally.

Neo-classical perspectives

Neo-classical theory of the firm assumes that the objective of the firm is to maximise profits, operating within a perfectly competitive market (Allen 1957). In this tradition, much of the mainstream financial management literature advocates the use of discounted cash flow techniques, the payback method, or the accounting rate of return method (e.g. Lumby 1994; Brien 1997; Thomas 2001). These approaches assume that there are capital projects to be appraised; that cash flows from projects aim to maximise owners' wealth; that management always act in the owners' best interest; that the future cash flow can be isolated/estimated; and that cash flows are discounted at the opportunity cost of capital. However, this type of literature hardly deals with how projects are generated and why projects are considered. The main inadequacy of this type of approach from the standpoint of this study is that it is explicitly normative, focusing on what firms should do, based on assumptions of profit maximisation and perfect knowledge. The treatment of uncertainty is also at variance with the way in which firms typically react to it in practice.

Behavioural/organisational perspectives

The behavioural theory of the firm focuses on decision-making processes, suggesting that the investment decisions of small firms may be guided by the objectives and behaviour of stakeholders. In this context, it has been suggested that decisions are influenced by factors such as how the workforce will cope with the resultant change, whether there is sufficient business to meet the new capacity, and the reliability of the equipment and its life span (Brophy and Shulman 1993), rather than engaging in complex appraisal methods. Behavioural and organisational perspectives emphasise that, in reality, information is far from perfect, with decision-makers possessing varying abilities and a range of motives. At the same time, this raises the question of how, in the absence of formalised methods, decisions are actually made. The central proposition of this chapter is that decision-making is based on knowledge acquired through experience, whilst being influenced by key stakeholders. As a consequence, relevant learning literature is briefly reviewed below.

Organisational learning perspectives

Although there is no single view as to what precisely constitutes learning, Gibb (1997: 15) suggests that it is 'the human processes by which skills, knowledge, habits and attitudes are acquired and altered in such a way that behaviour is modified'. Learning involves the acquisition, storage and interpretation of knowledge previously generated by others (Spender 1996a). Polanyi (1967), Spender (1996b), Grant (1996) and Leonard and Sensiper (1998) distinguish between tacit or implicit knowledge, which is not codified, and explicit, formal knowledge, which is codified. While Polanyi (1967) addressed tacit knowledge at an individual level, Nelson and Winter (1982) suggested it exists in group settings, embedded in organisational routines that no single person may understand completely. Organisations and firms evolve by adapting the body of knowledge shared by members, with much of the process taking place at the tacit level (Spender 1996a).

It may be argued that there is an organisational dimension to learning, even in the smallest company, because of the role of stakeholders (Wyer *et al.* 2000). In the absence of dominant power in the market-place, the owner-managed firm attempts to reduce the risk associated with uncertainty by building personal relationships of trust and confidence with its key stakeholders such as with customers, trade/equipment suppliers, funds providers and employees. It has been suggested that the small firm's ability to survive is a function of its ability to learn from these stakeholders, to build trust and interdependence with them, to use them to scan the wider business environment and to define, meet and bring forward their future needs (Gibb 1997).

It has been suggested that organisational learning is one of the neglected areas of small firm research (Chaston *et al.* 2001), which means that our knowledge and understanding of the interaction of learning and the entrepreneurship process is limited (Deakins 1998). In seeking to explain how small firms learn, Wyer *et al.* (2000) draw on Kelly's personal construct theory and contemporary learning theories, to demonstrate how strategic-level learning by owner-managers requires the building-up and constant changing of personal constructs and thus the capability and disposition to 'elaborate construct systems'.

Argyris and Schön (1978) offer a corresponding conceptualisation by considering Kelly's (1955) theory in terms of single- and double-loop learning. If change situations impact on a small firm owner-manager, he or she will use their existing personal constructs to cope with the change. On many occasions minor adjustments may enable the owner-manager to deal with the change, simply because a similar situation has been faced and dealt with in the past. This can be characterised as 'simple' (Stacey 1996) or single-loop learning, which takes place when the owner-manager has confirmed the validity of his or her current constructs by using them to make sense of a new situation.

However, sometimes change situations arise for which existing constructs are inadequate, requiring them to be extended through a process that involves questioning the underlying assumptions upon which the existing constructs are based. This is referred to as complex (Stacey 1996) or closed-loop learning, requiring change in the owner-manager's construct system. Innovative managers, for example, must regularly shift, break and create new paradigms of thinking for themselves (their personal construct), involving what is described as double-loop learning.

Organisational learning in small firms may often be unintentional, incidental or accidental, generating knowledge mainly from 'trial-and-error' decision-making processes, which may be appropriate in small firms under conditions of uncertainty (Matlay 2000). It is also a process that typically involves learning from peers; learning by doing; learning from feedback from customers; by copying; problem solving; opportunity taking; and also by learning from mistakes (Gibb 1997). Moreover, it may be viewed as a reflexive process, which co-creates the reality in which firms operate because they are affected not just by changes in the environment, but by their way of construing it (Hawkins 1995). It is also an adaptive process, emphasising that business owners continue with a course of action if the associated outcomes are positive or change their course of action if the associated outcomes are negative.

Since the study described below is concerned with real-world decision-making, it is grounded in behavioural theories of the firm, rather than being neo-classical. However, since the aim is to go beyond describing how decisions are made to better understand the factors shaping them, organisational learning literature is utilised and assessed as a basis for achieving additional insights. By applying organisational learning approaches to investment decision-making in small firms, the chapter contributes to an understanding of how knowledge is acquired and transferred by owner/managers, including what is learned, who it is learned from, and in what circumstances. In this regard, the chapter is part of a small but growing literature concerned with organisational learning in small firms.

Methodology and characteristics of case study companies

It is widely acknowledged that there is a need for grounded data collection in the study of entrepreneurship (Stockport and Kakabadse 1992), which has been reflected in a rapid growth in the use of qualitative methodologies over the past decade. Since the aim of the study on which this chapter is based was to gain insights into the processes of investment decision-making, a qualitative methodology was judged to be the most appropriate. Within this paradigm, an approach known as 'insider accounts' was selected, involving detailed accounts of the actions of owner-managers (Hammersley and Atkinson 1995), which enabled the behaviour and actions of owner-managers to be observed as they occurred (Shaw 1999). The selected method is compatible with the aim of seeking to add to existing understanding of the processes of decision-making by capturing the 'full range of data nuances and conditionality' when decisions were actually being made (Mason and Rogers 1997: 31).

The application of 'insider accounts' involved in-depth, semi-structured inter-views, supported by some direct observation, conducted longitudinally in eight case study companies. These firms were purposively selected from two contrast-ing sectors. A combination of printing and clothing firms was included, because of their contrasting technology bases, with considerable difference in the required investment levels. The philosophy underpinning 'insider accounts' is that the 'objects' studied are in fact 'subjects' and they themselves should produce accounts of their world. Therefore, 'insider accounts' can provide a basis for understanding the behaviour of small firms and the motivation of owner-managers, thus helping to answer basic questions relating to process. An important feature of the approach is its capacity to elicit descriptions, explanations and eval-uations of every aspect of owner-managers' actions. Thus, 'insider accounts' generate owner-manager's knowledge which can be tapped and treated as the basis of an alternative conception of appropriate techniques for smaller businesses.

The data collection was conducted longitudinally, with owner-managers being interviewed and observed three times over a period of 18 months, to build up case material on each company. The first interviews were semi-structured and exploratory in nature, focusing on 'sensitising propositions', generated through a combination of literature review and a brainstorming exercise (Jarvis *et al.* 1996). They established the initial boundaries of the research, as well as providing details of the owner-managers' background and personal biographies such as age, educa-tion, training and experience. They also included a summary of the development of the business to date, the owner-manager's definition of their business objec-tives and attitude to growth, and in particular the progress, plans and problems of the business.

The second and third interviews were more in-depth, focusing on investment decision-making, sources of investment finance and the difficulties faced in rais-ing such finance, investment appraisal techniques, and factors affecting choice of techniques. Although owner-managers were the prime focus of attention, other key informants such as key employees, business advisors and equipment suppliers were also interviewed. This helped in checking any conflicting evidence (Stockport and Kakabadse 1992). The interviews were allowed to flow as conver-sations with questions designed to elicit free-flowing narratives (Jarvis *et al.* 1996) around the topic of investment decision-making. Respondents were allowed free-dom in their responses and were encouraged to elaborate on their comments through the use of non-directive probes. The aim was to facilitate a conversation, giving the interviewee a good deal of leeway to talk in their own terms (Spence and Rutherfoord 2001), so as to understand how owner-managers learn within a wider context of business and personal growth (Cope and Watts 2000).

Apart from asking questions about their investment behaviour and on what was specifically learned from other stakeholders in the business, the researcher watched, listened and learned during the time spent in companies (Holliday 1992), which averaged about two hours per visit. This direct observation made it possible to observe the decision-making behaviour of owner-managers with respect to any particular investment. The interviews were spread over a period of 18 months between 1998 and 1999. Observations were limited to what the researcher could see when present at interviews, carried out through 'interrupted involvement' of the interviewee (Easterby-Smith *et al.* 1991: 100). Sometimes, the interviewee would break out to deal with other work, which enabled the researcher to observe working practices. Thus, observation allowed access to what owner-managers actually did in relation to what they said they did in the interview or what the theory and literature have suggested (Holliday 1992). For example, the owner-manager of Company 1 claimed that he does not liaise with anyone with respect to investment decisions, but was observed to liaise frequently with others such as the equipment supplier, a co-director, the production manager and peers, with evidence that their opinions were taken into consideration in making the final decision.

Profile of case study companies

The case study firms consist of eight limited companies, half in the printing and half in the clothing sector (as shown in Table 8.1). The oldest firm (printing firm) was established in 1924 and the youngest (clothing firm) in 1993. The smallest firm had six employees and a turnover of £0.5 million; the largest company had 50 employees and a turnover of £10 million. The frequency of purchase of equipment varied considerably. Two companies purchase equipment annually on average, two companies every two years, another two every three to four years, while the other two companies purchase equipment every five years, on average.

Empirical evidence of investment decision-making

Analysis of previous literature, together with data gathered in the initial interviews with owner-managers, suggests that investment decisions involve three main elements: the identification of the need to invest; evaluation of alternative choices; and the actual choice of alternatives. Although, in practice, the three elements are not necessarily separately identifiable, or sequential, the framework provides a convenient method of summarising the main empirical findings.

Identification of needs

An economically rational approach to decision-making suggests that the identification of a need to invest, for example, in a new piece of production equipment would be part of a rational planning process involving cost-benefit assessment. In practice, investment needs in the eight case study companies were identified mainly through the experience that owner-managers brought to the decision-making process. For example, the owner-manager of Company 4 stated:

> You weigh up the pros and cons. Again, it is experience. You have to follow what's going on, what equipment does what. We are guided by experience ...

Table 8.1 Summary profile of sample companies

Company	Sector	Year started	Legal status	Number of staff	Turnover	Capital expenditure	Frequency of purchase	Investment behaviour
1	Printing	1982	Limited	35	£3m	£2m	Yearly; £2m in last 2 years	Use gut-feeling Attend demonstrations Seek advice from equipment suppliers Inspect equipment in a working environment Seek opinion of a machine operator Seek opinion of finance companies Talk to other people in the industry Discussion with staff Feedback from customers
2	Printing	1966	Limited	20	£2m	£0.5m	4 to 5 years	Use gut-feeling Attend demonstrations Seek advice from equipment suppliers Inspect equipment in a working environment Seek opinion of a machine operator Seek opinion of finance companies Talk to other people in the industry Discussion with staff Sticking with what is known Feedback from customers
3	Printing	1924	Limited	17	£0.75m	£10k	3 to 5 years; 'depends on market needs'	Use gut-feeling Attend demonstrations Seek advice from equipment suppliers

4	Printing	1991	Limited	6	£0.5m	£40k	'no hard and fast rule, but on average every 2 years'	Inspect equipment in a working environment; Seek opinion of a machine operator; Seek opinion of finance companies; Talk to other people in the industry; Discussion with staff; Feedback from customers
5	Clothing	1982	Limited	50	£10m	£700k	Yearly; 'as and when needed'	Use gut-feeling; Seek advice from equipment suppliers; Sticking with what is known
6	Clothing	1993	Limited	35	£0.7m	£20k	4 to 5 years; £20k in past 2 years.	Use gut-feeling; Seek advice from equipment suppliers; Discussion with staff; Feedback from customers
7	Clothing	1974	Limited	20	£0.5m	£20k	2 to 3 years; £20k in last 2 years	Use gut-feeling; Seek advice from equipment suppliers; Sticking with what is known; Feedback from customers
8	Clothing	1991	Limited	11	£1m	£55k	'tend to be used for ever' £55k in past 2 years.	Use gut-feeling; Seek advice from equipment suppliers; Use gut-feeling; Seek advice from equipment suppliers; Sticking with what is known

In practice, our empirical evidence shows a heavy reliance on past experience of investment decision-making, which involves learning from previous decisions and mistakes (Deakins and Freel 1998). Experience also helps owner-managers to assess emerging market trends, contributing to an appraisal of their current production capacity:

> You look at the work you have already got and see whether you can do it more economically with a new piece of equipment or you have found the market outside is telling you that you haven't got the equipment to do that specific job. How much of it you are sending out and whether you want to get into that market.

(Owner-manager, Company 2)

In a recent purchase of a five-colour press, the owner-manager of Company 2 checked through everything they had done for the past twelve months, worked out the amount and type of work they had undertaken (i.e. from single colour to five colours), and worked out how much work they had subcontracted out and what had been done in-house. It was decided that the firm was better off with a machine with quicker turnout, slightly cheaper price and cheaper plate. As most of their work was between two colours and five colours, the five-colour machine was judged to be the most appropriate.

The estimation of financial needs was based on internally generated benchmarking and informal discussions with co-directors, key employees such as the production managers, and with equipment suppliers. The next stage was the identification of the sources of finance, although if finance is linked to equipment purchase this is not a separate stage. The search for the sources of finance was carried out by the owner-managers or the finance directors. The duration of the search varied from company to company but was generally brief and quick. They approached a number of finance companies (three at least) in order to ensure that the finance house dealt with was user-friendly. The following extract from the interview with the owner-manager of Company 2 gives some insight into the process:

> We approach a number of finance companies just to make sure that the finance house we are dealing with mainly is within reason of everyone else. They are not the cheapest, they are not the dearest, they are somewhere within the middle, and we are happy with them and we have a good relationship with their representative and the directors. They know us and they can trust us and we can talk to them and say that we've got problems, if we've got problems and ask them how to get out of it.

This demonstrates that the owner-managers were not particularly interested in the cheapest finance available, provided that the finance company knew them and their activities and can trust them. This supports the views expressed by the Bank of England (1999), which stressed access rather than the cost of finance as the key issue for small firms. Most of the finance houses were actually owned by equipment suppliers specialising in the industry. The significance of this is that in some cases the finance came as a package with the equipment that was being purchased. Finance providers tended to be those who the owner-managers believed were prepared to understand and empathise with their 'mode of life', and those who were prepared to treat them with respect if they had problems and to help them rather than hinder them. A number of the case study firms appeared to have established trust-based relationships with an equipment supplier over a number of years.

Evaluation of alternatives

Evaluating alternatives typically involved comparing the specifications of the machines under consideration, as well as their resale value and the relationship to their strategic vision for the development of the business, which was typically implicit. This process typically included attending demonstrations of equipment, which provided an opportunity to see the specifications and prices of equipment, as well as talking to other people in the industry and learning from their experience. This is illustrated by the following quotations:

> We attend demonstrations and talk to other people in the industry to know what they have got and what problems they have had.
>
> (Company 2)

> You learn a lot from demonstrations, from the experience of the suppliers. The ability to stand back to see what the machine can do is very important and very useful. ... At demonstrations we take what we consider to be the most difficult job and ask them to do it on the press for me and the operator to see how it works and how the various components work. If it looks okay and does what we consider to be a difficult job easily that goes to prove that it is a good machine.
>
> (Company 3)

> Take, for example, one company I met [at demonstration], they bought a machine for £900,000 over 5 years and it was in the image-setting side of things and basically it became obsolete after the first year.
>
> (Company 1)

These examples emphasise the informal nature of the learning experience for these owner-managers, who nevertheless have an interest in learning from others. Rather than being based on a formal appraisal technique, such as cost-benefit analysis, the choice of equipment is typically based more on an informal assessment of technical reliability, together with its capability in relation to the firm's production requirements. This is mainly because, for a small business owner, equipment must be technically reliable, easy to maintain and capable of producing products appropriate to the needs of its customer base. In other words, an informal approach is appropriate to their needs and encourages flexibility. It appears to be effective, although based on experiential learning rather than something that is formally taught.

Choice of alternatives

The final element of the decision-making process is choosing between alternatives. For non-routine investment decisions, owner-managers typically relied on technical advice from equipment suppliers, key employees and customers, as well as their own judgement.

The role of equipment suppliers

The role of equipment suppliers required some teasing out, since in several cases it emerged by the time of the third interview, although initially denied in some cases by owner-managers. For example, the owner-manager of Company 1 (as well as others) initially denied receiving advice from equipment suppliers, but by the third interview it became apparent that their role was considerable, particularly with respect to digital printing technology, which represented a major step into the unknown for the company. The owner-manager explained:

> They helped tremendously not only by providing us with advice about the CTP but also by providing technical support and training. They will probably continue to offer us the benefit of their experience for a long time. ... The advice and support gave us more confidence when we were going to buy our B2 Xeikon digital press. Our heavy dependence on them (equipment suppliers) has lessened as we now feel more able to cope with the technology ourselves. I now feel more confident to make these decisions myself.
>
> (Company 1)

The owner-manager of Company 1 believes that the advice enabled him to dissect, reflect, learn and act on the critical incident, thus leading to a change in behaviour. The role of the equipment supplier is one of facilitator that enables the owner-manager to change behaviour and attitude, modifying future actions as a result (Sullivan 2000). Overall, the role of equipment suppliers depended on the type of assets. If the assets involved were new technology, then the influence of equipment suppliers was more pronounced than with conventional technology, where greater familiarity with the technology on the part of the owner-manager was associated with less risk and uncertainty.

The role of key employees

Although key employees were involved in all three elements of the investment decision-making process, their role was most prominent at the evaluation stage, when they would attend demonstrations with owner-managers to check out equipment specifications and prices, as well as contributing to a technical assessment. In cases where an owner-manager is away from the 'sharp end' of production, machine operators may have more up-to-date technical knowledge than the owner-manager. This emphasises that investment appraisal did not involve cost-benefit analysis but rather simply appraising whether or not the equipment could do the job that it was supposed to do. In other words, the process was a technical appraisal rather than a financial one.

Behavioural and 'satisficing' approaches to decision-making enable entrepreneurs to learn what works and what does not work based on experience. In this respect, the finding is compatible with the analysis of financial management practices in small firms by Jarvis *et al.* (1996), who argue that, in practice, people often adopt a 'good enough' approach, that is, a decision that meets some minimum set of acceptable standards, determined by shared rules or norms, rather than attempting to achieve some optimal decision. The benchmarking threshold offers a variant on conventional, formal methods of investment decision-making, which assume the objective of simple profit maximisation.

The owner-manager of Company 3 reflected on a previous incident when he bought 'finishing' equipment,[1] which proved difficult to maintain due to a lack of spare parts. He admitted that the operator, who was responsible for using the equipment on a daily basis, had advised him against the purchase at the time, on the grounds that it would be difficult to maintain and may be unreliable. The owner-manager reflected:

> I was pretty heavy-handed in those days, taking decisions without seeking opinions and without listening to advice. In those days anybody who dared disagree with me or has a different opinion to mine was an enemy. For me it was a sign of weakness to consult my workers before making a decision. But now I have to realise that, that boy is much more up-to-date than me in terms of technical knowledge. When it comes to the technical reliability of a piece of kit he is the expert. I know that now and I don't mess him up. I cherish his expertise.
>
> (Company 3)

Whilst the management style of owner-managers often tends to be autocratic and underpinned by a reluctance to delegate decision-making (Burns 1996), in four of the companies (i.e. Companies 1, 2, 3 and 5), key employees were substantially involved in the investment decision-making process. Company 1 provides the best example where separate interviews with the owner-manager and production manager painted a similar picture:

> We [the owner-manager and the production manager] go and see some demos and look at different pieces of kit ... and think, well, will it work for us?
>
> (Owner-Manager, Company 1)

> We [the production manager and the owner-manager] go and look at different pieces of kit and then we say which one will slot in the easiest into the way we work already, and how much time is it going to take us to get us up and running on it and working 100 percent.
>
> (Production Manager, Company 1)

Use of the word 'we' by both the owner-manager and the production manager in the above quotes suggests a form of 'collective understanding' (Wyer and Mason 1998). The extent to which the opinion of the production manager was taken into account was apparent when the owner-manager revealed that a 'major incident' had taken place a few years previously when, contrary to the advice of the production manager, he had purchased a fully computerised Dainippon camera for £18,000, which was subsequently little used. The owner-manager recalled that at that time he had the problem of recognising and trusting the ability of key employees. The result was that the owner-manager not only made a poor investment decision, but the business suffered because of the tension, confusion and the internal conflict that the situation created. The owner-manager reflected on the situation and how he has learned from it:

> I have learned to trust him basically and to recognise that he is a huge asset to the company. I don't ignore him any more. I have come to respect his views and opinions, I have completely changed. ... Now if I want to buy any kit I call him to my office and ask him, 'What is your opinion about this kit? What do you think about this? What do you think about that? Have you considered this? Have you considered that?' And then we come to the conclusion that perhaps we should buy the equipment; that it is a good investment. I have definitely changed my style as far as management and decision-making is concerned.
>
> (Company 1)

It has been suggested that it is the ability to learn from mistakes that makes successful entrepreneurs (Sullivan 2000). Gaps in knowledge/competence have to be recognised and filled because 'what you cannot do yourself others can do, be they employees, partners, networks' (White 1999: 5). There was also evidence of the transfer of learning through team learning or 'collective meaning and understanding' (Wyer *et al.* 2000: 243). For example, the account of the sales manager in Company 2 provides an insight into this type of learning occurring when he referred to 'a weekend away' after Christmas, when the team stayed together in a hotel for the weekend sharing knowledge, ideas and opinions.

The owner-manager of Company 2 recalled the period when he took unilateral decisions, referring to an 'error of judgement' on his part when he 'single-handedly' purchased a two-colour lithographic Heidelberg MOZP (480 × 650 mm) at a cost of £140,000. It nearly sank the company because it became outdated as soon as it was purchased. The five-colour press they later bought was the most suitable for their operation. This realisation totally changed his attitude and perceptions:

> My attitude and perception have now changed. I now include directors in any major decisions and the 'weekend away' provides the opportunity for us to bang our heads together.
>
> (Company 2)

In this instance, team learning had taken place through sharing knowledge, opinions and ideas of how things work in the organisation and its operating environment (Massari *et al.* 1999), as an unconscious, informal process (Marsick and Watkins 1990). Nevertheless, it seems fair to argue that in Companies 1, 2, 3 and 5 there was some degree of collective sharing of knowledge, ideas and meanings. Although decisions may ultimately be made by one person (i.e. the owner-manager), he or she interacts with people within the organisation and collects information. This may involve seeking the views and technical advice of machine operators, even though ultimately they may choose to ignore them and basically make their own decision. However, the concept of 'collective meaning and sharing' was stronger in Companies 1, 2 and 5, which were larger companies than the rest of the case study firms and were also stronger performing firms in terms of sales turnover.

The role of customers

The role of customers in the investment decision-making process was significant both in the printing firms as well as the clothing firms. Two types of customer relationship can be distinguished in the two sectors. First, in the printing sector, it was individual customers having a specific role in the decision-making process. The ability to respond speedily to customer demands in Companies 1 and 2 (both printing firms), who increasingly wanted just-in-time printing, required the acquisition of new technology equipment. This includes direct digital colour and computer-to-plate (CTP) equipment, which was expensive, compared to clothing firms where equipment typically cost much less. To emphasise the role of customers' involvement in the decision-making process, the owner-manager of Company 1 commented that without customers we wouldn't be working and without customers we wouldn't be making money. Therefore, investment enables the firms to respond swiftly to customer demands. There was also investment designed to enable the firm to meet the needs of specific customers (e.g. the order for casual wear which required the use of twin-needle machines in Company 6).

Owner-managers learn from customers as part of a network and use them to scan the wider business environment and to define, meet and bring forward their future needs. For example, Company 5 ascertained the standard of quality of their product, which in turn determined the need for their investment, through a continuous feedback process between the customers and sales team and the rest of the management.

Second, there was subcontract relationship mainly in the cut-make-and-trim (CMT) clothing firms in which subcontracting is a feature of production. The role of customers in the investment decision-making process in clothing firms was mainly in the form of changing requirements of a major customer, affecting long-term bulk contracts, or obtaining orders or contracts from a new customer such as the orders received by Company 6. Although the customer was indeed a 'new market' for this company, there was no indication that investment was driven by a desire to enter a new market but rather a reaction to an opportunity. In other words, this was an application of an existing production process to a new opportunity (Smallbone *et al.* 1997).

Open-and closed-loop learning

Analysis of the empirical evidence suggests that a distinction between open- (or double-) and closed- (or single-) loop learning is useful in relation to how investment decision-making actually occurs in small manufacturing enterprises. Closed-loop learning arises from a situation that is similar to what has been dealt with in the past, while open-loop learning takes place when the situation is distinctively different from that experienced previously. In printing firms, for example, closed-loop learning was most evident when firms were replacing a printing press with another piece of equipment of similar technology. For example, the owner-manager of Company 2 emphasised that he is:

> Heidelberg born and bred. ... I normally buy Heidelberg from Germany because they are the best piece of equipment you can buy, and they hold value. . . . I have been in this trade since I was 11 and my first employer had a Heidelberg machine and I loved it. I have used other pieces of equipment and they are never as good as Heidelberg.

This is analogous to 'single-loop learning' (Argyris and Schön 1978), which applied to routine and immediate tasks or repetitive or 'lower-level learning' (Chaston *et al.* 2001). The quotation also illustrates that satisficing behaviour is occurring, with the owner-manager continuing to deal with an existing supplier as long as he is satisfied with the outcome. He only looks for change when he is faced with a critical event, such as a bad experience. The owner-manager has used Heidelberg presses throughout the time he has been involved in the industry. He is content to continue to buy Heidelberg equipment, because he considers these machines to be sound technically, have good residual value, and his familiarity with them eases maintenance and repair. Since he has found that these machines have worked well in the past, there is an assumption that they will continue to work. The experience here is that he sticks with the supplying company, the salesman and the finance package because it has worked for him so far.

In this context, closed-loop learning may be interpreted as 'expressive rationality', which is associated with notions of judgement and autonomy of owner-managers in pursuing ends considered worthy or valuable, suggesting that owner-managers can be creative individuals whose behaviour is shaped by experience. Closed- (or single-) loop learning appeared more common in the clothing sector than in the printing sector because production equipment was more basic and also more stable with respect to the technology base. In the clothing industry, there was more tendency for owner-managers to stick with what they had known in the past and to learn in a closed-loop situation, compared with the printing industry, where the pace of technological change has been quicker, with greater associated uncertainty for owner-managers.

Open- (or double-) loop learning was evident in the printing industry when existing conventional presses were replaced with digital technology or computer-to-plate (CTP) equipment. This represents a quantum leap for many businesses, taking the owner-manager into an area that he had not experienced before, not simply in terms of production but also in terms of markets and technical problems (Smallbone *et al.* 2000). Open- (or double-) loop learning involves the decision-maker stepping outside his or her existing terms of reference to assimilate knowledge that is potentially transferable to the situation currently faced, drawing on personal experience judged to be relevant and/or the experience and knowledge of others. Burgoyne and Hodgson (1983) describe this learning process as 'gradually eroding one belief and building another with a gradual accumulation of evidence and experience' (p. 398).

This is an interactive learning approach in the sense that owner-managers and key employees were learning from the experiences of each other and from equipment suppliers and peers. Open-loop learning can also be interpreted in the light of the 'procedural rationality' concept (Hargreaves Heap 1989; Jarvis *et al.* 1996). Here, the investment decision-making process was strongly influenced by industry-wide norms, which are shared expectations among those operating in the industry. Such norms provide explanations for behaviour that does not fall within the calculation of costs and benefits of particular causes of action of owner-managers.

Conclusions

The main empirical finding in this study is the key role of experiential learning in relation to investment decision-making in small manufacturing firms. This is reflected in the use of informal routines providing 'satisficing' solutions, which, although not explicitly rational, are boundedly rational, that is, they are rational within the context of owner-managers' perceptions, knowledge and experience.

Although none of the case study firms can be regarded as learning organisations, there was evidence of organisational learning in all of them, since they were learning from past experiences of owner-managers and/or from the experiences of others within their close network. Of particular interest in this regard are those firms where owner-managers admitted learning from mistakes made in the past, as well as those where the choice of equipment and decision-making methods typically make use of tried-and-tested informal routines, based on single-or closed-loop learning.

At the same time, tried-and-tested methods may be inadequate as a basis for effective decision-making, where decision-makers face situations that are outside their previous experience. This is where the willingness and ability of owner-managers to learn can be critical, because of the need for them to seek and be able to absorb appropriate knowledge, as well as the ability of key stakeholders to able to offer it. Whilst this approach shares many of the characteristics conceptualised as open-loop learning, learned procedures of the way these decisions are approached are also in evidence. This has been described as 'procedural rationality' (Hargreave Heap 1989), by which owner-managers are influenced by industry-wide norms and shared expectations, not because such practice is necessarily rational, but because it is considered an accepted practice in the industry, especially when decision-makers are faced with unfamiliar decisions.

By learning from experience, owner-managers were bringing together knowledge, skills, values and attitudes. In practice, they were learning by doing, by problem solving and opportunity taking, as well as learning from mistakes. It was this process of learning by experience that contributes to what respondents themselves often describe as gut-feeling, instinct, reflective thinking and judgement. At the same time, it must be recognised that learning by experience does not always result in positive solutions. It also often involves learning by trial and error, which is an adaptive process that provided the case study firms with an opportunity to evaluate outcomes associated with a course of action before deciding upon a future course of action.

The nature and extent of organisational learning in small firms depends upon the owner-manager's ability and willingness to develop their personal construct systems and change their existing 'mindset'. It can transpire through, for example, reflection and analysis of events that have taken place, which can initiate adjustment to their constructs, although it is more likely to occur, as Arrow (1962) has suggested, as a result of problem-solving activities. Key stakeholders with whom the owner-manager interfaces may also trigger adjustment to the constructs, whereby the owner-manager's perspective of a given situation is challenged by the stakeholder, offering the benefit of their experiences. If the individual is able to reflect and adjust in the light of the new insight, then the development and incorporation of new constructs takes place (Wyer *et al.* 2000). In this context, the potential for adopting an organisational learning perspective to enhance the understanding of how small businesses survive and develop appears high, although the empirical evidence available to demonstrate this hitherto is limited.

One of the issues raised by applying organisational learning perspectives to small firms concerns the relationship between individual learning by the owner-manager and learning by the organisation. Since all cases in this study involved owner-managers who were both main owners and main decision-makers, it could be argued that learning by the key individual that is applied within the organisation and learning by the organisation are inseparable. It would be interesting to analyse cases where management succession had occurred in order to see to what extent decisions within an organisation were based on learning that preceded a particular owner-manager, although this was not possible in the present study. However, it is the authors' view that it is legitimate to conceive of what is described as organisational learning, first, because of the fact that knowledge and experience of stakeholders in the organisations is drawn upon by owner-managers, and second, the focus of the investigation is on decisions within case study organisations.

Although a learning approach offers an attractive framework for interpreting the decision-making behaviour of small firms, its operationalisation presents methodological challenges. The 'insider accounts' methodology was chosen in recognition of the fact that much of the learning may be tacit and difficult to communicate (Nonaka 1994). Future research might focus on examining the extent to which the nature and extent of organisational learning is related to business performance, perhaps over a longer time period. Although a longitudinal dimension enabled verification of decision-makers' stated intentions with actions, as well as offering insights into processes that would not have been evident in single snapshot interviews, 18 months is arguably too short a time period to examine 'lumpy' decisions, such as those concerned with major capital purchases.

The study also shows the potential value of an 'insider accounts' methodology when undertaking process-oriented studies of management behaviour in small firms. The combination of in-depth interviews and observations repeated over an 18-month period has resulted in some unique insights into the nature and extent to which investment decisions are based on experiential learning. Although the extent of the observation that was possible was confined to intermittent visits, there were instances where the researcher was able to observe actions that differed from those previously described by decision-makers in answer to questions posed. In this instance, observation may be used as part of a process of triangulation.

Although not primarily a policy chapter, the evidence and analysis presented here does have some implications for policy, particularly with regard to the approach to and delivery of advice and training to small firms. The evidence presented suggests that, rather than focusing on formalised training courses teaching prescriptions, a more productive approach might be to place entrepreneurs into potential learning situations. This means creating a decision-making environment that is sensitive to the motives and values of owner-managers. It also involves gearing training activities to practical problems, tailor-made and specific to the business, in an in-house, informal manner.

Notes

1 A Setmaster (GST) Collator for £30,000.

References

Allen, R. (1957) *Mathematical Economics*. London: St Martin's Press.

Argyris, C. and Schön, D. A. (1978) *Organisational Learning: A Theory of Action Perspective*. Reading, MA: Addison-Wesley.

Arrow, K. (1962) 'The economic implications of learning by doing', Review of Economic Studies, 29(1), pp. 155–173.

Bank of England (1999) *Finance for Small Firms, a Sixth Report*, January.

Brien, M. O. (1997) 'Payback: a gulf between managerial accounting and financial theory in practice – a view from accountants and finance officers in Ireland. *International Journal of Accounting*, 32(2): 173–86.

Brophy, D. and Shulman J. (1993) Financial factors which stimulate innovation. *Entrepreneurship Theory and Practice*, Winter, Baylor University, 17(2): 61–75.

Burgoyne, J. and Hodgson, V. (1983) 'National learning and managerial action: a phenomenological study in the field setting. *Journal of Management Studies*, 20(3): 387–99.

Burns, P. (1996) 'The significance of small firms. In P. Burns, and J. Dewhurst. (eds), *Small Business and Entrepreneurship*. Basingstoke: Macmillan Press.

Chaston, I., Badger, B., Mangles, T. and Sadler-Smith, E. (2001) Organisational learning style, competencies and learning systems in small, UK manufacturing firms. *International Journal of Operations and Production Management*, 21(11): 1417–32.

Cope, J. and Watts, G. (2000) Learning by doing: an exploration of experience, critical incidents and reflection in entrepreneurial learning. *International Journal of Entrepreneurial Behaviour and Research*, 6(3): 104–24.

Deakins, D. (1998) Learning and the entrepreneur. *International Journal of Entrepreneurial Behaviour and Research*, 4(2): 85–87(editorial).

Deakins, D. and Freel, M. (1998) Entrepreneurial learning and the growth process in SMEs. *The Learning Organisation*, 5(3): 144–155.

Easterby-Smith, M., Thorpe, R. and Lowe, A. (1991) *Management Research: An Introduction,* Sage Publications, London.

Gibb, A. (1997) Small firms' training and competitiveness: building upon the small business as a learning organisation. *International Small Business Journal*, 15(3): 13–29.

Grant R. M. (1996) Toward a knowledge-based theory of the firm. *Strategic Management Journal*, 17(Winter Special Issue): 109–22.

Hammersley, M. and Atkinson, P. (1995) *Ethnography: Principles in Practice.* London: Routledge.

Hargreaves Heap, S. (1989) *Rationality in Economics.* Oxford: Blackwell.

Hawkins, P. (1995) The changing view of learning. In J. Burgoyne, M. Pedler and T. Boydell (eds), *Towards the Learning Company: Concepts and Practice.* New York: McGraw-Hill.

Holliday, R. (1992) Cutting new patterns for small firms research. In K. Caley, E. Chell, F. Chittenden and C. Mason (eds), *Small Enterprise Development Policy and Practice in Action.* London: Paul Chapman.

Jarvis, R., Kitching, J., Curran, J. and Lightfoot, G. (1996) *The Financial Management of Small Firms: An Alternative Perspective.* Association of Chartered Certified Accountants Research Report, London: No. 49.

Kelly, G. (1955) *The Psychology of Personal Construct*, vols 1 and 2. New York: Norton.

Leonard, D. and Sensiper, S. (1998) The role of tacit knowledge in group innovation. *California Management Review*, 40(3): 112–32.

Lumby, S. (1994) *Investment Appraisal and Financial Decisions.* London: Chapman & Hall.

Marsick, V. and Watkins, K. (1990) *Informal and Incidental Learning in the Workplace.* London: Routledge.

Mason, C. and Rogers, A. (1997) The business angel's investment decision: an exploratory analysis. In D. Deakins *et al.* (eds), *Small Firms Entrepreneurship in the Nineties.* London: Paul Chapman.

Massari, A., Lanzolla, G. and Taylor, B. (1999) Ciao! to the old ways (how to change culture). Paper presented at the 3rd Enterprise and Learning Conference, University of Paisley, November.

Matlay, H. (2000) Training and the small firm. In S. Carter, and D. Jones-Evans (eds), *Enterprise and Small Business: Principles, Practice and Policy.* London: Pearson Education.

Nelson, R. R. and Winter, S. G. (1982) *An Evolutionary Theory of Economic Change.* Cambridge, MA: Belknap Press, pp. 166, 400.

Nonaka, I. (1994) A dynamic theory of organisational knowledge creation. *Organisation Science*, 5(1): 14–37.

Polanyi, M. (1967) *The Tacit Dimension.* Garden City, NY: Anchor Books, p. 4.

Shaw, E. (1999) A guide to the qualitative research process: evidence from a small firm study. *Qualitative Market Research: An International Journal*, 2(2): 59–70.

Smallbone, D., Leigh, R. and North, D. (1995) The characteristics and strategies of high growth SMEs. *International Journal of Entrepreneurial Behaviour and Research*, 1(3): 44–62.

Smallbone, D., Baldock, R. and Fadahunsi, A. (1997) *Researching the Business Support Needs of Firms in the Printing and Packaging Industry.* Final Report to the British Printing Industry Federation, CEEDR, Middlesex University, London.

Smallbone, D., Baldock, R. and Supri, S. (2000) The implications of new technology for the skill and training needs of small and medium sized printing firms. *Education and Training*, 42(4): 299–307.

Spence, L. J. and Rutherfoord, R. (2001) Social responsibility, profit maximisation and small firm owner-manager. *Journal of Small Business and Enterprise Development*, 8(2): 126–39.

Spender, J. C. (1996a) Making knowledge the basis of a dynamic theory of the firm. *Strategic Management Journal*, 17(Winter Special Issue): 45–62.

Spender, J. C. (1996b) Competitive advantage from tacit knowledge? Unpacking the concept and its strategic implications. In B. Monsingeon, and A. Edmondson, (eds), *Organisational Learning and Competitive Advantage*, London: Sage pp. 56–73.

Stacey, R. D. (1996) *Strategic Management and Organisational Dynamics*. London: Pitman.

Stockport, G. and Kakabadse, A. (1992) Using ethnography in small firms research. In K. Caley, E. Chell, F. Chittenden and C. Mason (eds), *Small Enterprise Development Policy and Practice in Action*. London: Paul Chapman.

Storey, D., Watson, R. and Wynarczyk, P. (1989) *Fast Growth Small Businesses: Case Studies of 40 Small Firms in North East England*. Research Paper 67. London: Department of Employment.

Sullivan, R. (2000) Entrepreneurial learning and mentoring. *International Journal of Entrepreneurial Behaviour and Research*, 6(3): 160–75.

Thomas, R. (2001) Business value analysis: coping with unruly uncertainty. *Strategy and Leadership*, 29(2): 16–23.

White, I. (1999) Breeding entrepreneurs: a love match in Europe. Paper presented at the 3rd Enterprise and Learning Conference, University of Paisley, November.

Wyer, P. and Mason, J. (1998) The case for an organisational learning perspective to understanding the strategic development of small business. Paper presented at Enterprise and Learning Conference, Aberdeen, 10–11 September.

Wyer, P., Mason, J. and Theodorakopoulos, N. (2000) Small business development and the 'learning organisation'. *International Journal of Entrepreneurial Behaviour and Research*, 6(4): 239–59.

9 Sharing of tacit knowledge within top management teams in civic entrepreneurship

Patricia A. Rowe and Michael J. Christie

Introduction

This chapter contributes to our understanding of the sharing of tacit knowledge within organizational entrepreneurship. Organizational entrepreneurship can be divided into corporate and civic entrepreneurship (Kirby 2003: 21, 300). Existing research has focused on corporate entrepreneurship in middle management because the majority of intrapreneurial activity is perceived to occur at this level. Top management teams are also a focus for corporate entrepreneurship (Floyd and Woolridge 1999). However, this level of analysis is under-researched, in organizational entrepreneurship and in particular civic entrepreneurship. Specifically, there are few studies that empirically test managerial attitude that is an internal factor for organizational entrepreneurship (Hornsby *et al.* 1999). There are fewer studies that examine managerial attitude from the perspective of a top management team. This chapter draws on the research of top management teams of corporate entrepreneurship and applies this in the context of civic entrepreneurship.

Civic entrepreneurship

Civic entrepreneurship has been identified as the means by which public administration is recognized for being entrepreneurial and innovative (Drucker 1985: 201; Kirby 2003: 21). Civic entrepreneurship is a means by which governments are changing that requires greater innovation and leadership in public administration. This chapter develops and tests a factor of managerial attitude, namely leadership support. A congeneric one-factor model is presented together with a multilevel analysis of the leadership support factor. The relationship between leadership support and the sharing of tacit knowledge is significant at an individual level of analysis but not at the group level. OLS regression supported the main hypothesis, that leadership support has a direct positive effect on explication of tacit knowledge.

Civic entrepreneurship is salient during non-routine events that occur both in start-ups and with existing organizations undergoing renewal (Miles and Snow 1978). Entrepreneurial creativity may begin with the tacit intuition of an individual who is flooded with unconscious insight (Polanyi 1966). The entrepreneurial process begins with making this tacit insight explicit and sharing it with one or two individuals (Nonaka 1994; Floyd and Woolridge 1999).

Knowledge creation is as important in the process of self-renewal by a mature organization as in new start-ups, in shaping its strategic choices and in establishing its strategic intent (Zahra *et al.* 1999). Development of organizational knowledge occurs through learning both within a company and in the market–place. Integrating new knowledge by making it useful to the organization represents a new competence (Hamel and Prahalad 1994) that can lead to improved organizational performance (Grant 1996, 1997). An initial step in this process is the eliciting of tacit knowledge. The manner in which tacit knowledge is educed is not well researched. What is well recognized is the role of top management team activities in creating this knowledge (Burgelman and Sayles 1986; Zahra 1991).

Tacit knowledge is held in people's heads during start-ups or during organizational non-routine situations, like organizational renewal. It is the unarticulated knowledge that is the very basis of creativity and is not easily captured or codified (Leonard and Sensiper 1998). Thus, in beginning to explore a new idea, the civic entrepreneur triggers the knowledge creation component of organizational learning that is embedded in the collective, subjective experiences and historical interactions of organizational members (Weick 1979; Spender 1996; Floyd and Woolridge 1999).

Civic entrepreneurship is more likely when these dyads reflect a favourable exchange relationship. In more favourable relationships, the collaborative systems of inducements and contributions that emerge through dyadic interactions build a relationship based on mutuality, respect and trust that facilitates the sharing of tacit knowledge. In contrast, less favourable relationships in top management teams are characterized by a lack of mutuality, disrespect and mistrust that prevents the sharing of tacit knowledge that is critical (Zahra *et al.* 1999).

Tacit knowledge is critical to organizational survival during periods in which top management teams are confronted with complex and uncertain conditions. It is particularly important when they are faced with non-routine situations during which they engage in the generation of novel knowledge and novel routines (Nonaka and Takeuchi 1995; McGrath 2001). Leadership support in top management teams is needed to continually improve existing routines. The type of leadership support is critical in determining the capacity of a top management team to engage in exploratory learning so that they are better able to capitalize on knowledge in pursuit of competitive advantage (Bennis 1989; Hackman 1998; Zahra *et al.* 1999; McGrath 2001).

Top management teams that provide civic entrepreneurship, almost by definition, have to manage non-routine (unexpected) situations. That is, they need to operate as learning organizations (Zahra *et al.* 1999). They hold a unique position at the top of the organizational hierarchy as key decision-makers who operate in complex events and are presented with both team and non-team situations. Leadership support and the sharing of tacit knowledge are crucial for organizational success.

There is variation in the level of civic entrepreneurship of top management teams. Anecdotal evidence suggests that at the top levels, the individual agendas of senior executives are characterized by self-interest rather than cooperation on joint actions. Instead, individual executives represent disparate multiple subcultures that pursue functional agendas (Schein 1996; Katzenbach 1998; Robbins and Finley 2001). Moreover, they rely exclusively on the familiar discipline of executive leadership that typically overpowers the discipline required for team performance and depend upon crisis-type events to trigger team behaviour (Katzenbach 1998).

Not only is the purposeful behaviour of individuals central to the definition of corporate civic entrepreneurship (Stevenson *et al*. 1989; Zahra *et al*. 1999; Parry and Proctor-Thomson 2003). In this chapter we argue that the quality of purposeful interactions between the CEO and top management team members is also a key factor of corporate success. Internal relationships between the CEO and team members in top management teams can be perceived as a number of dyadic relationships between the CEO and each member of the leadership group (Graen and Scandura 1987; Graen and Uhl-Bien, 1995). Consequently, the dyadic relationship is the level of analysis in this study, rather than the individual level of analysis.

The key objective of the study reported in this chapter is to develop a better understanding of how to improve civic entrepreneurship in top management teams. In particular, the managerial attitude a CEO employs 'can create a climate in which conventional wisdom can be questioned and challenged and one in which errors are embraced rather than shunned in favor of safe low-risk goals' (Bennis 1989: 30). Thus, top management teams have opportunities, during unexpected, non-routine situations, to draw on the collective wisdom of the group to increase an organization's competences in assessing its markets or creating and commercializing new knowledge-intensive products, processes or services (Zahra *et al*. 1999).

A second objective is to examine the nature and extent of the explication of tacit knowledge in top management teams. This kind of knowledge is subjective and intuitive – something not easily visible and expressible. Examples include insights, intuitions and hunches. Tacit knowledge is deeply rooted in an individual's actions and experience as well as in the ideals, values or emotions he or she embraces. It has both a 'technical' and a 'cognitive' dimension. It is the cognitive dimension that this study examines. This cognitive dimension reflects an individual's image of reality (what is) and our vision for the future (what ought to be) (Nonaka and Takeuchi 1995: 8). Unlike the objective machine perspective, the perspective taken in this chapter includes a view of knowledge as including soft and qualitative elements. Within this view, the organization is perceived as a living organism (Morgan 1993). Within this context, evolving processes for sharing of tacit knowledge are critical.

The explication of tacit knowledge is argued by the authors to be a key process involved in the sharing of tacit knowledge. It is a measure of the degree to which team members report that they engage in explication of their tacit knowledge, to the consciousness of an executive team. Thus, they openly encourage each other to make explicit their novel ideas, insights and hunches. Much of the explication of tacit knowledge in executive teams arises through story-telling and is a product of reflection about past successes as well as past trials and tribulations (Brown and Duguid 2000). It can involve the cycling of stories about similar-looking challenges to build a synergy of ideas and insights as a means to, for example, effective decision-making and risk management.

Managerial attitude is one of several factors that appear to be consistently related to civic entrepreneurship activities (Damanpour 1991). In the existing literature, management support is a dimension of managerial attitude for which a scale has been developed and tested. It is the willingness of managers to facilitate entrepreneurial projects. Sources for these studies are low- to mid-level managers who provided perceptions of management support of entrepreneurial/intrapreneurial activity (Kuratko *et al.* 1990; Hornsby *et al.* 1999). In contrast to the management support construct, this study tests a second dimension of managerial attitude, namely the leadership support construct.

Leadership support is defined as the degree of support and consideration a person receives from his or her supervisor (Netemeyer *et al.* 1997). Leadership support operates when a leader instils pride, faith and respect among the top management team and provides individualized consideration for its members. CEOs' leadership support requires numerous roles in work settings, including initiating important activities, setting challenging but achievable goals, and providing timely feedback on performance.

At an organizational culture/climate level, leadership support can have a dual nature. First, it can be characterized by encouraging communication, valuing the input of employees and enhancing an organization's willingness to reflect critically on shared assumptions about organizational practices. This type of leadership support draws on the notion of interactional justice that refers to the sensitivity of the leader (reflected in his or her kindness and understanding) and the degree to which the communication regarding a particular procedure or outcome is perceived as fair and just (Erdogan *et al.* 2001). A supportive team leader facilitates the development of the knowledge that is critical to the civic entrepreneurship process to all top management team members and makes a commitment to organizational learning a high priority.

A second type of leadership support occurs with leaders who fail to support top management team members and who discourage two-way communication, interactional justice and organizational learning. These leaders are unlikely to accept challenges to their ways of doing things that are inherent to organizational learning. They are likely to display interactional facilitation that is consistent with a transactional approach to leadership.

Similar to interactional justice, path–goal theory suggests that a supportive leader provides guidance to his or her subordinates, treats them fairly, and considers their input valuable (House and Dessler 1974). A supportive leader encourages two-way communication, treats organizational members equitably, and values individuals' contributions to organizational performance (Singh 2000). Not surprisingly, leadership support is associated with high levels of trust towards supervisors and commitment to organizational goals (Podsakoff *et al.* 1993).

Leadership support characterized by interactional justice plays an important role in establishing organizational learning. By encouraging communication and valuing the input of employees, leaders can enhance the organization's willingness to reflect critically on shared assumptions about organizational practices. Leaders who fail to support employees and who discourage two-way communication are unlikely to accept challenges to their methods of management. A supportive leader, in contrast, will be able to communicate a well-defined vision for the organization and make learning a high priority (Pinto *et al.* 1998).

A few studies in the literature are indicative of a possible link between leadership support and organizational learning and are also suggestive of a possible link between leadership support and performance. For example, in a study involving work supervisors and employees, both internalization of organizational values and supervisor commitment are positively related to performance (Becker *et al.* 1996). However, the focus of Becker's study is task performance rather than intangible actions such as sharing of tacit knowledge.

In another study, more relevant to the research reported here, the quality of leader–member exchange between an individual employee and his supervisor was positively related to the degree to which the individual perceives dimensions of climate as supportive of innovative behaviour (Scott and Bruce 1994). These findings mirror findings when employees were the source of data collection (Amabile *et al.* 1996). These three studies are more relevant to this research than the Becker *et al.* (1996) study because they focus on the quality of the leader–member exchanges during episodes of innovation. By definition, innovation refers to the process of implementation of creative ideas within a team (Ramus and Steger 2000). It is during these episodes that double-loop learning is critical to the overall performance of a team. Double-loop learning is a type of learning identified in the organizational learning process (Argyris 1957). It occurs through insights and collective consciousness, occurs mostly at upper levels, and is critical to the development of new missions and new definitions of direction in a business (Fiol and Lyles 1985).

The public sector is increasingly utilizing the concepts of civic entrepreneurship. For example, in Australia, the competitive policy legislated by the Federal Government in 1993 marked a fundamental shift characterized by an expectation of civic entrepreneurship to expand the role of local government in a manner that establishes its commercial footing. The use of civic entrepreneurship in the public sector provides an opportunity to examine top management teams in a different context that adds knowledge to the literature.

The connection between tacit knowledge and the role of leadership support in creating and utilizing knowledge suggests the following hypotheses:

H1a: Leadership support has a direct, positive impact on the explication of tacit knowledge.

H1b: There is variation in the relationship between leadership support to explication of tacit knowledge at an individual level of analysis.

H1c: There is variation in the relationship between leadership support to explication of tacit knowledge at a team level of analysis.

The purpose of this study is to expand on previous research conducted by Hornsby *et al.* (1999) that examined the corporate entrepreneurship internal factor of managerial attitude and apply it in the case of this chapter to civic entrepreneurship. Our hypothesis is that leadership support, a dimension of managerial attitude that has not previously been tested, has a direct, positive impact on the explication of tacit knowledge. Since limited empirical studies exist concerning the connection between tacit knowledge and the role of leadership support in creating and utilizing knowledge, this chapter represents an early contribution to the literature.

Methods

The study reported in this chapter was undertaken with top management teams in local government authorities where the environment is changing, where CEOs and their top management teams not only have to manage their traditional stakeholders, but must also learn to promote an innovative organizational environment. To this end, top management teams in Queensland (Australia) local government manage infrastructure worth a total of more than US$22 billion across 125 local government authorities (Queensland Department of Local Government 2002). Establishing a commercial footing is dependent upon civic entrepreneurship in top management teams, rather than their being locked into traditional bureaucratic roles.

Sample and procedures

There are 125 local government authorities in Queensland. Of the 76 councils that responded to the questionnaire, 49 were located in rural regions. Many of these rural councils do not have a leadership group. Instead, activities such as engineering and planning in councils serving small communities are outsourced and the CEO has no permanent managers. This explains why only 16 of the 49 rural-based councils that responded to the questionnaire had responses from their CEO and at least two other top management team members. In contrast, of the 25 urban councils that responded, only 6 councils were excluded from multilevel, multivariate analysis because at least three leadership group members replied. The 38 councils that were excluded from multilevel multivariate analysis were made up of 28 CEOs and 31 other leadership group members. In summary, the data that were selected out for analysis were made up of leadership groups from 38 organizations where the CEO and at least two leadership group members responded. A cohort of 156 leadership group members was extracted from the total of 215 leadership group members who responded to the initial questionnaire. These data were analysed using MLwiN multilevel analysis software.

The survey was mailed to all local government CEOs in Queensland. In each package, there were five letters to members of the top management team, five information sheets assuring confidentiality, five surveys, and enough stamped envelopes for each respondent to independently return his or her survey. There was also the same survey for the CEO plus an individually addressed letter to each CEO requesting them to distribute the other five surveys to members of their top management teams. For each local council, the footer included a unique code for that particular local government authority. Some local government authorities phoned the first author requesting extra copies of the survey and these were duly forwarded. An exact percentage for the response rate is not possible because of variations in the number of leadership group members in the 125 local government authorities, ranging from one to thirteen. However, it is estimated that the total number of CEOs and leadership group members for the whole of Queensland is approximately 127 local government authorities × 4 leadership group members per authority = 508. Thus, an estimated 42 percent of the total population of leadership group members including CEOs in Queensland local government responded. This response rate exceeds the minimum requirement of 20 percent needed to be able to generalize to the population (Dillman 1978). The unit of analysis is the top management team. The research aims to examine the relationship between leadership support and the explication of tacit knowledge and the data were gathered from CEOs and members of their top management teams.

Survey instrument

The survey instrument consisted of several parts. The first part included the leadership support scale. Leadership support is a six-item scale adapted from Netemeyer *et al.* (1997) – a 5-point scale ranging from 1 = strongly agrees to 5 = strongly disagree (Cronbach's $\alpha = 0.91$).

The second section included a question regarding the explication of tacit knowledge. It asked: 'When interacting with other senior management team members, how often do you share tacit knowledge (hunches, insights and intuition) – "the wisdom inside our heads"?' This question used a 5- point rating scale of (1) never, (2) seldom, (3) sometimes, (4) often and (5) very often.

The third section focused on demographics. In particular, data were collected on age, gender, experience, education and affiliation. In this regard, Table 9.1 is a description of the sample.

In the first stage of the analyses, a confirmatory factor analysis was undertaken to determine construct validity for the leadership support scale. In particular, a one-factor congeneric measurement model was developed and tested for the leadership support scale. This involved model specification, parameter estimation

Table 9.1 Description of sample

Age range	Under 26 = 2%, 26–34 = 12%, 35–44 = 26%, 45–54 = 50%, >54 = 10%
Gender	Male = 195, female = 20
Range of experience	<1–37 years
Average experience	9.47 years
Education	No university degree = 14%, undergraduate degree = 37%, masters degree or MBA = 31%, PhD = 18%
Affiliation	Finance/administration = 44%, engineering = 26%, town planning = 7%, community services = 5%, other = 18%

and the use of weight vectors of factor-score regression coefficients for maximizing the reliability estimates of latent variables (Hill *et al.* 1993; Rowe 2002). Because the responses were categorical in nature and slightly skewed (Hill *et al.* 1993) the raw data were first analysed in PRELIS. PRELIS generates a correlation matrix of polychoric correlations for analysis in LISREL and also produces a weight matrix of asymptotic covariances of these estimated correlations for use in the asymptotically distribution-free WLS fit. These two matrices for the scale are then used in a LISREL run to estimate and test each one-factor congeneric model.

Estimating the model of the leadership support construct required examination of indicators to remove those that do not closely reflect the construct. We carried this out by identifying and eliminating the indicators with standardized residuals (>2.54), as recommended by Anderson and Gerbing (1988). High residuals imply that an indicator is not a good estimate of the observed data and thus will reduce the goodness-of-fit of the model. The goodness-of-fit statistics all indicate that the model fits the sample data well. The composite reliability of the model and explained variances indicate acceptable levels of reliability and validity. Details of these findings for the one-factor congeneric model are now elaborated.

Results

The parameter estimates and explained variance for items that closely reflect the leadership support scale are presented in Table 9.2. The lambda coefficient and error variance columns present the parameter estimate, standard errors in parentheses and *t*-values. The factor loadings for the items in the leadership support scale were strong (0.798 and above). The lambda coefficients are above a certain threshold (0.798). The indicator with the smallest error variance is Lead2 and the largest error variance is Lead4. Lead3 variance is between these two extremes.

Table 9.2 Parameter estimates for leadership support

Item	Lambda coefficient	Error variances (theta-delta)	Explained variance
Lead2	0.958 (0.020) 46.740	(a) 0.083 (b) (0.079) (c) 1.053	0.917
Lead3	0.887 (0.035) 25.241	(a) 0.213 (b) (0.093) (c) 2.299	0.787
Lead4	0.798 (0.038) 21.057	(a) 0.362 (b) (0.091) (c) 3.969	0.638
Lead6	0.854 (0.031) 27.848	(a) 0.270 (b) (0.086) (c) 3.135	0.730

(a) Parameter estimate, (b) standard error, (c) *t*-value.

Table 9.3 displays the fit statistics for the leadership support model. The model fits the data well ($\chi^2(2) = 1.18$, $p > 0.05$, AGFIH = 0.997 and RMR = 0.0113) and all items have very good item reliabilities (four at 0.80 or above). The measure of internal consistency (scale reliability $\alpha = 0.91$) is extremely good. Note also that the factor score regressions make substantive sense.

Table 9.3 Model goodness-of-fit statistics for leadership support

Chi-square (χ^2)	1.18
Degrees of freedom	2
Probability (p)	0.555
Goodness-of-fit index (GFI)	0.999
Root mean square residual (RMR)	0.0113
Root mean squared error of approximation (RMSEA)	0.0
Adjusted goodness-of-fit index (AGFI)	0.997
Comparative fit index (CFI)	1.000
Akaike information criterion (AIC)	20.000
Parsimonious goodness-of-fit index (PGFI)	0.200

The latent construct explains at least 64 percent of the indicator's variance, which suggests that the indicators are satisfactory measures of leadership support and have convergent validity (Nunnally and Bernstein 1994). The indicators also appear to have high reliability as evidenced by the composite reliability ($\alpha = 0.93$) and a moderate extracted variance estimate (0.77). Finally, the measures appear to be unidimensional as there was no correlation allowed between the indicators. Lambda estimates and error estimates are shown in Figure 9.1.

Table 9.4 presents the final measurement items and the factor score (FS) regressions for leadership support. The largest contribution to the latent construct of leadership support appears to be the item that reflects whether there is support from the CEO (factor score of 0.571). Consistent with the description of leadership support, the nature of the latent construct measured by these four items focuses on leader practices that are fair and just and understanding and that reflect high interactional justice.

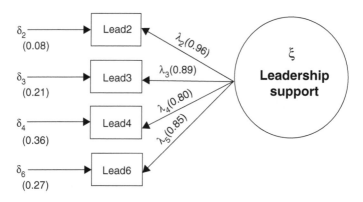

Figure 9.1 Congeneric one-factor model for leadership support.

Table 9.4 Final measurement items and factor score regressions for leadership support

Measure	FS	FS loadings
Lead2 There is support from our CEO.	0.571	0.547
Lead3 Our CEO will assist us when problems arise.	0.206	0.198
Lead4 Our CEO can be relied upon when things get tough.	0.109	0.105
Lead6 Our CEO is friendly and approachable.	0.157	0.150

In top management teams where leadership support was high, the interactions in dyads can be characterized by episodes of innovation in which there is a sharing of tacit knowledge (i.e. hunches, insights and intuitions). In contrast, in top management teams where leadership support is low, relationships are less trusting. Information processing but not the sharing of tacit knowledge occurs in these less favourable relationships. Unlike the interactions in relationships characterized by high leadership support, members are not likely to risk non-conformity or self-disclosure.

In stage two of the analyses, multilevel analysis was undertaken on the data. The data are inherently hierarchical because they examine interactions between top management team members. Consequently, to maximize measurement precision, the next step was to fit a two-level variance components models to ascertain whether the data have significant group-level variance. This was carried out in MLwiN. To determine the portion of variance in the leadership support construct due to between-group differences, a two-level variance components model was fitted, i.e. a null model. Using the subscript i to refer to a member of a top management team and the subscript j for the organization, this model was written in two parts a within-group, among-members part:

$$\gamma_{ij} = \beta_{0ij}\chi_0 + e_{ij}$$

and a between-group part:

$$\beta_{0ij} = \beta_{0j} + u_{0j}$$

where:

γ_{ij} is the dependent or response score for team member i in group j;

β_{0ij} is the intercept in the within-group relationship. It is the average level of team member's response for the group j;

e_{ij} is a random variable – assumed to have a mean of zero – representing the sum of all influences on γ_{ij};

χ_0 is a term that symbolizes a column vector of unities representing the response score of team members in the sample of groups;

β_{0j} is a coefficient of the mean response score of team members in the sample of groups. Since β_{0j} can vary across groups, β_{0j} is treated as a random variable at level 2.

By combining these two equations, a single equation version of the model can be written as follows:

$$\gamma_{ij} = \beta_{0ij}\chi_0 + {}_{(}u_{0j} + e_{ij)}$$

where $\beta_{0ij}\chi_0$ is the fixed part of the model and the bracketed residual term at level 2 (u_{0j}) and level 1 (e_{ij}) constitute the random part of the model.

The purpose of these equations is to model the group-dependence of team members on a specific response score. Hence, the intra-group correlation is given by $\rho = \sigma u_0^2 / (\sigma u_0^2 + \sigma e_0^2)$. This correlation provides an estimate of the proportion of the total variance in a team member's response score that is due to variation between groups. To determine the extent to which groups differ in their mean levels of a specific response score, the ratio of σu_0^2 estimate to its standard error $[se(\sigma u_0^2)]$ was referred to the usual Gaussian distribution (t-value) for gauging significance (t-value > 1.96 is significant). The two-level variance components analysis reported that 22 percent of the variance was at a group level in the leadership support construct as shown in Table 9.5.

Table 9.5 Mean, SE, *t*-value and % variance at both member and organizational levels for fitted two-level variance components model in MLwiN

Response variable −2*loglikelihood	Slope	Mean, SE and t-value	Member % variance	Group % variance
Leadership support loglikelihood (IGLS) = 291.344	0.328 (0.106)	4.153 (0.072) $\beta_{0ij} = 57.68$ $e_{0ij} = 7.68$ $u_{0j} = 2.25$	78%	22%

Relationship between leadership support and tacit knowledge

In stage three of the analyses, because the previous analysis confirmed the multi-level nature of the leadership support construct, a two-level covariance components model was analysed for the calculated leadership support score, using the single item for explication of tacit knowledge score as an explanatory variable. The explication of tacit knowledge score was calculated by allocating a high/low rating on a 5 point scale. High leadership support > 4 and low leadership support < 4. Next presented are the multilevel analysis findings for the leadership support score to explication of tacit knowledge score.

The fitted value of the common slope is significant (slope = 0.153, SE = 0.075). The intercepts of the lines vary (mean = 0.237, SE = 0.048). The overall *t*-value is significant (4.94). The *t*-value for the single-level analysis is also significant (7.78). However, the *t*-value for the group-level analysis is not significant. The key finding from this analysis is that Hypothesis 1a is confirmed that is, the relationship between leadership support and explication of tacit knowledge is significant. Hypothesis 1b is also confirmed that is, the variance is significant at an individual level of analysis. However, Hypothesis 1c was not significant. The variance between leadership support and explication of tacit knowledge is not significant at the group level.

Because the variance is not significant at a group level, the individual-level data were re-analysed using the ordinary least squares (OLS) regression technique in SPSS 10.1. The results are shown in Table 9.6. These findings also support H1a and H1b ($p < 0.001$).

Table 9.6 Regression analysis: explication of tacit knowledge as dependent variable

Variable	Entire sample, full model control and independent variables included (standardized coefficients)
Study variable: Leadership support	0.165**

$N = 215$, ** $= p < 0.001$

Discussion

The congeneric one-factor model provides a confirmatory factor analysis of the leadership support scale. This finding is a contribution to theory on civic entrepreneurship. In particular, it develops and tests this new dimension of managerial attitude. The leadership support construct explains the nature of managerial attitude in top management teams that operate in complex events and that are faced with non-routine situations that require the creation and utilization of new knowledge. Thus, the introduction of the leadership support scale enlarges our understanding of a key factor of civic entrepreneurship in top management teams, namely managerial attitude.

Next, the measurement properties of the leadership support scale when applied to top management teams are inherently multilevel in nature. The partitioning of individual-level variance and group-level variance is carried out to overcome this inherent multilevel nature of the unit of analysis, i.e. top management teams. The variance is significant for the leadership support factor at both levels of analysis. This finding is important because it supports the methodological argument that accounting for levels of analysis is critical if you want to avoid type I errors during the analysis of inherently nexted data (Rowe 2002).

The finding for the relationship between leadership support and the explication of tacit knowledge is significant at the dyadic level of analysis. This suggests that the sharing of tacit knowledge is dependent upon a top executive perceiving that interactional justice characterizes the quality of his or her relationship with a leader. The implication of this for management is that sharing of tacit knowledge is more likely if the work climate in which top management teams operate together is characterized by leadership support.

In the final set of analyses, OLS regression supported the main hypothesis, that leadership support has a direct positive effect on the explication of tacit knowledge. The results of this study largely support the association we expected to see between leadership support and the explication of tacit knowledge. Leadership support facilitates a climate in which the sharing of tacit knowledge can emerge. A further key contribution of this study was to successfully develop and test the leadership support construct as a dimension of managerial attitude in civic entrepreneurship.

Conclusion

Local government around the world is faced with increased pressures to be involved in the organization of economic development. Civic entrepreneurship in their top management teams is a key factor in the management of economic development. This study measures, through a survey, the relationship between a civic entrepreneurship internal factor (leadership support) and the explication of tacit knowledge. The hypothesis tested and supported is that there is variation in the explication of tacit knowledge (hunches, insights and intuition – 'the wisdom inside our heads') in leadership groups. These research findings have management implications for the way local government creates innovative top management teams to facilitate local economic and community development. In particular, the findings suggest that greater consideration be given to the selection of top management teams, the way managers are integrated into organizational decision-making processes, and the behaviours that are valued and rewarded in such teams.

References

Amabile, T. M., Conti, R., Coon, H., Lazenby, J. and Herron, M. (1996) Assessing the work environment for creativity. *Academy of Management Journal,* 39: 1154–84.

Anderson, J. C. and Gerbing, D. W. (1988) Structural equation modeling in practice: a review and recommended two-step approach. *Psychological Bulletin*, 103(3): 411–23.

Argyris, C. (1957) Some problems in conceptualizing organizational climate: a case study of a bank. *Administrative Science Quarterly*, 2: 501–20.

Becker, T. E., Billings, R. S., Eveleth, D. M. and Gilbert, N. L. (1996) Foci and bases of employee commitment: implications for job performance. *Academy of Management Journal,* 39(2): 464–82.

Bennis, W. (1989) *Why Leaders Can't Lead: The Unconscious Conspiracy Continues.* San Francisco: Jossey-Bass.

Brown, J. S. and Duguid, P. (2000) Balancing act: how to capture knowledge without killing it. *Harvard Business Review,* May: 73–80.

Burgelman, R. A. and Sayles, L. R. (1986) *Inside Corporate Innovation Strategy, Structure and Managerial Skills.* New York: The Free Press.

Damanpour, F. (1991) Organizational innovation: a meta-analysis of effects of determinants and moderators. *Academy of Management Journal*, 34(3): 555–91.

Dillman, D. A. (1978) *Mail and Telephone Surveys: The Total Design Method.* New York: Wiley.

Drucker, P. F. (1985) *Innovation and Entrepreneurship: Practice and Principles.* London: Pan Books.

Erdogan, B., Kraimer, M. L. and Liden, R. C. (2001) Procedural justice as a two-dimensional construct: an examination in the performance appraisal context. *Journal of Applied Behavioral Science*, 37(2): 205–22.

Fiol, C. M. and Lyles, M. A. (1985) Organizational learning. *Academy of Management Review*, 10: 803–13.

Floyd, S. W. and Woolridge, W. (1999) Knowledge creation and social networks in corporate entrepreneurship: the renewal of organizational capability. *Entrepreneurship Theory and Practice* 23(3): 123–43.

Graen, G. and Scandura, T. A. (1987) Toward a psychology of dyadic organizing. In L. L. Cummings and B. M. Staw (eds), *Research in Organizational Behavior*, Greenwich, CT: JAI Press, pp. 175–208.

Graen, G. and Uhl-Bien, M. (1995) Relationship-based approach to leadership: development of leader-member exchange (LMX) theory of leadership over 25 years: applying a multi-level multi-domain perspective. *Leadership Quarterly*, 6: 219–47.

Grant, R. M. (1996) Toward a knowledge-based theory of the firm. *Strategic Management Journal*, 17: 109–22.

Grant, R. M. (1997) The knowledge-based view of the firm: implications for managerial practice. *Long Range Planning*, 30 (3): 450–54.

Hackman, J. R. (1998) Why teams don't work. In R. S. Tindale *et al.* (eds), *Theory and Research on Small Groups*. New York: Plenum Press.

Hamel, G. and Prahalad, C. K. (1994) *Competing for the Future*. Boston: Harvard Business School Press.

Hill, P. W., Holmes-Smith, P. and Rowe, K. J. (1993) *School and Teacher Effectiveness in Victoria: Key Findings from Phase 1 of the Victorian Quality Schools Project.* Centre for Applied Educational Research, University of Melbourne.

Hornsby, J. S., Kuratko, D. F. and Montagno, R. V. (1999) Perception of internal factors for corporate entrepreneurship: a comparison of Canadian and US mergers. *Entrepreneurship Theory and Practice*, 24(2): 9–24.

House, R. J., and Dessler, G. (1974) The path-goal theory of leadership: some post hoc and a priori tests. In J. Hunt and L. Arson (eds), *Contingency Approaches to Leadership*, Carbondale, IL, Southern Illinois University Press: pp. 29–55.

Katzenbach, J. R. (1998) *Teams at the Top: Unleashing the Potential of Both Teams and Individual Leaders*. Boston: Harvard Business School Press.

Kirby, D. A. (2003) *Entrepreneurship*. London: McGraw-Hill.

Kuratko, D., Montagno, R. and Hornsby, J. (1990) Developing an entrepreneurial instrument for an effective corporate entrepreneurial environment. *Strategic Management Journal*, 11(Special Issue): 49–58.

Leonard, D. and Sensiper, S. (1998) The role of tacit knowledge in group innovation. *California Management Review*, 40(3): 112–32.

McGrath, R. G. (2001) Exploratory learning, innovative capacity, and managerial oversight. *Academy of Management Journal*, 44(1): 118–31.

Miles, R. E. and Snow, C. C. (1978) *Organizational Strategy, Structure and Process*. New York: McGraw-Hill.

Morgan, G. (1993) *Imaginization: The Art of Creative Management*, Newbury Park, CA: Sage.

Netemeyer, R. G., Boles, J. S., McKee, D. O. and McMurrian, R. (1997) An investigation into the antecedents of organizational citizenship behaviors in a personal selling context. *Journal of Marketing*, 61: 85–98.

Nonaka, I. (1994) A dynamic theory of organizational knowledge creation. *Organization Science*, 5(1): 14–37.

Nonaka, I. and Takeuchi, H. (1995) *The Knowledge-Creating Company: How Japanese Companies Create the Dynamics of Innovation*. New York: Oxford University Press.

Nunnally, J. C., and Bernstein, I. H. (1994) *Psychometric Theory* (3rd ed.), New York: McGraw-Hill.

Parry, K. W. and Proctor-Thomson, S. B. (2003) Leadership, culture and performance: the case of the New Zealand public sector. *Journal of Change Management,* 3(4): 376–99.

Pinto, J. K., Thoms, P., Traile, J., Palmer, T. and Govekar, M. (1998) *Project Leadership: From Theory to Practice.* Pennsylvania: Project Management Institute.

Podsakoff, P. M. Niehoff, B. P, MacKenzie, S. B. and Williams, M. L. (1993) Do substitutes for leadership really substitute for leadership? An empirical examination of Kerr and Jermier's Situational Leadership Model. *Organizational Behavior and Human Decision Processes*, 54(1): 1–44.

Polanyi, M. (1966) *The Tacit Dimension*. New York: Doubleday.

Queensland Department of Local Government (2002) *Councils at Work*. Retrieved 26 June 2002, from http://www.dlgp.qld.gov.au/local_govt/council_info/councils_at_work/ 26 June 2002.

Ramus, C. A. and Steger, U. (2000) The roles of supervisory support behaviors and environmental policy in employee ecoinitiatives at leading-edge European companies. *Academy of Management Journal,* 43(4): 605–26.

Robbins, H. and Finley, M. (2001) Some myths of effective teams. *Innovative Leader*, 10(4): 527.

Rowe, K. (2002) Estimating interdependent effects among multilevel composite variables in psychosocial research: an annotated example of the application of multilevel structural equation modeling. In N. Duan and S. Reise (eds), *Multilevel Modeling: Methodological Advances, Issues and Applications*. Mahwah, NJ: Lawrence, Erlbaum, 1–28.

Schein, E. H. (1996) Three cultures of management: the key to organizational learning. *Sloan Management Review*, 38(1): 9–20.

Scott, S. G. and Bruce, R. A. (1994) Determinants of innovative behavior: a path model of individual innovation in the workplace. *Academy of Management Journal*, 37(3): 580–607.

Singh, J. (2000) Performance productivity and quality of frontline employees in service organizations. *Journal of Marketing*, 64(4): 15–34.

Spender, J. C. (1996) Competitive advantage from tacit knowledge? Unpacking the concept and its strategic implications. In B. Mosingeon and A. Edmondson (eds), Organizational Learning and *Competitive Advantage*, London: Sage, pp. 56–73.

Stevenson, H. H., Roberts, M. J. and Grousbeck, H. I. (1989) Case 4-1 Michael Bregman. In *New Business Ventures and the Entrepreneur*. Homewood, IL: Irwin: pp. 33–61.

Weick, K. E. (1979) *The Social Psychology of Organizing*. New York: Random House.

Zahra, S. A. (1991) Predictors and financial outcomes of corporate entrepreneurship: an exploratory study. *Journal of Business Venturing*, 6(4): 259–85.

Zahra, S. A., Nielsen, A. P. and Bogner, W. C. (1999) Corporate entrepreneurship, knowledge, and competence development. *Entrepreneurship Theory and Practice*, 23(3): 169–90.

Section IV

Inter-organisational learning

10 Entrepreneurial knowledge flows and new venture creation

Paul N. Friga

Introduction

Entrepreneurship can be defined as the process by which new ventures are created (Gartner 1988). One of the most dominant research streams in the field of entrepreneurship is the study of antecedents to new venture creation (Reynolds and Miller 1992; Kreuger and Brazeal 1994; Venkataraman 1997). A primary research question in this area has been, 'What are the characteristics of entrepreneurs and the entrepreneurial learning processes that result in more incidents of business start-up efforts?' This chapter is an empirical examination of this topic. The focus of this chapter is the determination of the impact of knowledge flows in entrepreneurship, that is, the combination of general knowledge of the entrepreneur and the influx of new specific knowledge learned during the entrepreneurial process. Framed a bit differently, three specific research questions emerge that guide this investigation (performance in this case is defined as the incidents of new venture creation):

- How does general knowledge possessed by the entrepreneur affect new venture creation?
- How does the learning process during start-up activities affect new venture creation?
- What are the interaction effects of general and specific knowledge on new venture creation?

Although this topic has received dramatic growth in academic and practitioner attention over the past decade, there are some gaps in the literature. These gaps relate to the content of investigation and the methods utilized. Specific content deficiencies include the need to study entrepreneurship earlier in the process (to learn more about how new ventures come into being) and to consider not only the backgrounds and traits of entrepreneurs (considered general knowledge herein), but also the process of how the new venture is launched (considered new knowledge herein) (Gartner 1988; Venkataraman 1997). Weaknesses in the methods of published studies related to these issues include small sample sizes, unclear and varying performance measures and the lack of controls for moderating variables.

General knowledge of the entrepreneur is often operationalized as backgrounds and traits of entrepreneurs relating primarily to education and experience (Woodworth *et al.* 1969; Brush 1991; Jo 1996; Gartner 1999). Over the past twenty years, studies linking existing general knowledge to entrepreneurial performance have produced dramatically different or inconclusive results, as will be described later in this chapter. The testing of specific knowledge learned during the start-up process, often operationalized as formal assistance such as through small business assistance programs (Robinson 1982; Chrisman *et al.* 1987; Nahavandi and Chesteen 1988; 1989), has generated conclusions of positive links to performance, but the studies have been subject to small sample sizes with little or no control comparisons (e.g. entrepreneurs who do not seek assistance), leading to questionable validity.

Another opportunity for additional investigation relates the impact of general knowledge and specific knowledge on performance, when controlling for each other and studying interaction effects. The systematic study of main and interactive effects, which has not been adequately addressed in the literature, is the primary contribution of this chapter. 'By building off of three distinct literature bases – entrepreneurship, resource-based theory (RBT) and the knowledge-based view (KBV)/organizational learning (OL) – we are able to understand better how certain types of knowledge and mechanisms for transferring knowledge impact entrepreneurial performance'. The entrepreneurship literature is the anchor for the study, as it provides a population for testing, variables for consideration and impact opportunities in terms of strategies for individuals and macro-policy recommendations. The RBT and the KBV/OL inform the entrepreneurial literature by offering additional constructs and categories for study (general knowledge, specific knowledge and performance) and relationships to investigate (impact of specific knowledge on performance given general knowledge and the interaction effects of specific knowledge and general knowledge). The goal is to provide more explanatory power in this field of inquiry by building a more compelling model that not only includes variables previously tested independently, but also tests their combined direct and interaction effects.

The first section of this chapter sets the stage with a brief look at the key issues in the entrepreneurial literature and a general discussion of opportunities in existing theory for explaining the start-up phenomenon. This section is followed by a discussion of a conceptual model that guides this research project. Five hypotheses are presented from a review of the entrepreneurship and other supporting literature. Next, the testing is presented with a description of the dataset, methodology, and results. Finally, the discussion section describes conclusions, limitations, implications and further testing opportunities.

Theoretical backdrop

Entrepreneurship

The starting point for this investigation is a review of relevant entrepreneurial literature. Classic works described the importance of entrepreneurship and its role in US business history (Schumpeter 1934; Chandler 1962). In the 1980s, academic researchers began more formally studying entrepreneurship as a distinct literature base. Much of the early work focused on defining entrepreneurship and developing constructs for study. The field then struggled to identify common characteristics or traits of successful entrepreneurs for a number of years. Later analysis supported early claims that trait analysis was insufficient to explain entrepreneurial performance, as less than 7 percent of the variance in entrepreneurial performance was attributable to an entrepreneur's individual characteristics (Baum *et al.* 2001). A seminal piece in 1988 provided clarity on both of these issues (the definition of entrepreneurship and the study of traits). First, the definition offered for entrepreneurship was that of 'new venture creation' which helped identify parameters for entrepreneurship and also distinguished it from innovation (Gartner 1988; Venkataraman 1997). Second, there was a call to investigate not only entrepreneurs' backgrounds and traits but also the entrepreneurial start-up process and entrepreneurial behavior – especially the learning processes thereof (Gartner 1988).

Other researchers supported this expansion of focus to include both entrepreneurs' background and behavior. Cognitive factors were investigated (Schwenk 1988; Gatewood *et al.* 1995) as well as biases and heuristics (Busenitz and Barney 1997). The entrepreneurial background research continued during the 1980s with a focus on experience (Vesper 1980; MacMillan *et al.* 1985; Duchesneau and Gartner 1990) and education (Vesper 1980; Van de Ven *et al.* 1984; Stuart and Abetti 1990). This chapter will investigate both the background and behavior effects on new venture performance.

The final research area within the entrepreneurial literature covered in this chapter is the impact of external assistance on the start-up process. Studies have examined external assistance provided to entrepreneurs, with many claiming positive impact on new venture creation (Robinson 1982; Chrisman *et al.* 1987; Nahavandi and Chesteen 1988; and Chrisman 1999) and a few claiming less or no impact (Lamont 1972; Sandberg and Hofer 1987; Dennis and Phillips 1990). This chapter tests this tension and summarizes the varying constructs, methods and gaps in previous empirical papers.

Gaps in literature and areas for further investigation

A review of the entrepreneurial literature provides guidance as to where contribution opportunities exist. Specifically, there are five primary opportunities that led to the development of this particular research study. The first two opportunities represent gaps in the content of the literature and the next three represent problems in the methodologies of studies.

Study new venture creation earlier in the start-up process

Operating within our definition of entrepreneurship as the creation of a new venture or a distinct new business (Gartner 1988), much of entrepreneurial research could be better classified as small business research. Research on entrepreneurship is also often conducted as a study of the entrepreneur on an individual basis. This usually includes selection of existing entrepreneurs for study. The typical method for examining pre-venture activities is to survey entrepreneurs after the fact. This retrospective basis of data generation is limited as the responses are subject to recollection and survivorship bias.

The serious gap in knowledge about what takes place before the new venture is created, has been noted from sociological, psychological and strategic perspectives. Sociologists, in their study of organizations at the population level, note that decisions made at the earliest phase of organizational formation have long-lasting and often irreversible impact on the eventual performance (Aldrich *et al.* 1989). The psychology lens surfaces the importance of personality factors and cognitive sense-making during the start-up process (Learned 1992; Krueger and Brazeal 1994). Finally, strategy researchers hold that strategic planning and formal assistance during the start-up phase can impact performance (Robinson 1982; Chrisman 1999).

The reasons for the lack of study of the early stages of entrepreneurship are evident. The first problem is identification of the entrepreneur. Traditional studies have used data sources such as new business filings, small business assistance clients, and other such existing company databases. These approaches, however, only cover a small subset of the total entrepreneurs in existence at any given time (Aldrich *et al.* 1989). Another problem involves costly methodologies. Attempts to survey early-stage entrepreneurs are complicated and quite expensive (Chrisman 1999). In many cases, researchers have had to settle for smaller sample sizes and less statistical power. To truly study the early-stage entrepreneur, you must identify entrepreneurs who are actively trying to start a business and survey them during the process. Since only between 3 and 8 percent of the general population is involved with the creation of a new venture, this identification requires a large sampling set (Reynolds and Miller 1992). This chapter is entirely focused on the pre-venture process and is the result of a large-scale multiple-year research project over several years that includes an original sample of over 30,000 individuals (more thoroughly explained in the methodology section).

Study both entrepreneurial backgrounds and the start-up process

Many of the studies thus far in the field have focused on either backgrounds or the start-up process, but not both. Specific examples of these studies will be provided in the next section. The intent here is to advance the research stream by testing for direct and interactive effects of background conditions and learnings that occur during start-up activities. This is an area where the KBV/OL makes a theoretical contribution. For example, knowledge is often operationalized as an individual variable (Grant 1997) with links to performance and sources of knowledge, that go well beyond formal education. Thus it is important to consider additional sources of knowledge such as experience in the industry and formal assistance from trained professionals. This study includes traditional knowledge variables such as formal education as well as experience and assistance variables.

Increase the sample size

As previously discussed, it is difficult to obtain adequate sample sizes in entrepreneurial studies, given the difficulties in identifying individuals involved in the start-up process. For example, a review of the entrepreneurial literature related to topics covered in this chapter reveals relatively small sample sizes: education background testing – 71 (Carter *et al.* 1996); experience – 26 (Duchesneau and Cartner 1990) and 33 (Katz 1990); entrepreneurial intention – 20 (Bird 1988).

The study presented in this chapter involves a sample of over 30,000 individuals selected at random from the US population to yield a group of over 1,200 entrepreneurs (492 with usable entrepreneurship outcome variables). The random element of the selection is important to note as many of the studies in this field are based on convenience samples, such as all the firms seeking small business program assistance who respond to a survey. This will be discussed more thoroughly in the methodology section of this chapter.

Identify clear performance measures

The entrepreneurial field initially based its performance measures in a similar fashion to other more established disciplines such as economics and accounting. Traditional measures such as sales growth, profitability and return on investment, however, often led to more confusion than clarity, given the changing dynamics of an entrepreneurial organization and the difficulty of comparison. For example, sales growth is a difficult measure for entrepreneurs as start-up companies go through dramatic revenue swings and profitability often eludes new ventures for several years after start-up. Additionally, industry effects have been shown to have greater impact on performance than firm-specific characteristics in some cases.

As the field gravitates toward more study of the pre-venture process (based on a definition of entrepreneurship as the creation of a new venture or business entity), the dependent performance variables will likely change as well. Given the positive economic impact of new businesses in an economy and the clear delineation, the performance measurement is often the dichotomous variable of new venture creation/organizational formation (Learned 1992; Chrisman 1999).

Control for moderating effects

The issue of adequate controls during empirical testing represents the most significant opportunity for advancing theories. The vast majority of studies of entrepreneurial backgrounds (past general knowledge) and process (new specific knowledge learned) have been conducted in isolation without adequate controls. This makes generalization and comparison suspect. For example, experience has been cited as a major factor influencing new venture creation (Duchesneau and Gartner 1990; Stuart and Abetti 1990; Krueger 1993), but in these empirical studies, no controls were introduced for new experience gained during the start-up process or gleaned from the experience of others through advisement and/or consultation. And studies examining the impact of specific knowledge have traditionally not controlled for the effect of general knowledge (previous experience and/or education) (Chrisman *et al.* 1987; Nahavandi and Chesteen 1988; Chrisman 1999). Likewise, studies examining the effects of the educational backgrounds of entrepreneurs on performance (Cooper 1971; Brush 1991; Jo and Lee 1996) have not controlled for specific entrepreneurial-related education obtained during the start-up process such as with educational courses. In recent years, researchers have been addressing this issue with databases such as the one described herein that contain control samples.

The RBT and the KBV/OL will also aid in investigating this aspect. The RBT holds that it is the unique combination of resources that leads to competitive advantage (Penrose 1959; Barney 1996). The KBV suggests that knowledge-based resources are increasingly important for success in the modern age. OL provides arguments for the value of studying the learning process and its impact on performance. Thus, the combination of knowledge resources and their interactions represents an important avenue of research and is one of the primary contributions of this chapter.

The nascent entrepreneur and intention

With a goal of understanding pre-venture learning activities and antecedents, a researcher is faced with a challenging primary data-gathering situation. Relying on existing entrepreneurial organizations can only provide partial answers at best and efforts must be directed earlier in the process. Researchers have coined the term 'nascent entrepreneur' to represent an individual with intent to start a business (Reynolds and Miller 1992; Chrisman 1999), and this nascent entrepreneur has become the subject of several recent entrepreneurial investigations.

The construct of intention has been documented and tested in entrepreneurial literature over the past 13 years. Using certain psychological constructs, an entrepreneur's intention was first posited to have a direct effect on performance in a study based on interviews of 20 entrepreneurs (Bird 1988). Intention was also proposed as one of the four main properties in defining a new venture itself (Katz and Gartner 1988). Estimates of percentages of the general population with entrepreneurial intention range from 3 to 8 percent (Reynolds and Miller 1992 Dennis, 1997). Estimates of eventual links to performance (actual start-up) have been documented from 33 percent (Katz 1990) to 48 percent or more (Carter *et al.* 1996).

The model

Introduction and overview

The starting point for testing in this chapter is the nascent entrepreneur, who by definition possesses intention to start a business. The focus is on the general knowledge (background) and new specific knowledge learned during the start-up process (behavior). The direct relationships of each will be tested to support or refute previous empirical conclusions. The unique aspect of this model is the testing of potential moderating effects of each construct on the other's relationship to performance. This chapter will test the relationship between general knowledge and start-up occurrence, controlling for specific entrepreneurial knowledge learned during the start-up process. It will also test the moderating impact (if any) of general knowledge on the new knowledge start-up occurrence relationship and the interaction effects of specific and general knowledge.

This methodological contribution is important for a number of reasons. First, is the goal for increased explanatory power, multivariate investigations have become more common. By considering the effects of co-variation and partialling out effects of other variables, researchers gain a more accurate estimation of the impact of individual independent variables on dependent variables. The key question is, 'Will the general and specific knowledge effects on start-up occurrence hold when controlling for each other?' For example, for an entrepreneur with advanced education and significant experience, additional knowledge transfer attempts through formal counseling and/or classes may have more impact than they would have for a less educated or experienced entrepreneur. This is based on the theory of absorptive capacity that posts an increased ability to take advantage of new knowledge given more similar previous knowledge (Lane and Lubatkin 1998). It is also possible that an entrepreneur with less education or experience is more likely to take advantage of assistance programs, and therefore may alter start-up occurrence outcomes.

The dependent variable in this study is new venture creation status. Our dependent variable is a dichotomous variable of new venture creation – either the new venture was created or it was not. See Figure 10.1 for a diagram of the model guiding this research. Below is an explanation of each of the variables and specific hypotheses for testing.

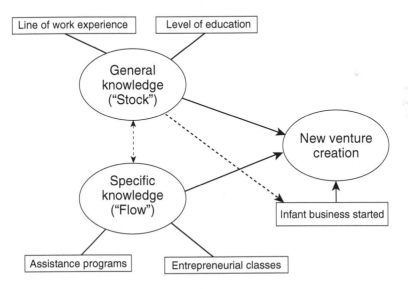

Figure 10.1 The entrepreneurial knowledge flows model.

General knowledge

In the entrepreneurial literature, general knowledge is often captured in the research stream by focusing on the certain events in an entrepreneur's background. Two primary indicators discussed and tested are an entrepreneur's experience and education – elements that constitute knowledge of past learnings. The construct of 'general knowledge' is then composed of two measurement variables: experience and the education gained prior to the point when a nascent entrepreneur acknowledges the intent to start a company and takes active steps towards starting a business. Another way to view the differentiation between general and new specific knowledge is to think of them as stocks and flows, which is a model developed in more established organizations (Dierickx and Cool 1989). Entrepreneurial organizations differ from large organizations as that their resource stock base is smaller – perhaps even just one individual – and they rely more on information flows. In this case, the stocks represent the background of the entrepreneur and the flows refer to the acquisition of additional knowledge (learning) resources through formal assistance programs and/or entrepreneurship classes.

The first general or 'stock' variable for study is experience. The study of experience has a deep history in entrepreneurial literature. In 1980, Karl Vesper reviewed several key studies on the topic and concluded that would-be entrepreneurs should 'seek work experience in several functional areas, preferably including marketing and finance as well as line-of-work and to take advantage of opportunities to participate in initiation of new ventures as educational trials in preparation for the 'main event' (Vesper 1980: 35).

A review of the key studies on the impact of experience indicates commonality in construct development but varying results. As shown in Table 10.1, most studies operationalize experience as a business function (e.g. marketing, finance, accounting, operations), entrepreneurial (first-hand experience with entrepreneurship or family exposure) and line-of-work (previous time spent working in the start-up industry). This chapter will focus on line-of-work experience, as it has a great deal of support in the literature as an explanatory variable related to projected success in new venture launches. This variable is also closely linked to the underlying absorptive capacity theory that suggests that the impact of new knowledge is dependent upon similar past experiences (Lane and Lubatkin 1998). 'Line-of-work' experience pertains to specific industry experience that is similar to the anticipated industry of the new venture. The line-of-work to performance relationship has been identified as an important variable in the literature (Lawyer *et al.* 1963; Brush 1991; Jo and Lee 1996).

The RBT offers insights into how specific resource combinations lead to competitive advantage that then translates to abnormally high returns (Barney 1996). The primary resource in new venture creation is the entrepreneur, and experience represents an aspect worthy of study. One aspect of experience is based upon the management position the entrepreneur is required to fulfill. Entrepreneurs are often called to play a number of roles in their start-up businesses, such as Chief Executive Officer (CEO). Another research stream providing input to this

Table 10.1 Entrepreneurial experience testing

Author	Operationalization	Results
Lawyer *et al.* (1963)	Line-of-work Business functions	Prior experience in the line-of-work and a variety of business functions leads to greater success in entry and subsequent survival
Brush (1991)	Line-of-work	Occupational experience linked to business survival and growth
Jo and Lee (1996)	Line-of-work Business functions	Mixed – managerial and entrepreneurial negative; line-of-work positive
Hoad and Rosko (1964)	Business functions	Prior experience, when combined with education, led to great success
Woodworth *et al.* (1969)	Business functions	Type of experience matters (selling, finance, other)
Shapero (1972)	Business functions	Variety of business functions helps performance
MacMillan *et al.* (1985)	Business functions General business	Study of 100 venture capitalists exhibited support for importance of 'track record'
Gartner (1999)	Business functions	Experience improves start-up performance
Duchesneau and Gartner(1990)	Business functions Exposure (parents) Prior entrepreneur	More successful entrepreneurs raised by entrepreneurial parents, broad business experience and prior entrepreneur experience
Collins and Moore (1970)	Prior entrepreneur	Experience with entrepreneurship impacts performance
Lamont (1972)	Prior entrepreneur	No support for added value of start-up experience
Van de Ven *et al.* (1984)	Prior entrepreneur	Start-up experience negatively linked to performance
Sandberg and Hofer(1987)	Prior entrepreneur	No significant influence of start-up experience on new venture performance
Krueger (1993)	Breadth/positiveness of experience	Prior exposure positively linked to performance

discussion is the study of top management in established organizations. Overall, empirical studies have shown support for the impact of the backgrounds of CEOs on the eventual performance of their respective firms. For example, years of service is posited as an explanatory variable in predicting corporate strategies and ultimate performance (Hambrick and Mason 1984). Theoretical support for the import of line-of-work experience could be that familiarity with the nuances of a particular industry (more knowledge) can lead to better focus on key issues, anticipation of potential problems, and connections to industry players.

The first hypothesis, then, attempts to incorporate the goal of entrepreneurship as the creation of a new venture and to describe the relationship of experience in that line-of-work:

H1:   Previous experience with the line-of-work/industry of the planned venture is positively related to the likelihood of new venture creation.

The other element of general knowledge is education. Although not tested as extensively as experience, an entrepreneur's education has been cited as an important background factor in predicting entrepreneurial start-up success. Early testing of education and the impact on entrepreneurial start-up success used 'one or more years of college' as the educational indicator (Hoad and Rosko 1964). The results showed that more successful entrepreneurs tended to have more advanced education (which led to the highest level of success when combined with experience). Also, they noted that education without experience led to a higher likelihood of failure, suggesting the need to test for interaction effects. Woodworth *et al.* (1969) also found support for a positive effect of more education on entrepreneurial success. Education also became a source of entrepreneurial ideas (Vesper 1979).

Continued investigation of this issue led to mixed results. Explanations for the variance in results could lie in the effect of certain controlling elements that have not been considered. Examples include gender and the nature of the type of start-up effort, such as those requiring more technical backgrounds. Education was found not to have significant impact for general firm formation (Sandberg and Hofer 1987) and even negative impact beyond the master's degree (Stuart and Abetti 1990). Other studies found the opposite effect and claimed that education has a positive impact on entrepreneurial performance. In a study of 191 women-owned businesses, education was found to affect business survival and growth (Brush 1991) and high-technology start-ups (Cooper 1971). One study found that education led to higher profitability but not higher growth (Jo and Lee 1996). A more recent study found support for education in general, linking it to increased new venture success (Gartner 1999).

Overall, education is generally considered to have an impact on new venture creation efforts. Theoretical support for this argument would be that the education indicator could represent other qualities that affect the likelihood of eventual new venture creation such as work ethic or intelligence quotient (IQ). It is clearly an important element of general knowledge and warrants testing for impact on performance. One of the potentially important control elements that must be considered is the impact of specific knowledge on the general knowledge attained through educational programs. For example, an entrepreneur with less education may be more apt to go to assistance programs for help during the entrepreneurial process, thereby increasing the chances of success in launching the new business.

The Top Management Team (TMT) literature base has investigated the impact of formal education and posits that the amount of formal education impacts performance (Hambrick and Mason 1984) by capitalizing on innovation gains due to the underlying differences of the individuals as represented by their educational pursuits. This provides additional support for the second hypothesis:

H2: Level of formal education is positively related to the likelihood of new venture creation.

Specific knowledge

Specific knowledge pertains to knowledge learned by the entrepreneur during certain activities occurring during the start-up process. Incorporating the RBT and the KBV/OL, it could be argued that entrepreneurial start-up efforts have significant gaps in their knowledge resource 'stocks' that can be greatly impacted by the flow of specific knowledge from formal assistance programs, which build on the collective experiences of years of working with start-up efforts. Research in this area increased during the 1990s, largely in response to the call for more behavior investigation (moving beyond traits and backgrounds). The RBT has surfaced as a useful lens to apply to the entrepreneurship literature and the issue of assistance programs (Chrisman and McMullan 2000). The research has generally focused on two areas: formal assistance programs and classes/workshops on entrepreneurship.

From a theoretical perspective, it would appear that there should be support for improved chances of new venture creation with the addition of new knowledge. This would be particularly true for new entrepreneurs seeking assistance on strategic or operational assistance. One of the major studies claiming support for outsider assistance was Robinson's paper in 1982. Outsider assistance improved an entrepreneur's chances of new venture creation due to better strategic planning (Robinson 1982). Table 10.2 summarizes other major research

Table 10.2 Entrepreneurial assistance program testing

Author	Testing	Results
Robinson (1982)	SBDC clients	Found support for support programs due to better strategic planning
Nahavandi and Chesteen (1988)	Mail survey of 123 SBDC clients	Behavior that results in accessing new knowledge results in better performance
Chrisman *et al.* (1987)	474 SBDC clients in GA/SC	Outsider assistance helped subsequent performance
Chrisman (1989)	249 SBDC clients	Strategic assistance valued; administrative and operating assistance not valued
Duchesneau and Gartner (1990)	Entrepreneurs	More successful entrepreneurs used assistance
Dennis and Phillips (1990)	High tech start-ups	No relationship at the state level of assistance and start-up performance
Coyle (1992)	Minnesota Outreach	Described assistance program efforts for entrepreneurs
Chrisman (1999)	SBDC clients	Outsider assistance increased number of new ventures

contributions related to the impact of formal assistance programs that are incorporated herein.

Most of the studies found support for the positive impact of assistance on entrepreneurial performance. One major exception was a high technology start-up investigation that indicated no significant impact of the assistance programs (Dennis and Phillips 1990). Theories suggest that in some cases the assistance does not prove valuable if it is not well grounded or if it is already known (Chrisman 1989). This suggests a need to test for interaction effects of general knowledge; however, none of the studies reviewed included controls for previous knowledge (addressed in the final two hypotheses). Overall, there seems to be support in the literature for a positive link between use of assistance programs and the chance of new venture creation:

H3:   Level of use of formal assistance programs is positively related to the likelihood of new venture creation.

Another element of entrepreneurial behavior that may impact the start-up process is the attainment of specific knowledge through entrepreneurial classes or workshops. Although this proposition has not been explicitly and empirically tested, it follows the same logic as the knowledge search through formal assistance programs as described above. This variable is distinct from general education as it pertains to a special topic of study – entrepreneurship. By exploring this variable, the inferred proposition inherent in the KBV of cumulative effects of knowledge resources, whereby more is better, can be tested. Accordingly, this leads to the next hypothesis:

H4:   Taking entrepreneurial-related classes/workshops during the start-up process is positively related to the likelihood of new venture creation.

Interaction effects

Another gap in the literature is the void of interaction effect testing of general and specific knowledge on start-up performance. Each has been tested in isolation, but not together. As a result, we may have an incomplete understanding of the relative importance of these independent variables and may miss important relationship issues that may lead to new conclusions about the new venture process.

The KBV/OL theoretical perspective offers some theoretical guidance that can inform our study of this process. Specifically, absorptive capacity is a research stream that analyzes the effectiveness of new specific knowledge on performance. Although typically analyzed at the organizational level, this concept offers lessons for individual study as well. For example, one key concept is that the existing general knowledge base greatly influences the ability to capitalize on new knowledge opportunities (Mangematin and Nesta 1999). It has also been suggested that the combinative capabilities for absorbing knowledge is directly related to the level of prior related knowledge (Van den Bosch et al. 1999). The RBT can also inform this argument. Specifically, research has shown that simultaneous pursuit of exploiting existing resources while exploring new resource combinations leads to increased performance (Wernerfelt 1984). The entrepreneurship setting offers a rich environment for testing the relationship between existing general and new resources of a more specific nature.

In our model, this leads to a potential moderating variable situation where general knowledge can moderate the impact of new specific knowledge on performance, given the absorptive capacity argument. By exploring these issues, we can develop a deeper understanding of the relative importance of types of knowledge and knowledge acquisition mechanisms on new venture creation. This also presents a more holistic understanding of the knowledge flows in the entrepreneurial process and results in a much fuller model with additional explanatory power. The final hypothesis is:

H5: The impact of specific entrepreneurial knowledge on the likelihood of new venture creation is moderated by previous general knowledge (higher levels of use of formal assistance programs and taking entrepreneurial classes will result in a higher likelihood of new venture creation given more experience and a higher level of general education).

Empirical testing

Dataset

The data for this study were gathered as part of an ongoing Panel Study of Entrepreneurial Dynamics (PSED) sponsored by the Entrepreneurial Research Consortium (ERC), which involves over 45 different international academic and government institutions. The population was a random selection of over 30,000 individuals who were surveyed by telephone and through the mail. General background information was gathered and summarized, specifically identifying which of the individuals were nascent entrepreneurs. The screening processes, along with women and minority over-sampling efforts, resulted in a sample group of 1,261 nascent entrepreneurs with over 800 variables and responses. Follow-up surveys were conducted after 12 months to evaluate the status of the start-up effort. Since the performance data are critical to this study, only cases with such information available were selected for study. This resulted in a final sample size of 492 entrepreneurs, with particular weightings based on their representation of the overall population. See an extensive discussion on the background and methodology in the book chapter by Reynolds in *Advances in Entrepreneurship, Firm Emergence, and Growth*, Vol. 4 (Reynolds 2000). Note that this is a dynamic database that continues to grow as annual follow-up interviews with the entrepreneurs continue for longitudinal purposes. The data used for this chapter were analyzed as of May 2001, and expansions and additional waves of data have been collected since that point.

The independent variables studied include experience in the start-up industry (EXP), years of education (EDU), contact with assistance programs (HELP) and entrepreneurship classes/workshops taken (CLASS). Experience (EXP) is the only continuous variable in the dataset as it represents total years of experience of the entrepreneur in the intended line of business. Education (EDU) represents the level of education the entrepreneur has achieved at the time of the survey. The education (EDU) variable is an interval variable that is based on the number of years of formal education achieved, with a range of 7 to 20. This variable is also analyzed in four categories for interaction effects with the following four categories: high school (hs), some college (hs+), college (coll) and graduate (grad). This allows for more explanatory power, and is chiefly helpful because using the single education (EDU) variable in logistic regression would force a straight line – a straight line would not be meaningful, as these data are not linear. Finally, the dependent variable is a nominal variable – a dichotomous assessment of whether or not a new venture was created (STAT).

Methodology and results

The first step of analysis was to review the data utilizing the frequency distributions and descriptive statistics. The software utilized was SPSS Version 10.0. The next step was to examine correlations to identify covariance relationships. Note that since most of these variables are nominal, great caution must be taken in reaching causation and directional conclusions. Finally, logistic regression was utilized to separate the main effects of the variables, general knowledge/new specific knowledge learned categories and interaction effects. Logistic regression was chosen over linear regression (such as ordinary least squares regression) primarily because the dependent variable is categorical and the predicated values are likely to lie outside the observed data range of 0–1. As the distributions of independent variables violate the multivariate normality assumption (see below), logistic regression was selected over discriminant analysis.

A review of the frequencies and descriptive statistics reveals the following observations. Experience (EXP) is skewed to the left with 25 percent of the entrepreneurs having no experience in the intended start-up industry and 40 percent having 2 years or less. This may be the result of respondents indicating a desire to change jobs and viewing entrepreneurship as a tool by which to do so. At the right end of the frequency distribution, those entrepreneurs with over 25 years of experience comprise only 10 percent of the entire population. This may suggest that as entrepreneurs age and become more established in their careers, they are less apt to consider attempting to launch a new business.

The education variable (EDU) is based on the number of years of education achieved by the entrepreneur. The minimum is 7 and the maximum is 20, with the majority between 12 and 16; these numbers represent high school, some college and college educations. To facilitate detailed interactions and testing between education levels (since the distribution of education years is not normal), additional dummy variables for education were created. The four sub-categories of education include: high school, some college, college degree and graduate. A separate analysis of these four categories of education seems to be distributed as we would expect given the US educational distribution – high school (15 percent), some college (41 percent), college degree (24 percent) and graduate (20 percent).

The two variables associated with new knowledge learned during the start-up process include HELP (contact with formal assistance programs) and CLASS (a class or workshop in entrepreneurship). Both variables are dichotomous responses, coded as 0 for no and 1 for yes. Only 17 percent of the entrepreneurs actually utilized formal assistance programs, while over 40 percent took a class or workshop related to entrepreneurship. This has implications for the reach of small business assistance programs (perhaps not as great as previously thought) and for studies that exclude entrepreneurs not seeking assistance in their sample populations (given the magnitude of this group, they should be incorporated in comparison and control modes).

Finally, 32 percent of the nascent entrepreneurs actually started the new venture within one year, which is slightly below previous estimates of between 33 percent (Katz 1990) and 48 (Carter *et al.* 1996). It is also interesting to note that of the 30,000 in the original sample, 1,261 were considered nascent entrepreneurs or 4 percent, which falls within previous estimates of between 3 and 8 percent (Reynolds and Miller 1992; Dennis 1997). See the full descriptive statistics in Table 10.3.

Table 10.3 Descriptive statistics

	N	Min.	Max.	Mean	S.Dev.	Yes (%)	No (%)
Experience (EXP)	486	0	60	9.16	10.66	N/A	N/A
Education (EDU)	491	7	20	14.98	2.08	N/A	N/A
High school (hs)	73	0	1	0.15	0.36	N/A	N/A
Some college (hs+)	199	0	1	0.40	0.49	N/A	N/A
College degree (coll)	119	0	1	0.24	0.43	N/A	N/A
Post college (grad)	100	0	1	0.20	0.40	N/A	N/A
Assistance (HELP)	491	0	1	0.17	0.38	17.1	82.9
Class/Workshop (CLASS)	492	0	1	0.41	0.49	40.9	59.1
Status of start-up (STAT)	492	0	1	0.33	0.47	32.8	67.2

The correlation analysis (see Table 10.4) was conducted to examine if these variables, many of which have been tested independently in the past, have intercorrelations that would affect conclusions about their respective contributions toward to explaining the incidents of new venture creation. Note that as all of these binary correlations include at least one nominal variable, directional conclusions should be drawn with caution. The experience variable (EXP) showed significant correlation to two sub-equation variables ('hs' or high school and 'grad' or graduate work), but not to education as measured on an interval basis between 7 and 20 (EDU, the education variable). Experience (EXP) was, however, significantly correlated to the use of formal assistance programs (HELP), such as the Small Business Development Association. This suggests that entrepreneurs of a particular experience level are more or less apt to seek assistance.

For example, on an intuitive level, it would seem reasonable that entrepreneurs with less experience would be more likely to seek help. The education sub-variables all correspond appropriately to the overall education variable, as one would expect. Two of the education sub-variables, 'hs' and 'grad,' also correlate with the assistance variable; this may be an area of investigation for future research.

One other correlation with significance worth noting is the link between the use of formal assistance programs (HELP) and the use of entrepreneurial class/workshop (CLASS). This could tie to underlying personality similarities such as motivation or the desire to learn. The most important finding from the correlation analysis is that all of the variables in isolation do not correlate with the dependent variable STAT, which indicates whether or not a new venture was created, except for one. HELP and STAT are correlated (Pearson correlation of 0.078 and significance of 0.042 at the 0.05 level), which implies some relationship between entrepreneurs who utilize assistance programs and those who successfully launch new ventures.

Another interesting finding comes from the logistic regression analysis. As shown in Table 10.5, three models were analyzed utilizing hierarchical logistic regression. 'Model 1' represents the general knowledge variables of education and experience. The results show that this model is insignificant and represents a low R-squared value between 0.005 and 0.006 (Cox and Nagelkerke, respectively), indicating that, at most, that only 0.6 percent of the variance could have attributed to these variables. The contribution of this finding is that the explanatory power of education and experience combined is not significant, which contradicts certain previous studies' claims of importance. 'Model 2,' which includes new knowledge variables of the use of formal assistance programs and taking an entrepreneurship course/workshop, does not improve the overall picture; 'Model 2' boasts an increase of chi square of only 2.989, a model R-squared of 0.011 to 0.015 (Cox and Nagelkerke, respectively) and overall insignificance. The contribution here is that, from a predictive perspective, those entrepreneurs seeking assistance and taking classes do not fall into a significantly different group as evaluated by the dependent variable of new venture creation. Finally, when interaction variables are introduced in 'Model 3,' there is a jump in explanatory power. The R-squared of the model is now between 0.039 and 0.055, which indicates that between 3.9 and 5.5 percent of the variance can be explained. Although this is still low, the change in chi square is 14.287. Although not significant as an explanatory model, this model has a dramatically higher chi square than those models not considering such interactions. A summary of the results is shown in Table 10.6.

Discussion

Conclusions

Perhaps the most interesting result from this analysis is the lack of empirical support for certain dominant theoretical propositions. Specifically, only one of the four independent variables, the use of formal assistance programs, had direct

Table 10.4 Correlations pearson correlation (sig.), 1 tailed test; bold denotes sig. (0.05/0.01)

	EXP	EDU	hs	hs+	coll	grad	HELP	CLASS	STAT
EXP	1								
EDU	0.065(0.078)	1							
hs	-0.097(0.016)	-0.63(0.000)	1						
hs+	0.038(0.202)	-0.388(0.000)	-0.344(0.000)	1					
coll	-0.061(0.092)	0.278(0.000)	0.236(0.000)	-0.466(0.000)	1				
grad	0.097(0.016)	0.744(0.000)	0.231(0.000)	0.417(0.000)	0.286(0.000)	1			
HELP	0.088(0.027)	0.184(0.000)	0.147(0.001)	0.009(0.422)	0.006(0.444)	0.149(0.000)	1		
CLASS	0.034(0.227)	0.039(0.195)	-0.070(0.062)	-0.060(0.092)	-0.04(0.163)	0.038(0.202)	0.210(0.000)	1	
STAT	0.012(0.397)	0.037(0.209)	0.018(0.348)	0.032(0.237)	0.007(0.438)	0.044(0.167)	0.078(0.042)	0.018(0.343)	1

Table 10.5 Logistic regression results

	Model 1	Model 2	Model 3
−2 log likelihood	607.303	604.314	590.027
Cox and Snell – R-squared	0.005	0.011	0.039
Nagelkerke – R-squared	0.006	0.015	0.055
Chi square	2.188	5.177	19.464
Chi square significance	0.823	0.638	0.193
Increase in chi square (block)	N/A	2.989	14.287
Increase in chi square sig. (block)	N/A	0.224	0.075
% class correct	67.8	67.8	69.1

Model 1=Experience+Education; *Model 2*=Model 1+Assistance+Classes; *Model 3*=Model 2+Interactions.

effects on the likelihood of new venture creation. This research project was designed to address many of the aforementioned weaknesses in the literature, specifically studying a greater number of entrepreneurs, studying them earlier in the process, and studying them with more controls than has been done in the past. After doing so the relationships and paradigms long held to be true in entrepreneurship, such as the belief that more education and relevant work experience will aid in entrepreneurial pursuits, are now called into question.

There are three primary conclusions from this research. First, general recipes for entrepreneurship success are dangerous and specific attribute theory is incomplete. Hypotheses 1 (experience affects incidence of new venture creation),

Table 10.6 Summary of results

Hypothesis Number	Description	Results
H1	Previous experience with the line-of-work/industry of the planned venture is positively related to the likelihood of new venture creation	Not supported
H2	Level of formal education is positively related to the likelihood of new venture creation	Not supported
H3	Level of use of formal assistance programs is positively related to the likelihood of new venture creation	Supported
H4	Taking entrepreneurial-related classes/worksh ops during the start-up process is positively related to the likelihood of new venture creation	Not supported
H5	The impact of new knowledge on the likelihood of new venture creation is moderated by previous knowledge (use of formal assistance programs and taking entrepreneurial classes will result in a higher likelihood of new venture creation given more experience and a higher level of education)	Supported

2 (education affects incidence of new venture creation), and 4 (taking entrepreneurial classes affects incidence of new venture creation) were not supported by the data, indicating that there are no significant arguments for prescribed recommendations relating to experience, education and classes to increase new venture creation. The logistic modeling, which included the explanatory power of the variables together, did not show significance; this lends further support to the need to search for additional explanatory variables and cautions not to rely on incomplete models claiming to predict entrepreneurial performance. Possible avenues for the development of additional variables that may help explain the ultimate performance of starting a business may lie in social network theory or more likely in the learning processes entrepreneurs undertake as they pursue their start-up objectives.

Second, formal assistance programs may indeed have impact on the incidence of new venture creation, given the support for Hypothesis 2 in this study. This finding is in alignment with previous studies drawing the same conclusion. The important contribution in this study is that the testing included entrepreneurs who sought the assistance as well as those who did not seek such help, which has not been tested previously. Since over 65 percent of the entrepreneurs in this study had only two years or less of relevant experience, and those with less experience are more likely to pursue assistance programs, this is a particularly important area for entrepreneurship policy recommendations. The analysis also surfaced data related to the use of such formal assistance programs, specifically that only 17 percent of nascent entrepreneurs took advantage of such programs. Further analysis into the availability, access and awareness of these programs may dramatically affect the number of start-ups in a particular region or country.

Third, interaction and moderation effects should be given more attention in studying these topics. Given the support for Hypothesis 5, certain entrepreneurs may benefit more from formal assistance and classes based on their respective backgrounds relating to education and experience. This lends partial support to absorptive capacity arguments that suggest that it is not the individual antecedents that are important, but the combination thereof. Or perhaps it is a case of 'necessary' but not 'sufficient.' This may represent the most intriguing finding from a research perspective. The use of the KBV and OL theoretical lens may inform entrepreneurship insofar as working toward a better understanding of why certain types of assistance have more impact on the likelihood of new venture creation. Ultimately, this may suggest a more tailored strategy toward assistance that is based upon the background of the respective entrepreneur. This would be an advancement in the causation arguments in entrepreneurship, which have moved from traits to process. Perhaps it is more important to continue to investigate both, and do so simultaneously for greater explanatory power in the creation of new ventures.

Future directions

Moving forward, this chapter introduces several topics for further investigation. For example, from a social network perspective, 'What is the impact of an entrepreneur's start-up team or social network on general or specific knowledge?' From a KBV perspective 'How might the specific breadth and depth elements of knowledge change the outcomes?' From a learning perspective, 'If exposure to knowledge opportunities does not differentiate the results, what specifically about the learning process itself may make the difference?' One of the goals of this chapter was to integrate multiple theoretical lenses to better inform the entrepreneurial literature, consistent with the call articulated by Shane and Venkataraman (2000) in their seminal entrepreneurial research paper. There is also an opportunity to use the findings here to test additional propositions related to TMT backgrounds and process links to performance – and both are important. Overall, the lack of significance of some of the historically important variables for new venture creation is a caution against general recipes for entrepreneurs and a call for more study of how the entrepreneurs truly learn what is necessary for success.

It is important to discuss some limitations of the current study. For example, logistics regression on panel data may be biased if the cases under study did not have the same probability to reach the end state. Additionally, the dependent variable in this study, new venture creation, may produce different results if the study included more time for the start-up process. Another tool that may be used on the PSED database or similar datasets for such investigations would be event history techniques. Finally, alternative measures exist that may alter the conclusions reached herein. Such measurement variables available, but not studied in this project, include work history, previous job title, number of years of paid experience, prior entrepreneurial experience, number of courses taken and school major. The primary purpose of this study was to begin the exploration of theoretical claims with one of the best emerging entrepreneurial databases available. As the database and performance tracking continues to grow and to be studied, more insights are sure to follow.

Studying the learning process could be a fruitful stream of research (Sexton *et al.* 1997). Although specific entrepreneurial traits may elude specification and verification, the emphasis on how and what entrepreneurs learn is clearly of import (Smilor 1997). Additionally, on a more positive note, this study confirms the impact of formal assistance programs in the enhancement of new venture creation likelihood, but the search for additional variables explaining the variance in new venture creation is a worthy pursuit. In fact, the PSED dataset contains additional variables for study as well. This study represents a contribution in that direction and provides empirical testing of certain entrepreneurial learning propositions.

Acknowledgment

Special thanks to Howard Aldrich, Richard Bettis, Jeffrey Covin, Hugh O'Neill, Michael Meeks Kelly Shaver and Anne York for their review and input related to ideas presented in this chapter.

References

Aldrich, H., Kalleberg A., Marsden, P. and Cassell, J. (1989) In pursuit of evidence: sampling procedures for locating new businesses. *Journal of Business Venturing,* 4(6): 367–87.

Barney, J. B. (1996) The resource-based theory of the firm. *Organization Science,* 7(5): 469.

Baum, R. J., Locke, E. A. and Smith, K. G. (2001) A multidimensional model of venture growth. *Academy of Management Journal,* 44(2): 292–303.

Bird, B. J. (1988) Implementing entrepreneurial ideas: the case for intention. *Academy of Management Review,* 13(3): 442–54.

Brush, C. D. (1991) Antecedent influences on women-owned businesses. *Journal of Managerial Psychology,* 6(2): 9–17.

Busenitz, L. W. and Barney, J. B. (1997) Differences between entrepreneurs and managers in large organizations: biases and heuristics in strategic decision-making. *Journal of Business Venturing,* 12(1): 9–20.

Carter, N. M., Gartner W. D. and Reynolds, P. D. (1996) Exploring start-up event sequences. *Journal of Business Venturing,* 11(3): 151–67.

Chandler, A. D. (1962) *Strategy and Structure.* Cambridge, MA: MIT Press.

Chrisman, J. J. (1989) Strategic, administrative, and operating assistance: the value of outside consulting to pre-venture entrepreneurs. *Journal of Business Venturing,* 4(6): 401–18.

Chrisman, J. J. (1999) The influence of outsider-generated knowledge resources on venture creation. *Journal of Small Business Management* 37(4): 42–58.

Chrisman, J. J. and McMullan, W. E. (2000) A preliminary assessment of outsider assistance as a knowledge resource: the longer-term impact of new venture counseling. *Entrepreneurship Theory and Practice,* Spring: 37.

Chrisman, J. J., Hoy, F. and Richard Jr, R. (1987) New venture development: the costs and benefits of public sector assistance. *Journal of Business Venturing,* 2(4): 315–29.

Collins, O. F. and Moore, D. G. (1970) *The Organization Makers: A Behavioral Study of Independent Entrepreneurs.* New York: Appleton-Century-Crofts.

Cooper, A. C. (1971) *The Founding of Technology-Based Firms.* Milwaukee, WI Center for Venture Management.

Coyle, P. (1992) Knowledge outreach program vitalizes small business growth. *Economic Development Review,* 10(1): 72–4.

Dennis, W. J. Jr. (1997) More than you think: an inclusive estimate of business entries. *Journal of Business Venturing,* 12(3): 175–96.

Dennis, W. J. Jr. and Phillips, B. D. (1990) The synergism of independent high technology business starts. *Entrepreneurship and Regional Development* 2:1–14.

Dierickx, I. and Cool, K. (1989) Asset stock, accumulation and sustainability of competitive advantage. *Management Science,* 35, 1504–11.

Duchesneau, D. A and Gartner, W. B. (1990) A profile of new venture success and failure in an emerging industry. *Journal of Business Venturing,* 5(5): 297–313.

Gartner, W. B. (1988) 'Who is an entrepreneur?' is the wrong question. *American Journal of Small Business* 12(4): 11–33.

Gartner, W. B. (1999) Predicting new venture survival: an analysis of 'Anatomy of a Startup' cases From Inc. Magazine. *Journal of Business Venturing,* 14(2): 215–32.

Gatewood, E. J., Shaver K. and Gartner, W. (1995) A longitudinal study of cognitive factors influencing start-up behaviors and success at venture creation. *Journal of Business Venturing* 10(5): 371–92.

Grant, R. M. (1997) The knowledge-based view of the firm: implications or management practice. *Long Range Planning,* 30(3): 450–4.

Hambrick, D. C. and Mason, P. A. (1984) Upper echelons: the organization as a reflection of its top managers. *Academy of Management Review*, 9(2): 193–206.

Hoad, W. and Rosko, P. (1964) *Management Factors Contributing to the Success and Failure of New Small Manufacturers*. Ann Arbor, MI: Bureau of Business Research, University of Michigan.

Jo, H. and Lee, J. (1996). The relationship between an entrepreneur's background and performance in a new venture. *Technovation*, 16(4): 161–72.

Katz, J. A. (1990) Longitudinal analysis of self-employment follow-through *Entrepreneurship and Regional Development*, 2: 15–25.

Katz, J. and Gartner, W. B. (1988) Properties of emerging organizations *Academy of Management Review*. 13(3): 429–42.

Krueger, N. F. Jr and Brazeal, D. (1994) Entrepreneurial potential and potential entrepreneurs. *Entrepreneurship Theory and Practice*, 18(3): 91–105.

Krueger, N. (1993). The impact of prior entrepreneurial exposure on perceptions. *Entrepreneurship Theory and Practice,* 18(1) 5–22.

Lamont, L. M. (1972). What entrepreneurs learn from experience. *Journal of Small Business Management*, 10(July): 254–60.

Lane, P. J. and Lubatkin, M. (1998) Relative absorptive capacity and inter-organizational learning. *Strategic Management Journal*, 19(5): 461–77.

Lawyer, K. *et al.* (1963) *Small Business Success: Operating Executive Characteristics*. Cleveland, OH: Bureau of Business Research, Case Western Reserve University.

Learned, K. E. (1992) What happened before the organization? *Entrepreneurship Theory and Practice*, 17(1): 39–49.

MacMillan, I. C., Siegel, R. and Subba Narasimha, P. (1985) Criteria used by venture capitalists to evaluate new venture proposals. *Journal of Business Venturing* Winter 119–29.

Mangematin, V. and Nesta, L. (1999) What kind of knowledge can a firm absorb? *International Journal of Technology Management*, 18(3–4): 149–72.

Nahavandi, A. and Chesteen, S. (1988) The impact of consulting on small business: a further examination. *Entrepreneurship Theory and Practice* 13(1): 29–41.

Penrose, E. (1959) *The Theory of the Growth of the Firm*. Oxford: Blackwell.

Reynolds, P. (2000) *Advances in Entrepreneurship, Firm Emergence, and Growth*, Vol. 4 Stamford, CT JAI Press.

Reynolds, P. and Miller, B. (1992) New firm gestation: conception, birth, and implications for research. *Journal of Business Venturing,* 7(5): 405–18.

Robinson, R. Jr (1982) The importance of 'outsiders' in small firm strategic planning. *Academy of Management Journal* 25(1): 30–94.

Sandberg, W. R. and Hofer, C. W. (1987) Improving new venture performance: the role of strategy, industry structure, and the entrepreneur. *Journal of Business Venturing*, 2(1): 5–28.

Schumpeter, J. A. (1934) *The Theory of Economic Development*. Cambridge, MA: Harvard University Press.

Schwenk, C. R. (1988) The cognitive perspective on strategic decision making. *Journal of Management Studies*, 25(1): 41–56.

Sexton, D. L., Upton, N. B., Wacholtz, L. E. and McDougall, P. P. (1997) Learning needs of growth-oriented entrepreneurs. *Journal of Business Venturing*, 12: 1–8.

Shane, S. and Venkataraman, S. (2000) The promise of entrepreneurship as a field of research Academy of Management Review. 25(1):217–26.

Shapero, A. (1982) Developing a high-tech complex through small company formations. *Survey of Business,* 18(1): 16–20.

Smilor, R. W. (1997) Executive Forum – Entrepreneurship: reflections on a subversive activity. *Journal of Business Venturing*, 12: 341–46.

Stuart, R. W, and Abetti P. (1990) Impact of entrepreneurial and management experience on early performance. *Journal of Business Venturing,* 5(3): 151–73.

Van de Ven, A. H., Hudson R. and. Schroeder D. M. (1984) Designing new business startups: entrepreneurial, organizational, and ecological considerations. *Journal of Management*, 10: 87–107.

Van den Bosch, A., Volberda, H. W. and de Boer, M. (1999) Coevolution of firm absorptive capacity and knowledge environment: organizational forms and combinative capabilities. *Organization Science*, 10(5): 551–68.

Venkataraman, S. (1997) The distinctive domain of entrepreneurhip reearch: an editor's perspective. J. A. Katz and J. Brockhauseds, *Advances in Entrepreneurship, Firm Emergence, and Growth* Greenwich, CT: JAI Press.

Vesper, K. H. (1979) New-venture ideas: do not overlook experience factor. *Harvard Business Review,* 57(4): 164.

Vesper, K. H. (1980) *New Venture Strategies*. Englewood Cliffs, NJ: Prentice Hall.

Wernerfelt, B. (1984) A resource-based view of the firm. *Strategic Management Journal*, 5(2): 171–81.

Woodworth, R. T. *et al.* (1969) *The Entrepreneurial Process and the Role of Accountants, Bankers and Lawyers*. Seattle School of Business, University of Washington.

11 Strategy making, organizational learning and performance in SMEs

Edward Gonsalves and Colin Gray

Introduction

Mintzberg and Waters' (1985) work on deliberate and emergent strategy formation is one of the primary pieces of literature in what has been described as the 'process' school of strategy. This chapter adopts a process-based approach when examining entrepreneurship strategies. It elaborates a typology of strategy formation processes based on Mintzberg's (1988) definition of strategy as a pattern in a stream of actions. The central themes and arguments are derived from a UK project (Gray and Gonsalves 2002), and build on Mintzberg and Waters' idea that 'emergent strategies imply learning that works' to hypothesize a relationship between senior managers' orientations to organizational learning, strategy making and environmental uncertainty. The chapter considers the methodological debate within entrepreneurial studies by attending to the structure–agency debate as duality rather than dualism. It also argues that a multidimensional approach to theorizing organizational learning will provide a more robust basis from which to deliver both diagnostic and normative models of learning within the field of entrepreneurship.

The empirical model integrates a 'configuration' perspective of firm strategy, which seeks to establish building blocks for theory construction. Configuration theories constitute a widespread body of literature on the tendency of organizational variable relationships towards 'ideal' types. The assumption is that active searches for new ways of operationalizing concepts lead to better correspondence between theory and measures, and that non-standard operationalizations of variables allow for relationship verification and external validity despite substantial methodological variation.

Researchers into SMEs (small and medium-size enterprises) are increasingly attending to the potential for the organizational learning concept to contribute to an understanding of entrepreneurship and entrepreneurial success. In developed market economies the antecedents for this growth in research are increasingly driven by two factors: first, the increasing emphasis at policy level on the need to promote entrepreneurial activity through education initiatives (Rae and Carswell 2001) and second, the increasing willingness by large firms and development agencies to participate in the establishment of entrepreneurial cultures within their networks of SME suppliers and customers (Gray 1998). Most of these reports readily admit that researching the process of organizational learning within entrepreneurial, SMEs remains long-term and problematic (Gray and Gonsalves 2002); however, an emerging consensus argues that further empirical study into these processes will help delineate and develop the concept of entrepreneurial learning.

This chapter attempts an integration of theoretical perspectives when hypothesizing relationships between the constructs of SME strategy making (Mintzberg 1978; Mintzberg and Waters 1985; Hart 1995), organizational learning (Crossan 1997; Easterby-Smith 1997), environmental uncertainty and performance in developing such a concept. The empirical description assumes a survey-based approach to theory testing and suggests SME managers' perceptions of their firms' characteristics and competitive environments as key measures. It adopts a process-based approach to describing the hypothesized relationships. The assumption is that a 'meta-theoretic' and integrative perspective enables researchers to conduct inquiries into SMEs that are at once consistent with previous researches in the field and sympathetic to concep-tualizing learning and strategy making as multidimensional and temporal phenomena.

We acknowledge therefore that the managers' responses to survey question-naires are a 'snapshot' of SMEs, which encompass codification of events in memory that bring to the present, and projected futures, impressions of the importance, duration, frequency and interdependencies that combine to produce the experience . . . of organization (Cairns *et al.* 2003: 129). As Kor and Mahoney (2000) note, in Penrosean approaches, 'The entrepreneurial imagination is influ-enced by experiences of interactions between managers and resources. Thus the firm is both pushed and pulled by the future' (p. 115).

Second, such an approach supports arguments in which actors' understandings of organizational phenomena, as reflected in their perceptions, may provide insights into organizational processes which are as valuable as studies into 'objective' strategic phenomena (Fombrun and Zajac 1987; Hooley *et al.* 1998). Finally, the survey-based approach is consistent with previous, albeit not solely SME-based, studies into the relationship between strategy making, competitive environments and firm performance (Miller and Friesen 1983; Mallory *et al.* 1997). These assumptions have guided the study when facing the methodological and definitional difficulties inherent in moving from verbal conceptualizations of a theory to the corresponding empirical investigation of that theory's central tenets (Venkatraman 1989). In doing so we attempt to fill some of the methodological gaps promulgated by theorists in each of the research domains considered. In particular, this makes explicit the research reality when working with the organizational learning construct, which in terms of empirically validated research remains dispersed (Lähteenmäki *et al.* 2001), and the strategy-making construct which, although more developed, continues to demand 'accuracy and parsimony' (Miller 1983: 772).

Conceptual reviews

SME strategy

Knowledge about SME management is fragmented (d'Amboise and Muldowney 1988). Robinson and Pearce (1984) note that 'the state of knowledge pertinent to the strategic management of SMEs is woefully inadequate. Most literature in this area is prescriptive, lacking a rigorous empirical base'. These gaps are attributable to the considerable methodological and theoretical volatility facing researchers in the field (Curran *et al.* 1992) (McKiernan and Morris 1993) and the theoretical limitations of ambiguous definitions of strategy, in much SME management literature.

The difficulty in conceptualizing leads to difficulties in operationalizing constructs for SMEs. Gibb and Scott (1985) draw attention to the confusion: 'What for example is the difference between a plan, a strategic plan, or for that matter just a simple strategy?' The question not only highlights the definitional confusion in the field, but is also witness to an overwhelming concern of analysing small business strategies as plans, that is, assuming strategic planning to be a proxy measure of, and an alternative to, strategic management (Pleitner 1989).

It is not the purpose of this chapter to consider arguments for and against the relative merits of prescribing strategic planning as an indispensable necessity for SME management. Instead we argue that all firms are engaged in 'strategic thinking', but not all have 'intended' strategies, that is to say, strategic plans. That smaller organizations tend to have implicit, intuitively derived strategies (Scott 1971; Mintzberg 1973) makes the distinction all the more important. SME research, especially at the conceptual level, will need to draw on developments in strategic theory if it is to adopt this broader and process-based perspective of strategy 'making/foming'.

Resource-based view of strategy

Strategy making and organizational learning are conceived in this study as potentially firm-specific endowments, a perspective that draws on the resource-based theory of the firm (Penrose 1959; Wernerfelt 1984) in which firms are perceived as bundles of differential resources replenished, diminished and sustained by managers as they exercise dynamic choices in their ongoing search for economic rents (Barney 1991). The resource-based view (RBV) accords greater weight to the positive role of entrepreneurial managerial discernment in explaining the sustainable competitive advantage of firms when compared to the emphasis placed on managers by traditional theories of industrial organization and strategic planning, and is consistent with the view of SME strategies as primarily process-based.

Hart (1995) notes that:

> The strategic significance of firm resources and capabilities has been heightened by recent observations that companies that are better able to understand,

nurture, and leverage core competencies outperform those that are preoccupied with more conventional approaches to [strategic] business planning ... (p. 989)

Conner's (1991) critique compares and contrasts the RBV to previous macro- and micro-economic schools of thought. For example, within the Schumpetarian proposition she contends that

firms exist primarily to seize competitive opportunity ... in order to make rival positions obsolete ... and that the purpose of the firms seeking radical innovation is tied to the possession of [a will to] monopoly power [thereby securing above normal returns in the long term] ... (p. 127)

From the Chicago School's perspective, firms exist not to obtain monopolistic positions through destruction of competitors, but to grow through the exploitation of competitive efficiency differentials in production and distribution. Hence, firm growth, size and scope are functions of this ability and the achievement of scale economies, rather than industry structure (Conner 1991).

In contrast to the above two perspectives, Conner (1991: 130) argues that transaction cost economic theorists (Williamson 1975) view the firm as an internally collusive entity legitimized into existence to save on costs attributable to that of market exchanges; that is, by

Forming an organization and allowing some authority (entrepreneur) to direct its resources, certain marketing costs are saved and thus firms exist to avoid [economize on] the costs of conducting the same exchange between autonomous market contractors ... they exist to avoid the costs of the market's pricing mechanism ... (p. 131)

Whilst acknowledging the relationship of the RBV to the above perspectives, as possible theories of the firm, Conner (1991) suggests that the former requires research efforts to pay increasing theoretical attention to managers' discernment in enabling their firms to generate rents as seekers of unique or otherwise costly-to-copy inputs.

Importantly, insufficient attention has been paid to the *'entrepreneurial vision, intuition and the creative act underlying such visions'* Conner (1991: 133). Conner (1991) argues strongly that from the resource-based perspective, reasons for firms' (notably the joint-stock company's) existence need not necessarily be explained as *avoiders of the negative*, but rather cumulative *creators of a positive*, independent of states of opportunism. The RBV therefore offers a positive theory of the firm's existence which turns on the advantages (over the market contract) in inter-component knowledge transplantation and creation-redeployment of specific assets ... (p. 141). In keeping with previous strategic management literature, the RBV places considerable emphasis on the role of underlying intra-firm-level, activity-based value linkedness/relatedness (Rumelt 1984; Markides and Williamson 1996; Mallory *et al.* 1997) to account for the potentially conscious or unconscious existence of gains.

Lastly, Conner (1991: 144) notes that the impacts that resource-based studies of the firm will have on the field of strategic management depends largely on the nature of how it is operationalized.

Of the four issues she highlights, two are pertinent to this research project. First, the search for explanations of differential firm returns needs to focus on differential inputs and capabilities, rather than similarities. The following section, which considers the role of management as a critical firm resource, attends to this possibility. Second, a distinction needs to be made between resources at stock and flow levels. We return to this issue later as we review and draw upon research (Crossan *et al.* 1993–2001) that explicitly recognizes such a distinction when proposing organizational learning processes as one of a firm's core capabilities (Prahalad and Hamel 1990).

We summarize the above in:

P1: The RBV of sustainable competitive advantage provides a sufficient and positive theoretical explanation of the firm within which to empirically study entrepreneurial strategic management.

The senior manager as entrepreneurial resource

The RBV also explicates the need to consider management's agency resource as part of the portfolio of strategically relevant resources that enable firms to generate rents (Barney 1991). In particular, the contribution of entrepreneurial acts of value linkedness, in achieving above-normal returns, relies on management's distinct abilities to make sense of their firms' stock of assets and manage the process by which resources are used and renewed . . . (Mahoney 1995: 92).

Castanias and Helfat (1991) argue that whilst much positivist agency literature about the management–ownership control split focuses on the plausible negative effects of managers acting in conflict with the interests of owners, the resource-based view is able to make the case for considering the mediating role of managerial rent collection methods in securing sustainable competitive advantage. For example, they highlight the case of Merck's CEO in developing and deploying an academically re-orientated R&D capability as a probable antecedent to Merck achieving, above-average returns on equity (Castanias and Helfat 1991: 158, 161).

By integrating deductive economic reasoning with a greater emphasis on the primary role of top managers, they suggest that, regardless of whether managerial skills are innate or learned, a 'congruent' model of managers' and owners' interests allows the possibility of a managerial rents framework which aligns the two. They therefore offer a *non-collusive* argument for the firm's existence. They suggest that arguments which encapsulate a mutual interest assumption may be allowed in developing RBV frameworks, and this need not violate the assumption of utility maximization. Drawing on Donaldson (1990), they note the similarity between their perspective and that of stewardship theory whereby managers are team players, and the optimal structure is one that authorizes them to act, given that they will act in the best interest of owners' (p. 377).

Whilst acknowledging the potential for conflicts of interest to subsume the economic assumption of utility maximization by both parties, the managerial rents framework provides a positive theory of management action when explaining possible sources of sustainable competitive advantage.

Building on the notion of the entrepreneurial manager as a firm resource, therefore, Mahoney (1995) argues that the resource-based view of the firm, grounded in Edith Penrose's inductive and deductive methodological approaches, is also a learning theory of the firm. In doing so he espouses the need to develop studies that combine perspectives from the domains of resource-based economic theory, strategic management dynamics and organizational learning. Specifically, he proposes a *resource-learning theory framework*, which, drawing on Spender's (1996) idea of firm-specific knowledge, suggests that differential, intra-firm learning configurations may offer a 'meta-competence' explanation of how firms generate sustainable rents:

> the management team may be rare in terms of firm-specific knowledge of individual managers as well as knowledge embedded in the team. Relatedly, the accumulation of firm specific knowledge may lead to imperfectly imitable advantages for firms that have assembled competent management teams. . . . Other managers and management teams will simply lack the knowledge of the particular circumstances and unique historical context in which actions need to be interpreted. (p. 92)

Although the nature of the research design reported here makes a path-dependency approach to organizational learning within the RBV framework impossible, we concur with the above arguments in

P2: The RBV of the firm posits a positive role for entrepreneurial management action and the possibility of viewing organizational learning processes as firm-specific, differential resources.

Organizational learning

The need for congruent and integrative studies across the domains has existed implicitly in the strategic management domain, with Shrivastava (1983, 1985, 1986), Fiol and Lyles (1985) and March (1991) recognizing the salient link that exists between learning processes within organizations and the predicaments of firm survival and growth. Mahoney's (1995) call for further integration between the fields of strategic management and organizational learning provides explicit encouragement for organizational scientists to adopt cross-disciplinarian views in developing exploratory empirical studies.

The following section describes one of the few research streams to attempt a conceptualization of the organizational learning process as both resource stock and flow (Direickx and Cool 1989: 1506) and therefore offers researchers the opportunity to examine the proposed association between strategic management and organizational learning that is consistent with the underlying resource-based view of the firm.

Multidimensional approaches to organizational learning

The 'learning organization' literatures tend towards over-prescriptive idealization of 'learning' in organizations. In other words, in these literatures, learning and change by and far is a given 'good' with little critique made of potential undesirable consequences of the implemented change programmes upon which much of this work relies (Argyris and Schön 1996).

Over the past decade, the disparate literatures on the subject have led to a plethora of definitional and theoretical suggestions, with little by way of empirical and measurement validation (Easterby-Smith 1997; Lähteenmäki *et al.* 2001). Crossan *et al.*'s (1993–2001) accumulated treatise on organizational learning and improvisation can be contrasted with the 'learning organization' ideal in that it represents a coherent programme of study, which enables researchers to design cross-sectional and empirical studies when testing normative claims made about the contribution of learning processes to firm success.

Crossan *et al.*'s (1995) case-based, inductively reasoned invitation to re-conceptualize organizational learning as a multidimensional theoretical construct, and Crossan and Hulland's (1997) measurement approach, underpins much of the research reported here (Figure 11.1). In particular, their proposals draw much greater attention to the possibilities and problems associated with unlearning and learning. They allow for verbal theories of the learning–performance link to be measured and tested, and acknowledge the possibility of 'negative consequence' explanations for the potential lack of empirical support.

The perspective-derived dimensions described below are closely associated with Crossan and Hulland's (1997) three *'pure-learning'* processes, and therefore may be asking respondents to report on organizational learning processes as stocks of firm resource (cognitive, constructive and constitutive), rather than the more difficult to capture learning flows (feedback and feed-forward). We differ from Crossan and Hulland (1997), in that we believe that the different processes, which account for individual, group and organizational accounts of learning, need to be accorded more methodological critique than Crossan *et al.* (1995–2001) suggest. In particular, we have found scant evidence (Gray and Gonsalves 2002) to indicate that (cross-sectional) surveys can 'uncover' the relationships and *enabling* tensions (Crossan and Hulland 1997) that allow for the pivotal transfer of change across these dimensions. The difficulty in capturing such tensions, we believe to be an artefact of our survey, quasi-experimental methods, and possibly a consequence of the difficulty and rarity faced in observing and interpreting such tension.

Our experience in using survey approaches suggests that the essentially unique and situational characteristics of tension-derived *turns in, and addition, of new* logics (Lähteenmäki *et al.* 2001: 120), probably best lend themselves to either anthropological approaches such as Leonard-Barton's (1992) studies, or the

'SPACE'	PROCESS	INPUT/OUTCOME (enabling mechanisms)
		Images
	Intuiting	*Metaphors*
		Experiences
INDIVIDUAL	'COGNITIVE'	
		Language
		Conceptual map
	Interpreting	
'Feed-forward' process		*Conversation/Dialogue*
GROUP	'CONSTRUCTIVE'	
'Feedback' process		*Shared understandings*
		Mutual adjustments
	Integrating	
		Interactive systems
ORGANIZATION	'CONSTITUTIVE'	
		Diagnostic systems
	Institutionalizing	*Routines*
		Rules & procedures

Figure 11.1 Levels and processes of organizational learning (adapted from Crossan *et al.* 1995: 525).

clinical-dialogical approaches offered by Senge (1990) and Schein (1993) in describing organization-wide change interventions. In particular, the complex, communicative processes of the feed-forward *and* feedback constructs described in the Crossan studies between the various dimensions, whilst easy to explain and represent to managers, have proved difficult to operationalize as valid content for the purpose of questionnaire-based studies.

We have, at the risk of conceptual fallibility, stretched these three 'pure' construct labels so as to make more explicit the process elements (cognitive, constructive, constitutive) of the constructs in our model, rather than solely the unit level of analysis – 'individual', 'social' and 'institutional'. We thereby make explicit our acceptance and recognition of the dynamic, indeterminate and paradoxical boundary that is otherwise implicit in many literatures. We accord significance to the need for a relaxation in the strong, dichotomous Cartesian dualism that has (hitherto) been the overwhelming assumption in 'behavioural' and 'cognitive' schools of organizational learning theory (Weick 1991). In particular, we argue that the reconsideration of change and learning as a 'duality' through the explanatory mechanisms of active, enacted sense-making (meaning-making and meaning-taking) generates a dynamic account of learning processes within firms.

Key learning dimensions

The dimensions described below are by definition partially consistent with the theoretical and empirical studies referred to in the previous section and incomplete. We build on the emphasis of the seminal theorists, from the diverse domains of organizational learning literatures in distinguishing between the dimensions. Whilst distinct, we realize the complex nature of organizational learning and the likelihood of significant overlap and interaction between the dimensions (Lähteenmäki *et al.* 2001: 124), but we are reluctant at this stage to develop a hierarchical, level-based approach to dimension analysis. We prefer to draw on Hooley *et al.*'s (1998) lateral typology of firm resource capabilities and assets in omitting the hierarchical dimension for the time being.

From the above we infer:

P3:   The disparate perspectives on learning processes within organizations necessitate a multidimensional approach for empirical studies into organizational learning as a firm-specific differential resource stock.

Individual-based personal-cognitive

Argyris' (1982, 1990, 1992) socio-technical constructions of organizational learning and individual defence routines form the bedrock of this dimension. Argyris and Schön (1978, 1996) construe most individuals as being involved in what they call Model I reasoning processes. In such instances, individuals make untested attributions, carry out unshared evaluations and offer solutions without recourse to example or illustration.

Argyris (1982) finds it difficult to imagine how in interpersonal exchanges we would be able to engage in double-loop learning, which involves questioning and changing governing conditions, given the characteristics of Model I reasoning that 'inhibits the exchange of relevant information and reduced sensitivity to feedback', (Edmondson 1996). His organizational learning turn comes when he notes that, as individuals skilled in Model I reasoning processes carry them into social systems such as organizations, they create organizational conditions that inhibit double-loop learning.

The organizational learning phenomenon in this argument depends on the 'if–then' reasoning processes of individuals that constitute the organization. Furthermore, the organizational environment in which individuals find their learning processes is a product of these very same reasoning processes. Edmondson (1996) notes:

> The problem is that individuals cause their own social systems to malfunction by virtue of their theories-in-use and at the same time O-I social systems 'cause' individuals to reason and act as they do. This is the logic underlying Argyris' case . . . a logic that accounts for the intractability of social systems. (p. 583)

According to these perspectives, only if and when the individuals constituting the organization begin to engage in Model II reasoning, allowing for double-loop learning processes, will organizations truly be capable of producing beneficial change. They argue that behaviour modification requires a change in individuals' theories in use. It is primarily individual change dependent, with the environment being a secondary influence on the change potentiality. The emphasis is not simply one of organizational design change, but more one of how individual logic structures can be changed.

The first dimension, then, personal cognitive learning (PCL), is conceived of having near equivalence to Crossan and Hulland's (1997) II process; it includes those capabilities and activities of the firm that consider members of the firm as individual learners. It is primarily about what resides in the mind of a person as a knowing individual. The content of such knowledge is dependent on what the individual knows, their past experiences, how those experiences are organized into knowledge structures, and what beliefs the individual has about those experiences. This individual cognition frames the individual's abilities to generate new organizational insights, ideas, information and action.

Traditionally the majority of corporate intervention models (through human resource and training initiatives) have concentrated their efforts on developing and changing individual cognitions. Such models depict the learner as a solo subject discovering, inventing and mastering the organizational world through mandate. In the majority of cases, the relationship between mandates and learners is formal and unidirectional and consists of discrete, non-negotiable communication boundaries between the two, with information being transferred from source (change/training programme) to passive recipient (targeted learners).

Group-based social-constructive

In contrast to the 'cognitivist' emphasis, constructivists (Cook and Yannow 1993; Brown and Duguid 1991; Lave and Wenger 1991) suggest there is a much greater urgency for organizational learning exercises to consider the learning that takes place in group bounded contexts. Organizational learning is inferred through observing how organizational groups engage in collective action. This then is a socio-cultural perspective of organizational learning. The organization's knowledge resides not in individuals' aggregate cognitions, but in the actions of individuals performing 'in congregate'. Organizational learning can occur independently of individuals but not in the absence of all individuals. For example, Cook and Yannow (1993) argue that the

> socio-cultural perspective and the cognitive perspective both include the study of individuals. The difference is one of focus . . . Within the cultural perspective, an individual does not hold organizational knowledge, nor do we see it as the aggregate knowledge of many individuals. What is known is known and made operational only by several individuals acting in congregate.

Brown and Duguid (1991), in discussing the idea of legitimate peripheral participation (Lave and Wenger 1990), refute the idea that there is a need for organizational learning interventions that rely solely on individuals' internalized schematic changes. This is because such an approach implies separation, involving some supposed external lesson crossing a boundary into the learner's mind. To act and communicate, individuals are constantly involved in changes that blend the 'internal' and 'external' exchanges characterized by the sharing of means rather than the 'ends' of internalized cause–effect logic.

Organizational learning is not solely driven by the need for individual self-identity, interests, preservation and sustainability in social groups (Weick 1979), but also by the need for organizational identity preservation, sustenance and acquisition. For them, such difficult to discern, stabilizing possibilities in the nature of organizational learning highlight the dangers of equating observed individual and/or organizational change with organizational learning in many descriptions of organization-wide change interventions.

Cook and Yannow (1993) reconsider Weick's (1979) account of the Duke Ellington Orchestra, which continued to thrive despite the annual turnover of its key personnel, including its founding members and leader. They argue that the orchestra not only survived because of what Weick describes as

> the audience recreating its concept of the Orchestra, but also because the Orchestra was able to preserve and sustain its identity through long-term organizational learning: specifically, the ongoing maintenance of the patterns of collective action among the players, intimately bound up in the performance itself, has enabled the organization to survive over the years and through a change in personnel because the Orchestra continued to learn what it needed to.

The second dimension, social constructive learning (SCL), then, emphasizes those capabilities and activities that consider firm members as socially embedded individuals. It recognizes the need for most individuals in most settings to engage in learning as a communal activity. It is not just that individuals must make knowledge their own in isolation, but that they must make it theirs in a community of those who have divergent and convergent aspirations around the content of that learning. The emphasis is not on personal knowledge interpretation, discovery and invention, but on the processes of argumentation and negotiation that allow for knowledge development and learning to occur within the medium of 'others'. The concern is with how knowledge develops through the social construction of meanings and through our everyday interactions with others, in which we represent back and forth to each other our negotiated sense of organizational realities. Knowing in this dimension is a process of negotiating and communicating sense not transmitting fully developed personal truths.

SCL strives to create environments in which individuals actively participate in ways that are intended to help them construct their own understanding of organizational problems and realities, rather than having change agents interpret organizational problems and ensure that individuals understand such problems as he or she (the change agent) has explained them. In SCL environments, learners are actively engaged in perceiving different perspectives, organizing and representing their own interpretations, reflecting the sense and meanings of communities to which they belong. This is not 'active' in the sense that individuals actively listen and then mirror the one correct view of organizational contexts (e.g. objectives, tasks, problems, etc.), but rather 'active' in the sense that learners must participate and interact with the surrounding environment in order to invent and negotiate.

Organization-based institutional-constitutive

The third dimension examined in this study, institutional constitutive learning (ICL), is an extension of the SCL idea that knowledge is built (Gray and Gonsalves 2002). It differs, however, in that idea, information and insight construction also occurs when organizational members politically engage in the construction of something external to themselves, or at least 'universal' to their firm – hence the term 'institutional', e.g. organizational charts, authority structure, support systems, formal procedures, committee and reporting mandates, and so on. The emphasis is on the external 'product' of constructive processes – the constitution of the firm. In the main, ICL criteria consist of those formal and informal, but publicly recognizable and accessible coordinating mechanisms – the political mechanisms and environments that may or may not limit the relevance and 'affectiveness' (Vince 2001) of organizational learning initiatives (Coopey and Burgoyne 2000).

The idea of politically constituted (constrained and enabled) learning partially recognises the emergent, deconstructive (Boje 1994) and social constructionist critiques of organizational learning as a domain of study. Studies in organizational learning from this perspective must not remain at risk of ignoring the wider context of the dominant capitalist premise (Boje 1994) that may sustain and/or threaten many of today's organizations. Easterby-Smith *et al*. (2000) note that 'this is a fundamental aspect and condition of learning both at the intra- and inter-organizational level . . . ' (p. 793).

For example, Bernstein and Beliveau (1996) found little evidence to suggest that independently owned pharmacies facing hostile (Covin and Slevin 1989) competitive environments benefited significantly from contracting with large institutional customers, whereas those that reconfigured their internal structures of coordination and joined prescription-buying group networks did benefit significantly. This dimension is consistent with and has near equivalence to Crossan *et al.*'s (1994, 1995) of process construct:

> Initially, this institutionalization is a means to leverage the learning of individuals. Structures, systems and procedures provide for the delegation of responsibility. New recruits can turn on these organization artifacts in a vicarious learning fashion instead of re-inventing the wheel. Over time, the individual and group learning become less dominant as the institutionalized learning at the organizational level begins to both guide and be modified by learning at the individual and group learning Crossan *et al*. (1994: 201).

In supporting the case for a multidimensional approach for the purposes of this study within firms, we suggest:

P4: Organizational learning can be conceptualized as a multi-dimensional construct partially consisting of 'personal cognitive learning' (PCL), 'social constructive learning' (SCL) and 'institutional constitutive learning' (ICL).

Hypotheses and test generation

Strategy making and organizational learning

The previous sections proposed a resource-based view of competitive strategic management and organizational learning as a multidimensional construct. The final proposition argued that for the field of organizational learning to progress, attempts at integrating such theoretical diversity will be of as much importance to the field as attempts to continue increasing the diversity of interpretations and explanations of the organizational learning construct (Easterby-Smith *et al*. 2001).

Establishing a construct's viability, however, is not only dependent on finding support (theoretical and empirical) for its internal consistency but also its relationship, in a broader explanatory framework, to other organizational fields of inquiry and constructs. Fiol and Lyles (1985), for example, argue that: 'The organization's strategic posture partially determines its learning capacity. Strategy determines the goals and objectives (deliberate or emergent) and the breadth of actions available for carrying out the strategy (intended, or realized)'. The aim now is to focus on the relationship implied by many literatures, from both domains of inquiry, to exist between organizational learning as a resource-based stock and strategic management, in particular strategy making. Strategic management literatures have increasingly focused on the roles played by learning in competitive strategy.

First, Cyert and March (1963) contend that the boundaries provided through strategic posturing influence learning and create a context for the perceptions and interpretations of the firm's competitive environment. A firm's strategic posture is conceptualized and operationalized variously in a number of strategic management literatures (Mintzberg 1973; Miles and Snow 1978; Covin and Slevin 1989). Generally, strategic postures are the firm's orientation and placement within its competitive environments when considered against criteria such as the firm's tendency toward proactiveness vis-à-vis competitors, innovation and risk-taking (Covin 1991). Strategic postures are also argued to be dependent on the choices made through the firm's individual, business-related decisions along these dimensions, and will include decisions regarding issues such as pricing, competitive response, financing, etc. (Covin 1991).

Second, Fiol and Lyles (1985: 805) maintain that the perceived strategic options are also a function of the firm's learning capacity. Therefore, although both strategy making and organizational learning are concerned with the relationship that a firm has with its environment in securing sustained competitive advantage, they are distinct constructs. The relationship between the two as conceptualized in leading literatures remains one of ambiguous, reciprocal causation. That is, whilst strategic management literatures have inferred organizational learning as a key process in managing for competitive advantage, very few have examined the actual learning resource-based processes within firms – that is, as an intra-firm capability. Contiguously, organizational learning theorists are increasingly recognizing their failures in integrating their frameworks with substantive business issues (Edmondson and Moingeon 1996).

Entrepreneurship, learning and strategy-making modes

Entrepreneurship as an 'invisible college' (Venkataraman 1997) of study has sought to establish boundaries through debates that may reflect the maturing and theoretical development of a young applied science. Venkataraman (1997) and Shane and Venkataraman (2000) contend that much of the scholarly work on entrepreneurship continues to rely on frameworks that are already in existence to explain and predict empirical phenomena. In particular, they argue that

> studies which focus solely in terms of whom the entrepreneur is and defining the field in terms of the individual alone [e.g. trait-theories which seek to answer questions about 'who is an entrepreneur?'] . . . ignore other process factors such as knowledge, cognitions and behaviours. . . .
>
> (Venkataraman 1997: 8)

Such an approach seeks to shift the focus from the 'Who is an entrepreneur debate?' to 'What is entrepreneurship?' and integrates a strong knowledge-based approach to the field in which learning processes for rent-generating discovery are a central tenet. It is consistent with their definition of entrepreneurship as a college of scholarly endeavour: *it seeks to understand how opportunities to bring into existence "future" goods and service are discovered, created and exploited . . .'(Venkataraman 1997: 3).*

Shane and Venkataraman's (2000) perspective implies a gap in the domain of entrepreneurship studies that is consistent with a learning process approach to entrepreneurship theory building. Such a definition is a positive theory of entrepreneurship and is congruent with the ideas of the positive resource-based theories of the firm and management discernment outlined above (Conner, 1991; Lichtenstein and Brush 2001). We go further in arguing that they imply *an entrepreneurial resource learning theory* of the firm strongly aligned to the firm resource-learning theories outlined above (Mahoney 1995), and recent literatures (Dess *et al.* 2003; Gray and Gonsalves 2002; Lichtenstein and Brush 2001; Morris *et al.* 2000; Rae and Carswell 2001). This study attempts to fill some of the void by operationalizing Mintzberg and Waters' (1985) deliberate-emergent typology to develop a core hypothesis for a study using a survey of SME firms.

Drawing on Mintzberg and Waters' (1982) study of strategic entrepreneurial success at Steinberg Inc., Mintzberg and Waters (1985) suggest that strategic learning is associated with emergent strategies: 'emergent strategy itself implies learning that works' (McKevitt *et al.* 1992). In addition, they argue that the entrepreneurial strategy-making modes (Mintzberg 1973; Hart 1995) will be particularly pertinent when managing for emergent strategies in firms operating in hostile and complex environments: 'Such behaviour is especially important when an environment is too unstable or complex to comprehend – or too imposing to defy' (McKevitt *et al.* 1992: 4). They make explicit the link between entrepreneurial strategy-making modes, learning, uncertain competitive environments and suggest that entrepreneurial firms with managers who value and recognize such linkages are likely to achieve performance success.

From the above, therefore, we are able to derive the following hypotheses:

H1: Firms engaged in entrepreneurial modes of strategy making, with positive orientations to intra-firm organizational learning, facing hostile competitive environments-will demonstrate evidence of sustainable competitive advantage.

H2: Firms engaged in non-entrepreneurial modes of strategy making, with positive orientations to intra-firm organizational learning,-facing stable competitive environments will demonstrate evidence of sustainable competitive advantages.

Configuration perspective of strategy and learning

The comprehensive attention given to the Mintzberg and Waters (1985) typology reflects a strong intuitive appeal but betrays a lack of empirical investigation and support for the theory (Doty *et al.* 1993). Configuration studie[1] (Venkatraman 1990) of strategy (Miles and Snow 1978; Mintzberg 1973, 1978, 1985) seek to operationalize building blocks for theory construction. The above framework and hypotheses fall into this general category of configuration research and forms the basis of an exploratory and descriptive study in the ongoing process of theoretical and empirical development.

At this stage of the research, we resist adopting a contingency approach (Gnyawali 2003) when testing the above hypothesis. First, although the measurement limitations of configuration versus contingency perspectives are recognised, Venkatraman (1989) notes that

> using exploratory perspectives (configurational approaches) that are less precise in specifying the functional form of fit 4 may be more appropriate in the earlier stages of seeking empirical support for hitherto verbalized concepts, but as the research stream matures, using confirmatory perspectives would be more appropriate. . . .

Second, typology theories do not hypothesize the relationships between 'ideal'-type patterns. Instead, they concentrate on emphasizing, and hypothesizing the relationship between 'type' and other multidimensional constructs. Doty and Glick (1994)[2] suggest that typological theories use 'types' to explain levels of dependent variables (e.g. performance). We disagree with this in the context of the deliberate-emergent typology. The position here is that the deliberate-emergent typology is not a normative theory of strategy. Rather, it aims to highlight hypothesized relationships between the strategy-making mode variable, and other, although not necessarily dependent, variables (e.g. learning, performance, environment).

Presenting the above perspectives of fit allows access to how we operationalize the problematic correspondence between the verbal construct definitions and statistical tests used to describe the strategy–learning–environment relationship.

Summary

The series of propositions outlined in this chapter provides a framework within which researchers can empirically test and shed further light on the diverse claims made about the process of intra-firm learning within the various domains of study. It seeks to provide a mechanism whereby the relationship between different learning processes and other value-based firm resources is evaluated and described. We have attended to the significant lack of empirical explication and testing of implied theories and models. In line with recent concerns, we have also emphasized our belief that the next wave of entrepreneurial resource-learning studies will need to complement their considerable conceptual gains and arguments with rigorous, exploratory measurement-based support.

The framework sustains the growing debate concerning the contribution of organizational learning as a multidimensional concept offering significant value to the field of enterprise inquiry, whilst acknowledging the limitations imposed by the divergent, methodological and philosophical sources of its key proponents. We have supported arguments for a cross-disciplinary, integrative approach to organizational learning by synthesizing coherent streams of argument across apparently disparate literatures and domains of inquiry into a congruent system of defendable, plausible and yet fallible propositions. In doing so, we hope not to have added to the hodge-podge of entrepreneurship research highlighted by Shane and Venkataraman (2000), but to have instead attempted a strong case for building empirical work that can contribute to their project by consistently exploring potential contributions contained within other fields of study.

Notes

1 Being explicit with perspectives and underlying assumptions of coalignment adopted by the research is critical because it determines the appropriate statistical test(s) to be used (see Venkatraman 1989, 1990).
2 Constructs as either form or pattern or multiple 'first-order' dimension coalignment (Doty and Glick 1994).

References

Argyris, C. (1982) The executive mind and double-loop learning. *Organizational Dynamics*, Autumn 5–22.
Argyris, C. (1990) *Overcoming Organizational Defences: Facilitating Organizational Learning*. Boston: Allyn Bacon.
Argyris, C. (1992) *On Organizational Learning*. Cambridge, MA: Blackwell.
Argyris, C. and Schön, D. A. (1974) *Theory in Practice: Increasing Professional Effectiveness*. San Francisco Jossey-Bass.
Argyris, C. and Schön, D. (1978). *Organizational Learning: A Theory of Action Perspective*. Reading, MA: Addison-Wesley.
Argyris, C. and Schön, D. (1996) *Organizational Learning II: Theory, Method, and Practice*. Reading, MA: Addison-Wesley.
Barney, J. B. (1991) Firm resources and sustained competitive advantage. *Journal of Management*, 17: 99–120.
Bernstein, E. and Beliveau, B. (1997) Strategies for hyper-competitive markets. *Journal of Business and Entrepreneurship*, October.
Boje, D. M. and Dennehy, R. F. (1994) *Managing in the Postmodern World: America's Revolution Against Exploitation*, 2nd ed. Dubuque, IA: Kendall/Hunt.
Brown, J. S. and Duguid, P. (1991) Organizational knowledge and communities of practice. *Organization Science*, 2(1): 40–57.
Cairns, G., McInnes, P. and Roberts, P. (2003) Organization space/time: from imperfect panoptical to heterotopian understanding. *Ephemera*, 32: 126–139.
Castanias, R. P. and Helfat, C. E. (1991) Managerial resources and rents. *Journal of Management,* 17: 155–71.

Conner, K. R. (1991) A historical comparison of resource-based theory and five schools of thought within industrial organization economics: do we have a new theory of the firm? *Journal of Management*, 17: 121–54.

Cook, S. D. N. and Yanow, D. (1996) Culture and organizational learning. In M. D. Cohen and L. S. Sproull (eds), *Organizational Learning*. Thousand Oaks, CA: Sage, pp. 430–59.

Coopey, J. and Burgoyne, J. (2000) Politics and organisational learning. *Journal of Management Studies*, 37(6): 869.

Covin, J. G. and Slevin, D. P. (1989) Strategic management of small firms in hostile and benign environments. *Strategic Management Journal*, 10: 75–87.

Covin, J. G. and Slevin, D. P. (1991) A conceptual model of entrepreneurship as firm behaviour. *Entrepreneurship: Theory And Practice*, 16(1): 7–24.

Crossan, M. and Bontis, N. (1998) The strategic management of organization learning. Working paper presented at Academy of Management, San Diego, CA.

Crossan, M. and Guatto, T. (1996) Organizational learning research profile. *Journal of Organizational Change Management*, 9(1): 107–12.

Crossan, M. and Hulland, J. (1997) Measuring organizational learning. Ivey working paper presented at Academy of Management, Boston, MA.

Crossan, M., Lane, H., White, R. and Djurfeldt, L. (1995) Organizational learning: dimensions for a theory. *International Journal of Organizational Analysis*, 3(4): 337–60.

Crossan, M., Lane, H. and White, R. (1999) An organizational learning framework: from intuition to institution. *Academy of Management Review*, 24(3): 522–37.

Curran, J., Jarvis, R., Blackburn, R. and Black, S. (1992) Networks and small firms: constructs, methodological strategies and some findings. *International Small Business Journal*, 11(2): 13.

Cyert, R. M. and March, J. G. (1963) *A Behavioral Theory of the Firm*. Englewood Cliffs, NJ: Prentice Hall.

D'Amboise, G. and Muldowney, M. (1988) Management theory for small business: attempts and requirements. *Academy of Management Review*, 13(2): 226.

Dess, G. G., Ireland, R. D., Zahra, S. A., Floyd, S. W., Janney, J. J. and Lane, P. J. (2003) Emerging issues in corporate entrepreneurship. *Journal of Management*, 29(3): 351–78.

Dierickx, I. and Cool, K. (1989) Asset stock accumulation and sustainability of competitive advantage. *Management Science*, 35: 1504–11.

Donaldson, L. (1990) A rational basis for criticisms of organizational economics. *Academy of Management Review*, 15: 395–401.

Doty, D. H. (1994) Typologies as a unique form of theory building: toward improved understanding and modelling. *Academy of Management Review*, 19(2): 230–51.

Doty, D. H., Glick, W. H. and Huber, G. P. (1993) Fit, equifinality, and organizational effectiveness: a test of two configurational theories. *Academy of Management Journal*, 36(6):1196.

Easterby-Smith, M. (1997) Disciplines of the learning organization: contributions and critiques. *Human Relations*, 50(9): 1085–1113.

Easterby-Smith, M., Crossan, M. and Nicolini, D. (2000) Organizational learning: debates past, present and future. *Journal of Management Studies*, 37(6): 783–96.

Edmonsdon, A. (1996) Three faces of Eden: the persistence of competing theories and multiple diagnoses in organizational intervention research. *Human Relations*, 49(5): 571–96.

Edmondson, A. and Moingeon, B. (1996) *Organizational Learning and Competitive Advantage*. London: Sage.

Fiol, C. and Lyles, M. (1985) Organizational learning. *Academy of Management Review*, 10(4): 803–13.

Fombrun, C. J. and Zajac, E. J. (1987) Structural and perceptual influences on intra-industry stratification. *Academy of Management Journal*, 30(1): 33–50.

Gibb, A. and Scott, M. (1985) Strategic awareness, personal commitment and the process of planning in the small business. *Journal of Management Studies*, 22(6): 597–629.

Gnyawali, D. R. and Stewart, A. C. (2003) A contingency perspective on organizational learning. *Management Learning*, 34 (1): 63–89.

Gray, C. W. J. A. (1998) *Enterprise and Culture*. London: Routledge.

Gray, C. W. J. A. and Gonsalves, E. (2002) Organizational learning and entrepreneurial strategy. *International Journal of Entrepreneurship and Innovation*, 3(1): 27–33.

Hart, S. L. (1995) A natural-resource-based view of the firm. *Academy of Management Review*, 20: 986–1014.

Hooley, G. J, Möller, K. and Broderick, A. J. (1998) Competitive positioning and the resource based view of the firm. *Journal of Strategic Marketing*, 6(2): 97–115.

Kor, Y. Y. and Mahoney, J. T. (2000) Penrose's resource-based approach: the process and product of research creativity. *Journal of Management Studies*, 37(1): 109–39.

Lähteenmäki, S., Toivonen, J. and Mattila, M. (2001) Critical aspects of organisational learning: research and proposals for its measurement. *British Journal of Management*, 12.

Lave, J. and Wenger, E. (1990) *Situated Learning: Legitimate Peripheral Participation*. Cambridge: Cambridge University Press.

Leonard-Barton, D. (1992) Core capabilities and core rigidities: a paradox in managing new product development. *Strategic Management Journal*, 13: 111–25.

Lichtenstein, B. M. B. and Brush, C. G. (2001) How do 'resource bundles' develop and change in new ventures? A dynamic model and longitudinal exploration. *Entrepreneurship Theory and Practice*, Spring: 37–58.

Mahoney, J. T. (1995) The management of resources and the resource of management. *Journal of Business Research*, 33: 91–101.

Mallory, G. R. and Gonsalves, E. (1995) Some strategies in uncertain environments: an empirical test of Mintzberg and Water's deliberate-emergent continuum. 9th British Academy of Management Conference, Sheffield.

Mallory, G., Gonsalves, E. and Sanderson, S. M. (1997) UK conglomerate performance a position paper British Academy of Management Conference, Sheffield.

March, J. G. (1991) Exploration and exploitation in organizational learning. *Organization Science*, 2: 71–87

Markides, C. C. and Williamson, P. J. (1996) Corporate diversification and organizational structure: a resource based view. *Academy of Management Journal*, 39: 340–67.

McKevitt, D., Asch, D. C., Cassells, E. and Mallory, G. R. (1992) Mintzberg and Waters Deliberate – emergent continuum in practice: an empirical study. British Academy of Management Conference, Bradford.

McKiernan, P. and Morris, C. (1993) Strategic planning and financial performance in the UK SMEs: does formality matter? British Academy of Management Conference.

Miles, R. E. and Snow, C. C. (1978) *Organizational Strategy, Structure and Process*, New York: McGraw-Hill.

Miller, D. and Friesen, P. (1983) Strategy-making and environment: the third link. *Strategic Management Journal*, 4 (2): 221–35.

Miller, D. and Friesen, P. (1984) *Organizations: A Quantum View*, Englewood Cliffs, NJ: Prentice Hall.

Mintzberg, H. (1973) Strategy making in three modes. *California Management Review*, 16: 44–58.

Mintzberg, H. (1978) Patterns in strategy formation. *Management Science*, 24(9): 934–49.

Mintzberg, H. and Waters, J. (1985) Of strategies deliberate and emergent. *Strategic Management Journal*, 16: 257.

Mintzberg, H., Otis, J., Shamsie, J. and Waters, J. (1988) Strategy of design: a study of architects in co-partnership. In J. Grant (ed.), Strategic Management Frontiers, Greenwich, CT: JAI Press.

Penrose, E. (1959) *The Theory of the Growth of the Firm*. New York: Wiley.

Pleitner, H. J. (1989) Strategic behaviour in small and medium-sized firms: preliminary considerations. *Journal of Small Business Management*, October.

Prahalad, C. K. and Hamel, G. (1990) The core competence of The corporation. *Harvard Business Review*, 90(3): 79–91.

Rae, D. and Carswell, M. (2000) Understanding entrepreneurial learning: a question of how? *International Journal of Entrepreneurial Behaviour and Research*, 6(3): 145–59.

Robinson, R. B. and Pearce II, J. A. (1984) Research thrusts in small firm strategic planning. *Academy of Management Review*, 9(1):128–137.

Rumelt, R. (1984) Towards a strategic theory of the firm. In R. Lamb (ed.), *Competitive Strategic Management*, Englewood Cliffs, NJ: Prentice Hall. pp. 556–70.

Schein, E. (1993) How can organizations learn faster? The challenge of entering the green room. *Sloan Management Review*, Winter.

Scott, B. (1971) *Stages of Corporate Development*, Case#9, 371–294, ICCH, Harvard

Senge, P. (1990) The leader's new work: building learning organizations, *Sloan Management Review*, 1990.

Shane, S. and Venkataraman, S. (2000) The promise of entrepreneurship as a field of research. *Academy Of Management Review*, 25(1): 217–26.

Shrivastava, P. (1987) Rigor and practical usefulness of research in strategic management. *Strategic Management Journal*, 8: 77–92.

Shrivastava, P. and Mitroff, I. I. (1984) Enhancing organisational research utilization: the role of decision makers' assumptions. *Academy of Management Review*, 9(1): 18–26.

Spender, J. C. (1996) Making knowledge the basis of a dynamic theory of the firm. *Strategic Management Journal*, 17: 45–62.

Venkataraman, S. (1997) The distinctive domain of entrepreneurship research: an editor's perspective. In J. Katz and R. Brockhaus (eds), *Advances in Entrepreneurship, Firm Emergence, and Growth*, Vol. 3. Greenwich, CT: JAI Press, p. 119–38.

Venkataraman, S., Van De Ven, A., Buckeye, J. and Hudson, R. (1990). Starting up in a turbulent environment: a process model of failure among firms with high customer dependence. *Journal of Business Venturing*, 5: 277–95.

Venkatraman, N. (1989) Strategic orientation of business enterprises: the construct, dimensionality, and measurement, *Management Science*, 35 (August): 942–62.

Venkatraman, N. (1989) The concept of fit in strategy research: toward verbal and statistical correspondence. *Academy of Management Review*, 14(3): 423–44.

Venkatraman, N. (1990) Performance implications of strategic coalignment: a methodological perspective. *Journal of Management Studies*, 27(1): 19–41.

Vince, R. (2001) Power and emotions in organizational learning. *Human Relations*, 54(10): 1325–51.

Weick, K. E. (1979) *The Social Psychology of Organizing*, 2nd ed. Reading, MA: Addison-Wesley.

Weick, K. E. (1991) The nontraditional quality of organizational learning. *Organization Science*, 2(1):

Wernerfelt, B. (1984) A resource-based view of the firm. *Strategic Management Journal*, 5: 171–80.

Williamson, O. E. (1975) *Markets and Hierarchies, Analysis and Antitrust Implications: A Study in the Economics of Internal Organization*. (New York): Free Press.

12 Absorptive capacity of knowledge-intensive business services

The case of architectural and engineering SMEs

Jan Waalkens, René J. Jorna and Theo Postma

Introduction and overview

The absorptive capacity (AC) of a firm is 'the ability of a firm to recognize the value of new, external information, assimilate it, and apply it to commercial ends' (Cohen and Levinthal 1990: 128). Lane *et al.* (2002) perceive AC as one of the most important constructs in organisational research of the past decades. They counted 189 papers that cite Cohen and Levinthal (1990) and conclude that there are three major shortcomings of this literature: '. . . limited attempts to revise the definition of AC, little attention to the actual process underlying absorptive capacity, and few attempts to measure it outside the R&D context'. In this chapter we address these shortcomings. First, we use a refined definition of AC (Zahra and George 2002). In this definition AC is divided into two elements, potential absorptive capacity (PACAP) and realised absorptive capacity (RACAP), the difference being related to organisational capabilities (or the lack thereof) that transform potential into realised innovation projects. Second, the process of individual learning and individual knowledge underlying organisational AC is modelled in terms of variables contributing to the AC of the firm. The way we deal with the third criticism is related to the second: we are interested in SMEs, which did not receive much attention in AC research until recently (Liao *et al.* 2003). They often lack R&D investment. We therefore introduce alternative indicators to supplement R&D expenditure in measuring AC. These indicators relate to the search behaviour or knowledge-gathering behaviour of the firm.

In the knowledge-based view, the firm can be defined in terms of its knowledge (Grant 1996). We take the knowledge-based view (KBV) as a point of departure. The KBV focuses on a firm's domain of knowledge use, transfer and development. The domain in which specific knowledge and problem-solving routines are applicable defines the scope of the firm. In this chapter we deal with *scope development* through AC, producing innovation as output. Through dynamic capabilities aimed at internal knowledge development and the use of absorptive capacity (acquisition and use of information new to the firm), the scope of a firm can be enlarged. Absorptive capacity is the base from which new or renewed things can be learned. It determines what may be learned from the external environment. Therefore, AC extends the cognitive scope of the individual, and through this, the cognitive scope of the organisation (Nooteboom 2000). In essence, absorptive capacity is about knowledge development, and is part of the innovation process. Innovation involves changing routines or creating new ones (Dosi and Egidi 1991). In order to be able to do this, firm members have to learn. Learning is therefore a condition for innovation. We are interested in innovative activity at the firm level. Two main forms of innovation are used: innovation projects aimed at *renewal* of products, processes and services, and innovation projects aimed at *new* products, processes and services. These forms of innovation can be seen as incremental and radical, respectively. Based on this innovation discussion, we define the main research question of this chapter as 'How does absorptive capacity relate to innovation and which factors account for differences in AC and innovation?'

The concept of absorptive capacity (Cohen and Levinthal 1990) was intended to be further developed to increase its usability, drawing on new insights. Zahra and George (2002) proposed to subdivide the concept of absorptive capacity into potential absorptive capacity and realised absorptive capacity (PACAP and RACAP, respectively). We adopt this re-conceptualisation: 'Potential capacity comprises knowledge acquisition and assimilation capabilities, and realized capacity centres on knowledge transformation and exploitation'. (Zahra and George 2002: 185). They posit that potential capacity provides firms with the strategic flexibility and the degrees of freedom to adapt and evolve in high-velocity environments. By doing so, potential capacity allows firms to sustain a competitive advantage even in a dynamic industry context. In terms of knowledge, PACAP is related to exploring the internal and external knowledge environment (the *search* for knowledge), while RACAP focuses on the effective exploitation and implementation of knowledge to achieve actual production and subsequent added value (the *use* of knowledge). We think that this re-conceptualisation is useful since, even though the two concepts are intimately related, they refer to two different kinds of routines. The first is about learning routines, while the second is about operating routines. According to March (1991), exploration and exploitation in firms have to be balanced in order to be effective. Too much exploration can harm continuity, because it is expensive, while too much exploitation can lead to a lack of strategic flexibility, risking failure in the long run.

Absorptive capacity is basically about knowledge acquisition, use and development and thus about learning. We address the issues of underlying search and learning processes of absorptive capacity and propose various alternative indicators of this concept by performing research into small and medium-sized knowledge-intensive business services (Miles *et al.* 1995), i.e. engineering and architectural SMEs in the construction sector. First, we chose this domain because it concerns a knowledge-intensive category. Second, innovation in this domain is often client-led; it depends, at least partly, on external information. Third, these firms produce a considerable amount of innovation.

In order to understand absorptive capacity, we first of all conceptualise the firm in the second section in terms of knowledge and routines, producing capabilities and dynamic capabilities. Absorptive capacity is a dynamic capability. To broaden our understanding of knowledge, knowledge is defined and its properties, which are relevant for this research, are discussed in the third section.

They relate to the possibility of *sharing* knowledge for innovation. In addition, the question 'How we can know that the firm has learned?' is answered. This leads to the definition of output variables on innovative activity of the firm. In the fourth section we explore the preconditions for *developing* knowledge of *individuals* and the stimulation of creative capacity. In fifth section we indicate the extent of and the way in which way the firm context supports learning and the development of absorptive capacity of an *organisation*. In the sixth section we trace the locus of absorptive capacity in an SME, in order to identify which person or persons should be the focus of research, as we want to know more about the knowledge development behaviour of the firm. We argue that only a limited number of people will be actively involved in formal innovation projects of the firm. Quantity of formal innovation projects is the dependent variable of absorptive capacity in this research. In the seventh section we draw conclusions with regard to alternative explanatory (independent) variables of absorptive capacity, based on insights in knowledge acquisition, use and development of (actors in) firms. The alternative variables are modelled in relation to their outcome of innovation projects and their commercial effects and are operationalised in order to conduct empirical research. The eighth section provides hypotheses on the relations in the model. The final section concludes with a short discussion on the preliminary findings of the empirical research. One has to keep in mind that the orientation of this chapter is first of all conceptual. At the time of writing this chapter, the analysis of gathered data is still in progress. Therefore, we only briefly discuss some preliminary findings. These findings, however, allow us to draw some conclusions on the usefulness of R&D as an explanatory variable of innovation in SMEs.

The firm in terms of knowledge and routines

According to Nelson (1991) and Nelson and Winter (1982), successful firms can be understood in terms of organisational routines, which define lower-order organisational procedures, and how these are coordinated. Next to this, there are higher-order decision procedures for choosing what is to be done at lower levels. 'The notion of a hierarchy of organisational routines is the key building block under our concept of core organisational capabilities. At any time the practised routines that are built into an organisation define a set of things the organisation is capable of doing confidently'. (Nelson 1991: 68). Basically, routines are sequences of activities that do not require attention or search behaviour in executing tasks.

Winter (2003) defines organisational capability as follows: 'An organisational capability is a high-level routine (or collection of routines) that, together with its implementing input flows, confers upon an organisation's management a set of decision options for producing significant outputs of a particular type' (Winter 2003: 991). Dynamic capabilities are the subset of the competences/capabilities, which allow the firm to create renewed or new routines, producing renewed and new products and processes, and respond to changing market circumstances. Capabilities consist of routines. Routines are behaviour that is learned, highly patterned, repetitive or quasi-repetitive, founded in part in tacit knowledge, with specific objectives. The opposite of a routine is ad hoc problem solving (Winter 2003). Capabilities are a matter of knowledge (Langlois 1992; Prahalad and Hamel 1994; Teece *et al.* 1997), and cannot be easily bought or sold in markets; knowledge resources have to be developed through *experience*. There is empirical evidence that the way production is organised by management inside the firm is the source of differences in firms' competence in various domains (Teece *et al.* 1997). Differences in coordinative routines and capabilities seem to have a significant impact on performance variables such as development cost, development lead times and quality. Significant firm-level differences suggest that routines related to coordination and resource use are firm-specific in nature.

The firm as we see it is governed by routines and has at least an operating capability and a marketing capability to connect to its markets. Its effectiveness is related to the effectiveness of its routines. If it is involved in innovation on a structural basis, it needs, next to these two basic capabilities, dynamic capabilities such as absorptive capacity. We expect, since the focus of the firm in the knowledge-based view is on efficiency, that the use of knowledge in an average firm prevails over the development of knowledge. For this reason the average firm has a tendency to favour exploitation processes and incremental innovation (March 1991) over radical innovation. Furthermore, the renewal of routines (improvement) has as output incremental innovation, and the process of improvement is *supportive* of routinisation. It is about single-loop learning (Argyris and Schön 1978): learning to do things better. More radical learning (double-loop) breaks up routines, replaces them or leads to installing new routines. The reason for this can probably be found in the nature of the average human being (Simon 1969). Radical learning is more difficult than incremental learning. Search processes are first of all primarily local, confined to the information the organisation has at its disposal in its own knowledge base. If problems cannot be resolved using internal data, information and competence, absorptive capacity comes into play. Absorptive capacity is first of all the *internal* ability to give meaning to external information. Without a proper knowledge frame, external information cannot be valued in relation to the improvement of task execution nor can it be cognitively internalised in order to produce improved skills.

Only a relatively small number of firm members will be engaged in formal and planned innovation activities (examples might be R&D and business development), since day-to-day exploitation operations and routines dominate the behaviour of the average firm. The abilities of these actors are of special interest to us and explain the knowledge development capability of the SME firm to a large degree (see also pp 259–60 on the locus of absorptive capacity in SMEs). Owner-managers, who are often responsible for innovation in their own company, control many of the smaller firms with up to 250 employees. His or her skills are crucial to the innovation process of the company. This person might be labelled the Chief Innovation Officer. In our conceptualisation we state that this person, who is responsible for innovation projects, being owner or not, is central to the innovation process. His or her absorptive capacity is one of the most important ingredients of the proposed construct Internal Knowledge Base.

We focus on preconditions and explanatory variables of the effective development of renewed and new routines. These routines are the knowledge resources of the firm and are collectively addressed as the knowledge base of the firm. The firm is first of all a collection of actors. For this reason, firm learning can only be understood by looking at how actors in firms learn: firm learning strongly resembles *individual* learning.

Knowledge defined, explored and measured at the level of the firm

We focus on external knowledge relevant to solving problems, which can lead to the successful execution of tasks. Therefore, the definition of Boekhoff (1997) is adopted: knowledge creates the possibility of the fulfilment of a task, in the present or in the future, by means of situation-dependent selection, interpretation and valuation of information. Knowledge is dynamic: 'Knowledge is essentially related to human action'. (Nonaka *et al.* 2000: 2). Knowledge is 'organisational' can only be meant metaphorically. In essence, knowledge can only be located in the mental domain (cognition) of individuals (Cohen and Levinthal 1990; Jorna 2002). These individuals possess cognitive structures for perception, interpretation and evaluation. According to Nooteboom (1996), perception produces data for interpretation:

> Interpretation entails the production of meaning, which transforms data to information, by fitting it into a stock of knowledge. Understanding connects and transforms information into beliefs or claims of causal or deductive insight. Knowledge is a meaningfully ordered stock of information (interpreted data), and understanding, *plus* [italics added] ability to transform it into action (skill), which yields performance.
>
> (Nooteboom 1996: 8)

Knowledge, information and data are closely connected (Jorna 2002). The raw material of data is the unformatted, unstructured material in the world. Data are such things as the various signals – acoustic, visual, tactile and otherwise – that are around us and that can be interpreted as (having) information. The relation between data and information formally is that information is a structuring of data that reduces uncertainty. The information value of a message is higher if it reduces more uncertainty. In a more informal way, it could be said that information is interpreted data. Knowledge is the interpretation of information in the eye of a certain beholder (by definition a human information-processing system), who brings in his own history, experiences and interpretation schemes. That is why the same information may lead to different knowledge for various individuals (Jorna 2002). This implies that sharing of knowledge is not easy and depends not only on the quality of the message and the sender, but also on the quality of prior related knowledge of the receiver. The ability to understand outside information can be developed through learning.

In all learning processes, knowledge is at least shared. In order to share knowledge, individuals need a common ground (common knowledge: Grant 1996) that enables them to understand each other. Nelson and Winter (1982) state that much of the detailed knowledge involved in routines is tacit, however. The sharing of tacit knowledge requires intensive interaction and in many cases the physical presence of actors involved in the sharing process (Jacobs 1999), because articulation of this kind of knowledge in, for instance, coded knowledge is difficult or even impossible. Coded knowledge can be transmitted at greater ease if the receiver understands the code. Senker (1995: 431) answers the question why tacit knowledge is so important in innovation processes:

> '[. . .] continuing dependence on tacit knowledge for innovation arises from the tendency for advances in knowledge and techniques to be associated with new tacit knowledge; from adherence to previous successful practice; from the lack of scientific or technological expertise within specific firms or sectors; and, possibly most commonly, from the *complexity* of systems'.

We can conclude that the sharing of knowledge, certainly in the case of knowledge for innovation, is not easy, and thus potentially slow and expensive. Knowledge sharing is an intrinsic part of learning. Another intrinsic part of learning is human creativity, which aids in internalising and assimilating absorbed knowledge, producing meaning and the possibility to deploy skills.

Yet, how can we tell whether a given population has effectively absorbed external information, and whether it has actually been internalised by individual cognitive structures? The simple and short answer that Boisot (1995: 209) provides is 'by the use to which it is put'. Therefore, in this research we choose to look at the outcome of AC, which is innovation at the level of the firm. We take the output variable of the number of innovation projects and their contribution to turnover in the last three years as the dependent variable, which is partly an economic variable. Statistical offices (e.g. in the Netherlands the Central Bureau of Statistics CBS 2001) also use this definition in large-scale research across OECD countries. The measure is inspired by the Frascati Manuals, a family of manuals of the OECD on how to measure innovation. We measure innovation at the firm level. In explaining absorptive capacity we adopt a multiple actor perspective. In the knowledge-based view (Grant 1996), innovation and learning is the exception to the rule, since the use of knowledge is leading in an exploitation process. Part of the explanation of the number of innovation projects can therefore be found at the level of input variables related to the behaviour of a limited number of actors, because other firm members are occupied in the execution of daily routines that yield the core competence of the firm. We are therefore interested in the learning behaviour of these individuals in particular.

Learning behaviour and learning of actors in firms

Cohen and Levinthal (1990) conclude, based on an extensive literature study, that learning skills and problem-solving skills are similar. They indicate the sort of necessary preconditions for successful learning do not differ from the preconditions required for problem solving and for the creative process.

'The prior possession of relevant knowledge and skills is what gives rise to creativity, permitting the sorts of associations and linkages that may have never been considered before' (Cohen and Levinthal 1990: 130). They conclude that creative capacity and absorptive capacity are so similar that there is little reason to differentiate their modes of development. The consequence for our research is that, because of their similarity, when we find indicator variables of the potential creativity of the firm, they might be considered also as indicator variables of the dynamic capability of absorptive capacity.

Routines are the skills of an organisation (Nelson and Winter 1982). Therefore, to understand the nature of the repertoire of organisational routines of the absorptive capacity of the firm, we have to understand more about learning skill development. Learning is a human activity. Based on the fact that all human productivity is knowledge-dependent, it is fundamental to assume that the critical input in production and the primary source of value is *knowledge that actors have* in organisations. According to Grant (1996), knowledge creation is an individual activity, following Simon (1991: 125): 'All learning takes place inside human heads; an organisation learns only in two ways:

a by the learning of its members, or
b by ingesting new members who have knowledge the organisation didn't previously have'.

In this research we follow this view on how firms learn, which means that the term 'organisational learning' will only be used in a metaphorical way. In analysing the dynamic capability of absorptive capacity, it implies opening the black box of the firm in this particular research to descend to the actor level in explaining *organisational* absorptive capacity and innovation.

For this reason we are firstly interested in the behaviour of actors in firms in general. The assumption in this research is that individuals in organisations are in general satisfiers. It is expected that these individuals on average choose the simplest solution involving the least effort. For this reason they are expected to be reluctant to employ internal R&D, since this is costly and risky (Smith 1995). Furthermore, routines favour incremental learning because they develop through repetitive and best practice and derive their strength from the fact that they 'automate' behaviour. We suppose, assuming that individuals in organisations are in general satisfiers, that they seek ways to fulfil their task in the easiest possible way by improving first of all the *efficiency* of task execution. Because maximising the use of rules, routines and other integration mechanisms that economise on communication and knowledge transfer enhances efficiency (Grant 1996), the productive firm and individual actors inside will be reluctant to engage in more radical learning, that is, *changing* rules. When problems occur, first of all the knowledge base of the firm is scanned to look for solutions. If localised search is unsuccessful, search activities expand over the borders of the firm into the network. These search activities can aim at both incremental and more radical learning. The network of the company and the existing corps of scientific (and technological) knowledge will be scanned, looking for solutions to problems.

Organisations are reluctant to engage in their own internal development processes, since this is risky and costly (Smith 1995).

The relevant learning of individuals to organisations is skill development related to organisational task execution. Innovation of task execution presupposes either improved task execution, the possibility of fulfilling new tasks, or a combination of both. Research on the memory of the individual (i.e. the knowledge base of the individual) suggests that accumulated prior knowledge increases the ability to put new knowledge into memory (acquisition of knowledge) (Anderson and Lebiere 1998). Next to this, the ability to recall and use it (Posner 1989) increases, and thus the necessary creativity of the individual has to increase at the same time. Human beings learn in firms by engaging in experience with the internal and external networks of the firm. Simple acquisition of knowledge is not enough for learning; appropriate contextual knowledge is needed to make new knowledge fully intelligible (Lindsday and Norman 1977; Grant 1996). It is insufficient to expose an individual briefly to relevant prior knowledge.

As far as learning skills are concerned, experience or performance on one learning task may influence and improve performance on subsequent learning tasks (Ellis 1965). Learning is cumulative, and learning performance is greatest when the object of learning is related to what is already known. Learning is therefore less effective in novel domains. What is actually well known by individuals will change only incrementally. The breadth of categories into which prior related knowledge is organised, the differentiation of those categories, and the linkages across them permit individuals to make sense of and, in turn, acquire new knowledge (Posner 1989). Fiol and Lyles (1994) indicate that a certain extent of disagreement is essential for corporate innovation. This is especially relevant when exploration of new knowledge is preferred to the exploitation of existing knowledge (March 1991).

For one actor, learning is a qualitative or quantitative change or progress (improvement) in one or more domains, but for a multi-actor system, learning essentially is also about some form of sharing knowledge, in many cases in the form of knowledge development. Learning in case of absorptive capacity is about both. The result of knowledge development is, in the firm context, improved for new routines in task execution, producing innovation as outcome. Actors inside firms learn through experiential learning (Kolb 1984). Experience (prior related knowledge), intensity of effort and diversity offer stimuli for learning and creative behaviour. The exchange of tacit knowledge usually presupposes the physical presence of actors. The direct experience with the operating and marketing process inside the firm is stored in the routines of the firm, in what we will call the Internal Knowledge Base. This is our first explanatory (independent) variable of the dynamic capability of absorptive capacity of the firm.

Absorptive capacity is related to organisational learning and is in essence always about the learning abilities of an individual actor or a multitude of actors in the case of *organisational* learning capabilities. Learning is time-consuming and deliberation hinders routinised behaviour. Reflection, one of four phases discerned by Kolb (1984) (next to experimentation, experience and conceptualisation), is clearly the opposite of routinising a task by exercising it in a patterned and prolonged way. Reflection merits learning, however. Learning is therefore less easy than routinised behaviour; it is time-consuming and thus costly.

Research shows that the knowledge development process is highly cyclical and interactive (Jacobs and Waalkens 2001) towards the environment of the firm. Up to 40 percent (Pavitt 1984) of information needed for innovation in firms stems from the environment of the firm. We argue that informal 'external knowledge' available to the firm in its network is therefore a second explanatory variable of the dynamic capability of the absorptive capacity of the firm. There is empirical proof that Formal Cooperation for innovation is also a variable related to external information for innovation, which is understandable considering the frequency, diversity and intensity of external contacts in this case. According to learning theory, these are preconditions for sharing and developing knowledge. We therefore choose the number of projects involving Formal Cooperation for inno-vation as our third explanatory variable. Based on our theoretical discussion, exploration and exploitation of both formal and informal contacts should contribute to the ability to innovate within the firm and to the enlargement of its cognitive scope.

Absorptive capacity of firms

In this section the absorptive capacity of firms is discussed. How can the firm context stimulate the development of knowledge of the individual? Organisational learning implies more than just the sum of the learning capabilities of individuals (Cohen and Levinthal 1990). Because the information-processing capabilities of organisations in many cases surpass the information- processing capacity of indi-viduals, organisations are able to innovate beyond the scope of single individuals. The knowledge diversity in the firm stimulates creativity and the learning poten-tial of the individual. According to Nooteboom (1996), the basis for learning is prior related knowledge, and learning is therefore more difficult in novel domains. We have already briefly discussed that innovations, which result from learning, can be incremental, involving stepwise improvements of what is already known (based on the established routines), or radical in the sense that the knowl-edge involved in the innovation is rather unfamiliar to the organisation. In this case, routines new to the firm are established. Within economic and organisa-tional literature, different degrees of learning are recognised. The distinction between 'single loop' versus 'double loop' (Argyris and Schön 1978) is perhaps the most widely known. Other distinctions include 'first-order' versus 'second-order' learning (Fiol and Lyles 1985) and 'exploitation' versus 'exploration' (Holland 1975; March 1991). Nooteboom (1996: 11) holds these distinctions to be synonymous with first- and second-order learning.

First order learning refers to the refinement of existing practice ('doing things better'), while second order learning refers to the emergence of a novel practice ('doing better things'). The first seems to be related to learning in the form of increased efficiency of an existing practice, and the second is related to new combinations in a newly emerging practice'.

Both kinds of learning are important to each organisation and potentially contribute to turnover and profit.

The diversity of knowledge inside the firm plays an important role. If there is uncertainty concerning the knowledge domains from which relevant and useful external information can be deduced, a diversified knowledge base offers a more robust base to learn. This is true because the chance that information gathered could be related to the prior related knowledge increases in case of a diversified knowledge base. Next to this, a diversified knowledge base facilitates the innovation process, because it permits individuals to make new links and relevant connections. Cohen and Levinthal (1990) consider the capacity to explore external knowledge as a critical component of innovative capabilities. They argue that the ability to evaluate and utilise outside knowledge is largely a function of the level of prior related knowledge.

At the most elementary level, this prior knowledge includes basic skills or even shared language but may also include knowledge of the most recent scientific or technological developments in a given field. Thus, prior related knowledge confers the ability to recognise the value of new information, assimilate it, and apply it to commercial or organisational ends. These abilities are a repertoire of routines that collectively constitute what can be called a firm's absorptive capacity. An organisation's absorptive capacity will depend on the absorptive capacities of its individual members, but is not resident in one single individual only: it depends on the links across a mosaic of the capabilities of various individuals, inside as well as outside the company. The knowledge base of organisations is divers in terms of capabilities, while these capabilities consist of the skills of more than one individual actor. An important question, therefore, in understanding the absorptive capacity of firms concerns the relation between the ability to share information and the diversity of knowledge of these individuals. Interactions between individuals who are each carriers of diverse and different knowledge structures will lead to new connections and associations and, together with that, to the capability to innovate at a level that exceeds the level of the individual. This only holds if there is enough overlap in the form of common, shared knowledge facilitating understanding. Cohen and Levinthal (1990) elaborate the effect of path dependency: they argue that if a firm has already developed some absorptive capacity in a particular area, it may more readily accumulate additional knowledge in the subsequent periods in order to exploit any critical external knowledge that may become available. Moreover, the possession of related expertise will permit the firm to better understand and therefore evaluate the importance of intermediate technological advances that provide signals as to the eventual merit of a new technological development. Absorptive capacity affects expectation formation, permitting the firm to predict more accurately the nature and commercial potential of technological advances. These revised expectations, in turn, condition the incentive to invest in absorptive capacity subsequently.

Critical knowledge to the firm is more than only technical knowledge. Marketing knowledge and production knowledge are also needed to assess whether an innovation can be exploited to commercial ends. The development of a network of internal and external business and communication relations facilitates the awareness of individuals about the knowledge and capabilities of other individuals, resulting in an enlargement of the absorptive capacity of the organisation. The concept of absorptive capacity has most often been applied to large firms. In that context, R&D is an established predictor variable of innovation activity, because it captures the knowledge behaviour in terms of expenditures related to innovation. If R&D expenses are high, propensity to gain experience with outside knowledge can also be high. In the context of SMEs it is known that about one-third of firms in the architectural and engineering sector spend money on R&D (Bilderbeek and Brouwer 2000). If companies innovate on a regular basis, without R&D spending, they can still develop a dynamic capability of absorptive capacity. Thus, R&D is not conditional for AC in SMEs. It is clear, though, that R&D spending is related to the level of AC in the case of large firms.

Effective learning extends the cognitive scope of the individual and it is reinforced in the firm environment if the right preconditions apply. Through effective learning of individuals, the cognitive scope of the organisation (Nooteboom 2000) can be enlarged. The scope of the firm can be enlarged through formal cooperation (strong ties) and through its counterpart, informal cooperation in the network of the firm (weak ties). Because of the empirical evidence of scope enlargement through formal cooperation (Teece *et al.* 1997; Nooteboom 1998, 2000), we choose Formal Cooperation as an explanatory variable next to the Internal and External Knowledge Base. The knowledge contacts involved in formal cooperation are relatively intense; accessible prior related knowledge is enlarged, while this pool of knowledge is in most cases more diversified than that of the single firm.

The picture for weak ties, and how they contribute to the ability to develop knowledge, is less clear. Efforts are in general less intense, but also the diversity of knowledge is an important ingredient for innovation. We expect that Formal Cooperation and External Knowledge Base are important in relation to new routines. Renewal of routines is probably more related to the Internal Knowledge Base in particular; it can be an outcome of localised search in the form of quality control, for instance, or of other internal feedback loops in the process. The capability to process information in knowledge in the Internal Knowledge Base is indispensable to assimilate, use and commercialise knowledge, whatever its origin, internal or external. A well-developed Internal Knowledge Base is a precondition for AC. Outside information cannot be understood without this crucial prior related knowledge.

The locus of AC in architectural and engineering SMEs

For our purpose, it is important to have an idea of which actor or actors are involved in the innovation capability in the case of architectural and engineering SMEs. Allen (1977) reports that in engineering agencies, information does not directly enter into the organisation. The knowledge base of organisations is diverse in terms of capabilities, while these capabilities on average consist of the skills of more than one individual actor. The interface with the environment is concentrated in one or a few boundary spanners. The stream of information is indirect, involving at least two steps. First, external information enters the organisation through 'technological gatekeepers', who read more, including relevant professional literature. These persons have more internal and external contacts than average employees. Second, boundary spanners have to translate outside information before it can be recognised and becomes useful to the production and marketing competences of the organisation.

While in principle every member of the organisation can be involved in single-loop learning, the responsibility for *innovation projects* at the level of the architectural and engineering firm, however, will be centralised in one or only a few gatekeepers and boundary spanners. In SMEs the head of the R&D department will fulfil the two roles of gatekeeper and boundary spanner, if the company is large enough and such a department is installed. In the case of a small company there might not be such a department, and it is possible that there is no formal R&D budget. In this case it is probable that the owner/manager fulfils both roles and can be considered a Chief Innovation Officer (CIO). In our empirical research we focus on the owner/manager or the person responsible for innovation projects at the board level.

We focus on this 'Chief Innovation Officer' who facilitates or initiates change and acts as a gatekeeper and a boundary spanner. He or she has the formal responsibility to engage in innovation projects. His or her search behaviour in terms of knowledge gathering and development are considered to be a crucial part of the absorptive capacity of the firm. However, this is not the whole story. Interaction between innovators and the rest of the firm is necessary: to put knowledge to work, the CIO needs the contribution of actors involved in the production and marketing units. With their help, innovations can be *commercialised* to have them contribute to turnover and profit. Because of the central position of the CIO, this person can report on his or her own knowledge development behaviour, as well as that of other relevant actors to innovation projects in his or her firm. The variable Internal Cooperation captures the perceived quality of the CIO in internal cooperation. We try to measure the satisfaction of the CIO in relation to the cooperation with the operations and marketing departments. We interpret this as a proxy of the ease of commercialisation of innovation projects. We define the moderator variable Internal Cooperation, therefore, as our final conceptual variable that influences the relationship between potential and realised absorptive capacity.

Modelling AC in the domain of architectural and engineering SMEs

Based on the discussion in the previous sections, we model absorptive capacity in the context of architectural and engineering SMEs as follows. We distinguish three explanatory (independent) variables: Internal Knowledge Base, Formal Cooperation in the network (with strong ties) and External Knowledge Base (with weak ties). R&D efforts and Internal Cooperation for innovation are moderating variables in our model. Next to these explanatory variables, three dependent variables are used. We first describe these dependent variables (numbered 1, 2 and 3) and then return to the independent variables (numbered 4, 5 and 6). After this, our moderating variables (numbered 7 and 8) are described.

The first dependent variable is the number of innovation projects aimed at *renewed* products, processes and services in the last three years (PACAP I), the second is the number of innovation projects aimed at *new* products, processes and services (PACAP II). The third dependent variable is the contribution of projects aimed at renewed and/or new products, processes and/or services (RACAP) to turnover. In our empirical research they are measured in the following way:

1 Number of innovation projects (in the last three years) aimed at renewed things, (PACAP I):

   a The number of projects in the last three years aimed at renewed products.
   b The number of projects in the last three years aimed at renewed processes.
   c The number of projects in the last three years aimed at renewed services.

   Adding these three items results in PACAP I, the number of projects aimed at renewed things.

2 Number of innovation projects (in the last three years) aimed at new things. (PACAP II):

   a The number of projects in the last three years aimed at new products.
   b The number of projects in the last three years aimed at new processes.
   c The number of projects in the last three years aimed at new services.

   Adding these three items results in PACAP II, the number of projects aimed at new things.

3 Contribution to turnover (RACAP):

   a Contribution to turnover of new and/or renewed products.
   b Contribution to turnover of new and/or renewed processes.
   c Contribution to turnover of new and/or renewed services.

   Adding these three items results in RACAP, the total contribution to turnover of projects on renewal and new things.

We refer to Figure 12.1 which depicts the conceptual model of AC. The model should be interpreted as follows. First, the Internal Knowledge Base is indispensable for the acquisition and subsequent use of external information. It permits the firm to recognise relevant information and to interpret it in order to generate value. Variables and indicators of Internal Knowledge Base are mentioned below and they are related to previous sections by means of a short comment.

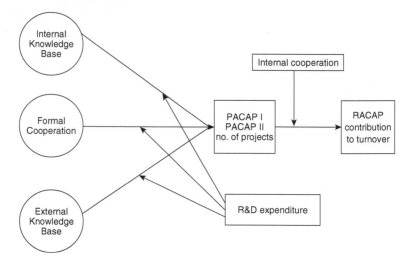

Figure 12.1 Conceptual model of absorptive capacity in architectural and engineering SMEs.

4   Internal Knowledge Base:

  a Level of technical education: technical skill training of the CIO.
  b Level of management education: management skill training of the CIO.
  c Working experience, general: general prior related knowledge of the CIO.
  d Working experience, building sector: specific prior related knowledge of the CIO.
  e Perceived level of technical know-how: specific prior related knowledge of the CIO.
  f Perceived level of knowledge of organisation: prior related knowledge of coordination of the CIO.
  g Perceived level of knowledge of the environment: additional prior related knowledge of marketing of the CIO.
  h Age of the firm: prior related knowledge in the firm of firm members in general.
  i Turnover per employee: firm competence.

The parts (aspects) (a)–(g) of the Internal Knowledge Base are indicators relating to the characteristics of the CIO (the individual), whose competence we perceive as of major importance to organisational AC in architectural and engineering firms. The age of the firm is meant as a proxy of the experience of the firm as a whole. The turnover per employee is a competence measure, indicating the firm's success in achieving commercial ends. We do not take profit as such an indicator, because this is often an indirect measure. Realised profits do not always end up in the books since these are often redirected and invested in the firm, partly due to the tax regime. The extent to which commercial ends are realised is in our opinion best measured by taking the turnover per employee. This indicator can be used as an indicator of firm competence, in the case of comparisons of competence of firms in the research sample. In this way the disturbing effect of firm size is eliminated. The label of the resulting (construct) variable is Internal Knowledge Base, INTKB.

The variable Formal Cooperation can aid in extending the cognitive scope of the company (i.e. external economies of cognitive scope: Nooteboom 2000). It is measured in the following way:

5   Formal Cooperation:

 a Cooperation is an important contributor to the knowledge production of our company (1 = don't agree at all, 5 = fully agree).
 b Does your company cooperate formally (contractual arrangements) for innovation?
 c If yes, how many formal cooperations were established in the last three years?

Measurement in the case of cooperation is straightforward. First, an opinion is asked about the value of cooperation for the respondent. Second, we asked whether the firm cooperated for innovation (contractually arranged) in the last three years. Third, we asked how many times such cooperation was established in the last three years (i.e. the years 1999–2002). The resulting variable is the Formal Cooperation for Innovation in the last three years: FCOOP. Through Formal Cooperation, valuable external information enters the company while through cooperation new knowledge is generated. Because of knowledge diversity and intensity of interaction the scope of participating individuals is enlarged, as is their innovating ability.

The External Knowledge Base relates the company to external information of the network, so that the firm (and innovating actors) can learn from this. Because, in general, solutions out of the network (through formal or informal cooperation) are more easily obtained than by doing R&D, it is expected that persons involved in problem solving will scan the network before they engage in R&D. The independent variable of External Knowledge Base (a construct) is inspired by the work of Landry *et al.* (2002) and consists of the following elements:

6   External Knowledge Base Personal (1 = don't agree at all, 5 = fully agree)–external links.

 A Relational asset index (possible transmission of specific, tacit knowledge):
  a I know personally professionals/managers in agencies of regional economic development.
  b I know personally professionals and managers in governmental agencies involved in economic development.
  c I know personally university/government researchers in the field of my products.

    d I know personally my clients and suppliers.
    e I am involved in a lot of personal contacts like in external meetings.

B   Participation asset index (intensity of effort, learning is difficult):

    a I participate a lot at the local level.
    b I participate a lot at the regional level.
    c I participate a lot at the national level.
    d I participate a lot at the international level.

In theory, personal interaction and intensity of effort are prerequisites for learning and innovation. The two indices A and B together form the measure for the External Knowledge Base Personal (EXKBP). EXKBP measures participation and intensity of the use of the external network of the gatekeeper by means of physical presence in meetings relevant to innovation activities. It relates to the possibility of sharing tacit knowledge. In addition to this sub-variable of External Knowledge Base Total (EXTKBT, our model variable External Knowledge Base), we constructed a sub-variable for firm contacts for research, External Knowledge Base of the Firm (EXKBF). This is assessed by the following index:

C   Research network index (knowledge sources, specific research environment):

    a We use a lot of research from public institutions.
    b We make use of institutions aimed at technology sharing.
    c We make a lot of use of the work of universities.
    d We make a lot of use of the work of polytechnics.
    e We use a lot of professional conferences and specialised literature.

6A and 6B include the possible transmission of tacit knowledge and relate to the fact that learning is difficult. Brief exposure to knowledge is not enough for knowledge development and learning. 6C relates to the diversity of the research knowledge network, which can lead to novel associations. 6C also includes the intensity of the use of different sources of information. Adding the five five-point scales results in the variable External Knowledge Base of the Firm (EXKBF). The resulting model variable External Knowledge Base Total (EXTKBT) is constructed by adding EXKBP and EXKBF divided by the number of their items. The resulting variable is the model variable EXTKBT that we consider as a proxy of external information relevant to the innovation process of the CIO and other firm members that can be obtained in order to facilitate the innovation process.

R&D is also a moderator variable in the conceptual model. Absorptive capacity is important in any company innovating on a regular basis, regardless of R&D. R&D expenditure will affect the internal knowledge base, the amount of formal cooperation, and the amount of information a company can extract 'informally' from its network by improving problem-solving routines. In addition to this, it will make the firm a more interesting party for formal cooperation in innovation, increasing the cognitive scope of the firm further. The following data are collected on R&D efforts:

7   Research and development:

   a Does your company have a formal R&D or business development department?
   b R&D expenditure as percentage of turnover.
   c R&D hours per year at the level of the company.

We start with the question whether or not the firm has a formal R&D or business development department. Keeping in mind the fact that about two-thirds of SMEs are known to actually have no expenditures on R&D, we try to complement this explanatory (moderating) variable of absorptive capacity by asking for hours spent on R&D activity. Both R&D expenditure divided by the number of employees (RDEXREL) and R&D hours divided by the number of employees (RDHOURR) will be examined in relation to the *relative* innovation production (data on innovation divided by the number of employees).

The four variables Internal Knowledge Base, Formal Cooperation, External Knowledge Base and R&D efforts together are expected to explain the number of innovation projects in the last three years, which is seen as the Potential AC (PACAP I and II). A second moderator variable, Internal Cooperation, moderates the relation between the number of projects and the contribution of new or renewed products, processes and services to turnover. This variable relates to the perceived quality of internal cooperation. It is the measurement of the satisfaction of the CZO in relation to cooperation with the operations, and marketing departments. It is measured in the following way:

8   Internal Cooperation (1 = don't agree at all, 5 = fully agree) – internal links.

   a My cooperation with the production department is good.
   b My cooperation with the Marketing department is good.

The moderator variable Internal Cooperation (INCOOP) moderates the relation between the number of projects and the contribution of new or renewed products, processes and services to turnover and profit. This variable relates to the perceived quality of internal cooperation, which we interpret as a proxy of the ease of commercialisation of innovation projects. It is obtained by adding the two five-point Likert scales. We argue that a high level of satisfaction on internal cooperation might indicate that the innovation process and commercialisation process run smoothly. Thus, it can explain successful exploration and subsequent exploitation. Only 25 per cent of innovation projects actually deliver in economic terms and contribute to commercial ends (Tidd *et al*. 1997). Many products, processes or services are technically speaking feasible but impossible to commercialise. The ability to exploit findings of explored knowledge to commercial ends is as important to an innovating firm as actual exploration in the form of innovation projects. It determines the economic value of these projects. In particular, the R&D marketing interface is known to be problematic. The contribution of innovation projects to turnover is therefore measured and labelled as realised absorptive capacity (RACAP). It relates to the use of external information in order to achieve a *contribution to commercial ends* in the form of contribution to turnover.

Hypotheses

Various hypotheses on relations of the four main explanatory variables in the model can be formulated. The six hypotheses below specify a number of relationships between the proposed explanatory variables and innovation outcomes in terms of number of projects (PACAP I and II) and their contribution to turnover (RACAP).

The internal knowledge base relates to the production, marketing and innovation capabilities of the firm. They are a crucial component of absorptive capacity; external information is useless unless there is a capability in the firm to recognise and embed the value, together with the ability to exploit this information in order to generate knowledge that can be commercialised. The resulting hypothesis relating to the variable internal knowledge base is:

H1: Higher scores on the internal knowledge base result in higher innovation production (PACAP I/II, RACAP).

Formal cooperation is supposed to increase the cognitive scope of a company (e.g. Teece *et al.* 1997; Nooteboom 2000). Therefore, more information can be obtained, and the quality of the processing of information can be enhanced. It is also expected that firms that cooperate formally are potentially more successful innovators. Since on average less than 50 per cent of the companies cooperate (CBS 2001), a comparison of cooperating firms versus firms that do not work in cooperation for innovation is feasible. The hypothesis is:

H2: Higher scores on Formal Cooperation result in a higher innovation production (PACAP I/II, RACAP).

Because of the diversity of external information and the frequency and intensity of contacts in which relevant information can be transmitted, the external knowledge base also increases the external cognitive scope of the firm. The availability of adequate external knowledge also affects innovation and the possibility of commercialisation, in particular where, new things are developed. The hypothesis is:

H3: Higher scores on the External Knowledge Base Total result in higher innovation production (PACAP II, RACAP).

Since the dominant type of knowledge development and sharing in innovation processes takes place through interaction, involving the physical presence of innovating actors is expected to contribute in particular to the problem-solving capacity of the firm. The variable External Knowledge Base Personal captures the personal interaction of the CIO with his or her network. The hypothesis is:

H4: Higher involvement in and use of the external network of the firm, involving the physical presence of actors, results in higher innovation production (PACAP I/II, RACAP).

In the conceptual model, R&D efforts moderate the relationships between the internal knowledge base, cooperation and the external knowledge base. This implies that, although there might be no R&D, there still can be a certain level of absorptive capacity. If there are any R&D efforts, this will reinforce the effect of the internal capability, the ability to cooperate and the ability to extract external knowledge from the network. The hypothesis is:

H5: Firms engaging formally in R&D have higher (innovation) production (PACAP I/II) than firms not undertaking formal R&D.

When it comes to internal cooperation we expect that the quality of cooperation of the CIO with the marketing and production department, is indicative of how successful the firm is in commercialising the results of innovation projects. The hypothesis is:

H6: Higher scores on internal cooperation (with production and marketing) result in higher scores on commercial success (RACAP).

Discussion and conclusion

If a firm interacts with and adapts to its environment on a structural basis, the firm needs absorptive capacity (AC) for new, external information. To understand AC, we first of all conceptualise the firm in terms of knowledge and routines, capabilities and dynamic capabilities. Absorptive capacity can be classified as a dynamic capability, which is the ability to learn from external innovation new to the firm. Learning is in this case the development of knowledge. Here, we define the output of absorptive capacity in terms of innovation projects and their effects on turnover. It may concern either incremental or radical innovation. We are interested in the factors that determine both potential and realised absorptive capacity (PACAP and RACAP). We define PACAP (I and II) as the number of innovation projects started on renewal (PACAP I) and on things new to the firm (PACAP II), respectively. These innovation projects can possibly be translated into business opportunities contributing to commercial ends. On the other hand, they can also fail to deliver the promise; for this reason, PACAP is therefore a necessary but not sufficient condition for realised absorptive capacity (RACAP). In the case of realised absorptive capacity the contribution of innovation to turnover of the firm can be measured, by which a contribution to commercial ends is realised. Only then is the phenomenon of absorptive capacity, as originally defined by Cohen and Levinthal (1990), fully grasped.

Although the classic indicator of absorptive capacity is R&D expenditure, we argue that in the case of SMEs, R&D expenditure is not an independent variable, but that it moderates knowledge-gathering behaviour. R&D expenditure is, in the case of SMEs, supplemental and not conditional. SMEs often lack formal R&D and for this reason we focus on additional explanatory variables, i.e. Internal Knowledge Base (measuring prior related knowledge), Formal Cooperation (formal collaboration with external parties), External Knowledge Base (the network of informal external relationships) and Internal Cooperation (the locus of absorptive capacity in an SME). The determination of the value of the alternative indicators of AC that we proposed is now in the phase of empirical testing. In May 2003 the data were gathered by means of a telephone inquiry into the sector of architectural and engineering SMEs. The response rate was 28 per cent out of 585 existing firms in the size class of 10–100 employees in the Netherlands. Preliminary results indicate the relevance of our approach. In all statistical tests performed, α is set at 0.05. In order to evaluate the capability for absorptive capacity and innovation, we selected 59 firms who claimed to innovate regularly, often or structurally. Firms that seldom or never innovate were omitted from the analysis because in these cases one cannot speak about a capability.

Our construct Internal Knowledge Base (INTKB) correlates significantly with PACAP1 ($r = 0.4$; $p < 0.05$, two-tailed). Our first hypothesis is that higher scores on the Internal Knowledge Base result in a higher innovation production in terms of PACAP I/II and RACAP. This hypothesis is therefore partly supported. Higher scores on the variable Formal Cooperation (FCOOP) should, according to our second hypothesis, result in higher scores on PACAP I/II and RACAP. We found the variable FCOOP to be significantly correlated to PACAP II ($r = 0.5$; $p < 0.05$, two-tailed), without significantly affecting PACAP I or RACAP. The construct of External Knowledge Base Total (EXTKBT) correlates significantly with PACAP II ($r = 0.4$; $p < 0.05$, two-tailed), without significantly affecting PACAP I or RACAP. In the case of our hypothesis on firms with formal R&D efforts (institutionalised in a department), we present a finding that is counter-intuitive: firms with an R&D department produce a significantly *lower* mean for PACAP II than that of firms without such a department (Mann-Whitney U, Wilcoxon W: $Z = -2.117$, sig. 0.034, two-tailed). Furthermore, we did not find any significant correlation between the absolute or relative R&D expenditure and the absolute or relative R&D hours with PACAP and RACAP. Our expectation based on these findings is that R&D efforts might have some relevance in the explanation of the innovation production of SMEs, but clearly to a lesser extent than in the case of large firms.

Referring to the role of tacit knowledge in innovation processes (sub-variable EXKBP of EXTKBT), we hypothesized that the physical presence of actors in innovation processes is crucial to obtain the required results. Again we find support for this hypothesis in relation to projects on new things, PACAP II ($r = 0.4$; $p < 0.05$, two-tailed). PACAP I and RACAP are not affected. Our variable Internal

Cooperation (INCOOP) shows no significant correlations with the innovation production in any respect. The proposed construct consists of only two items. The inter-item correlation is low, indicating that the two items might measure different things. This implies that adding the two items does not lead to a stable construct useful in our research at this moment.

In order to do research on absorptive capacity of SMEs, we needed additional variables other than R&D-related variables, because more than half of SMEs have no formal R&D department or expenditure. The preliminary findings in this research further illustrate the point that absorptive capacity of SMEs cannot be measured as in the case of large firms by measuring solely R&D expenditure. In addition to this, we did not find an expected correlation between the broader concept of R&D efforts in absolute or relative terms with the innovation production (PACAP and RACAP). We can conclude therefore that R&D efforts are unsuitable as a *direct* indicator variable of AC in SMEs. Therefore, at this point in time, we conclude that the use of our indicators on R&D efforts needs further attention in our final analysis.

This finding is important because it implies that measurement of absorptive capacity in the case of SMEs is virtually impossible if only indicators related to R&D are used. We therefore introduced Formal Cooperation as an additional variable that produces relevant results on PACAP II. Furthermore, Internal Knowledge Base and External Knowledge Base are found to be stable constructs related to PACAP I and PACAP II respectively. These three independent variables are directly related to knowledge gathering and knowledge development behaviour of actors in firms.

References

Allen, T. J. (1977) *Managing the Flow of Technology: Technology Transfer and the Dissemination of Technological Information Within the R&D Organization.* Cambridge MA: MIT Press.

Anderson, J. R. and Lebiere, C. (1998) *The Atomic Components of Thought.* Mahwah, NJ: Lawrence Erlbaum.

Argyris, C. and Schön, D. (1978) *Organizational learning.* Reading MA: Addison - Wesley.

Bilderbeek, R. and Brouwer, E. (2000) *Innovation Indicators for the Technical Engineering Industry: A Meso Perspective.* Utrecht: Dialogic.

Boekhoff, T. (ed.) (1997) *Managen van Kennis.* Deventer: Kluwer Bedrijfsinformatie BV.

Boisot, M. H. (1995) *Information Space: A framework for Learning in Organizations, Institutions, and Culture,* London: Routledge.

CBS (2001) *Kennis en Economie 2000, Onderzoek en Innovatie in Nederland* Amstardam: Elsevier Bedrijfsinformatie BV.

Cohen, W. M. and Levinthal, D. A. (1990) Absorptive capacity: a new perspective on learning and innovation. *Administrative Science Quarterly,* 35: 128–52.

Dosi, G. and Egidi, M. (1991) In G. Dosi (ed.), *Innovation, Organization and Economic Dynamics: Selected Essays.* Cheltenham: Edward Elgar, 2000.

Ellis, H. C. (1965) *The Transfer of Learning.* New York: Macmillan.

Fiol, C. M. and Lyles, M. A. (1985) Organizational learning. *Academy of Management Review,* 10(4): 85.

Grant, R. M. (1996) Toward a knowledge-based theory of the firm. *Strategic Management Journal,* 17 (Winter Special Issue): 112.

Holland, J. H. (1975) *Adaptation in Natural and Artificial Systems.* Ann Arbor: University of Michigan Press.

Jacobs, D. (1999) *Het Kennisoffensief: Slim Concureren in de Kenniseconomie* Deventer/ Alphen aan den Rijn: Samsom.

Jacobs, D. and Waalkens, J. (2001) *Innovatie²: Vernieuwingen in de Innovatiefunctie van Ondernemingen. Deventer: Kluwer.*

Jorna, R. (2002). De cognitieve kant van kennismanagement: over representaties, kennistypen, organisatievormen en innovatie. In P. van Baalen and M. Weggeman, *Kennis en Management.* Schiedam: Scriptum.

Kolb, D. A., Rubin, I. M. and McIntyre, J. M. (1984) *Experiential Learning.* Englewood Cliffs, NJ: Prentice Hall.

Landry, R., Amara, N. and Lamari, M. (2002) Does social capital determine innovation? To what extent? *Technological Forecasting and Social Change,* 69: 10.

Lane, J. L., Koka, B. and Pathak, S. (2002) A thematic analysis and critical assessment of absorptive capacity research. *Academy of Management Proceedings*, BPS, p. 4.

Langlois, R. N. (1992) Transaction-cost economics in real time. *Industrial and Corporate Change,* 1(1): 99–127.

Liao, J., Welsch, H. and Stoica, M. (2003) Organizational absorptive capacity and responsiveness: an empirical investigation of growth-oriented SMEs. *Entrepreneurship: Theory and Practice,* 28(1): 63–85.

Lindsay, P. H. and Norman, D. A. (1977) *Human Informatin Processing, Orlando, FL: Academic Press.*

March, J. G. (1991). Exploration and exploitation in organizational learning. *Organization Science* 2(1): 73.

Miles, I., Kastrinos, N. Bilderbeek, R., den Hertog, P., with Flanagan, K. and Huntink, W. (1995) *Knowledge-Intensive Business Services: Their Role as Users, Carriers and Sources of Innovation.* Luxembourg: Report to the EC DG XIII Sprint EIMS Programme.

Nelson, R. R. (1991) Why do firms differ, and how does it matter? *Strategic Management Journal,* 14, No. 8.

Nelson, R. R. and Winter, S. (1982) *An Evolutionary Theory of Economic Change,* Cambridge, MA: Harvard University Press.

Nonaka, I., Toyama, R. and Nagata, A. (2000) A firm as a knowledge-creating entity: a new perspective on the theory of the firm. *Industrial and Corporate Change,* 9(1–2): 2.

Nooteboom, B. (1996) *Towards a Cognitive Theory of the Firm, Issues and a Logic of Change* Groningen: SOM-School.

Nooteboom, B. (1998) *Management van Partnership–Over Allianties tussen Bedrijven.* Schoonhoven: Academic Service.

Nooteboom, B. (2000) *Learning and Innovation in Organizations and Economies,* Oxford: Oxford University Press.

Pavitt, K. (1984) Sectoral patterns of technical change: towards a taxonomy and a theory. *Research Policy* 13: 347.

Posner, M. I. (1989) *Foundations of Cognitive Science.* Cambridge, MA: MIT Press.

Prahalad, C. K. and Hamel, G. (1994) *Competing for the Future.* Cambridge, MA: Harvard Business School Press.

Senker, J. (1995) Tacit knowledge and models of innovation. *Industrial and Corporate Change,* 4(2): 431.

Simon, H. A. (1969) *The Sciences of the Artificial.* Cambridge, MA: MIT Press.

Simon, H. A. (1991) Bounded rationality and organizational learning. *Organization Science*, 2(1): 125–34.

Smith, K. (1995). Interactions in knowledge systems: foundations, policy implications and empirical methods. *STI Review*, no.16, OECD.

Teece, D. J., Pisano, G. and Shuen, A. (1997) Dynamic capabilities and strategic management. *Strategic Management Journal*, 18(7): 510.

Tidd, J., Bessant J. and Pavitt, K. (1997) *Managing Innovation: Integrating Technological, Market and Organizational Change.* Chichester: John Wiley.

Winter, S. G. (2003) Understanding dynamic capabilities. *Strategic Management Journal*, 24: 991.

Zahra, S. A. and George, G. (2002) Absorptive capacity: a review, re-conceptualisation, and extension. *Academy of Management Review* 27(2): 185.

13 The emergent nature of learning networks

Joakim Tell

Introduction

The focus in this chapter is on the potential for the university to formalise the use of informal learning methods, which better suit the needs of smaller enterprises. Here the network approach is used as a way of creating the dynamic process that characterises industrial estates, where relations between different players act as a source of inspiration and a sounding board in work on development issues and innovation. A learning network is defined as 'a platform for dialogue where researchers and SME managers come together and discuss and reflect upon different issues in their daily work, in order to initiate, follow and actively contribute to a joint development process'. Co-operation and different forms of dialogue[1] with other enterprises or public bodies are seen as important, in order to compensate for the disadvantages of competition that small enterprises often face when compared with larger enterprises. In this process the experience and knowledge to find new options and perspectives for tackling current problems have been used, in order to extend the necessary knowledge base and self-managing capacity.

Earlier studies of networks with a focus on learning and knowledge exchange (e.g. Emery 1987; Gustavsen 1992; Levin 1993), above all, demonstrate the power of innovation that comes from close relations between companies and universities and the importance of the dialogue in this connection. Some researchers, for instance Chaston and Mangles (2000), show that companies closely involved in networks adopt double-loop learning (Argyris and Schön 1978) to a greater extent in their daily work than companies without network contacts. However, there is a lack of studies between SMEs and universities that have closely followed and studied the long-term effects of co-operation 'from within' as has been done in this study. Further research in this area is required – studies that look into the different aspects of what organising such processes means, both in terms of organising principles and also in terms of the learning aspects.

The purpose of this chapter is to develop an understanding of how to organise learning networks between the university and managers of small traditional manufacturing enterprises, and a reflection upon what kind of learning this form of co-operation can lead to.

Theoretical framework

Networks

From a rational analytical viewpoint, the network metaphor is popular, as a means of analysing and understanding the connections between organisations, but also as a tool for explaining different processes of diffusion, such as the diffusion of innovation (Gustavsen and Ennals 1999). In this context, the concept of a network has proved to be a useful basis for exploring complex organisational phenomena, for example in issues such as the division of labour and co-ordination (Piore and Sabel 1984), or as one of several ways of explaining or understanding transactions between different actors (Williamson 1975) or industrial technological development (Håkansson 1987).

During the last twenty years, another way of using the concept of networks has developed. According to this theory, the network is seen as a development method, and not as an analytical tool. Of interest in this approach is not the network itself, but the process. One of the reasons for using the network in this way is discussed by Gustavsen (1993: 141), where he defines a productive structure (a network used as a development method) as a set of enterprises/organisations linked together and where 'the configuration of participants and links enables the structure to move to the forefront the type of concept-driven development characterising the leading edge in the field of productivity'. From my research perspective of networks, which are 'action-oriented and prescriptive', this was also the case. I use the notion of learning networks as a process of networking, which is defined as building relations between individuals, relations that are characterised by trust and commitment best understood from within the network itself. The idea behind the approach is that the participants, i.e. representatives from companies and researchers, jointly formulate problems and questions, and use each other's experience and knowledge to define options. This means that it is more a matter of creating an arena for reflection than of solving different technical and organisational problems. Like a so-called research circle,[2] 'the purpose should not primarily be to solve problems, but rather to examine them from as many angles as possible and thereby increase the existing knowledge of them' (Holmstrand and Härnstén 1996: 3).

One of the researchers who introduced the concept of a network into research on work and organisation was Herbst (1976: 35), who saw networks as a state where: 'Neither initial nor outcome state are specified in operational terms and the task was to achieve a more specificable task structure'.

In retrospect, Herbst's figure of a network (see Figure 13.1) visualises perfectly the search for a structure that developed during the development process in partnership with the SME managers. It is common that in the process of change the initial objective becomes more clearly structured and defined, and this has clearly characterised our use of the network concept.

$$? \; (?) \rightarrow ?$$

Figure 13.1 A network according to Herbst (1976: 35).

Learning

In the literature on learning, there is often a distinction made about the 'level' of learning (Fiol and Lyles 1985). Lower-level learning is focused learning that may be a mere repetition of past behaviours. Higher-level learning is the development of complex rules and associations regarding new actions, central norms, frames of reference and assumptions. One of the most widely spread and well-known distinctions of higher and lower levels of learning is Argyris and Schön's (1978) distinction between single-loop and double-loop learning. Adaptive and generative learning are concepts that describe different types/levels of learning, where the former is synonymous with single-loop learning and the latter with double-loop learning (Schein 1994). Lower levels of learning can be characterised as routine processes that occur through repetition in a familiar context. The consequences are behavioural outcomes.

Examples are institutional formal rules, adjustment in management systems, and problem-solving skills. 'Second-order transitions typically begin with a perceived crisis strong enough to "unfreeze" accepted interpretive schemes for at least some organizational members' (Bartunek 1984: 264). This typically happens when management practices are no longer successful, and management perceives a high task uncertainty. Higher levels of learning, on the other hand, can be characterised as non-routine processes, which occur through the use of heuristics and insights in an ambiguous context. The consequences are insights, heuristics and collective consciousness, and result in new missions and definitions, problem-solving skills, and the development of new myths, stories and cultures (Fiol and Lyles 1985). It is important to note that single-loop learning is not qualitatively less important than double-loop learning, but complementary, even though double-loop learning often is seen as 'better' in some of the organisational literature (Cook and Yanow 1993). Furthermore, double-loop learning does not always lead to changes in the daily life of organisations.

It can be argued that the learning situation of many managers in small companies is restricted due to prevailing conditions that block double-loop learning (Chaston and Mangles 2000). Learning of a higher level, i.e. double-loop learning, requires the learner to reframe, to develop new concepts and points of view, to cognitively redefine old categories, and to change standards of judgement. Such changes increase the learner's capacity to deal with situations in new ways and lay the foundation for developing radically new skills (Senge 1990).

There is a good deal of evidence that we cannot learn 'generatively' if we are totally preoccupied with coping and adapting (i.e. single-loop learning) while addressing internal questions (Schein 1994). Not only does this mean for an organisation that there must be some slack – some time available for double-loop learning – but equally important, there must be enough diversity concerning people, groups of people and subcultures to provide creative alternatives. The use of an inter-organisational network to question the guiding value system can be one way of overcoming the often-locked position internally that prevent learning in many enterprises.

Methodology

In order to examine if networks between small enterprises can be facilitated by the active involvement of a regional university, we (a colleague and I) initiated and participated in the development of two networks of small enterprises in our region. As part of the study, we focused on the exploration of alternative kinds of collaborative approaches. The selection of companies was initiated through an orientation phase during which we contacted small businesses in the region. We assessed the availability and need for various resources, as well as the interest of small businesses in developing collaborative structures. The study was done by means of a comprehensive questionnaire that was sent to 200 small manufacturing enterprises (10–99 employees). The result of the study showed that all companies expressed a strong need for more resources (e.g. technical, financial, personnel, etc.) and 75 percent stated that they would be interested in exploring collaborative relationships.

After the first phase, a participative exploration and design phase followed, in which extensive semi-structured interviews with 17 enterprises were conducted. The interviews resulted in a deeper understanding of the situation of small enterprises. Furthermore, the interviews developed a dialogue with the participating managers in which a first organisational network model was designed. After the construction of the network model, we entered the third phase in which the organisational network model was put into effect. The organising principle of the network model was that we met at a different company once a month for half a day. Each meeting focused on a minimum of two issues that were of particular concern to the 'host' company, but also of interest to the other companies. The meetings were organised into three parts: (a) the manager of the host company gave a presentation of the company and the issues he wished to raise, followed by a tour of the plant; (b) the participants addressed the questions of the host company in two heterogeneous groups with one of the managers of the host company and one researcher in each; (c) the meetings were concluded with a full discussion in the network group.

Ten small manufacturing companies (6–100 employees) formed two networks (five companies in each) together with us, representing the university. The companies were non-competitive, represented different technologies, and produced a variety of products. During more than six years of co-operation, we met in different constellations more than 100 times. At most meetings, the manager and the production manager have represented the companies, but employees have also, over time, been involved in the network. At these meetings, we have actively reflected upon different company-related possibilities and problems where the managers have used each other's experience and knowledge for new ideas and perspectives on how to develop their organisations.

Later, an additional two networks were initiated. The objectives were to draw on the experiences of the first two networks and to verify our knowledge about the networking process. The composition of these networks differed slightly from the first two. The third network consisted of five companies in the same industry, which was not the case in the first two networks. The fourth network organised four companies located in the same community, in contrast to the original networks that were geographically apart. These two networks also met approximately once a month to discuss company-related possibilities and concerns. All the networks drew upon research on group dynamics and models of change in organisations (e.g. the search conference method: Emery 1987), which provided a number of guiding principles. Through dialogue with the participating managers, the following basic principles were agreed upon: The network should be a relatively small assembly of individuals with democratic values, built on openness and willingness for long-term commitment towards collaboration; and actors should not have had prior work relationships with each other.[3] The network meetings have been applying a 'rotating chair', which has been a way of creating a sense of mutual responsibility in the group.

In the networks, the academics have been taking on different functions/roles. The university has had an administrative function – writing agendas together with the hosting managers, sending calls to meetings, and writing summaries of the meetings. The university has also had a legitimising function. In the early phases of the co-operation, our presence provided the participants with a sense of security. It was believed that the academic presence would guarantee that the goals of the network became objectively defined, and also that what was said in the network was not misused. Here the university representatives helped to build the necessary trust in the network by being what was perceived as a neutral partner. Over time in the co-operation, the university has also been keeping a focus on learning in the network.

In action research the researcher is a partner who provides an 'outside' point of anchorage that may be relevant for the 'inside'. 'Outside' means outside the traditional way of thinking, outside the operational and political context of the organisation. It does not necessarily mean 'representing' a university, or a discipline, or a particular field of expertise. However, one represents a different way of thinking, a different experience and a different set of narratives, which may be useful. One is involved in an ambiguous and problem-driven process. To what extent, when, and in what manner such an 'outside point of anchorage' is relevant depends on a combination of factors such as context, personality, relevant experience, type of issue to be addressed, and a kind of expertise that includes considerable tacit knowledge and, last but not least, is dependent on trust–trust that does not come with one's academic qualifications, but that has to be earned whilst working with the companies.

Empirical findings

During the first years of co-operation, we were often asked by colleagues why the companies participated in this kind of network and what they got out of it. We answered that this network fulfilled an important role in starting up different development projects and that the managers could learn from each other.

The question that followed was often: couldn't consultants arrange the same thing, and what was the use of bringing in the university?

When we asked the managers the same question, they brought up different aspects of why they found the network approach and the role of the university fruitful in this connection. First of all, to be a part of this network doesn't cost any money for the managers, except for the time that they put into the work (although time is a scarce resource for most managers, even scarcer than money in some respects). The network is further built upon a genuine interest of the managers in participating. When we 'recruited' managers to the network, we talked to a number of companies and identified a group of managers who searched for a group of other managers to meet and discuss everyday problems with. However, they did not know what kind of organisation could initiate and legitimate such a co-operation, which would have a focus on dialogue and not primarily a strict business focus. This meant, from an organising perspective, that it was more a matter of creating an arena for reflection than of solving different technical and organisational problems.

We also met managers who did not see any use for a network where the idea was to meet and reflect upon one's own organisation and others', and they did not want to participate either. That the network has functioned and produced interesting developments and learning is closely connected with the fact that those managers taking part are genuinely interested in trying this way of working and see the benefits. The approach would not have functioned if the managers did not see the point and really have a genuine interest in trying it out.

The managers noted that bringing in consultants to arrange this kind of work would cost money, which should put pressure on both the companies and consultants to really achieve and deliver something out of the network. The managers already work too much today, and they said that they did not need another group where they had to deliver, but a group where they could reflect upon their situation instead, and a forum where there was no real pressure on them to produce something. Having the university to legitimise the co-operation was one way of building up the necessary trust in order to gather the group in the first place. And since taking part in the network did not cost anything, it took away the pressure of having to deliver and created a relaxed atmosphere.

I felt dissatisfied when unable to give a convincing answer to the question of what this network contributed that other approaches could not do to the same extent. There was something in this approach other than uncertainty reduction and learning from each other that made the managers interested in this form of co-operation and want to continue, but I could not pinpoint it. It took me some time before I connected the question with a learning perspective and the ideas developed by Argyris and Schön (1978) of single- and double-loop learning. This has made it easier to understand and explain the benefits of the approach.

One way of visualising this is to consider what happened at the first network meeting. In retrospect, it was the very first network meeting, which, I think, had a major effect on the learning in the network, and explains why the managers found the approach so useful, even if they, and I, had problems in articulating this during the first years of co-operation.

Case 1: Questioning values

What happened during the first network meeting at one of the companies (we had all met once before at the university and discussed how we should practically work together, and the structural organisation of the networks: Lundberg and Tell 1997) was that the first company presented some of its current problems that were to be scrutinised by the other managers and by us.

At this network meeting the company raised two questions, one concerning a technical construction and the other about an organisational issue. When the manager had presented the two questions, he also gave an overview of the over-all situation of the company. During this presentation it emerged that the company had only one, though very significant, customer. The other managers participating at the meeting found this very remarkable, and brought up their doubts of just relying on one customer. The manager said that this was not the issue to be discussed and wanted the other managers to concentrate on the questions he had posed. But the other managers continued to repeat that the main problem for this company was not a technical construction or an organisational issue: its problem lay in the vulnerable situation of having to rely on only one customer. The manager hosting the meeting wanted to leave this question and continue, but the other managers did not want to let go of their opinion that this company needed to concentrate on the question of having only one customer.

Again in retrospect, this was the best thing that could have happened (even though, at the time, we thought that the idea of using networks to connect the university and SMEs would fail at the first meeting) – namely that at the first meeting, two issues became obvious for all of us. While perhaps not conscious, it was tacitly obvious what the network did contribute.

• First comes the question of problem-solving contra problem definition. It is frequently difficult for a small company (and for large companies as well) to understand where the problems really are. By re-contextualising the question, it became clear that it was not only possible but also necessary to reframe the issue.

When this situation was further examined, the meeting came to the conclusion that the two questions put forward by the company did not reflect the real issue faced by the company. Although the technology used by the company allowed a variety of products and a range of customers, its production system was totally geared towards this one particular customer. The big issue was that the company was very vulnerable (having only one customer), and diversification of production (making better use of the technology of the company) and an increase in the customer base were both essential. That is, a combination of product development and marketing was required.

• The second issue was the questioning of the ideas and values of the hosting manager. In this company, no one had questioned its having only one customer.

In the network, no manager was connected to any other by business or social relations (they did not know each other previously or have any business relations), and they could say what they felt without having to put their questions so as to suit someone's interests. The questioning made this manager realise (after half an hour) that he might look upon his company from another perspective, and concentrate on how to deal with this, which he did; and today, this customer still dominates, but the company now has its own profile with other customers, and is not totally dependent upon this large customer. Such learning is what Argyris and Schön (1978) refer to as double-loop learning, that is, a reframing of values and norms guiding one's actions.

Case 2: Questioning implicit ideas

To further visualise the learning that took place, a dialogue is presented that took place at a network meeting during the second year of co-operation. Part of a discussion illustrates the effects of gaining new perspectives and ideas for the internal development work through a dialogue across organisational borders. The discussion is about semi-autonomous workgroups. The issue focuses on how to lead such groups (it has been discussed for some time, but now some of the companies have launched 'live' projects in order to implement semi-autonomous workgroups). The manager of the host company is new at his post, but has prior experience as a manager in one of the other companies in the network.

The manager of the host company has raised the question of how to go on with the implementation of semi-autonomous workgroups, and the difficulties a company faces when dealing with leadership in that context. His implicit idea is to use permanent group leaders, but a question of how to tackle the issue of leadership in the groups is brought up by another manager. The question triggers a discussion concerning how the company feels about the leadership of the groups:

Visiting manager (A): Have you thought about rotating the leadership or having a permanent group leader, and anyway, are you offering all employees the possibility of becoming the group leader?

Visiting manager (B): To me it sounds like a good idea to rotate the leadership, as we are doing in our company.

Visiting manager (B): That will only lead to no one shouldering the responsibility of the group.

Researcher (X): If you rotate it's easier to implement a bonus system and other things on a group level. That is, the group is responsible. The group leader's function could also be rotated and anyone who wants could be offered the possibility to develop competence to lead the group.

Visiting manager (D): We have tried rotating group leaders. Some of the employees are taking an active part and some are not, others don't want to be part of such a system.

Manager of the host company: Yes, we have experienced that there are too few employees with the competence to be group leaders. We feel that we don't have … – but on the other hand – maybe it isn't a bad idea to rotate the leadership.

Researcher (Y): Maybe the employees who have been passive so far would step forward.

Visiting manager (B): It will show – exactly as you described earlier – that you thought the problem should be the assembly, but it didn't turn out that way, and it will be the same here. What you think will not work, will work just fine. We have had those experiences. We had a man who was completely impossible – 'a lone wolf' – who was responsible for running a machine, and he said, 'This is my machine, I have been here 20 years'. I was convinced that this man would not take any initiative, but he was the one who turned out to be the best.

Visiting manager (D): It is often those who complain that possess the best leadership abilities.

The manager of the host company: Yes, we have such a man – he always gives his perspective on everything. He has the potential to become a leader.

The manager of the host company continues: If you should try and 'eat the cookie and still have it', that is, to have a rotating group leader in the workshop, and a stationary group leader in the assembly. This idea feels satisfying. It doesn't have to be a permanent solution. You can say to the employees that you will give it a try. You can start rotating the leadership in the workshop and see how it works out.

The manager of the host company turns to the production manager and says: What do you think of this idea?

The production managers: Yes, to me it sounds like a good idea.

The manager continues: Good, we will try it!

As a result of this dialogue and the questioning of the implicit values, a rotating leadership was realised and semi-autonomous workgroups were implemented. One year after the meeting the production manager said the following on the outcome of using the networks as support when implementing semi-autonomous workgroups:

> We have semi-autonomous workgroups that work just fine. We would never have initiated this project without the support of the network, I am sure of that. I have gained a lot of assistance from the network, and I have seen that problems at the other companies have been the same as here. The implementation has not been as easy as you read in books. I began to see that problems related to a single person could grow and damage a whole group. The other companies have had the same problem, and from that you can learn a lot.

The manager continues saying that without the support of the other companies. '[w]e would not have been able to pull through the implementation due to the fact that we ran into more problems than we could handle on our own.'

It is important to note that not all network meetings has contained the feelings of 'eureka', but over time the work in the networks has oscillated between less productive meetings to meetings that have given a lot of insights and new ideas.

After working together for a while, it is easy to reach a point where people know each other too well and have mutual relations that make it difficult to be innovative any longer. We were not aware of this danger when initiating the network (or did not reflect on it enough), but it partly took care of itself when half of the managers who initially joined the network had left, for reasons such as changing workplace or other factors during the six years of co-operation. This change of managers has kept new ideas coming in.

During the time of co-operation, several internal development projects have been initiated in the companies, during which the network members have been used as a sounding board. Some of these projects (for instance, projects concerning the quality of the work environment, marketing strategies, reorganisation, and introduction of semi-autonomous groups) were carried out in some of the companies, while others were carried out together by all companies, such as:

- In the information technology (IT) project, the aim was to raise awareness of IT and its possibilities in supporting company development. Examples of activities in this project were getting an e-mail address and a company home-page. During the project some of the employees were given a crash course on the Internet.
- In the ISO 14001 project, the network focused on the implementation of ISO 14001. The participating companies supported the initiation of the ISO 14001 certification process in all participating companies, using each other and the network as an arena for joint reflection and support and as a resource pool.
- In the employee exchange programme, two to four employees from each company visited each other during a full day for mutual learning. The network of employees functioned in parallel with the network of managers, and led to a higher degree of incorporation of employees in the development work.

This network approach shows many similarities with other action strategies used in management training and development (cf. action learning (Revans 1980, 1982) and co-operative inquiry (Reason 1999)). On one important point, however, there is a difference that should be noted. The networks described in this chapter have not been constructed in order to solve a particular problem or to focus on a specific issue and to be ended thereafter. This approach is longitudinal and thus constitutes a somewhat different arena for learning that is more in line with what Senge (1994) labels a parallel learning system.

When asking the managers attending the network collaborations about the contribution of the network, they emphasise the importance of using the other network members' knowledge and experience to highlight and question their own specific problems in order to learn. In the network the managers, together with us representing academia, have reflected on their experiences from (among other things) different development projects. They have returned to their enterprises and used the network discussions as sources of inspiration for new actions, and they have then reflected on their new experiences in the network again. This process has been an ongoing loop between the company and network levels. As in many other management training approaches drawing on an action strategy, the combination of action (using, for example, real development projects as sources for experience) and reflection on action has shown itself to be an important characteristic of the learning process in these networks. Table 13.1 is a summary of the learning phases, key managerial issues, pitfalls and organising principles in the learning networks.

In this first phase, with managers committed to really wanting to try out the ideas of learning networks, the legitimising role of the university – and the fact that taking part did not cost anything (except time) and that the companies had no prior relations – created a trustful atmosphere and got the network started.

The prerequisites for learning have changed with time in the networks. At the beginning of the collaborations, the networks were primarily oriented towards specified goals of the network, e.g. the aim to increase company intellectual resources for product development, or the goal of getting support in purchasing IT solutions.

As time passed, trust increased between network members. In the wake of the interpersonal trust, a reciprocal and transparent milieu developed, which in turn established prerequisites for a receptive and confronting capacity between the managers, which led to higher-level learning. Using the vocabulary of Argyris and Schön, there was a change in the learning conditions in the networks towards Model II-like learning conditions. As a consequence of the changes in learning prerequisites, the 'return on investment' increased for the managers, since the learning outcome became qualitatively higher. This also established trust towards the learning process in itself.

The next phase was the activity in the network, characterised by reflection upon different development projects (single- and double-loop learning). The third phase is about achieving continuity in the network and still keeping the network innovative.

Organising the learning process in networks

For academic education and research at the university, closer co-operation with organisations and their members can have a positive impact, in the sense that it provides access to a deeper understanding of complex issues and produces actionable knowledge. Or, in the words of Argyris *et al.* (1985: ix), discussing action science 'creating usable knowledge is becoming an increasingly important topic in the social sciences. [. . .] Our focus is on knowledge that can be used to produce action, while at the same time contributing to a theory of that action'. The real-time aspect also provides opportunities for validating actionability in knowledge

Table 13.1 A summary of the three learning phases in the learning networks

	Phase 1: Initiating the networks?	Phase 2: The development process (?)	Phase 3: Continuity and new goals →?
Key managerial issues	• Committed management • University legitimises co-operation • No prior relations • No cost All of the above lead to a trustful atmosphere and an initiation of the learning networks	• An open and creative atmosphere • Single- and double-loop learning	• Uncertainty reduction • Initiative • Flexibility
Pitfalls	• Not achieving trustful openness • The managers not being committed	• The danger of getting stuck after the first meetings • Not achieving desired results	• The relations in the network become too strong between the members • Openness and the ability to be innovative decrease
Organising principles	• Action- and dialogue-oriented approach • The responsibility for the network rotates in the group • Take as a point of departure the problems that the companies face • Not too large groups (5–7 companies) • Two managers from each company to maintain continuity and commitment in the network	• Work with real action projects and reflect over them • The co-ordinator is important to push the work forward	• Network of networks (NON) • New managers join the network • Employees from companies join

Table 13.2 University and small enterprises meeting halfway in interdependent relations in learning networks

University	Learning networks	Small enterprises
Opens up to new roles	An arena for meeting halfway in interdependent relations	Join in networks
University takes on important different *roles*, such as a facilitator, consultant and academics, helping to build the necessary trust through being a neutral partner	The focus is on creating an arena for reflection rather than on solving different technical and organisational problems	By working with *networks* of *small enterprises* instead of a single enterprise in order to initiate change and development, it is possible to create an atmosphere of inter-organisational co-operation and *learning* through *dialogue*, characterised by *trust* and *commitment*
Guidelines for organising learning networks for the university • Access to interesting and relevant research questions in close co-operation with SMEs	The outcomes of learning networks	Outcomes on a managerial and company level • Internal and inter-organisational projects launched
Single-loop learning S.L. (action projects carried out in the companies) are used in order to reach out to the SMEs. Double-loop learning D.L. (a joint reflection in the network) is then possible to obtain through a dialogue on these action projects. This is an oscillation carried out over time, where the dialogue is used in order to produce trust and commitment.	Connecting mechanism is a reflection on joint actions in the network (see Figure 13.2 for further discussion)	Learning on a managerial and network level. Double-loop learning obtained both on an individual level and on a network level is closely connected with the single-loop learning and the projects carried out.

created through simultaneous creation and use. Table 13.2 gives an overview of the important concepts and ideas encapsulated in the use of the learning networks in order to reach out to small enterprises. This table highlights the importance for both parties of meeting halfway, in order to learn and develop from each other.

Organising a university-led learning network means leading a systematic and formalised interaction on a voluntary basis between SME managers. It is also a platform for dialogue where researchers and managers come together to discuss and reflect upon opportunities and problems in their daily work, which might lead to the creation of different inter-organisational and internal change processes. The idea is not necessarily to solve the problems, but to discuss them from as many angles as possible (problem definition). The basis for the development of the learning networks approach also incorporated the values and ideas of action research.

Conclusions and implications

The combination of action (using real development projects as boundary objects) and reflection (by means of trusting relations between network actors) has been shown to be an important condition in supporting the questioning of norms, values and world-views of the managers. The learning process in the network can be understood as described in Figure 13.2.

The observations tell us that the conditions in the learning process have changed in the networks during the time of collaboration. From a learning process point of view, it is possible to identify a shift, over time, from primarily focus single-loop to also include double-loop learning. The managers have learned and reflected on their own companies and different development projects, tried them out, and have then come back and reflected in the network again. This process has been an ongoing loop between the company and network level, and has, over time, fostered the questioning of values and norms by the participating managers. Long-term commitment to the network (i.e. the collaboration with

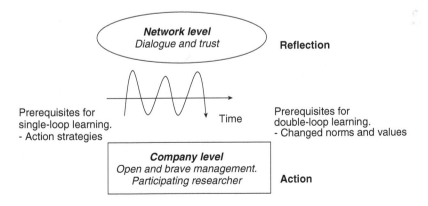

Figure 13.2 The learning process in a network.

other managers and researchers) establishes the necessary conditions for trust among the members of the network. In the wake of trust between the network actors, and by means of dialogue, an open-hearted and questioning milieu has originated. This has led to a movement of the learning conditions in the networks, which guide the network process.

By using the learning network as an arena for reflection, managers in small companies get support in the reflection process. This is an important ingredient in the learning process (Schön 1990). The network can be seen as a 'reflective tool'. It enables the learning of tacit knowledge between practitioners where both how (single-loop learning) and why (double-loop learning) are discussed. Important to mention here, however, is that in this discussion the initial reason why the SMEs joined was probably to learn action strategies on how to make their companies more effective, and not primarily double-loop learning. But what has made this work successful is the ability to connect these two levels through the dialogue-oriented approach used in the development process. If we had only concentrated on achieving double-loop learning, I think that the mangers would have left the network, because they would have had problems in seeing its practical utility. If we had only concentrated on single-loop learning, consultants and others could have been more effective in delivering solutions. The issue was the combination of the two, made possible through the trustful relations built in the network group, when no one of them had any prior relations with each other. Moreover, representing the university, we could facilitate this atmosphere of trust through the dialogue and the action-oriented research approach used.

Summarising the reflections on the characteristics of the learning process, my experience from observing networks over time indicates that there is a change in both the prerequisites for learning and in the learning itself. Learning in networks seems to exhibit an emergent nature and should therefore not be understood as a structure but as a process. I find that learning in this kind of approach has emergent characteristics and that the possibilities of exploiting the potential for higher-level learning that is inherent in group-based learning approaches are consequently increased over time.

Notes

1 'To the Greeks *dia-logos* meant a free flowing of meaning through a group allowing the group to discover insights not attainable individually. Dialogue differs from the more common "discussion", which has its roots in "percussion" and "concussion", literally a heaving of ideas back and forth in a winner-takes-all competition' (Senge 1990: 10).

2 'Put simply, a research circle is a study circle to which you add one or more researchers. The work centres on a certain problem that has been brought to the attention of the circle by a union or another group of practitioners'. (Holmstrand and Härnsten 1996: 3).

3 It might be worth noting the somewhat 'Scandinavian tradition' applied in the project (Gustavsen 1992). Although this issue is of interest, I will not elaborate further upon it in this chapter.

References

Argyris, C. and Schön, D. (1978) *Organisational Learning: A Theory of Action Perspective.* Reading MA: Addison-Wesley.

Argyris, C., Putnam, R. and Smith, D. (1985) *Action Science.* San Francisco: Jossey-Bass.

Bartunek, J. (1984) Changing interpretive schemes and organisational restructuring: the example of a religious order. *Administrative Science Quarterly*, 29: 355–72.

Chaston, I. and Mangles, T. (2000) Business networks assisting knowledge management and competence acquisition within UK manufacturing firms. *Journal of Small Business and Enterprise Development*, 7(2): 160–70.

Cook, S. D. N. and Yanow, D. (1993) Culture and organisational learning. *Journal of Management Inquiry*, 2(4): 373–90.

Emery, M. (1987) A Training Workshop on the Theory and Practice of Search Conferences. Canberra: Centre for Continuing Education, Australian National University.

Fiol, C. and Lyles, M. (1985) Organizational learning. *Academy of Management Review*, 10(4): 803–13.

Gustavsen, B. (1992) *Dialogue and Development: Theory of Communication, Action Research and the Restructuring of Working Life.* Assen: Van Gorcum.

Gustavsen, B. (1993) Creating productive structures: the role of research and development. In F. Naschold, E. R. Cole, B. Gustavsen, and H. van Beinum (eds), *Constructing the New Industrial Society.* Van Gorcum: Assen/Maastricht.

Gustavsen, B. and Ennals, R. (1999) *Work Organisation and Europe as a Development Coalition, Dialogues on Work and Innovation.* Amsterdam/Philadelphia: John Benjamins.

Håkansson, H. (1987) *Industrial Technological Development: A Network Approach.* London: Croom Helm.

Herbst, P. (1976) *Alternatives to Hierarchies.* Leiden: Martinus Nijhoff.

Holmstrand, L. and Härnsten, G. (1996) Democratic knowledge processes in working life, Presented at 4th Conference on Learning and Research in Working Life, Steyr, Austria, 1–4 July.

Levin, M. (1993) Creating networks for rural economic development in Norway. *Human Relations*, 46(2): 193–218.

Lundberg, M. and Tell, J. (1997) From practice to practice. *International Journal of Action Research and Organisational Renewal*, no. 2: 1–24.

Piore, M. and Sabel, C. (1984) *The Second Industrial Divide: Possibilities for Prosperity.* New York: Basic Books.

Reason, P. (1999) Integrating action and reflection through co-operative inquiry. *Management Learning*, 30(2): 207–226.

Revans, R. (1980) *Action Learning: New Techniques for Managers.* London: Blond & Briggs.

Revans, R. W. (1982) *The Origins and Growth of Action Learning.* London: Chartwell-Bratt.

Schein, E. (1994) *Organizational Learning as Cognitive Re-definition: Coercive Persuasion Revisited.* Cambridge, MA: MIT Sloan School of Management.

Schön, D. (1990) *The Reflective Practitioner.* New York: Basic Books.

Senge, P. M. (1990) *The Fifth Discipline.* New York: Currency Doubleday.

Senge, P. M. (1994) *The Fifth Discipline: The Art and Practice of the Learning Organization.* New York: Currency Doubleday.

Williamson, O. (1975) *Markets and Hierarchies: Analysis and Antitrust Implications.* New York: Free Press.

Section V

Learning, education and development

14 Being differently abled

Learning lessons from dyslexic entrepreneurs

Robert Smith

Introduction

Learning plays a crucial part in the development of entrepreneurial propensity and is inextricably linked to communication. An appreciation of the role of communication in entrepreneurial studies is increasing, albeit slowly, and in particular the pervasiveness of entrepreneurial narrative as a learning mechanism. For example, our knowledge of entrepreneurship is often grounded in cherished stories. These stories are built around accepted myths. One such myth of the 'poor boy' struggling to overcome communicational difficulties has long had anecdotal credence in entrepreneurial narrative. Indeed, it is part and parcel of the heroic construct of the entrepreneur and is an element of the basic script. This chapter[1] focuses upon weaving a more visible tapestry of the phenomenon from thread-like 'vignettes' collected from Internet articles, magazine columns and biographies. Although Reich (1987) cast doubt on the veracity of the 'poor-boy-making-good' storyline as a credible tale in the twenty-first century, vestiges of the narrative nevertheless remain.

If such 'poor boy' narratives no longer have persuasive power, should we now dispense with them? The author suggests that the answer is no and that there may be genuine psycho-social facets behind the pervasiveness of such myths which have yet to properly articulated. The poor-boy myth is an amalgam of many complicated social phenomena, such as class, gender, levels of education and marginality. Consequently, this chapter considers the impact of dyslexia and other learning difficulties on the communicational ability and styles of affected entrepreneurs. Learning difficulties per se are predominantly associated with masculinity (as is entrepreneurship) and in particular with childhood learning. Affected boys do not develop their potential to be enterprising and can drift into a life of delinquency and crime.[2] The question of why some boys raised in marginality turn to crime, whilst others overcome great odds to become entrepreneurs, has never been fully addressed. In less enlightened times dyslexia was viewed as a disability and those who were affected by it may not have fully understood its significance, or kept quiet about it for fear of invoking social consequences.

Entrepreneurial propensity has long been associated with the communicational concept of 'charisma' (the gift of grace) and charismatic people are generally regarded as being skilled orators. Not surprisingly, many successful entrepreneurs are also regarded as skilled raconteurs and storytellers, factors indicative of the importance of communication to entrepreneurial propensity. Many entrepreneurs are blessed with what Davis and Braun (1994) and Davis (1995) refer to as 'the gift of dyslexia'. The history of entrepreneurship is awash with examples of illiterate and dyslexic entrepreneurs who have succeeded despite (or because of) this 'gift'. This chapter views those with learning difficulties not as being disabled but as 'differently abled'. Rae (1999) argues that we learn to be entrepreneurial and Smilor (1997) that (action-based) learning is central to the entrepreneurial process, with effective entrepreneurs being exceptional learners. Indeed, many have a sponge-like ability to soak up vast quantities of information without drowning in detail. With the exception of work on entrepreneurial education and training there is relatively little research on specific aspects of learning in relation to entrepreneurship. As will be highlighted in this chapter, there is an interaction between learning and entrepreneurship as processes.

As will be demonstrated, a considerable number of entrepreneurs self-report having experienced such difficulties. These difficulties affect one's ability to communicate and appear to have a higher incidence in the male population. Although there is a hereditary aspect to many difficulties, secondary social and environmental influences appear to be more prevalent in determining life chances. It is also a difficult area to research, which perhaps explains the dearth of studies into it.

Such difficulties originate in childhood and early socialisation and if undiagnosed or untreated may lead to a narrowing of opportunities. Many such individuals may be branded as social misfits and consequently are drawn into a spiralling pattern of deviance and rebelliousness towards authority. On one hand we have the offending youth often associated with 'criminal families', and on the other we have the proverbial, enterprising 'child prodigy figure' associated with the 'entrepreneurial family'. From an examination of biographies and the life stories of persons who encounter learning disabilities, it is discernible that there exists in society a polarised and ideologically loaded 'double ethic' which discriminates between the privileged and underprivileged classes, viewing the symptoms created by the problem differently, according to class. In this view, dyslexic children from a working-class background were more prone to be considered as stupid and delinquent, whereas children from middle- and upper-class backgrounds were more likely to be considered to be special and thus gifted. We must be aware of ideological gildings, because Pollock and Walter (1993: 3) point out that communication is vital once, ideologically, intelligence has become associated with class, and in particular with the upper class as being of higher intelligence. Consequently, the inability to read and write has become associated with stupidity. Reading ability is a distinct social advantage. Yet exposure to a learning difficulty does not correlate to low IQ. This phenomenon has widespread implications for society, in that many potentially gifted children are not being channelled into socially productive and personally rewarding entrepreneurial occupations. Paradoxically, despite being associated with youth, entrepreneurship is very often a product of maturity. Pollock and Walter (1994: 22) also articulate that dyslexic children in later life have a propensity towards business acumen and are generally street-wise.

The findings of this present study are intriguing, revealing over fifty examples of entrepreneurs, chief executive officers and inventors who have self-reported experiencing learning difficulties such as dyslexia, ADD and ADHD. A contribution of this study is that it highlights specific communicational techniques adopted by these entrepreneurs to overcome their individual communicational deficits. These techniques, such as looking at the bigger picture learning from pictures the reliance upon memory, the preference for talking the avoidance of the written word, the refusal to work from a script, and so on, enable the individual entrepreneur to compete and often excel in an aggressive entrepreneurial milieu. These techniques turn disadvantage into a competitive advantage and imbue the dyslexic entrepreneur with a spontaneity and dramatic air, which characterise stereotypical notions of the entrepreneur. This chapter contributes to the collective knowledge of entrepreneurship by discussing a previously under-researched phenomenon.

The chapter has four sections. The first introduces the topic of dyslexia and other learning problems, providing a brief literature review/overview of the phenomenon and how it influences individual entrepreneurs. The second briefly considers the use of the Internet as an academic research tool/methodology. The third section demonstrates how dyslexia manifests itself into specific communicational traits. The chapter concludes with a discussion of implications and reflections on future research in this area. In particular, this chapter examines two research questions, namely:

- What are the links between entrepreneurship and dyslexia?
- Is it possible that dyslexics communicate differently from other people?

The hypothesis discussed is that there is a discernible link between entrepreneurial propensity and learning difficulties among a considerable number of entrepreneurs, which is worthy of further, more rigorous empirical research. We now turn to consider dyslexia and entrepreneurship.

Dyslexia and entrepreneurship

This section examines the research question, 'What are the links between entrepreneurship and dyslexia'. It commences by looking at specific learning difficulties, detailing some of the problems that they pose in relation to learning. Next, there is a brief literature review on the subject before turning to examine areas of existing entrepreneurship theory related to dyslexia. Overcoming marginality and disadvantage in then examined, followed by a look at learning difficulties and childhood. Dyslexia, storytelling and entrepreneurial propensity are that considered followed by next, executive functioning skills, and finaly a section on dyslexia and the 'crooked pathway' into crime. The links between the sections illustrate the potential scope for future studies.

Specific learning disabilities

Although this chapter concentrates upon dyslexia, other learning difficulties include attention deficit disorder (ADD), attention deficit hyperactivity disorder (ADHD), dyspraxia, dysphasia, autism, asperger's syndrome, emotional and behavioural difficulties (EBD) and challenging behaviour induced by family disadvantage. Learning difficulties are often an extremely private preserve, as indicated by Kerr (1973: 29–32), who highlighted the personal and collective embarrassment that dyslexia can cause. For those interested in the specific symptoms of dyslexia, dyspraxia and attention deficit disorders, see Table 14.1.

Table 14.1 Common signs of specific learning disorders

Disability	Symptoms
Dyslexia	Pre-school children may learn to talk later than other children and have difficulty in pronouncing or transposing words. They may be slow to develop a vocabulary, may have difficulty recalling words and with rhyming. They may be slow to learn the alphabet, numbers, days of the week, colours, shapes, and how to spell/write their name. They may be unable to follow multi-step directions, be slow to develop motor skills, and may have difficulty telling and or retelling a story in the correct sequence. They may find it difficult separating sounds in words or blending words together. Older children may have difficulty in connecting words and sounds or in decoding single words, may have difficulty spelling phonetically or may confuse small words. They may rely on memorising, guessing and context or have difficulty learning new vocabularies. They may consistently make reading and spelling errors, letter reversals, word reversals, inversions, transpositions and substitutions. They may transpose number sequences and confuse arithmetic signs. May have trouble remembering facts, have difficulty planning, organising and managing time, materials and tasks. May use an awkward pencil grip and have poor motor skills. Adults may hide reading problems, spell poorly or rely on others to correct bad spelling, may avoid writing, may be illiterate but may be very competent in oral language. They may rely upon and develop an excellent memory and have good people skills and intuitively read people very well. They may work in jobs well below their intellectual capacity and may be spatially talented and gravitate towards professions such as engineers, architects, artists, designers or crafts-based skills. They may be prone to left–right confusion, and mirror reversals of letters and words.
Dyspraxia	Symptoms include slowness, e.g. may be 8–12 years old before they can tie shoelaces, have difficulty dressing, be withdrawn in the company of other children, have untidy handwriting, be unable to assemble 'construction toys'. It also relates to difficulty in drawing, writing, buttoning and other motor skills,

Table 14.1 Common signs of specific learning disorders—cont'd

Disability	Symptoms
	sequencing or tasks that require fine movement skills. It is also associated with clumsiness and problems of language, perception and thought. It is estimated that up to 10 percent of the population experience the condition to one degree or another and it is four times more prevalent in boys than girls.
ADD and ADHD	Symptoms of ADHD are problems with attention and compulsive, hyperactive behaviour. It affects all aspects of life making children very unpopular and under-achieving. They suffer from low self-esteem and depression. Attention disorders relate to academic and behavioural problems of children with difficulty in focusing and maintaining attention. These can overlap with other conditions such as dyslexia, dyspraxia and speech and language disorders.

Source: Developed from material found on various Internet sites.

According to East and Evans (2001), children with special needs have particular strengths that manifest themselves as observable traits. An examination of such traits (see Table 14.2) suggests that they correlate to entrepreneurial traits. This is a key point in this chapter.

Table 14.2 Individual strengths manifested as traits

ADHD	Impulsive, restless and like to see finished work
Asperger's syndrome	Learn by rote but have difficulty with metaphors
Autistic spectrum disorder	Learn by rote and prone to fixate (interest in cars)
Cerebral palsy	Determination
Dyscalculia	Strong at art, oral work and reading but cannot learn by rote, may have difficulty reading and sequencing
Dyslexia	Strong performers at art, oral work and dramatic performance
Dyspraxia	Keen to do well
Aphasia	Strong art drawing
Semantic-pragmatic disorder	Learn by rote
Moderate learning difficulties (MLD)	Good readers
Left-handedness	Keen to do well

Irrespective of the learning difficulty studied, some generic consequences can be described. Communicational deficits may lead to a vicious circle characterised by lack of success/achievement, resulting in frustration and issues of low self-esteem, low self-confidence, fear of isolation, a sense of being different, bullying by peer groups, and inappropriate pressure from parents and authority figures. Often the problem manifests itself in specific problems such as truancy or self-harm. Literacy and numeracy are now taken for granted in modern Western societies, where reading and writing levels are now very high, but this was not always the case. In previous times the ability to read and write was a specific human and social capital exploited by social elites and was related to class position. Literacy equated to knowledge, power and wealth. Illiteracy was associated with poverty and the lower classes, as was crime in general. Many of those who were successful in breaking out of the cycle of poverty/deprivation/crime did so by virtue of self-education and other techniques of self-help eulogised in entrepreneur stories.

Other childhood illnesses interrupt schooling and can leave a legacy of impaired learning. Learning difficulties often occur in pairings. For instance, persons with dyslexia are commonly also dyspraxic. It is generally accepted that learning difficulties are risk factors in delinquency, and career failure in later life for children even with no conduct disorders. Approximately 80 percent of dyslexia is believed to be inherited (Hornsby, 1984) and ADD can be inherited, particularly through the male line.

Dyslexia is a neurological problem discovered by the English ophthalmologist. W. P. Morgan in 1896. The cause of the condition is unknown and there are varying degrees of dyslexia from mild, moderate to severe. The name is derived from the Greek words *dys* (trouble) and *lexia* (word). It manifests itself as difficulties in reading, writing and spelling. Research has shown that dyslexic brains are structured differently from lexic brains. Consequently, dyslexics often develop highly strategic and creative cognitive abilities. According to Reid and Kirk (2001) 'adult dyslexics have long been misunderstood and their considerable talents have often been unrecognised and unrealised'. It is a very complex condition and the form in which it manifests itself depends upon how much help, encouragement and support the individual is given, the level of parenting, schooling, how intelligent they are, their personality type and their socio-economic background. It is related to the ordering of the brain cells, and in particular an inefficient connection between the left and right halves of the brain.

A brief literature review

Academic research into entrepreneurship and dyslexia is in its infancy. Rawson (1968) researched the careers of dyslexic boys of middle-class professional backgrounds in Maryland and interestingly found that 13 percent became business executives and 7 percent eventually owned or managed their own business. Fortunately there is a wealth of anecdotal and autobiographical material. A search for academic articles specifically related to entrepreneurship and learning difficulties proved disappointing, with only one direct hit on an academic paper, namely that of Hlava (2003). However, the search also threw up various journalistic references printed in magazines, such as those by Morris (2002), and Tyson (2003), and also book titles, e.g. West (1999, 2001). The PhD thesis of Julie Logan (2001) on dyslexia and entrepreneurship was a seminal piece of research. Logan found that one in five entrepreneurs in her sample of respondents was dyslexic. Levander *et al.* (2001) have researched the incidence of ADHD in a sample of Swedish entrepreneurs, and the ongoing research of Uddin (2001–) looks at the link between adult literacy and income generation using a qualitative ethnographic approach to investigate the strategies adopted by non-schooled people to cope with their income-generating activities; it challenges the assumption that adults without schooling are a homogeneous mass of socially disabled people. Morris (2002), in an incisive article in *Fortune* magazine, examined dyslexia in the corporate world, discussing how business leaders with dyslexia overcome it by finding their own approach to success.

Those who have dyslexia are often referred to as visual thinkers, particularly if they are located in the professional classes. West (1999) notes that strong visual thinkers and dyslexics are always at the leading edge and critically discusses an interesting theory that many of the early dyslexics and strong visual thinkers who experienced language problems quit their schools and conventional towns and rushed to new frontiers where they pioneered new technologies – sailing ships, wind-or water-powered mills, railroads and telegraph lines, gold mines and oil fields. West highlights that these pioneers sought their fortune (in disproportionate numbers) in places like Australia, New Zealand, Canada, Texas, Alaska and California, and asks why so may technologists and entrepreneurs continue to fit this pattern.

West (2001) in a captivating article 'Dyslexic talents & Nobel Prizes' tells of the tradition of awarding Nobel Prizes for work associated with strong visual thinkers. West argues that the article counters perceived scientific wisdom that pictures are for non-professionals, laypersons and children. He narrates a wonderful story of inter-generational familial genius, in families in which dyslexia is an evident genetic factor. He discusses a familiar pattern of creative visuo-spatial abilities being developed in early life at the expense of linguistic ability – a genetic 'trade-off' effect. He discusses eight families, which over the generations have produced siblings who have excelled in creative occupations. Interestingly, these families are from privileged socio-economic backgrounds where the talk is of 'gifted children', not delinquents. He refers to these as 'visually orientated families', but one could equally refer to them as 'entrepreneurial families'. One family West discusses has produced, no fewer than four Nobel Laureates. It is apparent that these families trade on their specific social capital, across the generations.

However, to appreciate the influence of the subject on the entrepreneurial persona, one has to return to the seminal paper by Kets de Vries (1977), who articulated its consequences as manifested in enterprise (albeit without specifically mentioning learning disorders). The childhood stories that Kets de Vries narrates about the entrepreneurs he interviewed resonate with the reported experiences of many dyslexic people, for example, coming from an unhappy family background, feelings of displacement and isolation, being a misfit, feelings of rejection and marginality faced in a hostile world leading to the entrepreneur developing a yearning for control and achievement. The childhood of such entrepreneurs is a disturbing one filled with images of endured hardships, desertions, death, neglect and poverty. Such external factors may be easier to talk about than private learning difficulties.

Overcoming marginality

Overcoming marginality and humble beginnings are common themes in entrepreneur stories (see Kets de Vries 1977; Casson 1982; Smith 2002) and in narratives relating to learning disorders. For example, Hornsby (1984: 14) noted that in poor urban communities and isolated country districts there are a number of factors that accentuate the prevalence of learning difficulties. These include immigrant families, a poor grasp of the English language, large families, inadequate housing, poor diet, environmental pollution, lack of sleep, poor health, poor schooling, poverty, crime, and an apathy towards books and literacy. Hornsby highlights these and also a lack of availability of books and the problem of dyslexia being compounded by the inability of some parents themselves to read. Although Pollock and Walter (1994: xiii) state that dyslexia 'cuts across class, age and intelligence', there is nevertheless veracity in their statement that dyslexia may be related to social background because statistics show that difficulties are more common in poor areas than in affluent ones (ibid.: 14). Indeed, communicational isolation – whether geographical, social or mental – is an influencing factor. It is interesting that some of the very socio-economic factors discussed above are also the very conditions in which entrepreneurship appears to germinate and thrive in. Although it is difficult to evidence the preceding statement (other than anecdotally), nevertheless, marginality, ethnicity and poverty are all acknowledged as being factors that 'push' people into an entrepreneurial career path. Thus we begin to see links between dyslexia, social class and marginality – all of which may be important factors in the formation of entrepreneurial propensity.

Learning difficulties and childhood

Childhood is a time of restlessness, of questioning, of simplicity and of refreshing naïvety, during which the child begins to negotiate its own reality and to establish its own personal identity. No two children are really the same and it is easy for the child with learning difficulties to remain undetected as such. Interestingly, Leibovich and Saffo (2002), in referring to the childhood of the dyslexic entrepreneurs Bill Gates and John T. Chambers, labelled them both as 'restless kids' – an apt description for entrepreneurial behaviour. As discussed above, overcoming learning difficulties and communicational barriers is a common entrepreneurial theme. These barriers are commonly erected in childhood. The assertion of Smith (2002) that the entrepreneurial narrative itself is seldom encountered in childhood is germane to this study because it imposes another conceptual, mental barrier to children entering entrepreneurial occupations.

Attitudes to life are formed in childhood and learning difficulties first manifest themselves at this crucial time when learning is being consolidated. Interestingly, Pollock and Walter (1994: 148) point out that dyslexic children tire more easily than do non-dyslexic children, a fact that can reduce the amount of time they can concentrate – and hence the amount they can reasonably be expected to learn. Also, Kindlon and Thompson (1999: 7) report that the verbal abilities of girls develop faster than boys and that the gender stereotypes of male and female amplify the differences. Furthermore, Kindlon and Thompson (1999: 33–7) stress that boys are more prone to being misdiagnosed as having learning difficulties in early years or to fit the profile of troubled learners, with boys being two to four times more likely to be diagnosed as being hyperactive or suffering from ADHD. Official statistics suggest that boys account for 60 to 80 percent of those who suffer learning difficulties. Kindlon and Thompson refer to this as a 'black hole of failure'. An interesting contemporary theory is that the rate of dyslexia is the same for boys and girls but that the four to one ratio is explained because girls have fewer behavioural problems and work harder at school, therefore the misdiagnosis is social. Kindlon and Thompson (1999: 45) stress that boys suffer a double jeopardy, having a litany of harsh judgemental descriptors attributed to them, namely wilful, misbehaved and morally deficient.

School and learning are integral facets of childhood. Indeed, Hornsby (1984: 7–15) notes the importance of literacy as a key to success at school and in future employment. In the developed world, illiteracy is seen as a social handicap. Traditionally, in families from poor socio-economic backgrounds the problem was often ignored and the child withdrew into silent acceptance, often gravitating towards delinquency and a life of under-achievement. In more privileged families it was seen as a minor problem to be overcome and worked around, with such children being channelled into more creative activities that working-class families often could not afford. If one listens to the stories of dyslexic people in general, one finds a litany of sadness at their treatment by the education system. There are many such narratives in biography and posted on the Internet. The question as to why some people encounter discrimination whilst others are celebrated as geniuses must ultimately be a social phenomenon skewed by cultural factors. The twin ethics of achieving a good education and hard work can be hard taskmasters for those children who cannot concentrate on their schoolwork. The education system, with its emphasis on learning by rote and IQ tests, favours the linguistically and numerically privileged. Interestingly, Casson (1982: 356) recognises the role of education in entrepreneurial advancement but argues that it can disadvantage the entrepreneur by destroying their individuality. Educational systems are about conformity of learning, not encouraging individuality.

Many inspirational entrepreneurs and inventors have self-reported experiencing learning difficulties. For example, Richard Branson is on record as stating that at the age of eight he could not read and was beaten once or twice a week for doing poor school work or confusing the date of the Battle of Hastings Entrepreneur Zara Reid was called lazy at school because she could not read and write. She left school with no exams at all and instead learnt everything she knew by doing it and living it. Interestingly, she relies on a dictating machine. Clark (1977: 9) refers to Thomas Edison as being 'addled' or dyslexic, but despite this he was a prodigious reader of books and a fabled storyteller. Empathy, independence, imagination and optimism are all traits commonly found in the life stories of dyslexics as well as being considered as entrepreneurial traits.

Schooling can be a disturbing process for children with learning difficulties. Bullying, taunts and humiliation often form part and parcel of the learning process.

Take the case of entrepreneur Paul Orfalea, who failed a second grade and was forced to spend part of the third in a class of mentally retarded children; this one of the most illustrative stories that the author has encountered. According to Orfalea, when his classmates read aloud it was as if 'angels whispered words in their ears' (Morris 2002). The 'put-down' is a classic aspect of many stories told by entrepreneurs, and is usually associated with schooldays. For example, Clark (1977: 9) notes that the entrepreneur Thomas Edison suffered from the 'put-down' and was told that he 'would never make a success of anything'. Likewise, Sir Richard Branson tells a similar tale of a teacher who prophesied that he would either end up a being a millionaire or in jail. The put-down can act as a push or pull mechanism. Pollock and Walter (1994: 111) warn of the dangers of dyslexics developing secondary psychological problems such as withdrawal, truancy and delinquency.

Stanley (2000: 87) considers that many 'street-smart' entrepreneurs flout the cherished myth of high IQ = success. Indeed, he eulogises those millionaire self-made entrepreneurs who have succeeded with a SAT test below 900, endearingly labelling them his '900 Club'. He discusses the predominance of overcoming childhood marginality, hard work and the hard luck story in the personal narratives of self-made millionaires. Stanley (2000: 59) stresses that the 'halo that surrounds smart people often blinds us' and notes that many of the entrepreneurs with apparently lower intelligence employ considerable numbers of high-IQ people. He is not being disparaging of the intelligent, nor suggesting that they are not entrepreneurial, merely noting that those who have to struggle in life have to accentuate the qualities and characteristics they possess by hiring themselves. Stanley (2000: 9) further notes that there is a difference between the entrepreneurial origins and the final position of the legitimised millionaire entrepreneur, who as a class value education. He highlights that 90 percent of millionaires are college graduates with 52 percent possessing advanced degrees.

As a welcome counterbalance to the pessimistic narrative of dyslexia = difficulty = delinquency = crime, Kindlon and Thompson (1999: 51) argue that there is a history of great men who were notable misfits at school. This is a theme championed by West (1997) in his award-winning book, 'In the Mind's Eye'. Davies (1998) narrates the story of a dyslexic schoolboy who was told by teachers that he would never read or write but defied their predictions to become one of Britain's youngest entrepreneurs, founding a successful computer business. The story of child prodigy Dominic McVey is another inspirational tale. McVey started up a business from home aged 14 selling micro-scooters and at the age of 18 was worth £7 million. Yet at school he did not shine.

Dyslexia, storytelling and entrepreneurial propensity

According to Roddick (2000), storytelling ability is a fabled entrepreneurial trait. Stories can be told orally, and telling stories develops innate skills such as confidence and has a therapeutic quality. It is of relevance that one of the contemporary methods in dyslexia studies is the use of storytelling as a learning tool.

Encouraging the student with learning difficulties to read or concentrate on a story helps develops neural pathways. Simple stories with pictures are preferred as they are easier to concentrate upon. Importantly, short stories can be memorised. According to Pollock and Walter (1994: 107), dyslexics may have difficulty in following stories. They have to concentrate heavily upon them. Stories are important to them. Furthermore, Pollock and Walter (1994: 39–44) point out that reading and spelling utilise different neural pathways, as does the recognition of symbols; consequently, the dyslexic develops a propensity towards pictographic intelligence as opposed to ideographic intelligence. We shall return to this theme later. The entrepreneur as a voracious reader is a common theme in biographies and novels. Indeed, Kindlon and Thompson (1999: 4) note the importance of voracious reading in forming emotional literacy in boys, because reading connects us to a larger world beyond our own experiences and ideas. An inability to read may thus be a barrier to communicating effectively. Such an inability does not prevent one from engaging in the creative act of storytelling.

Executive functioning skills

Executive functioning (EF) skills are important to entrepreneurs and busy CEOs, allowing them to set goals, make and modify mental models of actions, organise activities, focus their attention selectively, and avoid impulses and distractions that sidetrack them from accomplishing their aim – in other words, to be single-minded in achieving tasks we set ourselves. What strikes one the most about such individuals is their single-mindedness and determination in overcoming environmental and situational obstacles to achieve their goals, whilst apparently being of 'two minds'. Many entrepreneurs are single-minded to the point of being obsessive and can appear to be silent and withdrawn to others. Yet they have an ability to operate simultaneously in two parallel worlds. For instance, the fabled entrepreneur Tony O'Reilly operated as a corporate executive with Heinz and as an Irish entrepreneur at the same time. Entrepreneurs have the mental capacity to cope with many plans simultaneously. It is perhaps executive functioning ability that sets them apart. According to Morris (2002), dyslexics learn humility and affinity, which are useful survival techniques in business/life.

Dyslexia and the 'crooked pathway' into crime

Establishing why some persons with learning and communicational difficulties overcome them to achieve productive success as entrepreneurs, inventors or scientists, whilst others succumb to destructive delinquent and criminal tendencies, is a question that, vexes many sociologists and parents. An appreciation of the link between entrepreneurship, dyslexia and crime already exists. An examination of Mafioso mythology also reveals that the link between illiteracy and crime can act as a spur to success. For instance, Hess (1998: 48–9) highlights the meteoric rise from humble beginnings of numerous 'Mafia Dons' such as Vito Cascio Fero, the son of a poor illiterate labourer; Giuseppe Genco Russo, a penniless goatherd who rose to riches; Nitto Minasola, a goatherd who started with two goats; Vincenzo Rimi, son of a shepherd, himself a cowherd who eventually rose to become a powerful cattle dealer; and Filippo Baltciglia, who rose from being a ceramic worker. Hess stresses that many of these now rich Mafiosi are illiterate e.g. Fero could not read and write and Minasola never attended school.

Reid and Kirk (2001) highlight the prevalence of dyslexia among the criminal population. This does not preclude criminals from becoming involved in entrepreneurial activity. Bolton and Thompson (2000: 196) discuss the interesting case study of George Reynolds, a reformed (Geordie) professional criminal who has become a successful entrepreneur/business magnate. Reynolds describes his former self as 'dyslexic, illiterate, backward and brainless . . . thief, bootlegger and bookmaker'. Reynolds prided himself in being a fast and decisive decision-maker. He was challenged in prison by a priest to utilise his considerable talents in legitimate business. He took the proffered advice and has never looked back. He started up an ice-cream round and through hard work diversified into shops, night clubs, manufacturing, engineering, and finally shipping. His business interests are now worth a reputed £250 million. Reynolds is a role model worthy of emulation. Another interesting study is that of dyslexic entrepreneur Kjell Inge Rokke, presented by Gibbs (2001). Rokke under-achieved at school and by the age of 16 was drifting into a life of petty crime until he ran away to sea to become a fisherman. Eventually he built up a fleet of trawlers and a thriving business in America before returning to his homeland, Norway, where he is regarded as both a hero and a villain, depending upon whose side of the story one believes. Both case studies are powerful illustrators of the link between crime, dyslexia and entrepreneurship.

Researching on the Internet

This section discusses the methodology, data collection techniques and research carried out. Although much of the material covered in the previous section frustratingly skims over the issues and may have appeared at times to have little factual basis, in places its elusive nature also impinges upon the choice of methodology. Initially, the author was concerned with the paucity of connecting theories and even considered that it may have been an artefact of collecting data from Internet and biographical sources.

Methodology

This chapter relies heavily on data gleaned from Internet sources. This collected material was used in conjunction with more formal academic texts and the biographies of entrepreneurs. By using the literature as a tentative theoretical orientation, the chapter considers the links between existing theories of entrepreneurial behaviour and explanations and the activities of dyslexic entrepreneurs. The methodology was designed to produce an initial explanatory framework to account for the apparent connections. The stories published on the Internet are used to illustrate and develop the formal academic theories. In this manner, the stories are applied to the theory to develop an explanatory theory about dyslexia and entrepreneurship. Distinctive patterns in the data emerged and these seem to reflect some existing theoretical behavioural models. Consequently the research extends and develops these models.

Using Internet data is often regarded as being methodologically unconvincing and less than rigorous to many experienced researchers. Be this at it may, it nevertheless tells a credible research story that could otherwise never have been told. Using the Internet or biographical data to examine phenomena and relationships that have been validated by previous, more conventional research is an accepted research method, but what does one do in the absence of such a corpus of validated material? There are a number of accepted methodologies, including constructing case studies/case stories. These were considered, but none could rival the sheer persuasive power of the fifty or so anecdotal entries located on the Internet. Granted, such anecdotal evidence is not a methodologically, systematic corpus of knowledge, but it paves the way for future research projects to build such a rigorous body of knowledge.

Another criticism may be the deliberate decision taken not to define such basic tenets as entrepreneur, entrepreneurship, marginality or deviance. This is because the subjects located on the Internet come from such a diverse span of occupations and time frames that imposing an all-encompassing definition was considered impossible. It sufficed for the purpose of the study that others had chosen to label them as entrepreneurs, inventors or chief executive officers. The only honest methodological approach open to the author was to use a narrative approach by telling a convincing research story. Storytelling is a time-honoured technique and is a wonderful method of teaching and learning.

The research

The actual research conducted on the Internet was carried out over a period of several days, using a combination of key words and phrases such as dyslexic entrepreneurs and so forth. This raised only one direct hit on an academic paper, namely Hlava (2003), but raised a considerable amount of related sites where brief mention was made of entrepreneurs to whom dyslexia was attributed. These sites included http://dys-add.com, http://dyslexiamylife.org and http://dyslexia.com, which list famous dyslexics. The content of some of the sites clearly mirrored each other and may have been copied from each other. The general tone of the dialogue contained on the sites was eulogistic, with the entrepreneurs being cited as shining examples for others with learning difficulties to follow. From these sites and from personal knowledge or previous research into biographies of entrepreneurs a list of entrepreneurs with learning difficulties was constructed. Incredibly, this grew to over fifty (see Table 14.3).

Taking cognisance of the advice of Harris (1997), it was necessary to triangulate the actual data found by the research. This was done by further Internet

Table 14.3 List of entrepreneurs/inventors/chief executive officers who have self-reported dyslexia or other learning difficulties

No	Name	Description
1	Charles Schwab	CEO/Entrepreneur of insurance brokerage Charles Schwab & Company. Was not diagnosed with dyslexia until in his forties when his son was also found to have dyslexia. The acute form of dyslexia manifested itself as a specific reading problem. He required to be tutored through school.
2	Sir Richard Branson	Founder of the Virgin group
3	Henry Ford	Founder of the Ford Motor company
4	Richard C. Strauss	Real estate financier
5	William Hewlett	Co-founder of Hewlett Packard
6	Paul J. Orfalea	The profoundly dyslexic founder of Kinko's
7	Ted Turner	President of Turner Broadcasting Systems
8	F. W. Woolworth	Founder of the Woolworth chain of shops
9	Craig McCaw	Wireless telecommunications entrepreneur and founder of McCaw Cellular
10	Mark Torrance	CEO of Musak Corporation
11	Malcolm Goodbridge III	Senior Vice President of American Express
12	Fred Friendly	Former CBS News President
13	William Doyle	Chairman, William Doyle Auction Galleries, New York
14	G. Chris Anderson	Vice Chairman of Paine Webber
15	William Wrigley Jr	Of the Wrigley chewing gum family
16	Russell Varian	The famous inventor
17	Zara Reid	Founder of CSI Promotions
18	John T. Chambers	CEO of Cisco Systems
19	Sir Alan Sugar	Founder of Amstrad
20	Anita Roddick	Co-founder of the Body Shop
21	James G Morgan. Jr	Attorney and legal entrepreneur
22	Franklin Benjamin	One of the founding fathers of enterprise
23	Alexander Graham Bell	The famous inventor
24	Albert Einstein	The famous inventor did not speak until the age of three
25	Thomas Edison	The famous inventor was unable to read until he was 12 years old
26	William Lear	Aviation engineer
27	Kjell Inge Rokke	The dyslexic Norwegian tycoon who walked away from a life of petty crime to build an American-based trawling empire before returning to his native land as an industrialist/tycoon.
28	Nelson A. Rockefeller	Attorney and Vice President of the US whose dyslexia forced him to hone his powers of concentration. He was an established artist/sculptor.
29	John D. Rockefeller	Father of the above, a dyslexic, prodigious entrepreneur and business titan
30	William Randolph Hearst	Founder of the Hearst Corporation
31	Steve Jobs	Founder of Apple Computers

Table 14.3 List of entrepreneurs/inventors/chief executive officers who have self-reported dyslexia or other learning difficulties—cont'd

No	Name	Description
32	George Reynolds	British entrepreneur and former criminal
33	Adam Faith	British entrepreneur, singer, actor and media star
34	Neil Holloway	Chief Executive of Microsoft UK
35	Bill Gates	CEO of Microsoft
36	Larry Ellison	Founder / CEO of Oracle
37	Ingvar Kamprad	Swedish businessman and founder of IKEA
38	Walt Disney	Founder of the Disney Corporation, animator and business mogul
39	Jackie Stewart	Formula One racing driver and entrepreneur
40	Wally Amos	Founder of a successful business, struggled against dyslexia and illiteracy problems
41	David Boies	Attorney and legal entrepreneur. He learned to read in the third grade and devoured *Marvel* comics, whose pictures provided clues to help him untangle the words.
42	Sam Walton	Founder of Wall-Mart
43	Martha Stewart	Founder of Martha Stewart Inc. struggled against dyslexia
44	John Reed	Led Citibank to the top of banking
45	Donald Winkler	Until recently head of Ford Financial
46	Gaston Caperton	Former governor of West Virginia and Head of the College Board
47	Diane Swonk	Chief economist at Bank One
48	Bill Samuels. Jr	President of the corporation Maker's Mark
49	Bill Dreyer	Inventor and biologist at Caltech
50	Peter Urs Bender	The Canadian self-help guru, businessman and promoter
51	Andrew Cardno	The New Zealand 'visual systems' entrepreneur who suffers from poor and dyslexia and learnt to read aged 10
52	Andrew Carnegie	Is said to have displayed ADD behavioural problems
53	Howard Hughes	The reclusive billionaire
54	James Dyson	Inventor of the Dyson vacuum cleaner and entrepreneur
55	Tommy Hilfiger	The clothes designer/entrepreneur
56	David Murdoch	CEO of Dole Foods
57	Raymond Smith	Former CEO of Bell Atlantic

research and by finding corroboration in the biographies of individual entrepreneurs to confirm that they did indeed have dyslexia or another learning difficulty. In most cases it was easy to verify the assertion merely by making an extended search using the names of the entrepreneurs. By checking these websites it was possible in the vast majority of instances to obtain corroborative references to their dyslexic tendencies. It must be stressed that this does not provide conclusive proof that the persons contained in the list are indeed dyslexic.[3] The main theme to emerge from the research was that entrepreneurs with specific learning difficulties appear to adopt specific communicational strategies.

Communicational strategies used by dyslexic entrepreneurs

This section is concerned with the question 'Is it possible that dyslexics communicate differently from other people?' Hornsby (1984: 12) acknowledges that 'dyslexics can often have exceptional skills and insights which are denied to other people'. Pollock and Walter (1994: 26) confirm that in dyslexics, 'intellectual grasp of facts, logic, reasoning, imagination, lateral thinking and creative skills may all be present to a very high degree'. In addition, Hornsby (1984: 122) stresses that, 'most dyslexics have above average spatial ability'. This increased level of spatial advantage can manifest itself as a skill or gift at recognising patterns and may be a factor in creative ability and in turn may feed entrepreneurial propensity. Hornsby (1984: 119) attributes dyslexics with having the traits of 'persistence, accuracy and speed at visual tasks'. These are characteristics with which successful entrepreneurs are often credited. It is also a common perception that the minds of many dyslexic people often work faster than their fingers. This is also a trait ascribed to many entrepreneurs.

According to Hlava (2003), herself an entrepreneur, entrepreneurs are different and tend to exhibit the following traits: rebelliousness, impulsiveness, they think outside the box, they view things turn a different point of view and are frequently dyslexic, upside-down thinkers. The dyslexic New Zealand entrepreneur Andrew Cardno refers to dyslexics as 'eclectic people'. Dyslexia affects self-confidence and dyslexics are often characterised as loners–a fabled entrepreneurial trait. Although it is often argued that entrepreneurs are born, not made, and that there are possibly biological underpinnings to entrepreneurship, it is a practice into which one can be socialised–therefore it can be learned from experience.

Interestingly, like entrepreneurs, no two dyslexics are alike, each have their own eclectic weaknesses and strengths. However, entrepreneurs and executives with specific learning disorders appear to utilise certain communicational strategies to help them cope. According to Morris (2002), dyslexic executives possess a distinctly different way of processing information that gives them an edge in a volatile, fast-moving world. There are generic and individual varieties. Generic ones include soaking up information in other ways than print (orally and visually vacuuming up information); minimising the amount of time they have to spend reading; utilising newspapers, short magazine articles, and summaries; and making use of environmental scanning. Those who can read and write prefer not to do so, thereby preserving their time/energies. Information grazing is a common technique. Many problems are idiosyncratic, for example, Gaston Caperton who has difficulty in dialing telephone numbers, and Diane Swonk who obsessively checks her calculations at least five times (Morris 2002). Entrepreneurs turn dyslexic deficits into advantages. Morris relates a wonderful story told by Diane Swonk's former boss and mentor at Bank One, who considered that Swonk had a 'third eye' because her predictions invariably came true. According to Morris, Bill Samuels adheres to the old adage 'Many times in business, different is better than better . . . And we dyslexics do different without blinking an eye.' Similarly, Morris tells the fascinating story of Paul Orfalea, who recalls that his mother used to console him by saying that when everybody grows up, 'The A students work for the B students. The C students run the businesses. And the

D students dedicate the buildings'. It is a wonderfully inspirational statement mirroring the sentiments of Stanley (2000) that most successful entrepreneurs originate from students who overcome difficulties at school. It is evident that 'differently abled' entrepreneurs utilise individual techniques to overcome their difficulties; see Table 14.4, adapted from the article by Morris (2002), for an appreciation of specific communicational strategies adopted by individual entrepreneurs.

Table 14.4 Specific communicational strategies adopted by entrepreneurs

Sir Richard Branson	Writes important details on his hand to overcome bad memory **(P)**
	Does not use computers **(B)**
	Uses Filofax **(B)**
	Bluffs way through problems **(B)**
	Avoids maths **(B)**
David Boies	Learns by listening/Socratic dialogues **(O)**
	Uses teaching/learning tools **(B)**
	Highly selective about information input and revises points of importance **(B)**
	Memorises key points **(B)**
	Looks at the big picture as a story and envisages how it will end **(P)**
	Contextualises elements of the story where they fit best **[C]**
	Commits everything to memory and because he does not work from a script seldom goes wrong. This enables him to be dramatic/flexible and to improvise **[C and B]**
	Wanders around themes **[C]**
Charles Schwab	Learns plots and characters in books from pictures **(P)**
	Fast-forwards past the smaller, logical steps of sequential thinkers **[C]**
	Synthesizes things differently and more quickly than other people **[C]**
	Concentrates on the end result **(B)**
	Shortcuts rigorous step-by-step process beloved of sequential thinkers **[C]**
Bill Dreyer	Thinks in 3-D Technicolor pictures instead of words **(P)**
	Likens his dyslexia to having CAD (computer-aided design) in your brain **(P)**
Donald Winkler	Performs mental warm-up exercise each morning **[C]**
	Practices trigger words that confuse him **[C]**
Craig McCaw	Hires 'translators' to turn his intuitive concepts and ideas into reality and interpret his ideas to linear thinkers **(B)**
	Relies on his conceptual thinking **[C]**
	Grabs abstract information from the environment, often being unaware of its origin **[C]**
	Minimises reading/writing to conserve energy **(B)**
	Grasps maximum meaning from minimum content/context **[C]**
	Scan reads pulling out meaning **[C]**
	Alternating between apparent disinterest and maniacal focus **(B)**

Table 14.4 Specific communicational strategies adopted by entrepreneurs—cont'd

John T. Chambers	Hires 'details people' as linear thinkers and analysts **(B)**
	Builds a team to shore up his weaknesses **(B)**
	Refuses to get bogged down in details **[C]**
	Relies on his wife for telephone numbers **(B)**
	Uses GPS as he gets lost easily **(B)**
	Prefers voicemail to e-mail as it is so much easier to understand and visualise by hearing **(O)**
	Prefers summaries in three pages or less with major points highlighted in yellow **(P)**
	Does not keep paper records **(O)**
Paul J. Orfalea	Hid lack of reading ability until 40 and refused to show anyone his handwriting **(B)**
	Cultivated a casual, can't-be-bothered-with-it management style that allowed him to avoid the written word **(B)**
	Delegated tasks requiring reading **(B)**
	Avoided the corporate office and instead went from place to place observing, talking to customers, making changes **(B)**
Bill Samuels. Jr	Surrounds himself with verbal people who like to talk **(O)**
	Cannot write but can organise old information into a different pattern easily **(B)**
	Utilised homespun advertisement campaigns

Source: Adapted from Morris (2002).
Key, **(P)** = Pictorial; **(O)** = Orality; **(B)** = Behavioural; **[C]** = Cognitive.

A contribution of this study is that it highlights specific communicational techniques adopted by these entrepreneurs to overcome their individual communicational deficits. These techniques, such as looking at the bigger picture, learning from pictures, the reliance upon memory, the preference for talking, the avoidance of the written word, the refusal to work from a script, and so on, enable the individual entrepreneur to compete and often excel in an aggressive entrepreneurial milieu, turning disadvantage into a competitive advantage. Interestingly, many of these techniques are associated with 'pictorial' thinking, 'orality', and 'cognitive' and 'behavioural' activity. There is a need to test this tentative formation using empirical research methods to see if these methods of communicating are replicated in the strategies of other dyslexic entrepreneurs.

The subject of dyslexia and entrepreneurship was raised in the BBC2 television programme *Mind of the Millionaire,* screened at 9 pm, on Tuesday, 7 October. 2003. Interestingly, the programme highlights that educational qualifications are not necessary to become an entrepreneur. The presenter, Dr Adrian Atkinson, discussed several 'non-specific dyslexic characteristics' such as (1) not being dependent upon a script; (2) appearing to others to be behaving 'off the wall'; (3) repeatedly challenging authority; (4) breaking or changing the rules; (5) asking questions not in the script; (6) refusing to seek permission; (7) using a pragmatist to bounce ideas off; and (8) being 'street-smart'. Most of these are fabled entrepreneurial traits. Using a specially commissioned survey of entrepreneurs, the presenter posited some interesting statistics, namely that 61 percent of entrepreneurs were lazy or average at school, 53 percent came from underprivileged backgrounds, and 73 percent did not care what others thought of them. Many were given a free rein by parents to behave differently despite educational disappointments. Interestingly, two out of the five entrepreneurs featured tested positive for dyslexia. It was claimed that the rate of dyslexia among entrepreneurs (as a genre) was four times higher than the national average.

When one takes into account other methods of communication used by entrepreneurs, such as projecting theatrical and dramaturgical imagery, semiotic exhibitionism, storytelling, as well as techniques of embellishment such as self-publicity, authoring one's own legend, and the fabrication of fable, as identified by Smith (2003: 11–13), then it could be argued that perhaps differently abled entrepreneurs do communicate differently. The entrepreneurs are not behaving differently, but merely enacting what is normal to them. The research provides the basis of a tentative theoretical/psychological model that can be used to assess potential entrepreneurs and channel them into appropriate methods of learning/expression. It is now time to draw the discussion to a close by considering implications and reflecting upon the research.

Implications and reflections on the research

The implications of the study could prove to be far-reaching, because unlike entrepreneurship per se, specific learning difficulties can be screened for and those people with the psychological gift of pictorial thinking could be encouraged to embark upon an entrepreneurial career path. Dyslexic entrepreneurs such as Sir Richard Branson are often presented as an iconic symbol to encourage would-be entrepreneurs to emulate them. However, is it fair to expect them to emulate the entrepreneurial style of another, which may be influenced by biological underpinnings of a learning disorder? An appreciation of the biological underpinnings of entrepreneurial action is increasing. For instance, White *et al.* (2003) studied the effect of the male hormone testosterone upon entrepreneurial propensity. Testosterone is associated with enterprising behaviour and also with aggression, violence and deviance. Could dyslexia and other learning difficulties be linked to other biological underpinnings such as testosterone?

The chapter also highlights the false logic/ideological underpinning of the 'double ethic' which holds that working class and other disadvantaged persons with learning difficulties are branded as delinquents and propelled towards a life of crime, whereas those from a more privileged socio-economic background are raised as special for their talents. From the perspective of entrepreneurial learning it is apparent that we need to adopt a different pedagogical approach to teaching and understanding such 'differently abled' entrepreneurs. Indeed, there are pedagogical ramifications in respect of how we teach entrepreneurship. The flexibility and the ability to adapt displayed by such entrepreneurs allows them to excel in conditions of change and uncertainty, upon which the entrepreneurial

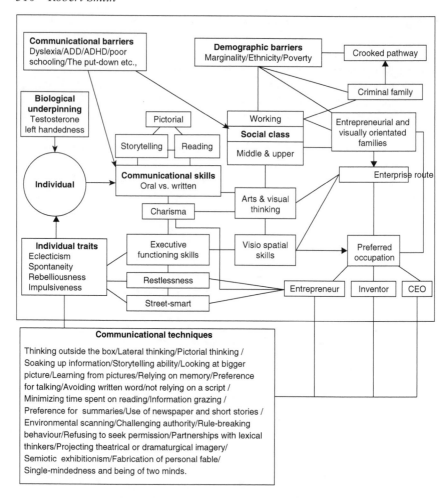

Figure 14.1 Learning from a conceptual framework/mapping approach.

process thrives. We would be wise to heed the lessons learned from these differently abled entrepreneurs. Consequently, it is fitting to end this chapter with a pictorial representation/mapping of the topics covered (see figure 14.1).

Notes

1 An earlier version of this chapter entitled 'Being differently abled: entrepreneurs and dyslexia – an exploratory study using the Internet' was presented at an International Research Seminar' at Groupe ESC Clermont on 29 March 2004. I am indebted to Alistair R. Anderson and other reviewers for their help in developing this chapter.
2 Considering the aspects that lead to crime lies outwith the remit of this chapter, although certain examples are cited where they impinge upon entrepreneurial propensity.

3 It is appreciated that there are ethical dilemmas raised in conducting such research and that there is a need to confirm the specific details of the alleged disorder located on the Internet. This will entail contacting the persons and conducting follow-up research to clarify or refute the assertions.

References

Bolton, B. and Thompson, J. (2000) *'Entrepreneurs: Talent, Temperament, Technique'*. London: Butterworth-Heineman.

Casson, M. (1982) *'The Entrepreneur'*, Oxford: Martin Robertson.

Clark, R. W. (1977) *'Edison: The Man Who Made the Future'*. London: MacDonald & Jones.

Davies, C. (1998) Unteachable boy runs 60,000 firm. *Daily Telegraph*, 18 September.

Davis, R. (1995) *'The Gift of Dyslexia'*. London: Souvenir Press.

Davis, R. D. and Braun E. M. (1994) 'The Gift of Dyslexia', California, Souvenir Press Ltd.

East, V. and Evans, L. (2001) *'At a Glance: A Quick guide to Children's Special Needs'*. Birmingham: Questions Publishing.

Gibbs, W. (2001) Maximum Overdrive, *Scanorama* magazine, June: 72–7.

Harris, R. (1997) Evaluating Internet research sources, www.Virtualsalt.com, version date: 17 November 1997.

Hess, H. (1998) Mafia and Mafiosi: Origin, Power and Myth, translated by Ewald Osers. London: C. Hurst & Co.

Hlava, M. M. K (2003) Expanding partnerships for small-and medium sized enterprises (SME's) needed: the right kind of support abstract located on the Internet (accessed 30 June 2003).

Hornsby, B. (1984) *Overcoming Dyslexia: A Straightforward Guide for Families and Teachers*. London: Marin Dunitz.

Kerr, J. (1973) *Crime and dyslexia Criminologist*, 8(29).

Kets de Vries, M. F. R. (1977) The entrepreneurial personality: a person at the crossroads *Journal of Management Studies*, 14 (1): 34–57.

Kindlon, D. and Thompson, H. (1999) *Raising Cain: Protecting the Emotional Life of Boys*. Harmondsworth, Middlesex: Penguin Books.

Leibovich, M. and Saffo, P. (2002) *The New Imperialists: How Five Restless Kids Grew Up to Virtually Rule the World*. Englewood Cliffs, NJ: Prentice Hall.

Levander, A., Raccuia, I. and Hamrefors, S. (2001) Entrepreneurial profiling, stimuli, reaction, action: a cognitive approach to entrepreneurship paper presented at the 11th Global Conference on Entrepreneurship Research, EM Lyon, France, 26–27 April.

Logan, J. (2001) Entrepreneurial success: a study of the incidence of dyslexia in the entrepreneurial population and the influence of dyslexia on success. PhD Dissatating Bristol University.

Morris, B. (2002) Overcoming dyslexia, *Fortune* magazine, 28 April.

Pollock, J. and Waller, E. (1994) *Day to Day Dyslexia in the Classroom*. London and New York: Routledge

Rae, D. (1999) Understanding how people learn to be entrepreneurial, Paper presented at the 22nd ISBA Conference, Leeds Metropolitan University, 17–19 November.

Rawson, M. (1968) *Developmental Language Disability Adult Accomplishments of Dyslexic Boys* Baltimore: John Hopkins Uncertainty Press.

Reich, R. B. (1987) Entrepreneurship reconsidered: the team as a hero *Harvard Business Review*, 65(3), 77–83.

Reid, G. and Kirk, J. (2001) *Dyslexia in Adults: Education and Employment* London: John Wiley.

Roddick, A. (2000) *Business as Unusual.* London: Thorsons.

Smilor, R. (1997) *Entrepreneurship 2000* Upstart Publishing. Chicago

Smith, R. (2002) Inspirational tales: propagating the entrepreneurial narrative amongst children Paper presented at the Babson-Kauffman Entrepreneurship Research Conference, Boulder, CO June.

Smith, R. (2003) Constructing the heroic/fabled entrepreneur: a biographical analysis Paper presented at the Babson-Kauffman Entrepreneurship Research Conference, Babson College, Boston MA, June.

Stanley, T. J. (2000) *The Millionaire Mind.* Kansascity: Andrews McMeel.

Tyson, E. (2003) 'View from the top – Charles Schwab – everybody's broker'. Internet magazine article from the *Stanford Business School Magazine.*

Uddin, A. (2001–ongoing) The development of literacy and other practices for income generation and for the improvement of the living conditions of the poor: a case study of two Bangladeshi villages PhD dissertation, University of Nottingham.

West, T. G. (1997) *In the Mind's Eye* Amherst, NY: Prometheus Books.

West, T. G. (1999) The abilities of those with reading disabilities: focusing on the talents of people with dyslexia. Chapter 11 *Reading and Attention Disorders Neurobiological Correlates.* In D. D. Duane (ed.). Baltimore, York Press Based on a conference sponsored by the National Dyslexia Research Foundation.

West, T. G. (2001) Dyslexic talents & Nobel Prizes. February issue of *ACM-SIGGRAPH Computer Graphics.*

White, R. E., Thornhill, S. and Hampson, E. (2003) Entrepreneurs and evolutionary biology: the relationships between testosterone and new venture creation Paper presented at the Babson Kauffman Entrepreneurship Research Conference, Babson College, Boston, MA, June.

TV programme

Mind of the Millionaire, BBC2, Tuesday, 7 October 2003.

Websites

http://www.dyslexiamylife.org
http://dys-add.com.symptoms
http://www.dyslexia.com

15 Starting from scratch

Understanding the learning outcomes of undergraduate entrepreneurship education

Sandra L. Fisher, Mary E. Graham and Marc Compeau

Introduction

Entrepreneurship education in business schools is experiencing tremendous growth, and there are many innovative programs at the college level (Newton and Henricks 2003). Several factors support this trend. First is a general shift in teaching methods away from programmed instruction in favor of experiential learning (Schank *et al*. 1999). As business schools look to implement experiential learning, entrepreneurship is emerging as a natural fit for this instructional technique. Many of the courses in university entrepreneurship programs rely upon experiential or 'learning by doing.' For example, at Babson College, one of the top-ranked institutions in the United States for entrepreneurship education (Newton and Henricks 2003), some courses require students to start and run actual businesses (www.babson.edu).

Second, entrepreneurship education has benefited from the involvement of entrepreneurs through organizations such as the US Association for Small Business and Entrepreneurship and the Kauffman and Coleman Foundations, and through special centers of entrepreneurship housed within universities. These institutions support a broad spectrum of entrepreneurship education, including providing funding for various educational programs and supporting social and community investment. These efforts have helped increase the visibility of entrepreneurship as a profession and as a field of academic study.

Third, the academic literatures on management science and entrepreneurship have supported entrepreneurship education by expanding the conceptual and empirical knowledge base available to the field. Researchers have been refining models of entrepreneurship that could be used as foundational frameworks in entrepreneurship courses (see Shane and Venkataraman 2000; Zahra and Dess 2001). Others are moving beyond trait models of entrepreneurship toward a consensus that elements of entrepreneurship, can in fact be learned (Timmons 1995; Baron and Markman 2000). In addition, researchers are generating empirical results with implications for entrepreneurial decision-making (e.g. Jack and Anderson 1999) and developing valid measures of constructs, such as corporate entrepreneurship environment (Hornsby *et al*. 2002).

Unfortunately, while there is much descriptive information available on entrepreneurship education innovations and programs, there is little research on realized learning outcomes or the effectiveness of various educational programs. The research that does exist on learning outcomes appears rather fragmented, with different sets of researchers focusing on unique and often disparate learning outcomes. We contend that there is a great need to review the existing material on entrepreneurial learning outcomes and attempt to organize it. Doing so would permit consideration of different types of learning outcomes (e.g. knowledge versus skill), which is necessary in order to specify what changes in instructional approaches may be needed; and by content (e.g. market research, business plans), which will guide curriculum design and improvement. An important side benefit of organizing learning outcomes is the facilitation of knowledge sharing among academic researchers, practitioners and educators (Rynes *et al.* 2001) by permitting them to discuss issues from a common framework. In summary, the primary purpose of our chapter is twofold: (1) to begin structuring the wide array of potential learning outcomes and goals in a way that facilitates continuous improvement efforts for entrepreneurship education; and (2) to acknowledge the contributions and perspectives of the academic and business communities and improve communication across these important constituencies.

As the appropriate learning outcomes for entrepreneurial programs may differ depending on the target audience (Leitch and Harrison 1999), this chapter examines a homogeneous student cohort: undergraduate students at one university. An undergraduate focus has the added benefit of providing much-needed information to colleges and universities that have experimented with substituting entrepreneurship courses for traditional introductory management principles classes, or that have only recently added undergraduate entrepreneurship majors (e.g. Hofstra University: Newton and Henricks 2003). However, this effort may inform other types of entrepreneurship education as well.

We begin with a definition and review of the research on entrepreneurship education. Consulting the views of entrepreneurs and academics, we identify desired learning outcomes of entrepreneurship education. To systematically incorporate these views into entrepreneurship education design and outcomes evaluation, we rely upon an established, outcomes-based learning typology (Kraiger *et al.* 1993). This framework has logical implications for the methods of instruction and assessment that will facilitate cognitive, skill-based and affective types of learning. The framework also fits nicely with the learning content recommendations by academics and entrepreneurs, which will permit us to derive implications for curriculum content. To demonstrate the value of this learning outcomes typology in the entrepreneurship education context, we describe a study in which we apply it to two undergraduate entrepreneurship courses. The results of the study demonstrate how a formal, theory-based framework can be used to develop and assess entrepreneurial learning.

Entrepreneurship education

There are many forms of education that carry the entrepreneurship label, likely due to the relative newness of entrepreneurship programs, and ambiguity in the definitions of entrepreneurship (Jack and Anderson 1999; Shane and

Venkataraman 2000) and entrepreneurs (Pink 2001). University programs range from limited course offerings to comprehensive programs with substantial course offerings and a wealth of entrepreneurship resources (Newton and Henricks 2003). This variation presents a challenge for researchers seeking to identify and examine student learning outcomes that are generalizable to other programs.

We address this challenge in several ways. First, we begin with a clear definition of entrepreneurial education: 'the process of providing individuals with the concepts and skills to recognize opportunities that others have overlooked, and to have the insight, self-esteem, and knowledge to act where others have hesitated' (CELCEE 2003). This definition is consistent with that of frequently cited entrepreneurship education researchers (Gibb 1993; Garavan and O Cinneide 1994a). Second, we adapt and apply a learning outcomes framework to evaluate the learning outcomes of two undergraduate classes that are at the far end of the experiential spectrum. The classes rely heavily on experiential learning methods in that students start and run actual businesses, and receive funds from and report to real investors. Results on intensive courses such as these can serve as benchmarks for other courses and programs.

Learning outcomes of entrepreneurship education

Solid instructional design and effective evaluation of learning require clear specification of learning outcomes (Gagne *et al.* 1992; Brown and Gerhardt 2002). It is unfortunate that while there is much attention to instructional methods in entrepreneurship education (e.g. Rae 2000; Raffo *et al.* 2000), less attention has been paid to the actual learning outcomes. Kolb (1984) offered an overarching model for experiential learning that presents learning as interplay between education, work and personal development. This holistic model adapts fairly easily to the entrepreneurship education context (e.g. Jones-Evans *et al.* 2000), but it leaves unspecified what learning will result from each factor and from the interaction of factors. We suggest an approach that begins with the definition of learning outcomes, from which it is possible to make informed choices about instructional and evaluation techniques.

To ensure a comprehensive look at learning outcomes relevant to entrepreneurship, we conducted an extensive search of the academic literature, business press and other sources that suggested potential learning outcomes of entrepreneurship education courses. We looked to see what academics were saying, based on both research and teaching experiences, about the skills, knowledge and other attributes required for entrepreneurial success. From entrepreneurship-related business sources we searched for entrepreneurs' opinions regarding what made them successful and recommendations they had for others wanting to be entrepreneurs. The results of our review are described below.

For the most part, the literature on entrepreneurship-related learning outcomes tended to be in the form of relatively unorganized lists and not based in theory or a well-defined conceptual foundation. We first examined the academic literature explicitly focusing on entrepreneurship education. Rae (2000) offers many learning themes as part of a model of entrepreneurial learning: confidence and self-efficacy, personal values and motivation, goal-setting and achievement, a personal theory, skills and knowledge, learning through social relationships, and the ability to learn quickly and actively. But others delineate fewer, more general learning outcomes. Gibb (1993) suggests only three learning areas: opportunity seeking, problem solving and self-confidence. Jack and Anderson (1999) suggest that university-based entrepreneurship programs should 'build critical theoretical knowledge about entrepreneurship and . . . endow students with the management skills necessary for an entrepreneurial career' (p. 8). Garavan and O Cinneide (1994a, 1994b) suggest that high-quality entrepreneurship education programs should include learning outcomes related to knowledge and skills/competencies, and attitudes regarding risk planning and uncertainty. Brush *et al.* (2003) presented a model of the entrepreneurship content domain in their discussion on doctoral-level entrepreneurship education. This model helped specify the different processes critical to entrepreneurship, including opportunity exploration, exploitation and recognition, venture creation and wealth creation. However, the focus of their discussion was on creating entrepreneurship *scholars* rather than entrepreneurs per se.

From the research-oriented perspective, we located only two formal studies that explicitly examined learning outcomes of undergraduate entrepreneurship students. Daly (2001) found a high degree of active learning and cooperation among students in a course in which students started and managed Internet businesses. Garavan and O Cinneide (1994b) examined six entrepreneurship education programs across several countries and concluded that the programs emphasized cognitive learning and skill-based learning. However, both of these studies were somewhat limited in their focus and lacked a conceptual framework for understanding the results.

Other studies focused on attributes or skills related to entrepreneurial success. Baron (2000) noted the importance of personal attributes such as adaptability, but also social competence skills including impression management and persuasiveness. Timmons (1995) described six key entrepreneurial attitudes and behaviors that can be acquired, including determination, leadership, opportunity obsession, tolerance of risk, creativity and motivation to excel. Eggers (1995) focused more on the business-specific skills, including creating a business plan, financial management, marketing and motivating others. Baum *et al.* (2001) conducted a study examining venture growth as their definition of entrepreneurial success, and found that tenacity, proactivity and passion for work were three traits associated with success. Further work conducted by Baum and Locke (2003) concluded that skill in obtaining the necessary resources was also critical to success. Shook *et al.* (2003) presented an organizing model of the enterprising individual, examining psychological factors such as personality, beliefs and values, individual characteristics such as demographics and education, and cognitions, including both content and process. They suggest that these factors will explain key entrepreneurial decisions and behaviors, noting that a greater understanding of how entrepreneurial knowledge structures develop and how entrepreneurs make decisions would be useful in advancing the field.

Other researchers focused more on the concept of corporate entrepreneurship, or encouraging entrepreneurial behaviors among managers in existing organizations. In this context, Echols and Neck (1998) noted the importance of motivation to pursue opportunity. While this may be viewed as an individual difference rather than a learning outcome, Echols and Neck implied that this motivational tendency could be enhanced with the appropriate organizational and reward structures, suggesting it is reasonable to treat it as a learning outcome. Thornberry (2002) focused on 'the three major activities of entrepreneurs, namely: opportunity identification; shaping; and capturing' (p. 334). Based on his experience in training managers in four companies, Thornberry reported that most individuals, if properly motivated, could learn these things, with development of a business plan being the most teachable aspect of the process.

In addition to the perspective of academic researchers, we also examined the views of experienced entrepreneurs, primarily by reading or viewing interviews published in various formats. Many of the experienced entrepreneurs focused on personal skills and attributes as important factors related to their success. They noted qualities such as enthusiasm, creativity, persistence, persuasiveness and dealing with frustration in a constructive way (Gendron 2000; EVO Knowledge 2002; Staff 2003). Interpersonal skills mentioned frequently included listening skills, leadership and networking. Several of the entrepreneurial sources also listed specific business-related skills such as conducting market research, writing a business plan, getting financing and quantifying risks (DiCarlo 2002; EVO Knowledge 2002; Singer 2002).

During the cataloging of potential learning outcomes, it became even clearer that inclusion of multiple stakeholders (i.e. entrepreneurs, researchers and educators) was vital to our goal of developing a comprehensive understanding of entrepreneurship education learning outcomes. For example, entrepreneurial and research-oriented sources mentioned the importance of enthusiasm, passion or the entrepreneurial spirit (e.g. Baum *et al.* 2001; EVO Knowledge 2002). In contrast, more pedagogically focused experts were careful to note that an important outcome of entrepreneurship education is to allow the students to form their own opinions of entrepreneurship as a step toward deciding if this is an activity in which they wish to engage in the future (Roberts 2003). We also discovered that some entrepreneurs were skeptical of the extent to which formal business education would result in many of the key learning outcomes, especially those related to interpersonal skills. For example, according to Richard Rebh, CEO and chairman of Floorgraphics, business school does not teach you important things like 'how to manage people, how to sell, how to work through personal issues with employees' (Singer 2002: 2).

From this review of entrepreneurship learning outcomes, we conclude that there is extensive information currently available that provides a useful starting point for understanding desired outcomes of entrepreneurship learning. However, there is no conceptually grounded, parsimonious framework to guide specification and examination of student learning outcomes. It is unclear how educators should integrate entrepreneurship learning outcomes into courses or other learning experiences, how they should be sequenced, and how success should be measured. Applying a typology of learning outcomes may help to organize this litany of potential outcomes into a more coherent structure that would allow for more effective treatment of these issues in terms of curriculum design, continuous improvement and outcomes evaluation.

A learning outcomes framework

There are a number of different ways to think about organizing and categorizing learning outcomes. Early work on learning focused on operant conditioning (i.e. the work of Pavlov and Skinner), which sought to explain individuals' behavioral responses to environmental stimuli (Weiss 1990). Later in the twentieth century, cognitive and educational psychologists broadened the focus to include two types of learning outcomes, explicit (or tacit) and implicit knowledge (Reber 1989; Seger 1994). Explicit knowledge consists of individuals' verbal or concrete representations of concepts or ideas. Implicit knowledge, on the other hand, is a more abstract representation of a concept or process, and individuals may not always be able to easily retrieve or describe that knowledge (Seger 1994). In a similar vein, Anderson (1982) suggested that learners must first develop declarative, or verbal, knowledge about concepts before developing the more complex procedural knowledge of how to do things. Educational psychologists have offered a variety of learning typologies as well. For example, Gagne *et al.* (1992) offer a learning system that incorporates five types of learned human capabilities, including verbal knowledge, motor skill and attitude, and nine types of learning outcomes (e.g. discrimination, defined concepts, rules). Thus, across these disparate literatures, there appears to be a general consensus that it is important to consider a range of learning outcomes.

The theories and models reviewed above provide a foundation for understanding general types of learning and the multiple processes by which individuals learn. However, in order to identify and evaluate the learning outcomes, and specifically the learning outcomes of entrepreneurship courses, additional specificity is needed. For this we sought a framework that acknowledges many concepts and processes from cognitive psychology regarding learning and skill acquisition, but which can also be easily tailored to learning in undergraduate entrepreneurship courses. We decided to use and adapt a classification scheme by Kraiger *et al.* (1993) that meets these criteria. This framework is designed for use in educational and training settings, and had been used to evaluate the learning outcomes of undergraduates (Schmidt and Ford 2003; Towler 2003). The Kraiger *et al.* framework is useful for understanding entrepreneurial learning outcomes in several respects. In its use of *three* types of broad learning outcomes — cognitive, skill-based and affective – this framework balances recognition of multiple types of learning with parsimony. Relatedly, this framework facilitates discussion and description of concepts and skills applicable to the business world, whereas the more cognitive theories have traditionally focused on very narrow learning tasks such as artificial grammars and pattern recognition (Seger 1994). At the same time, the framework's explicit recognition of cognitive learning may provide a necessary counterweight to the emphasis on skill-based learning by entrepreneurs.

The cognitive category of the framework includes learning outcomes that are largely knowledge-based (Kraiger *et al.* 1993). These outcomes could include verbal knowledge, knowledge organization and cognitive strategies, and are similar to the explicit or declarative knowledge types discussed previously. Skill-based outcomes are more behavioral, looking at tasks learners can actually perform. These outcomes are similar to implicit or procedural types of learning outcomes. Affective outcomes include two main subcategories; attitudinal and motivational outcomes. Attitudinal outcomes reflect changes in learner attitudes toward the content, and could include development of an attitude toward a new object, or a change in an attitude that was already held. Motivational outcomes reflect the learner's approach to future tasks, including self-efficacy. The inclusion of these affective or motivational outcomes makes this framework particularly relevant to the entrepreneurial context, as motivational factors appear to play an important role in entrepreneurial success (e.g. Rae 2000; Baum and Locke 2003).

Each of these learning outcomes could potentially be relevant to entrepreneurship education. Cognitive outcomes could include factual knowledge such as different types of organizational structures, important parts of a business plan, and the difference between revenue and profits. Skill-based outcomes could include delivering a persuasive sales presentation, developing a complete business plan, and resolving interpersonal conflict. Affective outcomes could include expressing an interest in marketing activities, feeling confident about one's ability to be a leader, and being motivated to start one's own business. This framework is ideal for understanding learning outcomes for purposes of continuous improvement because the three types of learning imply different improvement interventions. For example, a deficiency in cognitive learning regarding cash flow statements would suggest a need to improve the information on cash flow statements taught to students, including how the statements work and why they are important. However, a deficiency in skill-based learning regarding cash flow statements would suggest a need to increase student use of and practice with these statements.

To flesh out the Kraiger *et al.* (1993) framework with learning outcomes specific to entrepreneurship education, we categorized the information from academic and entrepreneur stakeholders (see Table 15.1). Consistent with Kraiger *et al.*, the preliminary undergraduate entrepreneurship learning outcomes framework presented in Table 15.1 is divided into the three broad types of learning outcomes: cognitive, skill-based and affective. Within these outcome types, we have organized the proposed learning outcomes into two broad content areas: *business-specific* content and *interpersonal/personal* content. Business-specific content addresses the aspects of entrepreneurship that are unique to the business world, including topic areas such as business planning, finance, accounting, marketing and strategy. The interpersonal/personal content addresses concepts related to how the entrepreneur interacts with other people, including leadership, motivation, conflict resolution and communication, as well as personal factors

Table 15.1 Preliminary undergraduate entrepreneurship learning outcomes framework

Learning type	Learning content
Cognitive	*Business-specific content* Understanding risk Knowledge of how to get things done without resources Basics of accounting, finance, technology, marketing *Interpersonal/personal content* Knowledge of personal fit with entrepreneurship career
Skill-based	*Business-specific content* Conducting market research, assessing the marketplace Marketing products and services Recognizing and acting on business opportunities Creating a business plan, including a financial plan Obtaining financing Developing a strategy Identifying strategic partners Risk management *Interpersonal/personal content* Persuasion, getting people excited about your ideas Listening Setting priorities (goal setting) and focusing on goals Defining and communicating a vision Leadership, motivating others Active learning Dealing with customers Managing people Resolving conflict Adapting to new situations, coping with uncertainty
Affective	*Business-specific content* Entrepreneurial spirit Passion for entrepreneurship Self-efficacy for entrepreneurship Commitment to business venture *Interpersonal/personal content* Self-confidence, self-esteem Need for achievement, motivation to excel

Note: Sources used to create this table are marked with an asterisk in the reference list.

such as self-efficacy and personal career choices. Categorization by content areas will further enhance definition of appropriate learning outcomes by emphasizing that there are multiple types of learning outcomes within a given content area. For example, learning outcomes related to conflict resolution could include knowledge regarding grievance procedures, how to conduct mediation, and/or self-efficacy for one's ability to act as a mediator.

The cognitive section of the preliminary framework is focused primarily on the understanding and awareness of basic business concepts, including understanding the concept of risk (Eggers 1995; DiCarlo 2002), knowledge of how to get things done without resources (DiCarlo 2002), and the basics of accounting, finance and other core business disciplines (Singer 2002). On the interpersonal side, one important learning outcome from the academic perspective was knowledge of the extent to which entrepreneurship would provide a good fit with one's preferences and career goals (Roberts 2003).

The skill-based outcomes were the greatest focus of the expert sources we examined. Important skill-based learning outcomes in the business-specific content area included conducting market research (DiCarlo 2002), recognizing and acting on business opportunities (Gibb 1993; Eggers 1995), creating business and financial plans (Singer 2002; Thornberry 2002), and marketing products and services (Timmons 1995). Interpersonal skill-based outcomes noted by the experts focused on communication skills such as persuasion, listening, resolving conflict, and defining and communicating a vision (Timmons 1995; Gendron 2000; Singer 2002; Baum and Locke 2003; Staff 2003). Setting priorities (i.e. goal setting) and focusing on goals were also viewed as key learning outcomes (Rae 2000; Staff 2003). Several sources suggested that management behaviors such as staffing, managing people and budgets, and establishing a formal management system were relevant (Eggers 1995; Moore 2000; EVO Knowledge 2002).

It is important to note that many of the skill-based learning outcomes described by the expert sources could and should be translated into cognitive, intermediate learning outcomes for novices (Anderson 1982). For example, novice entrepreneurs would likely need to have some factual knowledge about conducting market research (e.g. what it is, what sources can be used) before fully developing and automatizing that skill. Similarly, identifying strategic partners was mentioned by several sources as an important skill for entrepreneurs (Tropman and Morningstar 1989; Baron and Markman 2000; Roberts 2003). In the end state, this is a skill-based learning outcome. However, in preliminary stages, students must become aware of the importance of this activity, and perhaps even learn some steps or approaches for accomplishing it (i.e. cognitive learning).

The affective learning section includes business-related learning outcomes such as entrepreneurial spirit, passion for entrepreneurship (Thornberry 2002; Baum and Locke 2003), and commitment to the business venture (Timmons 1995; Krass 1999). Several academic sources mentioned self-efficacy as a key affective outcome (e.g. Baum and Locke 2003). While self-confidence and self-esteem are more general concepts that are critical to entrepreneurship (Gibb 1993), self-efficacy is best conceptualized as context-specific, meaning that an individual's self-efficacy will differ from activity to activity (Locke and Latham 2002). Therefore, this fits in the business-specific content category.

In summary, use of the Kraiger *et al.* framework in entrepreneurial education permits a coherent specification of desired learning outcomes. Next, we apply this preliminary framework of learning outcomes to the assessment of undergraduate education.

Application of the framework

To illustrate an application of this framework in an existing entrepreneurship education program, we used it as part of an ongoing effort to evaluate and refine two undergraduate entrepreneurship courses, in which we posed the following exploratory questions. Because of the untested nature of the recommendations by entrepreneur and academic experts, we focus on the categorization of learning outcomes in two courses, and an initial comparison of the outcomes with the expert recommendations. The next steps – formal curriculum and instructional method revisions – are beyond the empirical scope of the chapter. Our primary focus is the following:

1   What types of learning (i.e. cognitive, skill-based, affective) and specific learning content occurs in experiential entrepreneurship courses?
2   How does this learning compare to the entrepreneurship learning outcomes suggested in Table 15.1?

Our second focus is on potential interrelationships between the three types of learning outcomes and on how individual differences might affect learning. Since entrepreneurial course content (e.g. business plan development) can span all learning types (i.e. cognitive, skill-based, affective), we might expect correlations in learning across types. Thus, we ask:

3   What are the interrelationships among the three types of entrepreneurial learning?

In addition, the literature on aptitude–treatment interactions strongly suggests that students do not all react to learning environments in the same way (Fleishman and Mumford 1989). And the entrepreneurship literature has a long history of focusing on traits as a key determinant of pursuing entrepreneurial ventures and achieving success in these ventures (Baum and Locke 2003). While our study design perhaps prevents definitive disentangling of the effects of affective learning and individual differences, we begin to explore the above questions. Thus, we present our fourth research question:

4   Will self-esteem, entrepreneurial spirit and organizational structure preference affect learning outcomes?

Method

Research setting and sample

The sample consisted of 113 undergraduate students enrolled in two entrepreneurship courses at Clarkson University: a required first-year course and an elective second-year course. In the first-year course, each student becomes a member of a company of approximately 20–25 students. Each company begins by assessing the market potential for a product or service, preparing a detailed business plan, and presenting its business plan to an investment board that can approve start-up capital up to $2,500 for each company. This loan must be paid back before the end of the academic year. If the company receives approval for funding, they begin the process of ordering inventory, scheduling labor, designing a marketing campaign and negotiating with vendors, while simultaneously dealing with teamwork and leadership issues.

Classroom time is divided between work on the small businesses and more traditional educational activities. Throughout the year, students are introduced to elements of business theory and practice (e.g. organizational structure, performance goals and rewards, basic accounting concepts and procedures) via lectures, class discussion, textbook readings and guest speakers. This background material is intended to help the students attain the cognitive learning outcomes needed to understand and address the business situations they are experiencing on a day-to-day basis. During the class periods devoted to work on the businesses, instructors are available to advise the students on planning, operational and problem-solving issues. Instructors take great care to limit their role to the facilitation of team activities rather than being active participants in the decision-making process.

In the second-year course, a select group of 24 sophomore business students are again challenged to create, build and run a start-up company. During the course of the academic year students structure the company, share in collaborative creative thinking, undertake extensive market research and launch a product or service. This course is unique in two key ways. First, students are expected to develop a larger, more complex company than in the first-year course, using more resources (up to $10,000). Second, these students live and work together in a designated wing of a university residence hall, in a state-of-the art, corporate-like, resource center. Thus, the students experience the additional challenge of the group dynamics inherent in a living and learning environment. This live-in environment is intended to more closely replicate the real work environment in a start-up company than a few one-hour classes scattered throughout the week. In such an environment, students must learn to deal with a more intense range of organizational and behavioral issues such as teamwork, conflict resolution, leadership, communication and problem solving. Activities in this course are limited to developing and running the business; they do not include the more traditional classroom activities such as lectures and guest speakers that are a part of the first-year course.

Participants in the study were 90 first-year students and 23 second-year students enrolled in these courses at Clarkson University, a small private university located in a small town in the northeastern United States. Nearly all of the first-year students are recent high school graduates, and were 18 years old at the time of the study. The majority of the students were male. Sixty-nine percent of the first-year students were male, and 64 percent of the second-year students were male. Data on the ethnic composition of the participants were not available, but 10 percent of students in the university's undergraduate population as a whole are from ethnic backgrounds other than White. All of the participants had declared business majors, ranging from Financial Information and Analysis to Business and Technology Management to e-Business. Students were not required to participate in the study. However, as an incentive for participation, students received one entry into a random drawing for $150 at the end of the semester for each completed survey they returned.

Data collection and measures

Data were collected in two ways. First, brief e-mail surveys were sent to the students five times during the spring semester, approximately every two weeks. Students were asked to describe the most important thing they had learned in the class during the past week. This learning question was open-ended, allowing students to describe any type of learning outcome. Response rates ranged from 41 percent to 22 percent across the five e-mail data collection periods. In all, 78 of the 113 participants responded to at least one e-mail survey. In combination with the learning specified by the entrepreneurial experts in Table 15.1, the e-mail results also served as a foundation for a written survey on learning outcomes.

During the last week of the semester, participants completed a written survey containing a structured learning assessment and several attitudinal and individual difference measures. The response rate for this survey was 88 percent among the first-year students and 100 percent among the second-year students, which resulted in 100 respondents for the written survey. The structured learning assessment asked students to indicate the extent to which they had acquired knowledge (i.e. cognitive learning) and improved certain skills (i.e. skill-based learning) in relevant business areas. An example knowledge item is 'Financial analysis'. The 25 knowledge items were evaluated using a five-point rating scale that ranged from 'Learned nothing' to 'Gained extensive knowledge of this topic.' An example skill item is 'Lead a group or team.' The 20 skill items were rated on a five-point scale ranging from 'No improvement' to 'Can now perform this almost effortlessly.' The second-year students were also asked an open-ended question about what they learned from the second-year experience that they did not learn in the first-year course. See the Appendix for a complete copy of the survey.

The attitudinal and individual difference constructs measured in the final survey were Intent to Transfer, Entrepreneurial Spirit, Entrepreneurial Learning, Self-Esteem and Organizational Structure Preference. All of these scales were used with a five-point rating scale ranging from 'Strongly disagree' to 'Strongly agree.' Intent to Transfer was assessed with a three-item measure developed for this study in which participants were asked to indicate the extent to which they would use their learning from this course in the future. An example item is 'I plan to use the concepts and skills I learned in [this course] in future business pursuits.' The Entrepreneurial Spirit and Entrepreneurial Learning scales were both developed for this study based on the emotions and attitudes associated with positive affect and excitement toward entrepreneurship. The Entrepreneurial Spirit scale consisted of seven items intended to measure each participant's attitude toward entrepreneurship. Example items are 'I am confident in my ability to start a new business' and 'Risk-taking is exciting.' The Entrepreneurial Learning scale contained four items intended to measure many of the same concepts as the Entrepreneurial Spirit scale, but directly attributed the attitude change to the entrepreneurial course. An example item from this scale is 'The [course] experience has shown me that I can handle the risk involved in starting a business.' Self-Esteem was measured with Rosenberg's (1965) ten-item scale. Organizational Structure Preference was measured using a six-item scale based on Veiga and Yanouzas

(1979) that examines preferences for mechanistic or organic structures. An example of a mechanistic-related item is 'I prefer to work in an organization where work methods and procedures are clearly specified.' We included this measure because of an expected correlation between preference for organic structures and entrepreneurship learning, since organic structures are more likely to provide the decision-making discretion necessary for responding quickly to recognized entrepreneurial opportunities.

Data analysis

E-mail survey

We examined frequencies of learning outcomes from the e-mail surveys by coding participants' responses to the open-ended learning questions, according to content and type of learning. Content of the learning outcome was defined as the various business topics (e.g. marketing, human resources) or interpersonal/personal topics (e.g. leadership, teamwork, career choices) covered in the courses. Type of learning was defined as cognitive, skill-based or affective as defined by Kraiger *et al.* (1993). Pairs of trained coders consisting of the first two authors and a master's -level graduate student coded each e-mail response. Because many of the open-ended responses were lengthy and multi-faceted, coders could list up to two learning types and two content areas for each entry. Responses could also be coded 'No learning' when a response was provided but it did not describe any actual learning that had taken place. The coding pairs reviewed the results for agreement, discussing any disagreements and coming to a consensus decision on the final type(s) and content area(s) for each entry. The average agreement across all five data collection periods was 89 percent.

Written survey analysis

We computed scale scores for the attitudinal and individual difference variables by averaging the items for each of the scales. We also constructed two variables representing indexes of overall cognitive learning and skill-based learning, which was computed by taking the mean score across all the items in each respective learning type. Analysis of the written survey data consisted of correlational analysis, differences in means tests (t tests) between the learning types, and comparisons of first-year and second-year student results. To minimize our chances of capitalizing on Type I error in the series of t tests, we used the more conservative significance value of $p < 0.01$ when interpreting the results.

Results

E-mail surveys

We first examined the results from the e-mail surveys to answer our first research question concerning types of learning in the experiential entrepreneurship courses. Participants listed cognitive-based learning outcomes most frequently

($n = 169$, 67 percent), followed by affective outcomes ($n = 48$, 19 percent) and skill-based outcomes ($n = 24$, 10 percent). Eleven responses (4 percent) contained no learning outcomes. Examining the second question, a visual comparison of these results with Table 15.1 suggests that entrepreneurship experts appear to be emphasizing skill-based learning to a greater degree than was reported by the participants in these two courses.

Table 15.2 presents a complete listing of the responses coded by content categories. The most frequently listed content areas were interpersonal relationships ($n = 50$, 21.5 percent), getting work done ($n = 30$, 13 percent), communication ($n = 24$, 10 percent) and accounting ($n = 24$, 10 percent). Overall, content areas of an interpersonal nature were mentioned more frequently than the business-oriented content areas. Visual comparison of Table 15.2 results with Table 15.1 content areas indicated that there was substantial overlap between the content of student learning and the content specified by the experts.

Written survey

Means, standard deviations and reliability coefficients for the attitudinal, transfer, self-esteem and learning variables assessed on the final written survey are presented

Table 15.2 Learning outcomes from e-mail surveys

Business-specific content			Interpersonal/personal content		
Content area	Freq.	%	Content area	Freq.	%
Accounting	24	10.3	Dealing with interpersonal relationships	50	21.6
Finance	18	7.8	Getting work done (planning work activities, delegation)	30	12.9
Product development	16	6.9	Communication (oral, written)	24	10.3
Organizational structure	8	3.4	Leadership/motivating others	10	4.3
Developing/implementing a business plan	7	3.0	Power and politics	7	3.0
Marketing	7	3.0	Business-oriented problem-solving and decision-making	6	2.6
Business content – other	6	2.6	Personal career choices	6	2.6
Risk	3	1.3	Interpersonal content – other	6	2.6
Ethics, ethical responsibility	2	0.9			
Human resources	2	0.9			

Note: Frequency indicates number of times content category was mentioned by participants in the e-mail surveys. Results include participants from both courses across all data collection periods.

in Table 15.3. Reliability coefficients range from 0.72 to 0.85, and so were determined to be acceptable. Correlations among the variables are also presented in Table 15.3. Looking at the composite learning indices, the three types of learning appeared to be related, addressing our third research question. Entrepreneurial learning was positively correlated with both cognitive learning ($r = 36$; $p < 0.01$) and skill-based learning ($r = 0.51$; $p < 0.01$), indicating that those who learned about entrepreneurship also obtained entrepreneurship-related knowledge and skills. The correlation between the cognitive and skill-based learning indices was 0.73 ($p < 0.01$). Students who reported significant cognitive learning also tended to report significant skill-based learning. Thus, it appears that the entrepreneurial, or affective, types of learning were more strongly related to skill-based versus cognitive learning. We then examined the item-level learning type data comprising these two indexes, which are presented in Table 15.4.

There were no significant differences between the first-year and second-year students when looking at the composite learning scores ($p > 0.05$). Independent samples t tests performed on the individual learning items revealed several significant differences between the two student groups. The first-year students reported greater learning on three cognitive items (all $p < 0.01$): factual learning related to (a) persuasion and sales techniques, (b) financial analysis and (c) market analysis. First-year students also reported greater learning ($p < 0.01$) on two skill-based items: (a) conducting a financial analysis for a company, and (b) conducting a market analysis. The second-year students reported greater learning ($p < 0.01$) on two cognitive items: factual learning related to (a) business ethics and (b) adapting to change. We also note that there were no differences in the amount of interpersonal/personal content learned by the students, but that first-year students reported learning more in terms of business content than did second-year students ($p < 0.01$). There were no mean differences between the two groups on the attitudinal, intent to transfer and self-esteem scales ($p > 0.05$).

Across both groups, intentions for transfer were very high ($M = 4.53$, SD = 0.53, for each group), indicating that both first- and second-year students felt they would be able to transfer knowledge and skills learned in these courses to other situations. Intent to transfer was correlated with both cognitive learning ($r = 0.35$, $p < 0.01$) and skill-based learning ($r = 0.52$, $p < 0.01$), suggesting that those who experienced greater learning were more confident about their ability to apply these concepts later.

To answer our fourth research question looking at the relationship between individual differences and learning outcomes, we examined the correlations among these variables. Self-esteem was significantly correlated with skill-based learning ($r = 0.29$, $p < 0.01$), but not with cognitive learning ($r = 0.17$, NS). Organizational structure preference was correlated with entrepreneurial learning ($r = -0.22$, $p < 0.05$), but not with either of the other learning types. Entrepreneurial spirit was not significantly correlated with cognitive learning, but was positively related to skill-based learning ($r = 0.32$, $p < 0.01$).

Table 15.3 Scale descriptives and correlations – written survey

	Mean	SD	1	2	3	4	5	6	7
1 Entrepreneurial spirit	3.88	0.64	(0.82)						
2 Entrepreneurial learning	3.93	0.70	0.66**	(0.74)					
3 Organizational structure preference	3.21	0.72	−0.33**	−0.22*	(0.77)				
4 Self-Esteem	4.10	0.60	0.28**	0.27**	−0.12	(0.85)			
5 Transfer intentions	4.53	0.53	0.50**	0.59**	−0.18	0.27**	(0.72)		
6 Cognitive learning composite	4.00	0.51	0.13	0.36**	0.09	0.17	0.35**	(0.75)	
7 Skill-based learning composite	3.76	0.61	0.32**	0.51**	−0.04	0.29**	0.52**	0.73**	(0.84)

Note: $n=100$. Reliability of scales presented in the diagonal (coefficient alpha for 1–5, split half for 6 and 7). * $p < 0.05$. ** $p < 0.01$.

Table 15.4 Item-level learning data

Cognitive learning items (factual learning in each of these areas)	Mean	SD
Leadership tools	4.17	0.73
Teamwork	4.43	0.76
Principles of written communication	3.82	0.89
Principles of oral communication	3.98	0.82
Processes for conflict management	3.94	0.90
Persuasion and sales techniques	3.62	0.99
Financial analysis	3.74	1.05
Market analysis	3.91	0.99
Value of diversity	3.36	1.10
Business ethics	3.91	1.03
Entrepreneurial career options	4.11	0.99
Adapting to change	4.03	0.90
Developing and implementing a business plan	4.53	0.72
Problem-solving methods	4.08	0.83
Using personal contacts to get things done	3.86	0.93
Organizational structure	4.19	0.75
Goal setting	4.32	0.79
Motivation	4.13	0.90
Risk analysis	3.90	0.97
Project management	3.96	0.91

Skill-based learning items (behavioral learning in each of these areas)	Mean	SD
Contribute to a team	4.10	0.82
Lead a group or team	3.76	1.09
Manage my own time and responsibilities	3.84	0.95
Persuade others of my point of view	3.66	0.91
Make effective decisions	3.88	0.82
Make effective oral presentations	3.70	1.02
Write clearly and effectively	3.51	0.92
Resolve conflict between people	3.60	0.99
Deal with uncertainty	3.56	0.83
Manage my own stress	3.45	1.14
Conduct a financial analysis for a company	3.34	1.20
Conduct a market analysis	3.60	1.10
Choose a career that will be right for me	3.26	1.05
Sell a product or service	3.85	1.02
Approach activities confidently	3.95	0.93
Listen to what others are really saying	4.02	0.93
Use personal contacts to get things done	3.65	1.04
Motivate myself to get work done	3.69	1.05
Identify and analyze risk	3.67	0.89
Set realistic goals	3.94	0.95
Adapt to changing situations	4.01	0.90
Work with others who are different from me	4.17	0.92
Conduct business ethically	3.83	1.06
Solve new or difficult problems	3.91	0.74
Work across teams and functions	4.01	0.90

Note: $n = 100$.

Discussion

The primary purpose of this chapter was to review and apply an established learn-ing typology to inform our understanding of entrepreneurship education learning outcomes. To enhance the application of the typology, we drew on the collective wisdom of entrepreneurs and academics, who provided a relatively convergent list of desired learning content for entrepreneurship courses (see Table 15.1). These experts emphasized skill-based types of learning in both business content areas (e.g. creating a business plan) and interpersonal/personal content areas (e.g. adapt-ing to new situations). To a lesser degree, they acknowledged the importance of cognitive and affective learning to entrepreneurial education. For example, they indicated that entrepreneurs needed to learn some basics of accounting and other business functions, and understand concepts such as risk.

The Kraiger *et al.* (1993) learning typology of cognitive, skill-based and affective learning types was straightforward to apply in an entrepreneurial education context. Use of the typology reinforced the fact that learning content could take the form of any of the three learning types. That is, business content or interper-sonal/personal content could take the form of cognitive, skill-based or affective learning. Through our e-mail data collection efforts, students reported experienc-ing all three types of learning, and their learning overlapped with almost all of the content areas specified by the entrepreneurs and academics. However, the students tended to emphasize cognitive learning (i.e. knowledge and facts) to a much greater degree than the experts. We attribute this finding partly to the fact that first- and second-year undergraduate students are typically at earlier stages of learning than the experts, combined with the fact that cognitive learning generally has to precede skill-based learning (Anderson 1982; Ackerman 1987). These findings have implications for curriculum design in that novices may have to be exposed to basic information on business and interpersonal/personal topics before they can acquire and use many of the skills related to these areas in an entrepreneurial setting. We note, however, that this is likely an iterative process, such that introductory information serves as a foundation for basic skill develop-ment, which in turn can facilitate more complex cognitive learning. On the other hand, this finding could also be an artifact of our data collection method to the extent that students find it easier to recall and report cognitive learning.

Results from the final written survey confirmed that students experienced substantial cognitive and skill-based learning across many entrepreneurship-related content areas specified by the experts. They also reported a high degree of entrepreneurial learning (a form of affective learning) in the form of interest in entrepreneurship and self-efficacy in relation to business start-ups. Students' greatest cognitive learning occurred in the area of teamwork and in developing a business plan. For example, on the topic of business plan development, students reported on average that they 'learned a moderate amount' to 'gained extensive knowledge of this topic' ($M = 4.53$, SD = 0.72). The least amount of cognitive learning occurred in the area of 'valuing diversity' with students reporting that they 'learned some basic facts about it' ($M = 3.36$, SD = 1.1). Ironically, they reported the greatest amount of skill-based learning in the area of 'working with others who are different from me' ($M = 4.17$, SD $= 0.92$). This apparent contradiction may stem from perceived differences between the concepts of 'valuing diversity' and 'working with others.' Alternatively, this finding may support Reber's (1989) research on implicit learning, in which it is suggested that knowledge does not have to be acquired consciously. Consistent with our expectations there was substantial correlation between all three types of learning: entrepreneurial spirit and learning (i.e. a form of affective learning), cognitive learning and skill-based learning. This bodes well for the entrepreneurship courses from which survey data were drawn, in that students appear not only to understand entrepreneurial concepts, but also developed skills and affect related to entrepreneurship.

Results on the intent of students to transfer learning to other classes and settings were very favorable, consistent with the intent of experiential learning (Kolb 1984). This is a positive finding, particularly in light of continued concerns about transfer in educational environments (Baldwin and Ford 1988). We suggest including intent to transfer as a stated learning objective in entrepreneurship courses.

There were several interesting differences between the first-year and second-year students that are consistent with different objectives of the two entrepreneurship courses. First-year students reported greater cognitive and skill-based learning on introductory business topics such as sales techniques, financial analysis and market analysis. Second-year students reported greater cognitive learning on more complex topics such as ethics and adapting to change, in line with the higher stakes and living/learning focus of the second-year course.

Second-year students' responses to the open-ended question on the final survey offered some interesting insight as well. First, it appears that the second-year experience reinforced what students had learned in their first-year entrepreneurship class, increasing their confidence to actually use the knowledge and skills in the future. For example, one student attributed learning the 'amount of risk involved in a business' to the second-year course. Another second-year student reported learning from the course the 'importance of being both realistic and aspiring.' Finally, the students perceived that living together, while an additional source of stress, helped them improve their communication, teamwork and conflict resolution skills.

Our use of the Kraiger *et al.* (1993) typology to categorize student learning outcomes resulted in a clear picture of the learning that occurred in two undergraduate entrepreneurship courses. This initial step lays the foundation for subsequent identification of curriculum design needs and areas for improvement. Importantly, the typology we used is rooted in theories of learning and cognition, which provide a solid foundation for understanding entrepreneurial-related learning. In addition, the framework is parsimonious in that it categorizes learning into just three types, and it permits curriculum designers and program evaluators to make the essential distinction between learning type and learning content. As such, the Kraiger *et al.* framework could be quite useful to continuous improvement efforts in entrepreneurship education (Goldstein and Ford 2002). This is because educators are able to address learning *content* deficiencies with curriculum re-design and learning *type* deficiencies with different instructional approaches. For example, student learning in financial analysis was relatively low across both cognitive ($M = 3.63$, SD $= 0.99$) and skill-based ($M = 3.34$, SD $= 1.20$) learning types, suggesting that additional or new forms of information on financial analysis are needed in these courses. If only the skill-based learning had been found to be low, future iterations of the course might have focused on more skill-creating instructional methods such as opportunities to model effective teamwork behaviors, peer assessment of teamwork behaviors, and performance planning to improve these behaviors.

Finally, results confirm that it is possible to teach knowledge and skills related to entrepreneurship, as well as enhance interest in the topic (Timmons 1995; Baron and Markman 2000). This is consistent with the findings of Peterman and Kennedy (2003) suggesting that entrepreneurial education can increase participants' perceptions of the desirability of entrepreneurship. At the same time, our findings indicate that particular individual differences are correlated with the amount of learning and intent to transfer this learning (see Table 15.3). Students high in self-esteem and entrepreneurial spirit reported experiencing greater entrepreneurial and skill-based learning and substantially higher intentions to transfer their learning. This finding suggests that students with higher self-esteem were better able to take advantage of the educational experience and develop their entrepreneurship-related skills. If so, individuals with high self-esteem and entrepreneurial spirit may learn and transfer more than others, which has implications for entrepreneurship education program design and the selection of students for entrepreneurship courses. Clearly, there appears to be a relationship between individual differences and entrepreneurship learning that remains to be more fully specified.

Limitations and future research

We acknowledge several limitations of our chapter that would be important to redress in future research. First, while we believe that our examination of entrepreneur and academic expert views on entrepreneurship resulted in a representative list of learning outcomes, future work in this area should rely on a more systematic survey of these sources. For example, it is possible that the experienced entrepreneurs included in our review may have been biased in their reports of attributes and skills needed for entrepreneurial success, focusing only on those individual differences that were present or absent in their own experiences rather than considering the field of entrepreneurship more broadly. Thus, the learning outcomes in this study should be looked upon as an initial specification of learning outcomes particular to experiential undergraduate entrepreneurship courses, as a first step toward identifying ideal mixes of content areas and learning types in entrepreneurship education (Garavan and O Cinneide 1994a).

Second, our results may not be generalizable to all entrepreneurship courses because they reflect the undergraduate experiences in entrepreneurship courses at one university. Some aspects of the course design in this situation may limit generalizability to other entrepreneurial situations. For example, students were divided into teams of 20–25 people to start their companies. We suspect it is rare for start-ups in the real world to involve such a large team. The findings are most effectively generalized to other undergraduate entrepreneurship courses at the far end of the experiential spectrum, or classes with a similar course design. We encourage future research on graduate-level entrepreneurship education, as well as entrepreneurship courses utilizing a range of learning methods. Additionally, we encourage research that explicitly examines learning outcomes relevant to novice entrepreneurs. We anticipate that the overall framework would still be generalizable to other audiences, although the specific outcomes may need to be adjusted depending on the knowledge, skills and experience individuals bring to the table. We acknowledge as well that the use of other learning outcomes frameworks (e.g. the more detailed framework of Gagne *et al.* 1992) may have resulted in somewhat different results than our study. Future research may wish to further validate and compare models of training and learning outcomes in entrepreneurial education contexts.

We would have preferred to use a more complete research design (Schwab 1999), but pre-test data did not exist and there were no additional business students at this university to serve as a comparison group for members of the first-year class. Future research should employ as rigorous a design as is feasible in a field setting. Additionally, our student data were self-reported, so we obtained only one perspective regarding each student's learning outcomes. While we addressed this somewhat with two data collection methods over a period of several months, future research could gather data from other sources such as peer and instructor evaluations of student learning outcomes. Finally, because it is more difficult for students to assess attitudinal learning via self-reports (versus the two other types of learning), we were less able to distinguish actual learning versus individual differences in the affective area, with the exception of the entrepreneurial learning measure. At a minimum we were able to generate preliminary benchmarking and correlational data on entrepreneurial attitudes.

We also encourage future research on the dynamics behind student learning, particularly the skill development process. A question particularly relevant to the topic of entrepreneurship pertains to the timing of learning. In our study we regarded learning as a semester-long event, but it is possible that what students learned in the courses will be fully realized only as they learn more or gain life and work experience. It would be interesting to conduct follow-up studies with students to determine the extent to which they do actually transfer their learning to other courses, business ventures and career opportunities. To illustrate, we could envision the declaration of one second-year student that 'I learned that I will never again work in an organization with so many politics' evolving into a different learning outcome in the future; perhaps 'I learned that most organizations have politics.'

Finally, the debate regarding what business content and interpersonal/personal content can be taught and which abilities and individual differences are less malleable appears active. Thus, the entrepreneurship community would welcome further systematic research on this topic. We encourage future researchers of learning outcomes to rely on the Kraiger *et al.* and similar learning typologies as means of organization and to enhance generalizability across contexts. Additional studies specifying and documenting learning outcomes are needed, and this effort would be quite useful to the many entrepreneurship courses in existence.

Conclusion

The goal of this chapter was to provide a coherent structure for organizing student learning in entrepreneurship to facilitate curriculum design, course and program evaluation, and continuous improvement. The Kraiger *et al.* (1993) learning typology provides a parsimonious framework grounded in learning theory and cognition that can be used effectively for these purposes. Categorization of undergraduate student learning outcomes from two experiential learning courses using this learning typology revealed substantial cognitive, behavioral and affective learning on many topics central to entrepreneurship. Thus, while undergraduate students may be 'starting from scratch' in entrepreneurship courses, these experiences can be designed to provide them with a solid foundation of the knowledge, skills and attitudes necessary to be an entrepreneur or to apply entrepreneurial principles within organizations.

Acknowledgment

The authors gratefully acknowledge research assistance by Kristen Clauss on this project. We thank Amy Beekman and two anonymous reviewers for helpful comments on earlier versions of this chapter. We also thank the Shipley Center for support in completing the project. Note: The first two authors contributed equally to the chapter.

References

References marked with as asterisk indicates sources used to develop the preliminary framework in Table 15.1.

Ackerman, P. L. (1987) Individual differences in skill learning: an integration of psychometric and information processing perspectives. *Psychological Bulletin*, 102: 3–27.
Anderson, J. R. (1982) Acquisition of a cognitive skill. *Psychological Review*, 89: 369–406.
Babson College Academic Programs in Entrepreneurship http://www2.babson.edu/babson/babsoneshipp.nsf/Public/academicprograms, accessed April 29, 2003.
Baldwin, T. T. and Ford, J. K. (1988) Transfer of training: a review and directions for future research. *Personnel Psychology*, 41: 63–105.
*Baron, R. A. (2000) Psychological perspectives on entrepreneurship: cognitive and social factors in entrepreneurs' success. *Current Directions in Psychological Science*, 9: 15–18.
*Baron, R. A. and Markman, G. D. (2000) Beyond social capital: how social skills can enhance entrepreneurs' success. *Academy of Management Executive*, 14: 106–15.
*Baum, J. R. and Locke, E. A. (2003) The relationship of entrepreneurial traits, skill, and motivation to subsequent venture growth. Paper presented at the 18th Annual Conference of the Society for Industrial and Organizational Psychology, Orlando, FL.

*Baum, J. R., Locke, E. A. and Smith, K. G. (2001) A multidimensional model of venture growth. *Academy of Management Journal*, 44: 292–303.

Brown, K. G. and Gerhardt, M. W. (2002) Formative evaluation: an integrative practice model and case study. *Personnel Psychology*, 55: 951–84.

*Brush, C. G., Duhaime, I. M., Gartner, W. B., Stewart, A., Katz, J. A., Hitt, M. A., Alvarez, S. A., Meyer, G. D. and Venkataraman, S. (2003) Doctoral education in the field of entrepreneurship. *Journal of Management*, 29(3): 309–31.

CELCEE (2003) The Center for Entrepreneurial Leadership Clearinghouse on Entrepreneurship Education (www.celcee.edu/about) accessed April 28, 2003.

Daly, S. P. (2001) Student-operated internet businesses: true experiential learning in entrepreneurship and retail management. *Journal of Marketing Education*, 23: 204–15.

*DiCarlo, L. (2002) Teaching the school of hard knocks. *Forbes.com*. (Oct.), retrieved October 16, 2002, from http://www.forbes.com.

*Echols, A. E. and Neck, C. P. (1998) The impact of behaviors and structure on corporate entrepreneurship. *Journal of Managerial Psychology*, 13: 38–48.

*Eggers, J. H. (1995) Developing entrepreneurs: skills for the 'wanna be', 'gonna be', and 'gotta be better' employees. In M. London (ed.), *Employees, Careers, and Job Creation*. San Francisco: Jossey-Bass pp. 165–84.

*EVO Knowledge, Inc. (2002) *Leading New Ventures: Entrepreneurship and Intrapraneurship* [training video]. Chicago.

Fleishman, E. A. and Mumford, M. D. (1989) Individual attributes and training performance. In I. L. Goldstein (ed.) *Training and Development in Organizations*, San Francisco: Jossey-Bass pp. 183–255.

Gagne, R. M., Briggs, L. J. and Wager, W. W. (1992) *Principles of Instructional Design* 4th ed. New York: Harcourt Brace Jovanovich.

*Garavan, T. N. and O'Cinneide, B. (1994a) Entrepreneurship education and training programmes: a review and evaluation – Part 1. *Journal of European Industrial Training*, 18(8): 3–12.

*Garavan, T. N. and O'Cinneide, B. (1994b) Entrepreneurship education and training programmes: a review and evaluation – Part 2. *Journal of European Industrial Training*, 18(11): 13–21.

*Gendron, G. (2000) The origin of the entrepreneurial species. *Inc.* (Feb.), Retrieved February 6, 2003, from http://www.inc.com.

*Gibb, A. A. (1993) The enterprise culture and education. Understanding enterprise education and its links with small business, entrepreneurship and wider educational goals. *International Small Business Journal*, 11: 11–34.

Goldstein, I. L. and Ford, J. K. (2002) *Training in Organizations* 4th ed. Belmont, CA: Wadsworth.

Hornsby, J. S., Kuratko, D. F. and Zahra, S. A. (2002) Middle managers' perception of the internal environment for corporate entrepreneurship: assessing a measurement scale. *Journal of Business Venturing*. 7(3): 253–73.

*Jack, S. L. and Anderson, A. R. (1999) Entrepreneurship education within the enterprise culture: producing reflective practitioners. *International Journal of Entrepreneurial Behaviour and Research*, 5: 1–13 [electronic version]. Retrieved April 23, 2003, from the ProQuest database.

Jones-Evans, D., Williams, W. and Deacon, J. (2000). Developing entrepreneurial graduates: an action-learning approach. *Education and Training*, 42: 282–8.

Kolb, D. A. (1984) *Experiential Learning Experience as the Source of Learning and Development*. Englewood Cliffs, NJ: Prentice Hall.

Kraiger, K., Ford, J. K. and Salas, E. (1993) Application of cognitive, skill-based, and affective theories of learning outcomes to new methods of training evaluation. *Journal of Applied Psychology*, 78: 311–28.

*Krass, P. (1999) *The book of Entrepreneurs' Wisdom*. New York: John Wiley.

Leitch, C. M. and Harrison, R. T. (1999) A process model for entrepreneurship education and development. *International Journal of Entrepreneurial Behaviour and Research*, 5: 83–109.

Locke, E. A. and Latham, G. P. (2002) Building a practically useful theory of goal setting and task motivation: a 35-year odyssey. *American Psychologist*, 57: 705–17.

*Moore, D. P. (2000) *Careerpreneurs: Lessons from Leading Women Entrepreneurs on Building a Career Without Boundaries*. Palo Alto, CA: Davies-Black.

Newton, D. and Henricks, M. (2003) Can entrepreneurship be taught? *Entrepreneur*, April: 62–71.

Peterman, N. E. and Kennedy, J. (2003) Enterprise education: influencing students' perceptions of entrepreneurship. *Entrepreneurship Theory and Practice*, 28(2) 129–44.

Pink, D. H. (2001) *Free Agent Nation: How America's New Independent Workers Are Transforming the Way We Live*. New York: Warner Books.

*Rae, D. (2000) Understanding entrepreneurial learning: a question of how? *International Journal of Entrepreneurial Behaviour and Research*, 6: 145–59 [electronic version].

Raffo, C., Lovatt, A., Banks, M. and O'Connor, J. (2000) Teaching and learning entrepreneurship for micro and small businesses in the cultural industries sector. *Education and Training*, 42: 356–65.

Reber, A. S. (1989) Implicit learning and tacit learning. *Journal of Experimental Psychology: General*, 118: 219–35.

*Roberts, J. S. (2003) *Entrepreneurship Then and Now* [DVD]. Columbia College Chicago: The Coleman Foundation

Rosenberg, M. (1965) *Society and the Adolescent Self-Image*. Princeton, NJ: Princeton University Press.

Rynes, S., Bartunek, J. M. and Daft, R. L. (2001) Across the great divide: knowledge creation and transfer between practitioners and academics. *Academy of Management Journal*, 44: 340–55.

Schank, R. C., Berman, T. R. and MacPherson, K. A. (1999) Learning by doing. In C. M. Reigeluth (ed.), *Instructional-Design Theories and Methods*. Vol. II. Mahwah, NJ: Erlbaum.

Schmidt, A. M. and Ford, J. K. (2003) Learning within a learner control training environment: the interactive effects of goal orientation and metacognitive instruction on learning outcomes. *Personnel Psychology*, 56: 405–29.

Schwab, D. P. (1999) *Research Methods for Organizational Studies*. Mahwah, NJ: Erlbaum.

Seger, C. A. (1994) Implicit learning. *Psychological Bulletin,* 115(2): 163–96.

*Sexton, D. L. and Smilor, R. W. (1986) *The Art and Science of Entrepreneurship*. Cambridge, MA: Ballinger.

Shane, S. and Venkataraman, S. (2000) The promise of entrepreneurship as a field of research. *Academy of Management Journal*, 25: 217–26.

*Shook, C. L., Priem, R. L. and McGee, J. E. (2003) Venture creation and the enterprising individual: a review and synthesis. *Journal of Management*, 29(3): 379–99.

*Singer, T. (2002) Where did you learn to grow a company? *Inc*. (Oct.15), retrieved March 26, 2003, from http://www.inc.com.

*Staff (2003) Entrepreneurs: born or made? A conversation with Herb Kelleher of Southwest Airlines. *Babson Insight*, retrieved March 26, 2003, from http://www.babsoninsight.com.

*Thornberry, N. E. (2002) Corporate entrepreneurship: teaching managers to be entrepreneurs. *Journal of Management Development*, 22(4): 329–44.

*Timmons, J. (1995) *New Venture Creation: Entrepreneurship in the 21st Century*. Boston: McGraw-Hill/Irwin.

Towler, A. J. (2003) Effects of charismatic influence training on attitudes, behavior, and performance. *Personnel Psychology*, 56: 363–81.

*Tropman, J. E. and Morningstar, G. (1989) *Entrepreneurial Systems for the 1990's*. Westport, CT: Quorum Books.

Veiga, J. F. and Yanouzas, J. N. (1979) *The Dynamics of Organization Theory: Gaining a Macro Perspective*. St. Paul, MN: West.

Weiss, H. M. (1990) Learning theory and industrial and organizational psychology. In M. D. Dunnette and L. M. Hough (eds), *Handbook of Industrial and Organizational Psychology*, Palo Alto, CA: Consulting Psychologists Press Vol. 1, 171–222.

Zahra, S. and Dess, G. G. (2001) Entrepreneurship as a field of research: encouraging dialogue and debate. *Academy of Management Review*, 26: 8–10.

Appendix: Structured learning assessment

Section I. Factual learning

In this section, we are interested in how this course has impacted your knowledge – have you learned facts or pieces of information that you didn't know at the beginning of the course? **Please circle the response that best describes your level of factual learning in each of these areas.**	Learned nothing	Was exposed to the topic	Learned some basic facts about it	Learned a moderate amount	Gained extensive knowledge of this topic
1. Leadership tools	1	2	3	4	5
2. Teamwork	1	2	3	4	5
3. Principles of written communication	1	2	3	4	5
4. Principles of oral communication	1	2	3	4	5
5. Process for conflict management	1	2	3	4	5
6. Persuasion and sales techniques	1	2	3	4	5
7. Financial analysis	1	2	3	4	5
8. Market analysis	1	2	3	4	5
9. Value of diversity	1	2	3	4	5
10. Business ethics	1	2	3	4	5
11. Entrepreneurial career options	1	2	3	4	5
12. Adapting to change	1	2	3	4	5
13. Developing and implementing a business plan	1	2	3	4	5
14. Problem solving metthods	1	2	3	4	5
15. Using personal contacts to get things done	1	2	3	4	5
16. Organizational structure	1	2	3	4	5
17. Goal setting	1	2	3	4	5
18. Motivation	1	2	3	4	5
19. Risk analysis	1	2	3	4	5
20. Project management	1	2	3	4	5
21. Other _____	1	2	3	4	5

Section II. Skills and abilities

In this section, we are interested in how this course has impacted your behavior – can you do things now that you couldn't do at the beginning of the course? **Please circle the response that best describes your level of behavioral improvement in the skills and abilities described below.**	No improvement	Made one or two minor improvements	Made some improvements	Made substantial improvements	Can now perform this almost effortlessly
1. Contribute to a team.	1	2	3	4	5
2. Lead a group a team.	1	2	3	4	5
3. Manage my own time and responsibilites.	1	2	3	4	5
4. Persuade others of my point of view.	1	2	3	4	5
5. Make effective decisions.	1	2	3	4	5
6. Make effective oral presentations.	1	2	3	4	5
7. Write clearly and effectively.	1	2	3	4	5
8. Resolve conflict between people.	1	2	3	4	5
9. Deal with uncertainty.	1	2	3	4	5
10. Manage my own stress.	1	2	3	4	5
11. Conduct a financial analysis for a company.	1	2	3	4	5
12. Conduct a market analysis.	1	2	3	4	5
13. Choose a career that will be right for me.	1	2	3	4	5
14. Sell a product or service.	1	2	3	4	5
15. Approach activities confidently.	1	2	3	4	5
16. Listen to what others are really saying.	1	2	3	4	5
17. Use personal contacts to get things done.	1	2	3	4	5
18. Motivate myself to get work done.	1	2	3	4	5
19. Identify and analyze risk.	1	2	3	4	5
20. Set realistic goals.	1	2	3	4	5
21. Adapt to changing situations.	1	2	3	4	5
22. Work with others who are different from me.	1	2	3	4	5
23. Conduct business ethically.	1	2	3	4	5
24. Solve new or difficult problems.	1	2	3	4	5
25. Work across teams and functions.	1	2	3	4	5
26. Other ————————————	1	2	3	4	5

Section III: Attitudes and feelings

	Strongly Agree				
In this last section, you will see questions about your attitudes and feelings toward several issues.	Agree				
	Neither Agree nor Disagree				
Please indicate the *extent to which you agree with* the following statements by circling the appropriate number.	Disagree				
	Strongly Disagree				
1. I am confident in my ability to start a new business.	1	2	3	4	5
2. I plan to use the concepts and skills I learned in SB113/114 in future <u>coursework.</u>	1	2	3	4	5
3. I would like to start my own business someday.	1	2	3	4	5
4. I plan to use the concepts and skills I learned in SB113/114 in future <u>business pursuits.</u>	1	2	3	4	5
5. I enjoy facing challenges.	1	2	3	4	5
6. I plan to use the concepts and skills I learned in SB113/114 in my future <u>career</u>.	1	2	3	4	5
7. Risk-taking is exciting.	1	2	3	4	5
8. I am confident in my ability to play a leadership role in team activities.	1	2	3	4	5
9. The risk involved in starting a company is too stressful for me.	1	2	3	4	5
10. I can handle the risk involved in starting a business.	1	2	3	4	5
11. I have good ideas that will be successful in the marketplace.	1	2	3	4	5
12. On the whole, I am satisfied with myself.	1	2	3	4	5
13. At times I think I am no good at all.	1	2	3	4	5
14. I feel that I have a number of good qualities.	1	2	3	4	5
15. I am able to do things as well as most people.	1	2	3	4	5
16. I feel I do not have much to be proud of.	1	2	3	4	5
17. I certainly feel useless at times.	1	2	3	4	5
18. I feel that I'm a person of worth, at least on an equal basis with others.	1	2	3	4	5
19. I wish I could have more respect for myself.	1	2	3	4	5
20. All in all, I am inclined to feel that I am a failure.	1	2	3	4	5
21. I take a positive attitude toward myself.	1	2	3	4	5
22. The SB113/114 experience has made me want to start my own business someday.	1	2	3	4	5
23. The SB113/114 experience has shown me that I can handle the risk involved in starting a business.	1	2	3	4	5
24. The SB113/114 experience has shown me that I have good ideas that can be sucessful in the marketplace.	1	2	3	4	5
25. The SB113/114 experience has made me more interested in business.	1	2	3	4	5
I prefer to work in an organization where:					
26. Goals are defined by managers at higher levels.	1	2	3	4	5
27. Work methods and procedures are clearly specified.	1	2	3	4	5
28. Top management makes the important decesions.	1	2	3	4	5
29. My career is pretty well planned out for me.	1	2	3	4	5
30. My length of service is almost as important as my level of performance	1	2	3	4	5
31. Management is able to provide the information I need to do my job well.	1	2	3	4	5

Index